# Thinking and Writing
# about Poetry

# Thinking and Writing about Poetry

## MICHAEL MEYER

*University of Connecticut*

**Bedford/St. Martin's**
A Macmillan Education Imprint

Boston • New York

**For Bedford/St. Martin's**

*Vice President, Editorial, Macmillan Higher Education Humanities:* Edwin Hill
*Editorial Director for English and Music:* Karen S. Henry
*Executive Editor:* Vivian Garcia
*Senior Developmental Editor:* Christina Gerogiannis
*Production Editor:* Deborah Baker
*Production Supervisor:* Robert Cherry
*Marketing Manager:* Joy Fisher Williams
*Copyeditor:* Bev Miller
*Indexer:* Steve Csipke
*Director of Rights and Permissions:* Hilary Newman
*Senior Art Director:* Anna Palchik
*Cover Design:* William Boardman
*Composition:* Cenveo Publisher Services
*Printing and Binding:* RR Donnelley and Sons

Manufactured in the United States of America.

0  9  8  7  6  5
f  e  d  c  b  a

*For information, write:* Bedford/St. Martin's, 75 Arlington Street, Boston, MA 02116 (617-399-4000)

ISBN 978-1-4576-8750-1

For My Wife
Regina Barreca

## About Michael Meyer

Michael Meyer, Emeritus Professor of English, taught writing and literature courses for more than thirty years — since 1981 at the University of Connecticut and before that at the University of North Carolina at Charlotte and the College of William and Mary. In addition to being an experienced teacher, Meyer is a highly regarded literary scholar. His scholarly articles have appeared in distinguished journals such as *American Literature, Studies in the American Renaissance,* and *Virginia Quarterly Review.* An internationally recognized authority on Henry David Thoreau, Meyer is a former president of the Thoreau Society and coauthor (with Walter Harding) of *The New Thoreau Handbook,* a standard reference source. His first book, *Several More Lives to Live: Thoreau's Political Reputation in America*, was awarded the Ralph Henry Gabriel Prize by the American Studies Association. He is also the editor of *Frederick Douglass: The Narrative and Selected Writings.* He has lectured on a variety of American literary topics from the University of Cambridge to Peking University. His other books for Bedford/ St. Martin's include *The Bedford Introduction to Literature,* Eleventh Edition; *The Compact Bedford Introduction to Literature,* Tenth Edition; *Literature to Go,* Second Edition; *Poetry: An Introduction,* Seventh Edition; and *Thinking and Writing about Literature,* Second Edition.

# Preface for Instructors

*Thinking and Writing about Poetry* is a concise guide to reading canonical and contemporary poetry that also treats every stage of the writing process for composing essays about poetry — from generating topics to documenting sources. This book has developed and grown out of the widely adopted *Poetry: An Introduction*, Seventh Edition. Though *Thinking and Writing about Poetry* is a new book, major portions of it have been class-tested in hundreds of literature courses and carefully revised and refined over seven editions. Common to both books are the assumptions that understanding literature — through reflection, discussion, and writing — enhances its enjoyment and that literature offers a valuable and unique means of apprehending life in its richness and diversity. Over the years, scores of instructors have offered valuable comments on questionnaires indicating that any book with high aspirations to inspire students to become lifelong readers of imaginative literature, as well as more thoughtful and skillful writers, had also better provide enticing selections along with clear, practical advice about thinking and writing about literature. This book is designed to do just that.

This text is flexibly organized into three parts that may be taught consecutively or in any order you prefer. "Elements of Poetry" — the first eleven chapters — is devoted to the elements of poetry. The second part, "Approaches to Poetry," consists of a pair of chapters that feature two different approaches to poetry: an in-depth study of Robert Frost and a thematic case study on humor and satire — as well as a collection of poems that emphasizes canonical works. And the third part, "Critical Thinking and Writing about Poetry," discusses strategies for critical thinking, reading, and writing about literature that can be assigned selectively throughout the course. Sample student papers and hundreds of assignments appear in the text, offering students the support they need to write about poetry.

*Thinking and Writing about Poetry* accommodates many teaching styles and addresses the needs of today's poetry classrooms. Among its features are contemporary poets commenting directly to students about how they read and write, and a new online resource, *LaunchPad Solo for Literature*, that offers instructors more options for teaching and students even more help for exploring, enjoying, and writing about literature.

# FEATURES OF *THINKING AND WRITING ABOUT POETRY*

## Teachable poems your students will want to read

Chosen for their appeal to students, *Thinking and Writing about Poetry*'s rich and diverse selections range from the classic to the contemporary and include such gems as Cornelius Eady's "The Supremes," Mary Oliver's "The Poet with His Face in His Hands," and Kay Ryan's "Turtle." The poems represent a variety of periods, nationalities, cultures, styles, and voices — from the serious to the humorous and from the canonical to very recent works. Classic works by John Donne, Robert Frost, Elizabeth Bishop, Langston Hughes, and others are generously represented. In addition, there are many contemporary selections from well-regarded writers including Sherman Alexie, Sharon Olds, Natasha Trethewey, and Denise Duhamel.

## Many options for teaching, learning — and enjoying

In its abiding effort to make literature come to life for students and the course a pleasure to teach for instructors, *Thinking and Writing about Poetry* includes these helpful features:

**A clear, lively discussion of the elements of poetry**    Eight of the first eleven chapters are devoted to the elements of poetry — diction, tone, images, figures of speech, symbols, sounds, rhythm, and poetic forms. Each of these chapters begins with a focused, student-friendly discussion of the element interspersed with lively examples that show students how that element contributes to the poem's effects and potential meanings. At the end of these chapters is a mini-anthology of poems for further study, each accompanied by questions for critical thinking and writing.

**Useful connections between popular and literary culture**    The text draws carefully on examples from popular culture to explain the elements of poetry, inviting students to relate to literature through what they already know. Writing assignments that help students draw connections between popular culture and more canonical works appear after each example. The examples include greeting-card verse and contemporary song lyrics, such as Bruce Springsteen's "Devils & Dust."

**Two engaging chapters that offer two different kinds of approaches to poetry**    The first, an in-depth study of Robert Frost that includes multiple works along with commentaries, draft manuscript pages, photos, and provocative contextual materials; the second, a case study on satire and humor demonstrating that serious poems can be funny and that comic poems can be thoughtful. These poems — whether slyly subtle or even savage — are likely to assure readers that laughter can engender thought as well as pleasure.

**Accessible coverage of a variety of critical approaches to poetry**    For instructors who wish to incorporate literary theory into their courses, Chapter 15, "Critical Strategies for Reading," introduces students to a variety of critical strategies, ranging from formalism to cultural criticism. In brief examples, the approaches are applied in analyzing Robert Frost's "Mending Wall" and other works so that students will have a sense of how to use these strategies in their own reading and writing.

**Plenty of help with reading and writing about poetry**    Seven chapters on reading and writing about poetry ensure that students get the help they need, beginning — in the book's introduction and first chapter — with how to approach a poem and think critically about it. Annotated versions of several poems — William Hathaway's humorous "Oh, Oh," Elizabeth Bishop's widely taught "Manners," and John Donne's classic sonnet "Death Be Not Proud" — model for students the kind of critical reading that leads to excellent writing about poetry. Chapters 2 and 11 take students through every step of the writing process, from generating topics to documenting sources — while sixteen sample papers throughout the book model the results. (See the "Resources for Reading and Writing about Poetry" chart on the inside back cover.) For students who need help with researched writing, Chapter 17, "The Literary Research Paper," offers detailed advice for finding, evaluating, and incorporating print and electronic sources in a paper. It also includes the most current MLA documentation guidelines.

**Hundreds of questions and assignments**    First Response prompts, Considerations for Critical Thinking and Writing questions, Connections to Other Selections questions, Critical Strategies questions, and Creative Response questions — give students many opportunities for thinking and writing. In addition, these helpful checklists offer questions and suggestions for reading and writing about poetry:

- Suggestions for Approaching Poetry (Ch. 1, p. 26)
- Questions for Responsive Reading and Writing (Ch. 2, p. 45)
- Suggestions for Scanning a Poem (Ch. 8, p. 177)
- Questions for Writing about an Author in Depth (Ch. 12, p. 250)
- Questions for Arguing Critically about Literature (Ch. 16, p. 353)
- Questions for Revising and Editing (Ch. 16, p. 360)
- Questions for Incorporating Secondary Sources (Ch. 17, p. 390)

## A rich selection of readings

The carefully selected poems represent canonical, multicultural, contemporary poetry. Complementing the many classic works that have long made classroom discussion come alive are numerous works not frequently anthologized, such as Jim Tilley's "The Big Questions" and Lisa Parker's "Snapping Beans." Featuring many of the most engaging poets of the twenty-first century, the selections include plenty of poems on daily life and contemporary issues such as Sherman Alexie's "The Facebook Sonnet" (on friendship and connection today), and Harryette Mullen's "Dim Lady" (a modern and memorable take on William Shakespeare's "My mistress' eyes are nothing like the sun").

## *Reading and writing advice from contemporary poets*

Brief selections throughout the book titled "When I Read" and "When I Write" were written especially for my anthologies by poets and are directed to students. This advice and insight gives students a unique opportunity to hear from many notable poets, like Martín Espada, Tony Hoagland, and Marilyn Nelson. Students will learn about how these writers work, about their reading habits, and perhaps most importantly, about what drives them to be poets.

## ACKNOWLEDGMENTS

This book has benefited from the ideas, suggestions, and corrections of scores of careful readers who helped transform various stages of an evolving manuscript into a finished book and into subsequent editions. I remain grateful to those I have thanked in prefaces of *The Bedford Introduction to Literature*, particularly to the late Robert Wallace of Case Western Reserve University. I would also like to give special thanks to Ronald Wallace of the University of Wisconsin and William Henry Louis of Mary Washington College. In addition, many instructors who have used *Poetry: An Introduction* responded to a questionnaire about the book — which led to the creation of this one. For their valuable comments and advice I am grateful to James Anderson, Johnson & Wales University; Jonathan Barron, University of Southern Mississippi; Kay Berry, Dixie High School; Jonathan Blake, Worcester State University; Douglas Crawford-Parker, University of Kansas; Melissa Criscuolo, Florida Atlantic University; Mark Crosby, Kansas State University; Louis Gallo, Radford University; Christine Grogan, University of South Florida; James Hausman III, South Fayette Township School District High School; Jane Hilberry, Colorado College; Audrey Lapointe, Ohio University; Kimmy Palmiotto, Suffern High School; Luivette Resto, Cerritos College; James Scoles, University of Winnipeg; Donald Sheehy, Edinboro University of Pennsylvania; and V. Andrew Wright, University of Detroit–Mercy.

I am also indebted to those who cheerfully answered questions and generously provided miscellaneous bits of information. What might have seemed to them like inconsequential conversations turned out to be important leads. Among these friends and colleagues are Raymond Anselment, Barbara Campbell, Ann Charters, Irving Cummings, William Curtin, Margaret Higonnet, Patrick Hogan, Lee Jacobus, Greta Little, George Monteiro,

Brenda Murphy, Joel Myerson, Rose Quiello, Thomas Recchio, William Sheidley, Milton Stern, Kenneth Wilson, and the dedicated reference librarians at the Homer Babbidge Library, University of Connecticut.

I am particularly happy to acknowledge the tactful help of Roxanne Cody, owner of R. J. Julia Booksellers in Madison, Connecticut, whose passion for books authorizes her as the consummate matchmaker for writers, readers, and titles. It's a wonder that somebody doesn't call the cops.

I continue to be grateful for what I have learned from teaching my students and for the many student papers I have received over the years that I have used in various forms to serve as good and accessible models of student writing.

At Bedford/St. Martin's, my debts once again require more time to acknowledge than the deadline allows. Charles H. Christensen, Joan Feinberg, Denise Wydra, Edwin Hill, Karen Henry, Vivian Garcia, and Maura Shea influenced this project with their intelligence, energy, and sound advice. As my developmental editor, Christina Gerogiannis expertly kept the book on track and made the journey a pleasure to the end; her valuable contributions richly remind me how fortunate I am to be a Bedford/St. Martin's author. Editorial assistant Cara Kaufman gracefully handled a variety of editorial tasks. Permissions were deftly arranged by Kalina Ingham, Arthur Johnson, Martha Friedman, and Susan Doheny. The difficult tasks of production were skillfully managed by Deborah Baker. Bev Miller provided careful copyediting, and Anne True and Angela Morrison did more-than-meticulous proofreading. I thank all of the people at Bedford — including Billy Boardman, who designed the cover, and Joy Fisher Williams, the marketing manager — who helped make this formidable project a manageable one.

Finally, I am grateful to my sons Timothy and Matthew for all kinds of help, but mostly I'm just grateful they're my sons. And for making all the difference, I thank my wife, Regina Barreca.

— Michael Meyer

# GET THE MOST OUT OF YOUR COURSE WITH *THINKING AND WRITING ABOUT POETRY*

***Thinking and Writing about Poetry*** doesn't stop with a book. Bedford/St. Martin's offers resources that help you and your students get even more out of your book and course. You'll also find convenient instructor resources, and even a nationwide community of teachers. To learn more about or to order any of the following products, contact your Bedford/St. Martin's sales representative, visit **macmillanhighered.com/myrep**, or visit **macmillanhighered.com/meyerpoetry/catalog**.

## *Assign* LaunchPad Solo for Literature — *the online, interactive, guide to close reading*

**macmillanhighered.com/meyerpoetry/catalog**

To get the most out of *Thinking and Writing about Poetry*, assign it with *LaunchPad Solo for Literature*, which can be packaged at **no additional cost.** With easy-to-use and easy-to-assign modules, reading comprehension quizzes, and engaging author videos, *LaunchPad Solo for Literature* guides students through three common assignment types: responding to a reading, comparing and contrasting two or more texts, and instructor-led collaborative close reading. Get all our great resources and activities in one fully customizable space online; then use our tools with your own content.

## *Package one of our best-selling brief handbooks at a discount*

Do you need a pocket-sized handbook for your course? Package *Easy Writer* by Andrea Lunsford or *A Pocket Style Manual* by Diana Hacker and Nancy Sommers with this text at a 20% discount. For more information, go to **macmillanhighered.com/easywriter/catalog** or **macmillanhighered.com/pocket/catalog.**

## *Teach longer works at a nice price*

Volumes from our Literary Reprint series — the Case Studies in Contemporary Criticism series, Bedford Cultural Edition series, the Bedford Shakespeare series, and the Bedford College Editions — can be shrinkwrapped with *Thinking and Writing about Poetry* at a discount. For a complete list of available titles, visit **macmillanhighered.com/literaryreprints/catalog.**

## *Trade Up and save 50%*

Add more value and choice to your students' learning experiences by packaging their Bedford/St. Martin's textbook with one of a thousand titles from our sister publishers, including Farrar, Straus and Giroux and St. Martin's Press — at a discount of 50% off the regular price. Visit **macmillanhighered.com/tradeup** for details.

## *Access your instructor resources and get teaching ideas you can use today*

Are you looking for professional resources for teaching literature and writing? How about some help with planning classroom activities?

**Download your instructor's manual**    This comprehensive manual offers teaching support for every selection, useful for new and experienced instructors alike. Resources include commentaries, biographical information, and writing assignments, as well as teaching tips from instructors who have taught with the book, additional suggestions for connections among the selections, and thematic groupings with questions for discussion and writing. The manual is available online at **macmillanhighered.com/meyerpoetry /catalog.**

**TeachingCentral**    We've gathered all of our print and online professional resources in one place. You'll find landmark reference works, sourcebooks on pedagogical issues, award-winning collections, and practical advice for the classroom — all free for instructors and available at **macmillanhighered .com/teachingcentral.**

**LitBits Blog: Ideas for Teaching Literature and Creative Writing**    Our popular LitBits blog — hosted by a team of instructors, poets, novelists, and scholars — offers a fresh, regularly updated collection of ideas and assignments. You'll find simple ways to teach with new media, excite your students with activities, and join an ongoing conversation about teaching. Go to **macmillanhighered.com/litbits.**

**Order content for your course management system**    Content cartridges for the most common course management systems — Blackboard, Canvas, Angel, Moodle, Sakai, and Desire2Learn — allow you to easily download Bedford/St. Martin's digital materials for your course. For more information, visit **macmillanhighered.com/coursepacks.**

# Brief Contents

# Contents

## 7. Sounds

## 11. Combining the Elements of Poetry: A Writing Process   237

## Approaches to Poetry   247

## 12. A Study of Robert Frost   249

## 13. A Thematic Case Study: Humor and Satire    282

## 14. A Collection of Poems    296

# Critical Thinking and Writing about Poetry    325

# Thematic Contents

## KEY TO THEMES

### Fear

### Loss and Grief

### Violence, War, and Peace

# Reading
# Imaginative Literature

Poetry does not need to be defended,
any more than air or food needs to be
defended.
—LANGSTON HUGHES

Granger, NYC.

## THE NATURE OF LITERATURE

Literature does not lend itself to a single tidy definition because the making of it over the centuries has been as complex, unwieldy, and natural as life itself. Is literature everything that has been written, from ancient prayers to graffiti? Does it include songs and stories that were not written down until many years after they were recited? Does literature include the television scripts from *Modern Family* as well as Shakespeare's *King Lear*? Is literature only writing that has permanent value and continues to move people? Must literature be true or beautiful or moral? Should it be socially useful?

Although these kinds of questions are not conclusively answered in this book, they are implicitly raised by the poems included here. No definition of literature, particularly a brief one, is likely to satisfy everyone because definitions tend to weaken and require qualification when confronted by the uniqueness of individual works. In this context it is worth recalling Herman Melville's humorous use of a definition of a whale in *Moby-Dick* (1851). In the course of the novel Melville presents his imaginative and symbolic whale as inscrutable, but he begins with a quotation from Georges Cuvier, a French naturalist who defines a whale in his nineteenth-century

1

study *The Animal Kingdom* this way: "The whale is a mammiferous animal without hind feet." Cuvier's description is technically correct, of course, but there is little wisdom in it. Melville understood that the reality of the whale (which he describes as the "ungraspable phantom of life") cannot be caught by isolated facts. If the full meaning of the whale is to be understood, it must be sought on the open sea of experience, where the whale itself is, rather than in exclusionary definitions. Although they may be helpful, facts and definitions do not always reveal the whole truth.

Despite Melville's reminder that a definition can be too limiting and even comical, it is useful for our purposes to describe literature as a fiction consisting of carefully arranged words designed to stir the imagination. Stories, poems, and plays are fictional. They are made up — imagined — even when based on actual historic events. Such imaginative writing differs from other kinds of writing because its purpose is not primarily to transmit facts or ideas. Imaginative literature is a source more of pleasure than of information, and we read it for basically the same reasons we listen to music or view a dance: enjoyment, delight, and satisfaction. Like other art forms, imaginative literature offers pleasure and usually attempts to convey a perspective, a mood, a feeling, or an experience. Writers transform the facts the world provides — people, places, and objects — into experiences that suggest meanings.

Consider, for example, the difference between the following factual description of a snake and a poem on the same subject. Here is the *Webster's Collegiate Dictionary* definition:

> any of numerous limbless scaled reptiles (suborder Serpentes or Ophidia) with a long tapering body and with salivary glands often modified to produce venom which is injected through grooved or tubular fangs.

Contrast this matter-of-fact definition with Emily Dickinson's poetic evocation of a snake in "A narrow Fellow in the Grass":

A narrow Fellow in the Grass
Occasionally rides —
You may have met Him — did you not
His notice sudden is —

The Grass divides as with a Comb —          5
A spotted shaft is seen —
And then it closes at your feet
And opens further on —

He likes a Boggy Acre
A floor too cool for Corn —          10
Yet when a Boy, and Barefoot —
I more than once at Noon

Have passed, I thought, a Whip lash
Unbraiding in the Sun

When stooping to secure it                                    15
It wrinkled, and was gone —

Several of Nature's People
I know, and they know me —
I feel for them a transport
Of cordiality —                                               20

But never met this Fellow
Attended, or alone
Without a tighter breathing
And Zero at the Bone —

    The dictionary provides a succinct, anatomical description of what a snake is, whereas Dickinson's poem suggests what a snake can mean. The definition offers facts; the poem offers an experience. The dictionary description would probably allow someone who had never seen a snake to sketch one with reasonable accuracy. The poem also provides some vivid subjective descriptions—for example, the snake dividing the grass "as with a Comb"—yet it offers more than a picture of serpentine movements. The poem conveys the ambivalence many people have about snakes—the kind of feeling, for example, so evident on the faces of visitors viewing the snakes at a zoo. In the poem there is both a fascination with and a horror of what might be called snakehood; this combination of feelings has been coiled in most of us since Adam and Eve.

    That "narrow Fellow" so cordially introduced by way of a riddle (the word *snake* is never used in the poem) is, by the final stanza, revealed as a snake in the grass. In between, Dickinson uses language expressively to convey her meaning. For instance, in the line "His notice sudden is," listen to the *s* sound in each word and note how the verb *is* unexpectedly appears at the end, making the snake's hissing presence all the more "sudden." And anyone who has ever been surprised by a snake knows the "tighter breathing / And Zero at the Bone" that Dickinson evokes so successfully by the rhythm of her word choices and line breaks. Perhaps even more significant, Dickinson's poem allows those who have never encountered a snake to imagine such an experience.

    A good deal more could be said about the numbing fear that undercuts the affection for nature at the beginning of this poem; the point here is that imaginative literature gives us not so much the full, factual proportions of the world but rather some of its experiences and meanings. Instead of defining the world, literature encourages us to try it out in our imaginations.

## THE VALUE OF LITERATURE

Mark Twain once shrewdly observed that a person who chooses not to read has no advantage over a person who is unable to read. In industrialized societies today, however, the question is not who reads, because nearly everyone can and does, but what is read. Why should anyone spend precious time with literature when there is so much reading material available that provides useful information about everything from the daily news to personal computers? Why should a literary artist's imagination compete for attention that could be spent on the firm realities that constitute everyday life? In fact, national best-seller lists include collections of stories, poems, or plays much less often than they do cookbooks and, not surprisingly, diet books. Although such fare may be filling, it doesn't stay with you. Most people have other appetites, too.

Certainly one of the most important values of literature is that it nourishes our emotional lives. An effective literary work may seem to speak directly to us, especially if we are ripe for it. The inner life that good writers reveal in their characters often gives us glimpses of some portion of ourselves. We can be moved to laugh, cry, tremble, dream, ponder, shriek, or rage with a character by simply turning a page instead of turning our lives upside down. Although the experience itself is imagined, the emotion is real. That's why the final chapters of a good adventure novel can make a reader's heart race as much as a 100-yard dash or why the repressed love of Hester Prynne in Nathaniel Hawthorne's *The Scarlet Letter* is painful to a sympathetic reader. Human emotions speak a universal language regardless of when or where a work was written.

In addition to appealing to our emotions, literature broadens our perspectives on the world. Most of the people we meet are pretty much like ourselves, and what we can see of the world even in a lifetime is astonishingly limited. Literature allows us to move beyond the inevitable boundaries of our own lives and cultures because it introduces us to people different from ourselves, places remote from our neighborhoods, and times other than our own. Reading makes us more aware of life's possibilities as well as its subtleties and ambiguities. Put simply, people who read literature experience more life and have a keener sense of a common human identity than those who do not. It is true, of course, that many people go through life without reading imaginative literature, but that is a loss rather than a gain. They may find themselves troubled by the same kinds of questions that reveal Daisy Buchanan's restless, vague discontentment in F. Scott Fitzgerald's *The Great Gatsby:* "'What'll we do with ourselves this afternoon?' cried Daisy, 'and the day after that, and the next thirty years?'"

Sometimes students mistakenly associate literature more with school than with life. Accustomed to reading it in order to write a paper or pass an examination, students may perceive such reading as a chore instead of a pleasurable opportunity, something considerably less important than studying for the "practical" courses that prepare them for a career. The study of literature, however, is also practical because it engages you in the kinds of problem solving important in a variety of fields, from philosophy to science and technology. The interpretation of literary texts requires you to deal with uncertainties, value judgments, and emotions; these are unavoidable aspects of life.

People who make the most significant contributions to their professions — whether in business, engineering, teaching, or some other area — tend to be challenged rather than threatened by multiple possibilities.

Instead of retreating to the way things have always been done, they bring freshness and creativity to their work. F. Scott Fitzgerald once astutely described the "test of a first-rate intelligence" as "the ability to hold two opposed ideas in the mind at the same time, and still retain the ability to function." People with such intelligence know how to read situations, shape questions, interpret details, and evaluate competing points of view. Equipped with a healthy respect for facts, they also understand the value of pursuing hunches and exercising their imaginations. Reading literature encourages a suppleness of mind that is helpful in any discipline or work.

Once the requirements for your degree are completed, what ultimately matters are not the courses listed on your transcript but the sensibilities and habits of mind that you bring to your work, friends, family, and, indeed, the rest of your life. A healthy economy changes and grows with the times; people do, too, if they are prepared for more than simply filling a job description. The range and variety of life that literature affords can help you to interpret your own experiences and the world in which you live.

To discover the insights that literature reveals requires careful reading and sensitivity. One of the purposes of a college literature class is to cultivate the analytic skills necessary for reading well. Class discussions often help establish a dialogue with a work that perhaps otherwise would not speak to you. Analytic skills can also be developed by writing about what you read. Writing is an effective means of clarifying your responses and ideas because it requires you to account for the author's use of language as well as your own. This book is based on two premises: that reading literature is pleasurable and that reading and understanding a work sensitively by thinking, talking, or writing about it increase the pleasure of the experience of it.

Understanding its basic elements — such as point of view, symbol, theme, tone, and irony — is a prerequisite to an informed appreciation of literature. This kind of understanding allows you to perceive more in a literary work in much the same way that a spectator at a tennis match sees more if he or she understands the rules and conventions of the game. But literature is not simply a spectator sport. The analytic skills that open up literature also have their uses when you watch a television program or film and, more important, when you attempt to sort out the significance of the people, places, and events that constitute your own life. Literature enhances and sharpens your perceptions. What could be more lastingly practical as well as satisfying?

## THE CHANGING LITERARY CANON

Perhaps the best reading creates some kind of change in us: we see more clearly; we're alert to nuances; we ask questions that previously didn't occur to us. Henry David Thoreau had that sort of reading in mind when he remarked in *Walden* that the books he valued most were those that caused him to date "a new era in his life from the reading." Readers are sometimes changed by literature, but it is also worth noting that the life of a literary work can also be affected by its readers. Melville's *Moby-Dick,* for example, was not valued as a classic until the 1920s, when critics rescued the novel from the obscurity of being cataloged in many libraries (including Yale's) not under fiction but under cetology, the study of whales. Indeed, many writers contemporary to Melville who were important and popular in the nineteenth century — William Cullen Bryant, Henry Wadsworth Longfellow, and James Russell Lowell, to name a few — are now mostly unread; their names appear more often on elementary schools built early in the twentieth century than in anthologies. Clearly, literary reputations and what is valued as great literature change over time and in the eyes of readers.

Such changes have steadily accelerated as the literary *canon* — those works considered by scholars, critics, and teachers to be the most important to read and study — has undergone a significant series of shifts. Writers who previously were overlooked, undervalued, neglected, or studiously ignored have been brought into focus in an effort to create a more diverse literary canon, one that recognizes the contributions of the many cultures that make up American society. Since the 1960s, for example, some critics have reassessed writings by women who had been left out of the standard literary traditions dominated by male writers. Many more female writers are now read alongside the male writers who traditionally populated literary history. This kind of enlargement of the canon also resulted from another reform movement of the 1960s: the civil rights movement sensitized literary critics to the political, moral, and esthetic necessity of rediscovering African American literature, and more recently Asian and Hispanic writers have been making their way into the canon. Moreover, on a broader scale the canon is being revised and enlarged to include the works of writers from parts of the world other than the West — a development that reflects the changing values, concerns, and complexities of recent decades, when literary landscapes have shifted as dramatically as the political boundaries of much of the world.

.   .   .

No semester's reading list — or anthology — can adequately or accurately echo all the new voices competing to be heard as part of the mainstream literary canon, but recent efforts to open up the canon attempt to sensitize readers to the voices of women, minorities, and writers from all over the world. This development has not occurred without its urgent advocates or passionate dissenters. It's no surprise that issues about race, gender, and class often get people off the fence and on their feet (these controversies are discussed further in Chapter 15, "Critical Strategies for Reading"). Although what we regard as literature — whether it's called great, classic, or canonical — continues to generate debate, there is no question that such controversy will continue to reflect readers' values as well as the writers they admire.

# The Elements of Poetry

# 1

# Reading Poetry

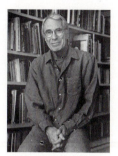

Ink runs from the corners of my mouth,
There is no happiness like mine.
I have been eating poetry.
— MARK STRAND

## READING POETRY RESPONSIVELY

Perhaps the best way to begin reading poetry responsively is not to allow yourself to be intimidated by it. Come to it, initially at least, the way you might listen to a song on the radio. You probably listen to a song several times before you hear it all, before you have a sense of how it works, where it's going, and how it gets there. You don't worry about analyzing a song when you listen to it, even though after repeated experiences with it, you know and anticipate a favorite part and know, on some level, why it works for you. Give yourself a chance to respond to poetry. The hardest work has already been done by the poet, so all you need to do at the start is listen for the pleasure produced by the poet's arrangement of words.

Try reading the following poem aloud. Read it aloud before you read it silently. You may stumble once or twice, but you'll make sense of it if you pay attention to its punctuation and don't stop at the end of every line where there is no punctuation. When you finish reading it, think about why it's called "Snapping Beans."

## Lisa Parker (b. 1972)

### *Snapping Beans*                                        *1998*

*For Fay Whitt*

I snapped beans into the silver bowl
that sat on the splintering slats
of the porchswing between my grandma and me.
I was home for the weekend,
from school, from the North,                                    5
Grandma hummed "What A Friend We Have In Jesus"
as the sun rose, pushing its pink spikes
through the slant of cornstalks,
through the fly-eyed mesh of the screen.
We didn't speak until the sun overcame                          10
the feathered tips of the cornfield
and Grandma stopped humming. I could feel
the soft gray of her stare
against the side of my face
when she asked, *How's school a-goin'?*                         15
I wanted to tell her about my classes,
the revelations by book and lecture,
as real as any shout of faith
and potent as a swig of strychnine.
She reached the leather of her hand                             20
over the bowl and cupped
my quivering chin; the slick smooth of her palm
held my face the way she held tomatoes
under the spigot, careful not to drop them,
and I wanted to tell her                                        25
about the nights I cried into the familiar
heartsick panels of the quilt she made me,
wishing myself home on the evening star.
I wanted to tell her
the evening star was a planet,                                  30
that my friends wore noserings and wrote poetry
about sex, about alcoholism, about Buddha.
I wanted to tell her how my stomach burned
acidic holes at the thought of speaking in class,
speaking in an accent, speaking out of turn,                    35
how I was tearing, splitting myself apart
with the slow-simmering guilt of being happy
despite it all.
I said, *School's fine.*
We snapped beans into the silver bowl between us                40

and when a hickory leaf, still summer green,
skidded onto the porchfront,
Grandma said,
*It's funny how things blow loose like that.*

### CONSIDERATIONS FOR CRITICAL THINKING AND WRITING

1. FIRST RESPONSE. Describe the speaker's feelings about starting a life at
   college. How do those feelings compare with your own experiences?
2. How does the grandmother's world differ from the speaker's at school?
   What details especially reveal those differences?
3. Discuss the significance of the grandmother's response to the hickory
   leaf in line 44. How do you read the last line?

The next poem creates a different kind of mood. Think about the title,
"Those Winter Sundays," before you begin reading the poem. What associations do you have with winter Sundays? What emotions does the phrase
evoke in you?

### ROBERT HAYDEN (1913–1980)

## *Those Winter Sundays*                                    1962

Sundays too my father got up early
and put his clothes on in the blueblack cold,
then with cracked hands that ached
from labor in the weekday weather made
banked fires blaze. No one ever thanked him.                    5

I'd wake and hear the cold splintering, breaking.
When the rooms were warm, he'd call,
and slowly I would rise and dress,
fearing the chronic angers of that house,

Speaking indifferently to him,                                  10
who had driven out the cold
and polished my good shoes as well.
What did I know, what did I know
of love's austere and lonely offices?

Does the poem match the feelings you have about winter Sundays?
Either way, your response can be useful in reading the poem. For most of
us, Sundays are days at home; they might be cozy and pleasant experiences
or they might be dull and depressing. Whatever they are, Sundays are more
evocative than, say, Tuesdays. Hayden uses that response to call forth a
sense of missed opportunity in the poem. The person who reflects on those
winter Sundays didn't know until much later how much he had to thank his

father for "love's austere and lonely offices." This is a poem about a cold past and a present reverence for his father — elements brought together by the phrase "Winter Sundays." *His* father? You may have noticed that the poem doesn't use a masculine pronoun; hence the voice could be a woman's. Does the gender of the voice make any difference to your reading? Would it make any difference about which details are included or what language is used?

What is most important about your initial readings of a poem is that you ask questions. If you read responsively, you'll find yourself asking all kinds of questions about the words, descriptions, sounds, and structure of a poem. The specifics of those questions will be generated by the particular poem. We don't, for example, ask how humor is achieved in "Those Winter Sundays" because there is none, but it is worth asking what kind of tone is established by the description of "the chronic angers of that house." The remaining chapters in this part of the book will help you formulate and answer questions about a variety of specific elements in poetry, such as speaker, image, metaphor, symbol, rhyme, and rhythm. For the moment, however, read the following poem several times and note your response at different points in the poem. Then write down a half-dozen or so questions about what produces your response to the poem. To answer questions, it's best to know first what the questions are, and that's what the rest of this chapter is about.

## JOHN UPDIKE  (1932–2009)

### *Dog's Death*                                                    *1969*

She must have been kicked unseen or brushed by a car.
Too young to know much, she was beginning to learn
To use the newspapers spread on the kitchen floor
And to win, wetting there, the words, "Good dog! Good dog!"

We thought her shy malaise was a shot reaction.                          5
The autopsy disclosed a rupture in her liver.
As we teased her with play, blood was filling her skin
And her heart was learning to lie down forever.

Monday morning, as the children were noisily fed
And sent to school, she crawled beneath the youngest's bed.              10
We found her twisted and limp but still alive.
In the car to the vet's, on my lap, she tried

To bite my hand and died. I stroked her warm fur
And my wife called in a voice imperious with tears.
Though surrounded by love that would have upheld her,                    15
Nevertheless she sank and, stiffening, disappeared.

Back home, we found that in the night her frame,
Drawing near to dissolution, had endured the shame
Of diarrhoea and had dragged across the floor
To a newspaper carelessly left there. *Good dog.*                    20

Here's a simple question to get started with your own questions: What would the poem's effect have been if Updike had titled it "Good Dog" instead of "Dog's Death"?

## THE PLEASURE OF WORDS

The impulse to create and appreciate poetry is as basic to human experience as language itself. Although no one can point to the precise origins of poetry, it is one of the most ancient of the arts, because it has existed ever since human beings discovered pleasure in language. The tribal ceremonies of peoples without written languages suggest that the earliest primitive cultures incorporated rhythmic patterns of words into their rituals. These chants, very likely accompanied by the music of a simple beat and the dance of a measured step, expressed what people regarded as significant and memorable in their lives. They echoed the concerns of the chanters and the listeners by chronicling acts of bravery, fearsome foes, natural disasters, mysterious events, births, deaths, and whatever else brought people pain or pleasure, bewilderment or revelation. Later cultures, such as the ancient Greeks, made poetry an integral part of religion.

Thus, from its very beginnings, poetry has been associated with what has mattered most to people. These concerns — whether natural or supernatural — can, of course, be expressed without vivid images, rhythmic patterns, and pleasing sounds, but human beings have always sensed a magic in words that goes beyond rational, logical understanding. Poetry is not simply a method of communication; it is a unique experience in itself.

What is special about poetry? What makes it valuable? Why should we read it? How is reading it different from reading prose? To begin with, poetry pervades our world in a variety of forms, ranging from advertising jingles to song lyrics. These may seem to be a long way from the chants heard around a primitive campfire, but they serve some of the same purposes. Like poems printed in a magazine or book, primitive chants, catchy jingles, and popular songs attempt to stir the imagination through the carefully measured use of words.

Although reading poetry usually makes more demands than does the kind of reading we use to skim a magazine or newspaper, the appreciation of poetry comes naturally enough to anyone who enjoys playing with words. Play is an important element of poetry. Consider, for example, how the following words appeal to the children who gleefully chant them in playgrounds:

> I scream, you scream
> We all scream
> For ice cream.

These lines are an exuberant evocation of the joy of ice cream. Indeed, chanting the words turns out to be as pleasurable as eating ice cream. In poetry, the expression of the idea is as important as the idea expressed.

But is "I scream . . ." poetry? Some poets and literary critics would say that it certainly is one kind of poem because the children who chant it experience some of the pleasures of poetry in its measured beat and repeated sounds. However, other poets and critics would define poetry more narrowly and insist, for a variety of reasons, that this isn't true poetry but merely ***doggerel***, a term used for lines whose subject matter is trite and whose rhythm and sounds are monotonously heavy-handed.

Although probably no one would argue that "I scream . . ." is a great poem, it does contain some poetic elements that appeal, at the very least, to children. Does that make it poetry? The answer depends on one's definition, but poetry has a way of breaking loose from definitions. Because there are nearly as many definitions of poetry as there are poets, Edwin Arlington Robinson's succinct observations are useful: "[P]oetry has two outstanding characteristics. One is that it is undefinable. The other is that it is eventually unmistakable."

This comment places more emphasis on how a poem affects a reader than on how a poem is defined. By characterizing poetry as "undefinable," Robinson acknowledges that it can include many different purposes, subjects, emotions, styles, and forms. What effect does the following poem have on you?

## WILLIAM HATHAWAY (B. 1944)

### Oh, Oh                                                    *1982*

My girl and I amble a country lane,
moo cows chomping daisies, our own
sweet saliva green with grass stems.
"Look, look," she says at the crossing,
"the choo-choo's light is on." And sure
enough, right smack dab in the middle
of maple dappled summer sunlight
is the lit headlight — so funny.
An arm waves to us from the black window.
We wave gaily to the arm. "When I hear
trains at night I dream of being president,"
I say dreamily. "And me first lady," she
says loyally. So when the last boxcars,

© William Hathaway.

named after wonderful, faraway places,
and the caboose chuckle by we look
eagerly to the road ahead. And there,
poised and growling, are fifty Hell's Angels.

15

# A SAMPLE CLOSE READING
## *An Annotated Version of "Oh, Oh"*

After you've read a poem two or three times, a deeper, closer reading—line by line, word by word, syllable by syllable—will help you discover even more about the poem. Ask yourself: What happens (or does not happen) in the poem? What are the poem's central ideas? How do the poem's words, images, and sounds, for example, contribute to its meaning? What is the poem's overall tone? How is the poem put together?

You can flesh out your close reading by writing your responses in the margins of the page. The following interpretive notes offer but one way to read Hathaway's poem.

The title offers an interjection expressing strong emotion and foreboding.

The informal language conjures up an idyllic picture of a walk in the country, where the sights, sounds, and tastes are full of pleasure.

The carefully orchestrated *d*'s, *m*'s, *p*'s, and *s*'s of lines 6–8 create sounds that are meant to be savored.

Filled with confidence and hope, the couple imagines a successful future together in exotic locations. Even the train is happy for them as it "chuckle[s]" in approval of their dreams.

## WILLIAM HATHAWAY (B. 1944)
### *Oh, Oh*                1982

My girl and I amble a country lane,
moo cows chomping daisies, our own
sweet saliva green with grass stems.
"Look, look," she says at the crossing,
"the choo-choo's light is on." And sure          5
enough, right smack dab in the middle
of maple dappled summer sunlight
is the lit headlight — so funny.
An arm waves to us from the black window.
We wave gaily to the arm. "When I hear          10
trains at night I dream of being president,"
I say dreamily. "And me first lady," she
says loyally. So when the last boxcars,
named after wonderful, faraway places,
and the caboose chuckle by we look              15
eagerly to the road ahead. And there,
poised and growling, are fifty Hell's Angels.

The visual effect of the many *o*'s in lines 1–5 (and 15) suggests an innocent, wide-eyed openness to experience while the repetitive *oo* sounds echo a kind of reassuring, satisfied cooing.

"Right smack dab in the middle" of the poem, the "black window" hints that all is not well.

Not until the very last line does "the road ahead" yield a terrifying surprise. The strategically "poised" final line derails the leisurely movement of the couple and brings their happy story to a dead stop. The emotional reversal parked in the last words awaits the reader as much as it does the couple. The sight and sound of the motorcycle gang signal that what seemed like heaven is, in reality, hell: Oh, oh.

Hathaway's poem serves as a convenient reminder that poetry can be full of surprises. Full of confidence, this couple, like the reader, is unprepared for the shock to come. When we see those "fifty Hell's Angels," we are confronted with something like a bucket of cold water in the face.

But even though our expectations are abruptly and powerfully reversed, we are finally invited to view the entire episode from a safe distance — the distance provided by the delightful humor in this poem. After all, how seriously can we take a poem that is titled "Oh, Oh"? The poet has his way with us, but we are brought in on the joke, too. The terror takes on comic proportions as the innocent couple is confronted by no fewer than *fifty* Hell's Angels. This is the kind of raucous overkill that informs a short animated film produced some years ago titled *Bambi Meets Godzilla*: you might not have seen it, but you know how it ends. The poem's good humor comes through when we realize how pathetically inadequate the response of "Oh, Oh" is to the circumstances.

As you can see, reading a description of what happens in a poem is not the same as experiencing a poem. The exuberance of "I scream . . ." and the surprise of Hathaway's "Oh, Oh" are in the hearing or reading rather than in the retelling. A *paraphrase* is a prose restatement of the central ideas of a poem in your own language. Consider the difference between the following poem and the paraphrase that follows it. What is missing from the paraphrase?

## ROBERT FRANCIS (1901–1987)

### *Catch*                                                              1950

Two boys uncoached are tossing a poem together,
Overhand, underhand, backhand, sleight of hand, every hand,
Teasing with attitudes, latitudes, interludes, altitudes,
High, make him fly off the ground for it, low, make him stoop,
Make him scoop it up, make him as-almost-as-possible miss it,          5
Fast, let him sting from it, now, now fool him slowly,
Anything, everything tricky, risky, nonchalant,
Anything under the sun to outwit the prosy,
Over the tree and the long sweet cadence down,
Over his head, make him scramble to pick up the meaning,               10
And now, like a posy, a pretty one plump in his hands.

Paraphrase: A poet's relationship to a reader is similar to a game of catch. The poem, like a ball, should be pitched in a variety of ways to challenge and create interest. Boredom and predictability must be avoided if the game is to be engaging and satisfying.

· · ·

A paraphrase can help us achieve a clearer understanding of a poem, but, unlike a poem, it misses all the sport and fun. It is the poem that "outwit[s] the prosy" because the poem serves as an example of what it suggests poetry should be. Moreover, the two players — the poet and the reader — are "uncoached." They know how the game is played, but their expectations do not preclude spontaneity and creativity or their ability to surprise and be surprised. The solid pleasure of the workout — of reading poetry — is the satisfaction derived from exercising your imagination and intellect.

That pleasure is worth emphasizing. Poetry uses language to move and delight even when it includes a cast of fifty Hell's Angels. The pleasure is in having the poem work its spell on us. For that to happen, it is best to relax and enjoy poetry rather than worry about definitions of it. Pay attention to what the poet throws you. We read poems for emotional and intellectual discovery — to feel and to experience something about the world and ourselves. The ideas in poetry — what can be paraphrased in prose — are important, but the real value of a poem consists in the words that work their magic by allowing us to feel, see, and be more than we were before. Perhaps the best way to approach a poem is similar to what Francis's "Catch" implies: expect to be surprised, stay on your toes, and concentrate on the delivery.

# A SAMPLE STUDENT ANALYSIS

## Tossing Metaphors Together in Robert Francis's "Catch"

The following sample paper on Robert Francis's "Catch" was written in response to an assignment that asked students to discuss the use of metaphor in the poem. Notice that Chris Leggett's paper is clearly focused and well organized. His discussion of the use of metaphor in the poem stays on track from beginning to end without any detours concerning unrelated topics (for a definition of *metaphor*, see p. 103). His title draws on the central metaphor of the poem, and he organizes the paper around four key words used in the poem: "attitudes, latitudes, interludes, altitudes." These constitute the heart of the paper's four substantive paragraphs, and they are effectively framed by introductory and concluding paragraphs. Moreover, the transitions between paragraphs clearly indicate that the author was not merely tossing a paper together.

Chris Leggett

Professor Lyles

English 203-1

9 November 2015

Tossing Metaphors Together in Robert Francis's "Catch"

The word *catch* is an attention getter. It usually means something is

about to be hurled at someone and that he or she is expected to catch it.

*Catch* can also signal a challenge to another player if the toss is purposefully

difficult. Robert Francis, in his poem *Catch*, uses the extended metaphor of two

boys playing catch to explore the considerations a poet makes when "tossing

a poem together" (line 1). Line 3 of "Catch" enumerates these considerations

metaphorically as "attitudes, latitudes, interludes, [and] altitudes." While regular

prose is typically straightforward and easily understood, poetry usually takes

great effort to understand and appreciate. To exemplify this, Francis presents

the reader not with a normal game of catch with the ball flying back and forth

in a repetitive and predictable fashion, but with a physically challenging game

in which one must concentrate, scramble, and exert oneself to catch the ball, as

one must stretch the intellect to truly grasp a poem.

The first consideration mentioned by Francis is attitude. Attitude, when

applied to the game of catch, indicates the ball's pitch in flight—upward,

downward, or straight. It could also describe the players' attitudes toward each

other or toward the game in general. Below this literal level lies *attitude*'s

meaning in relation to poetry. Attitude in this case represents a poem's tone.

A poet may "Teas[e] with attitudes" (3) by experimenting with different tones

to achieve the desired mood. The underlying tone of "Catch" is a playful one,

set and reinforced by the use of a game. This playfulness is further reinforced

by such words and phrases as "[t]easing" (3), "outwit" (8), and "fool him" (6).

Considered also in the metaphorical game of catch is latitude, which,

when applied to the game, suggests the range the object may be thrown—how

high, how low, or how far. Poetic latitude, along similar lines, concerns a poem's

breadth, or the scope of topic. Taken one level further, latitude suggests freedom

from normal restraints or limitations, indicating the ability to go outside the

norm to find originality of expression. The entire game of catch described in

Francis's poem reaches outside the normal expectations of something being

merely tossed back and forth in a predictable manner. The ball is thrown in

almost every conceivable fashion, "Overhand, underhand . . . every hand" (2).

Exploration
of the mean-
ing of the
word *catch*.

Thesis
statement
identifying
purpose
of poem's
metaphors.

Reference
to specific
language
in poem,
around
which the
paper is
organized.

Introductory
analysis of
the poem's
purpose.

Analysis of
the meaning
of *attitude* in
the poem.

Discussion
of how the
attitude
metaphor
contributes
to poem's
tone.

Analysis of
the meaning
of *latitude* in
the poem.

Other terms describing the throws—such as "tricky," "risky," "Fast," "slowly," and "Anything under the sun"(6-8)—express endless latitude for avoiding predictability in Francis's game of catch and metaphorically in writing poetry.

> Discussion of how the latitude metaphor contributes to the poem's scope and message.

During a game of catch the ball may be thrown at different intervals, establishing a steady rhythm or a broken, irregular one. Other intervening features, such as the field being played on or the weather, could also affect the game. These features of the game are alluded to in the poem by the use of the word *interludes*. *Interlude* in the poetic sense represents the poem's form, which can similarly establish or diminish rhythm or enhance meaning. Lines 6 and 9, respectively, show a broken and a flowing rhythm. Line 6 begins rapidly as a hard toss that stings the catcher's hand is described. The rhythm of the line is immediately slowed, however, by the word "now" followed by a comma, followed by the rest of the line. In contrast, line 9 flows smoothly as the reader visualizes the ball flying over the tree and sailing downward. The words chosen for this line function perfectly. The phrase "the long sweet cadence down" establishes a sweet rhythm that reads smoothly and rolls off the tongue easily. The choice of diction not only affects the poem's rhythmic flow but also establishes through connotative language the various levels at which the poem can be understood, represented in "Catch" as altitude.

> Analysis of the meaning of *interlude* in the poem.

> Discussion of how the interlude metaphor contributes to the poem's form and rhythm.

While *altitudes* when referring to the game of catch means how high an object is thrown, in poetry it could refer to the level of diction, lofty or down-to-earth, formal or informal. It suggests also the levels at which a poem can be comprehended, the literal as well as the interpretive. In Francis's game of catch, the ball is thrown high to make the player reach, low to "make him stoop" (4), or "Over his head [to] make him scramble" (10), implying that the player should have to exert himself to catch it. So too, then, should the reader of poetry put great effort into understanding the full meaning of a poem. Francis exemplifies this consideration in writing poetry by giving "Catch" not only an enjoyable literal meaning concerning the game of catch, but also a rich metaphorical meaning—reflecting the process of writing poetry. Francis uses several phrases and words with multiple meanings. The phrase "tossing a poem together" (1) can be understood as tossing something back and forth or the process of constructing a poem. While "prosy" (8) suggests prose itself, it also means the mundane or the ordinary. In the poem's final line the word *posy* of course represents a flower, while it is also a variant of the word *poesy*, meaning poetry, or the practice of composing poetry.

> Analysis of the meaning of *altitudes* in the poem.

> Discussion of how the altitude metaphor contributes to the poem's literal and symbolic meanings, with references to specific language.

Leggett 3

Francis effectively describes several considerations to be taken in writing poetry in order to "outwit the prosy" (8). His use of the extended metaphor in "Catch" shows that a poem must be unique, able to be comprehended on multiple levels, and a challenge to the reader. The various rhythms in the lines of "Catch" exemplify the ideas they express. While achieving an enjoyable poem on the literal level, Francis has also achieved a rich metaphorical meaning. The poem offers a good workout both physically and intellectually.

> Conclusion summarizing ideas explored in paper.

Leggett 4

Work Cited

Francis, Robert. "Catch." *Thinking and Writing about Poetry*. Ed. Michael Meyer. Boston: Bedford/St. Martin's, 2016. 16. Print.

Before beginning your own writing assignment on poetry, you should review Chapter 2, "Writing about Poetry: From Inquiry to Final Paper," and Chapter 16, "Reading and the Writing Process," which provides a step-by-step overview of how to choose a topic, develop a thesis, and organize various types of writing assignments. If you are using outside sources in your paper, you should make sure that you are familiar with the conventional documentation procedures described in Chapter 17, "The Literary Research Paper."

How does the speaker's description in Francis's "Catch" of what a reader might expect from reading poetry compare with the speaker's expectations concerning fiction in the next poem, by Philip Larkin?

## Philip Larkin (1922–1985)

### *A Study of Reading Habits*                    *1964*

When getting my nose in a book
Cured most things short of school,
It was worth ruining my eyes
To know I could still keep cool,
And deal out the old right hook                              5
To dirty dogs twice my size.

Later, with inch-thick specs,
Evil was just my lark:
Me and my cloak and fangs
Had ripping times in the dark.                               10
The women I clubbed with sex!
I broke them up like meringues.

Don't read much now: the dude
Who lets the girl down before
The hero arrives, the chap
Who's yellow and keeps the store,                            15
Seem far too familiar. Get stewed:
Books are a load of crap.

In "A Study of Reading Habits," Larkin distances himself from a speaker whose sensibilities he does not wholly share. The poet — and many readers — might identify with the reading habits described by the speaker in the first twelve lines, but Larkin uses the last six lines to criticize the speaker's attitude toward life as well as reading. The speaker recalls in lines 1–6 how as a schoolboy he identified with the hero, whose virtuous strength always triumphed over "dirty dogs," and in lines 7–12 he recounts how his schoolboy fantasies were transformed by adolescence into a fascination with violence and sex. This description of early reading habits is pleasantly amusing, because many readers of popular fiction will probably recall having moved through similar stages, but at the end of the poem, the speaker provides more information about himself than he intends to.

As an adult the speaker has lost interest in reading because it is no longer an escape from his own disappointed life. Instead of identifying with heroes or villains, he finds himself identifying with minor characters who are irresponsible and cowardly. Reading is now a reminder of his failures, so he turns to alcohol. His solution, to "Get stewed" because "Books are a load of crap," is obviously self-destructive. The speaker is ultimately exposed by Larkin as someone who never grew beyond fantasies. Getting drunk is consistent with the speaker's immature reading habits. Unlike the speaker, the poet understands that life is often distorted by escapist fantasies, whether through a steady diet of popular fiction or through alcohol. The speaker in this poem, then, is not Larkin but a created identity whose voice is filled with disillusionment and delusion.

The problem with Larkin's speaker is that he misreads books as well as his own life. Reading means nothing to him unless it serves as an escape from himself. It is not surprising that Larkin has him read fiction rather than poetry because poetry places an especially heavy emphasis on language. Fiction, indeed any kind of writing, including essays and drama, relies on carefully chosen and arranged words, but poetry does so to an even greater extent. Notice, for example, how Larkin's deft use of trite expressions and slang characterizes the speaker so that his language reveals nearly as much about his dreary life as what he says. Larkin's speaker would have no use for poetry.

What is "unmistakable" in poetry (to use Robinson's term again) is its intense, concentrated use of language — its emphasis on individual words to convey meanings, experiences, emotions, and effects. Poets never simply process words; they savor them. Words in poems frequently create their own tastes, textures, scents, sounds, and shapes. They often seem more sensuous than ordinary language, and readers usually sense that a word has been hefted before making its way into a poem. Although poems are crafted differently from the ways a painting, sculpture, or musical composition is created, in each form of art the creator delights in the medium. Poetry is carefully orchestrated so that the words work together as elements in a structure to sustain close, repeated readings. The words are chosen to interact with one another to create the maximum desired effect, whether the purpose is to capture a mood or feeling, create a vivid experience, express a point of view, narrate a story, or portray a character.

Here is a poem that looks quite different from most **verse**, a term used for lines composed in a measured rhythmical pattern, which are often, but not necessarily, rhymed.

## ROBERT MORGAN (B. 1944)

### *Mountain Graveyard*                                                            1979

*for the author of "Slow Owls"*

*Spore Prose*

| | |
|---|---|
| stone | notes |
| slate | tales |
| sacred | cedars |
| heart | earth |
| asleep | please |
| hated | death |

Though unconventional in its appearance, this is unmistakably poetry because of its concentrated use of language. The poem demonstrates how serious play with words can lead to some remarkable discoveries. At first glance "Mountain Graveyard" may seem intimidating. What, after all, does this list of words add up to? How is it in any sense a poetic use of language? But if the words are examined closely, it is not difficult to see how they work. The wordplay here is literally in the form of a game. Morgan uses a series of **anagrams** (words made from the letters of other words, such as *read* and *dare*) to evoke feelings about death. "Mountain Graveyard" is one of several poems that Morgan has called "Spore Prose" (another anagram) because he finds in individual words the seeds of poetry. He wrote the poem in honor of the fiftieth birthday of another poet, Jonathan Williams, the author of "Slow Owls," whose title is also an anagram.

The title, "Mountain Graveyard," indicates the poem's setting, which is also the context in which the individual words in the poem interact to provide a larger meaning. Morgan's discovery of the words on the stones of a graveyard is more than just clever. The observations he makes among the silent graves go beyond the curious pleasure a reader experiences in finding that the words *sacred cedars*, referring to evergreens common in cemeteries, consist of the same letters. The surprise and delight of realizing the connection between *heart* and *earth* are tempered by the more sober recognition that everyone's story ultimately ends in the ground. The hope that the dead are merely asleep is expressed with a plea that is answered grimly by a hatred of death's finality.

Little is told in this poem. There is no way of knowing who is buried or who is looking at the graves, but the emotions of sadness, hope, and pain are unmistakable — and are conveyed in fewer than half the words of this sentence. Morgan takes words that initially appear to be a dead, prosaic list and energizes their meanings through imaginative juxtapositions.

The following poem also involves a startling discovery about words. With the peculiar title "l(a," the poem cannot be read aloud, so there is no sound, but is there sense, a **theme** — a central idea or meaning — in the poem?

## E. E. CUMMINGS (1894–1962)

### l(a

1958

l(a

le
af
fa

ll
s)
one
l

iness

## CONSIDERATIONS FOR CRITICAL THINKING AND WRITING

1. FIRST RESPONSE. Discuss the connection between what appears inside and outside the parentheses in this poem.
2. What does Cummings draw attention to by breaking up the words? How do this strategy and the poem's overall shape contribute to its theme?
3. Which seems more important in this poem — what is expressed or the way it is expressed?

Although "Mountain Graveyard" and "l(a" do not resemble the kind of verse that readers might recognize immediately as poetry on a page, both are actually a very common type of poem, called the **lyric**, usually a brief poem that expresses the personal emotions and thoughts of a single speaker. Lyrics are often written in the first person, but sometimes — as in "Mountain Graveyard" and "l(a" — no speaker is specified. Lyrics present a subjective mood, emotion, or idea. Very often they are about love or death, but almost any subject or experience that evokes some intense emotional response can be found in lyrics. In addition to brevity and emotional intensity, lyrics are also frequently characterized by their musical qualities. The word *lyric* derives from the Greek word *lyre*, meaning a musical instrument that originally accompanied the singing of a lyric. Lyric poems can be organized in a variety of ways, such as the sonnet, elegy, and ode (see Chapter 9), but it is enough to point out here that lyrics are an extremely popular kind of poetry with writers and readers.

The following anonymous lyric was found in a sixteenth-century manuscript.

## ANONYMOUS

### *Western Wind*                                            *ca. 1500*

Western wind, when wilt thou blow,
The small rain down can rain?
Christ, if my love were in my arms,
And I in my bed again!

This speaker's intense longing for his lover is characteristic of lyric poetry. He impatiently addresses the western wind that brings spring to England and could make it possible for him to be reunited with the woman he loves. We do not know the details of these lovers' lives because this poem focuses on the speaker's emotion. We do not learn why the lovers are apart or if they will be together again. We don't even know if the speaker is a man. But those issues are not really important. The poem gives us a feeling rather than a story.

A poem that tells a story is called a ***narrative poem***. Narrative poetry may be short or very long. An ***epic***, for example, is a long narrative poem on a serious subject chronicling heroic deeds and important events. Among the most famous epics are Homer's *Iliad* and *Odyssey*, the Old English *Beowulf*, Dante's *Divine Comedy*, and John Milton's *Paradise Lost*. More typically, however, narrative poems are considerably shorter, as is the case with the following poem, which tells the story of a child's memory of her father.

---

**WHEN I WRITE** "There are lots of things that are going on in the world, in your room, or in that book you didn't read for class that could set you on fire if you gave them a chance. Poetry isn't only about what you feel, it's about what you think, and about capturing the way the world exists in one particular moment." — REGINA BARRECA

---

# REGINA BARRECA (B. 1957)
## Nighttime Fires    1986

© Nicolette Theriault.

When I was five in Louisville
we drove to see nighttime fires. Piled
    seven of us,
all pajamas and running noses, into the
    Olds,
drove fast toward smoke. It was after my
    father
lost his job, so not getting up in the
    morning
gave him time: awake past midnight, he
    read old newspapers
with no news, tried crosswords until he
    split the pencil
between his teeth, mad. When he heard
the wolf whine of the siren, he woke my mother,
and she pushed and shoved                                    10
us all into waking. Once roused we longed for burnt wood
and a smell of flames high into the pines. My old man liked
driving to rich neighborhoods best, swearing in a good mood
as he followed fire engines that snaked like dragons
and split the silent streets. It was festival, carnival.      15

If there were a Cadillac or any car
in a curved driveway, my father smiled a smile
from a secret, brittle heart.
His face lit up in the heat given off by destruction
like something was being made, or was being set right.        20
I bent my head back to see where sparks

ate up the sky. My father who never held us
would take my hand and point to falling cinders that
covered the ground like snow, or, excited, show us
the swollen collapse of a staircase. My mother                    25
watched my father, not the house. She was happy
only when we were ready to go, when it was finally over
and nothing else could burn.
Driving home, she would sleep in the front seat
as we huddled behind. I could see his quiet face in the          30
rearview mirror, eyes like hallways filled with smoke.

This narrative poem could have been a short story if the poet had wanted to say more about the "brittle heart" of this unemployed man whose daughter so vividly remembers the desperate pleasure he took in watching fire consume other people's property. Indeed, a reading of William Faulkner's famous short story "Barn Burning" suggests how such a character can be further developed and how his child responds to him. The similarities between Faulkner's angry character and the poem's father, whose "eyes [are] like hallways filled with smoke," are coincidental, but the characters' sense of "something . . . being set right" by flames is worth comparing. Although we do not know everything about this man and his family, we have a much firmer sense of their story than we do of the story of the couple in "Western Wind."

Although narrative poetry is still written, short stories and novels have largely replaced the long narrative poem. Lyric poems tend to be the predominant type of poetry today. Regardless of whether a poem is a narrative or a lyric, however, the strategies for reading it are somewhat different from those for reading prose. Try these suggestions for approaching poetry.

## Suggestions for Approaching Poetry

1. Assume that it will be necessary to read a poem more than once. Give yourself a chance to become familiar with what the poem has to offer. Like a piece of music, a poem becomes more pleasurable with each encounter.

2. Pay attention to the title; it will often provide a helpful context for the poem and serve as an introduction to it. Larkin's "A Study of Reading Habits" is precisely what its title describes.

3. As you read the poem for the first time, avoid becoming entangled in words or lines that you don't understand. Instead, give yourself a chance to take in the entire poem before attempting to resolve problems encountered along the way.

4. On a second reading, identify any words or passages that you don't understand. Look up words you don't know; these might

include names, places, historical and mythical references, or anything else that is unfamiliar to you.

5. Read the poem aloud (or perhaps have a friend read it to you). You'll probably discover that some puzzling passages suddenly fall into place when you hear them. You'll find that nothing helps, though, if the poem is read in an artificial, exaggerated manner. Read in as natural a voice as possible, with slight pauses at line breaks. Silent reading is preferable to imposing a te-tumpty-te-tum reading on a good poem.

6. Read the punctuation. Poems use punctuation marks — in addition to the space on the page — as signals for readers. Be especially careful not to assume that the end of a line marks the end of a sentence, unless it is concluded by punctuation. Consider, for example, the opening lines of Hathaway's "Oh, Oh":

> My girl and I amble a country lane,
> moo cows chomping daisies, our own
> sweet saliva green with grass stems.

Line 2 makes little or no sense if a reader stops after "own." Keeping track of the subjects and verbs will help you find your way among the sentences.

7. Paraphrase the poem to determine whether you understand what happens in it. As you work through each line of the poem, a paraphrase will help you to see which words or passages need further attention.

8. Try to get a sense of who is speaking and what the setting or situation is. Don't assume that the speaker is the author; often it is a created character.

9. Assume that each element in the poem has a purpose. Try to explain how the elements of the poem work together.

10. Be generous. Be willing to entertain perspectives, values, experiences, and subjects that you might not agree with or approve of. Even if baseball bores you, you should be able to comprehend its imaginative use in Francis's "Catch."

11. Try developing a coherent approach to the poem that helps you to shape a discussion of the text. See Chapter 15, "Critical Strategies for Reading," to review formalist, biographical, historical, psychological, feminist, and other possible critical approaches.

12. Don't expect to produce a definitive reading. Many poems do not resolve all the ideas, issues, or tensions in them, and so it is not always possible to drive their meaning into an absolute corner. Your reading will explore rather than define the poem. Poems are not trophies to be stuffed and mounted. They're usually more elusive. And don't be afraid that a close reading will damage the poem. Poems aren't hurt when we analyze them; instead, they come alive as we experience them and put into words what we discover through them.

A list of more specific questions using the literary terms and concepts discussed in the following chapters begins on page 45. That list, like the suggestions just made, raises issues and questions that can help you read just about any poem closely. These strategies should be a useful means for getting inside poems to understand how they work. Furthermore, because reading poetry inevitably increases sensitivity to language, you're likely to find yourself a better reader of words in any form — whether in a novel, a newspaper editorial, an advertisement, a political speech, or a conversation — after having studied poetry. In short, many of the reading skills that make poetry accessible also open up the world you inhabit.

You'll probably find some poems amusing or sad, some fierce or tender, and some fascinating or dull. You may find, too, some poems that will get inside you. Their kinds of insights — the poet's and yours — are what Emily Dickinson had in mind when she defined poetry this way: "If I read a book and it makes my whole body so cold no fire can ever warm me, I know that it is poetry. If I feel physically as if the top of my head were taken off, I know that it is poetry." Dickinson's response may be more intense than most — poetry was, after all, at the center of her life — but you, too, might find yourself moved by poems in unexpected ways. In any case, as Edwin Arlington Robinson knew, poetry is, to an alert and sensitive reader, "eventually unmistakable."

## BILLY COLLINS (B. 1941)

### *Introduction to Poetry*                                          1988

I ask them to take a poem
and hold it up to the light
like a color slide

or press an ear against its hive.

I say drop a mouse into a poem                                        5
and watch him probe his way out,

or walk inside the poem's room
and feel the walls for a light switch.

I want them to water-ski
across the surface of a poem                                          10
waving at the author's name on the shore.

But all they want to do
is tie the poem to a chair with rope
and torture a confession out of it.

They begin beating it with a hose                                     15
to find out what it really means.

### Considerations for Critical Thinking and Writing

1.  FIRST RESPONSE. In what sense does this poem offer suggestions for approaching poetry? What advice does the speaker provide in lines 1–11?

2.  How does the mood of the poem change beginning in line 12? What do you make of the shift from "them" to "they"?

3.  Paraphrase the poem. How is your paraphrase different from what is included in the poem?

4.  CREATIVE RESPONSE. Write a poem that describes your own experience reading and encountering poetry.

## POETRY IN POPULAR FORMS

Before you try out these strategies for reading on a few more poems, it is worth acknowledging that the verse that enjoys the widest readership appears not in collections, magazines, or even anthologies for students, but in greeting cards. A significant amount of the personal daily mail delivered in the United States consists of greeting cards. That represents millions of lines of verse going by us on the street and in planes over our heads. These verses share some similarities with the poetry included in this anthology, but there are also important differences that indicate the need for reading serious poetry closely rather than casually.

The popularity of greeting cards is easy to explain: just as many of us have neither the time nor the talent to make gifts for birthdays, weddings, anniversaries, graduations, Valentine's Day, Mother's Day, and other holidays, we are unlikely to write personal messages when cards conveniently say them for us. Although impersonal, cards are efficient and convey an important message no matter what the occasion for them: I care. These greetings are rarely serious poetry; they are not written to be. Nevertheless, they demonstrate the impulse in our culture to generate and receive poetry.

In a handbook for greeting-card freelancers, a writer and past editor of such verse began with this advice:

> Once you determine what you want to say — and in this regard it is best to stick to one basic idea — you must choose your words to do several things at the same time:
>
> 1.  Your idea must be expressed as a complete idea; it must have a beginning, a middle, and an end.
>
> 2.  There must be coherence in your verse. Every line must be linked logically and smoothly with its neighbors.
>
> 3.  Your expressions . . . must be conversational. High-flown language rarely comes off successfully in greeting-card writing.
>
> 4.  You must write with emphasis — and something else: enthusiasm. It's necessary to create interest in that all-important first line. From that point on, writing your verse is a matter of developing your idea and

bringing it to a peak of emphasis in the last line. Occasionally you will find that you have shot your wad too early in the verse, and whatever you say after that point sounds like an afterthought.

5. You must do all of the above and at the same time make everything come out right in the meter-and-rhyme department.[1]

This advice is followed by a list of approximately fifty of the most frequently used rhyme sounds accompanied by rhyming words, such as *love, of, above* for the sound *uv.* The point of these prescriptions is that the verse must be written so that it is immediately accessible — consumable — by both the buyer and the recipient. Writers of these cards are expected to avoid any complexity.

Compare the following greeting-card verse with the poem that comes after it. "Magic of Love," by Helen Farries, has been a longtime favorite in a major greeting-card company's "wedding line"; with different endings it has been used also in valentines and friendship cards.

If you're college age, you might not send very many greeting cards at this point in your life, though the card industry figures that you will once you get married or start a household. You might also prefer mailing — or e-mailing — cards that include more humor and sarcasm than you'll find in the example that follows, but the vast majority of older consumers enjoy sending the sort of traditional card written by Helen Farries.

## HELEN FARRIES (1918–2008)

### *Magic of Love*                                     *date unknown*

There's a wonderful gift that can give you a lift,
It's a blessing from heaven above!
It can comfort and bless, it can bring happiness —
It's the wonderful MAGIC OF LOVE!

Like a star in the night, it can keep your faith bright,          5
Like the sun, it can warm your hearts, too —
It's a gift you can give every day that you live,
And when given, it comes back to you!

When love lights the way, there is joy in the day
And all troubles are lighter to bear,                              10
Love is gentle and kind, and through love you will find
There's an answer to your every prayer!

May it never depart from your two loving hearts,
May you treasure this gift from above —
You will find if you do, all your dreams will come true,           15
In the wonderful MAGIC OF LOVE!

---

[1] Chris Fitzgerald, "Conventional Verse: The Sentimental Favorite," *The Greeting Card Writer's Handbook*, ed. H. Joseph Chadwick (Cincinnati: Writer's Digest, 1975), 13, 17.

# John Frederick Nims (1913–1999)

## *Love Poem*                                                  *1947*

My clumsiest dear, whose hands shipwreck vases,
At whose quick touch all glasses chip and ring,
Whose palms are bulls in china, burs in linen,
And have no cunning with any soft thing

Except all ill-at-ease fidgeting people:                          5
The refugee uncertain at the door
You make at home; deftly you steady
The drunk clambering on his undulant floor.

Unpredictable dear, the taxi drivers' terror,
Shrinking from far headlights pale as a dime                       10
Yet leaping before red apoplectic streetcars —
Misfit in any space. And never on time.

A wrench in clocks and the solar system. Only
With words and people and love you move at ease.
In traffic of wit expertly maneuver                                15
And keep us, all devotion, at your knees.

Forgetting your coffee spreading on our flannel,
Your lipstick grinning on our coat,
So gaily in love's unbreakable heaven
Our souls on glory of spilt bourbon float.                         20

Be with me, darling, early and late. Smash glasses —
I will study wry music for your sake.
For should your hands drop white and empty
All the toys of the world would break.

### Considerations for Critical Thinking and Writing

1. **FIRST RESPONSE.** Read these two works aloud. How are they different? How the same?

2. To what extent does the advice to would-be greeting-card writers apply to each work?

3. Compare the two speakers. Which do you find more appealing? Why?

4. How does Nims's description of love differ from Farries's?

In contrast to poetry, which transfigures and expresses an emotion or experience through an original use of language, the verse in "Magic of Love" relies on **clichés** — ideas or expressions that have become tired and trite from overuse, such as describing love as "a blessing from heaven above." Clichés anesthetize readers instead of alerting them to the possibility of fresh perceptions. They are used to draw out **stock responses** — predictable, conventional reactions to language, characters, symbols, or situations; God, heaven, the flag, motherhood, hearts, puppies, and peace are some often-used objects of stock responses. Advertisers manufacture careers from this sort of business.

Clichés and stock responses are two of the major ingredients of sentimentality in literature. **Sentimentality** exploits the reader by inducing responses that exceed what the situation warrants. This pejorative term should not be confused with *sentiment*, which is synonymous with *emotion* or *feeling*. Sentimentality cons readers into falling for the mass murderer who is devoted to stray cats, and it requires that we not think twice about what we're feeling because those tears shed for the little old lady, the rage aimed at the vicious enemy soldier, and the longing for the simple virtues of poverty might disappear under the slightest scrutiny. The experience of sentimentality is not unlike biting into a swirl of cotton candy; it's momentarily sweet but wholly insubstantial.

Clichés, stock responses, and sentimentality are generally the hallmarks of weak writing. Poetry — the kind that is unmistakable — achieves freshness, vitality, and genuine emotion that sharpen our perceptions of life.

Although the most widely read verse is found in greeting cards, the most widely *heard* poetry appears in song lyrics. Not all songs are poetic, but a good many share the same effects and qualities as poems. Consider these lyrics by Bruce Springsteen.

## Bruce Springsteen (b. 1949)

### Devils & Dust                                      2005

I got my finger on the trigger
But I don't know who to trust
When I look into your eyes
There's just devils and dust
We're a long, long way from home, Bobbie                5
Home's a long, long way from us
I feel a dirty wind blowing
Devils and dust

I got God on my side
I'm just trying to survive                              10
What if what you do to survive
Kills the things you love
Fear's a powerful thing
It can turn your heart black you can trust
It'll take your God filled soul                         15
And fill it with devils and dust

Well I dreamed of you last night
In a field of blood and stone
The blood began to dry
The smell began to rise                                 20
Well I dreamed of you last night, Bobbie

In a field of mud and bone
Your blood began to dry
The smell began to rise

We've got God on our side                                         25
We're just trying to survive
What if what you do to survive
Kills the things you love
Fear's a powerful thing, baby
It'll turn your heart black you can trust                          30
It'll take your God filled soul
Fill it with devils and dust

Now every woman and every man
They want to take a righteous stand
Find the love that God wills                                       35
And the faith that He commands
I've got my finger on the trigger
And tonight faith just ain't enough
When I look inside my heart
There's just devils and dust                                      40

Well I've got God on my side
And I'm just trying to survive
What if what you do to survive
Kills the things you love
Fear's a dangerous thing                                          45
It can turn your heart black you can trust
It'll take your God filled soul
Fill it with devils and dust

Yeah, it'll take your God filled soul

Fill it with devils and dust                                      50

## Considerations for Critical Thinking and Writing

1. FIRST RESPONSE. How do images of war and the phrases that are repeated evoke a particular mood in this song?

2. Do you think this song can accurately be called a narrative poem? Why or why not? How would you describe its theme?

3. How does your experience of reading "Devils & Dust" compare with listening to Springsteen singing the song (available on *Devils & Dust*)?

4. Surely not all manifestations of poetry in popular culture represent good poetry. Does bad poetry undercut good poetry? Does it cheapen its value? At this point in your study of poetry — the beginning — how do you define a good poem or a bad poem?

5. What is your favorite poem? Where did you first encounter it? Why is it important to you? Alternatively, if you can't come up with a favorite poem, why can't you?

## Perspective

### ROBERT FRANCIS (1901–1987)

## *On "Hard" Poetry*                                                  1965

When Robert Frost said he liked poems hard he could scarcely have meant he liked them difficult. If he had meant difficult he would have said he didn't like them easy. What he said was that he didn't like them soft.

Poems can be soft in several ways. They can be soft in form (invertebrate). They can be soft in thought and feeling (sentimental). They can be soft with excess verbiage. Frost used to advise [writers] to squeeze the water out of a poem. He liked poems dry. What is dry tends to be hard, and what is hard is always dry, except perhaps on the outside.

Yet though hardness here does not mean difficulty, some difficulty naturally goes with hardness. A hard poem may not be hard to read but is hard to write. Not too hard, preferably. Not so hard to write that there is no flow in the writer. But hard enough for the growing poem to meet with some healthy resistance. Frost often found this healthy resistance in a tight rhyme scheme and strict meter. There are other ways of getting good resistance, of course.

And in the reader too, a hard poem will bring some difficulty. Preferably not too much. Not enough difficulty to completely baffle him. Ideally a hard poem should not be too hard to make sense of, but hard to exhaust its meaning and its beauty.

"What I care about is the hardness of the poems. I don't like them soft, I want them to be little pebbles, but placed where they won't dislodge easily. And I'd like them to be little pebbles of precious stone — precious, or semiprecious" ([Robert Frost] interview with John Ciardi, *Saturday Review*, March 21, 1959).

Here is hard prose talking about hard poetry. Frost was never shrewder or more illuminating. Here, as well as in anything else he ever said, is his flavor.

What contemporary of his can you imagine saying this or anything like it?

In 1843 Emerson jotted in his journal: "Hard clouds and hard expressions, and hard manners, I love."

From *The Satirical Rogue on Poetry*

### CONSIDERATIONS FOR CRITICAL THINKING AND WRITING

1. What is the distinction between "hard" and "soft" poetry?

2. Explain whether you would characterize Bruce Springsteen's "Devils & Dust" (p. 32) as hard or soft.

3. CREATIVE RESPONSE. Given Francis's brief essay and his poem "Catch" (p. 16), write a review of Helen Farries's "Magic of Love" (p. 30) as you think Francis would.

# POEMS FOR FURTHER STUDY

## MARY OLIVER (B. 1935)

### *The Poet with His Face in His Hands*                    2005

You want to cry aloud for your
mistakes. But to tell the truth the world
doesn't need any more of that sound.

So if you're going to do it and can't
stop yourself, if your pretty mouth can't                      5
hold it in, at least go by yourself across

the forty fields and the forty dark inclines
of rocks and water to the place where
the falls are flinging out their white sheets

like crazy, and there is a cave behind all that               10
jubilation and water fun and you can
stand there, under it, and roar all you

want and nothing will be disturbed; you can
drip with despair all afternoon and still,
on a green branch, its wings just lightly touched             15

by the passing foil of the water, the thrush,
puffing out its spotted breast, will sing
of the perfect, stone-hard beauty of everything.

#### CONSIDERATIONS FOR CRITICAL THINKING AND WRITING

1. FIRST RESPONSE. Describe the kind of poet the speaker characterizes. What is the speaker's attitude toward that sort of poet?

2. Explain which single phrase used by the speaker to describe the poet most reveals for you the speaker's attitude toward the poet.

3. How is nature contrasted with the poet?

---

**WHEN I WRITE** "When I'm creating a story, I try to keep writing until I finish a draft — same for a poem, but I don't set aside a specific block of time. When the inkling of a poem is there, I write. When it's not, I go for a walk until it arrives." — JIM TILLEY

---

## JIM TILLEY (B. 1950)

### *The Big Questions*                                        2011

The big questions are big only
because they have never been answered.
Some questions, big as they seem,
are big only in the moment,
like when you're hiking a trail alone                          5

and you encounter a mammoth
grizzly who hasn't had lunch
in a fortnight, and he eyes you
as the answer to his only big question.
Life turns existential, and you can't                                    10

help questioning why you are here —
in this place on this planet
within this universe —
at this precise time,
or why he is, and you know he's not,                                    15

even for a moment, wondering
the same thing, because he's already
figured it out. And you, too,
know exactly what to do.
So, this can be a defining moment,                                      20

but not a big question,
because no one ever figures those out.
Still, one day when someone does,
might it not be a person like you
staring down a bear looking for lunch?                                  25

### Considerations for Critical Thinking and Writing

1. **FIRST RESPONSE.** What are the "big questions" raised in this poem?
2. Explain whether or not you think the bear and his "lunch" have much in common.
3. How does Tilley's use of language create a poem that is philosophically serious as well as genuinely funny?

### Connection to Another Selection

1. To what extent does Mary Oliver's "The Poet with His Face in His Hands" (p. 35) also raise the existential question of "why you are here"?

## Alberto Ríos (b. 1952)

### *Seniors*                                                   1985

Alberto Ríos.

William cut a hole in his Levi's pocket
so he could flop himself out in class
behind the girls so the other guys
could see and shit what guts we all said.
All Konga wanted to do over and over
was the rubber band trick, but he showed
everyone how, so nobody wanted to see

anymore and one day he cried, just cried
until his parents took him away forever.
Maya had a Hotpoint refrigerator standing                           10
in his living room, just for his family to show
anybody who came that they could afford it.

Me, I got a French kiss, finally, in the catholic
darkness, my tongue's farthest half vacationing
loudly in another mouth like a man in Bermudas,                     15
and my body jumped against a flagstone wall,
I could feel it through her thin, almost
nonexistent body: I had, at that moment, that moment,
a hot girl on a summer night, the best of all
the things we tried to do. Well, she                                20
let me kiss her, anyway, all over.

Or it was just a flagstone wall
with a flaw in the stone, an understanding cavity
for burning young men with smooth dreams —
the true circumstance is gone, the true                             25
circumstances about us all then
are gone. But when I kissed her, all water,
she would close her eyes, and they into somewhere
would disappear. Whether she was there
or not, I remember her, clearly, and she moves                      30
around the room, sometimes, until I sleep.

I have lain on the desert in watch
low in the back of a pick-up truck
for nothing in particular, for stars, for
the things behind stars, and nothing comes                          35
more than the moment: always now, here in a truck,
the moment again to dream of making love and sweat,
this time to a woman, or even to all of them
in some allowable way, to those boys, then,
who couldn't cry, to the girls before they were                     40
women, to friends, me on my back, the sky over me
pressing its simple weight into her body
on me, into the bodies of them all, on me.

### Considerations for Critical Thinking and Writing

1. FIRST RESPONSE. Comment on the use of slang in the poem. Does it surprise you? How does it characterize the speaker?

2. How does the language of the final stanza differ from that of the first
   stanza? To what purpose?

3. Write an essay that discusses the speaker's attitudes toward sex and life.
   How are they related?

CONNECTION TO ANOTHER SELECTION

1. Think about "Seniors" as a kind of love poem and compare the speaker's voice here with the one in T. S. Eliot's "The Love Song of J. Alfred Prufrock" (p. 304). How are these two voices used to evoke different cultures? Of what value is love in these cultures?

## ALFRED, LORD TENNYSON (1809–1892)

### *Crossing the Bar*                                                    1889

Sunset and evening star,
    And one clear call for me!
And may there be no moaning of the bar,°                            *sandbar*
    When I put out to sea,

But such a tide as moving seems asleep,                                  5
    Too full for sound and foam,
When that which drew from out the boundless deep
    Turns again home.

Twilight and evening bell,
    And after that the dark!                                        10
And may there be no sadness of farewell,
    When I embark;

For tho' from out our bourne of Time and Place
    The flood may bear me far,
I hope to see my Pilot face to face                                      15
    When I have crost the bar.

#### CONSIDERATIONS FOR CRITICAL THINKING AND WRITING

1. FIRST RESPONSE. How does Tennyson make clear that this poem is about more than a sea journey?

2. Why do you think Tennyson directed to his publishers to place "Crossing the Bar" as the last poem in all collections of his poetry?

3. Discuss the purpose of the punctuation (or its absence) at the end of each line.

CONNECTION TO ANOTHER SELECTION

1. Compare the speaker's mood in "Crossing the Bar" with that in Dylan Thomas's "Do Not Go Gentle into That Good Night" (p. 204).

Edgar Allan Poe (1809–1849)

## *The Raven*                                                1845

Once upon a midnight dreary, while I pondered, weak and weary,
Over many a quaint and curious volume of forgotten lore,
While I nodded, nearly napping, suddenly there came a tapping,
As of some one gently rapping, rapping at my chamber door.
" 'Tis some visiter," I muttered, "tapping at my chamber door —          5
　　　　　　　　　　　　　　Only this, and nothing more."

Ah, distinctly I remember it was in the bleak December,
And each separate dying ember wrought its ghost upon the floor.
Eagerly I wished the morrow; — vainly I had tried to borrow
From my books surcease of sorrow — sorrow for the lost Lenore —          10
For the rare and radiant maiden whom the angels name Lenore —
　　　　　　　　　　　　　　Nameless here for evermore.

And the silken sad uncertain rustling of each purple curtain
Thrilled me — filled me with fantastic terrors never felt before;
So that now, to still the beating of my heart, I stood repeating          15
" 'Tis some visiter entreating entrance at my chamber door —
Some late visiter entreating entrance at my chamber door; —
　　　　　　　　　　　　　　This it is, and nothing more."

Presently my soul grew stronger; hesitating then no longer,
"Sir," said I, "or Madam, truly your forgiveness I implore;          20
But the fact is I was napping, and so gently you came rapping,
And so faintly you came tapping, tapping at my chamber door,
That I scarce was sure I heard you" — here I opened wide the door; —
　　　　　　　　　　　　　　Darkness there, and nothing more.

Deep into that darkness peering, long I stood there wondering, fearing          25
Doubting, dreaming dreams no mortal ever dared to dream before;
But the silence was unbroken, and the darkness gave no token,
And the only word there spoken was the whispered word, "Lenore!"
This *I* whispered, and an echo murmured back the word, "Lenore!"
　　　　　　　　　　　　　　Merely this, and nothing more.          30

Then into the chamber turning, all my soul within me burning,
Soon I heard again a tapping somewhat louder than before.
"Surely," said I, "surely that is something at my window lattice;
Let me see, then, what thereat is, and this mystery explore —
Let my heart be still a moment and this mystery explore; —          35
　　　　　　　　　　　　　" 'Tis the wind, and nothing more!"

Open here I flung the shutter, when, with many a flirt and flutter,
In there stepped a stately raven of the saintly days of yore;
Not the least obeisance made he; not an instant stopped or stayed he;

But, with mien of lord or lady, perched above my chamber door —                  40
Perched upon a bust of Pallas° just above my chamber door —
                          Perched, and sat, and nothing more.

Then this ebony bird beguiling my sad fancy into smiling,
By the grave and stern decorum of the countenance it wore,
"Though thy crest be shorn and shaven, thou," I said, "art sure no craven,     45
Ghastly grim and ancient raven wandering from the Nightly shore —
Tell me what thy lordly name is on the Night's Plutonian shore°!" —
                          Quoth the raven, "Nevermore."

Much I marveled this ungainly fowl to hear discourse so plainly,
Though its answer little meaning — little relevancy bore;                      50
For we cannot help agreeing that no sublunary being
Ever yet was blessed with seeing bird above his chamber door —
Bird or beast upon the sculptured bust above his chamber door,
                          With such name as "Nevermore."

But the raven, sitting lonely on the placid bust, spoke only                   55
That one word, as if his soul in that one word he did outpour.
Nothing farther then he uttered — not a feather then he fluttered —
Till I scarcely more than muttered, "Other friends have flown before —
On the morrow *he* will leave me, as my hopes have flown before."
                          Quoth the raven, "Nevermore."          60

Wondering at the stillness broken by reply so aptly spoken,
"Doubtless," said I, "what it utters is its only stock and store,
Caught from some unhappy master whom unmerciful Disaster
Followed fast and followed faster — so, when Hope he would adjure,
Stern Despair returned, instead of the sweet Hope he dared adjure —           65
                          That sad answer, "Nevermore!"

But the raven still beguiling all my sad soul into smiling,
Straight I wheeled a cushioned seat in front of bird, and bust, and door;
Then upon the velvet sinking, I betook myself to linking
Fancy unto fancy, thinking what this ominous bird of yore —                   70
What this grim, ungainly, ghastly, gaunt, and ominous bird of yore
                          Meant in croaking "Nevermore."

This I sat engaged in guessing, but no syllable expressing
To the fowl whose fiery eyes now burned into my bosom's core;
This and more I sat divining, with my head at ease reclining                   75
On the cushion's velvet lining that the lamplight gloated o'er,
But whose velvet violet lining with the lamplight gloating o'er,
                          *She* shall press, ah, nevermore!

---

41 *Pallas:* Pallas Athena, the goddess of wisdom and the arts.     47 *Plutonian shore:* The dark underworld ruled by Pluto in Greek mythology.

Then, methought, the air grew denser, perfumed from an unseen censer
Swung by angels whose faint foot-falls tinkled on the tufted floor.          80
"Wretch," I cried, "thy God hath lent thee — by these angels he hath sent thee
Respite — respite and Nepenthe° from thy memories of Lenore!
Let me quaff this kind Nepenthe and forget this lost Lenore!"
                              Quoth the raven, "Nevermore."

"Prophet!" said I, "thing of evil! — prophet still, if bird or devil! —          85
Whether Tempter sent, or whether tempest tossed thee here ashore,
Desolate, yet all undaunted, on this desert land enchanted —
On this home by Horror haunted — tell me truly, I implore —
Is there — *is* there balm in Gilead?° — tell me — tell me, I implore!"
                              Quoth the raven, "Nevermore."   90

"Prophet!" said I, "thing of evil! — prophet still, if bird or devil!
By that Heaven that bends above us — by that God we both adore —
Tell this soul with sorrow laden if, within the distant Aidenn,°
It shall clasp a sainted maiden whom the angels name Lenore —
Clasp a rare and radiant maiden whom the angels name Lenore."          95
                              Quoth the raven, "Nevermore."

"Be that word our sign of parting, bird or fiend!" I shrieked, upstarting —
"Get thee back into the tempest and the Night's Plutonian shore!
Leave no black plume as a token of that lie thy soul hath spoken!
Leave my loneliness unbroken — quit the bust above my door!          100
Take thy beak from out my heart, and take thy form from off my door!"
                              Quoth the raven, "Nevermore."

And the raven, never flitting, still is sitting, still is sitting
On the pallid bust of Pallas just above my chamber door;
And his eyes have all the seeming of a demon that is dreaming,          105
And the lamp-light o'er him streaming throws his shadow on the floor;
And my soul from out that shadow that lies floating on the floor
                              Shall be lifted — nevermore!

82 *Nepenthe:* A numbing drug.      89 *Gilead:* An allusion to medicinal healing in Jeremiah 8:22.      93 *Aidenn:* Eden.

### CONSIDERATIONS FOR CRITICAL THINKING AND WRITING

1. FIRST RESPONSE. How do the word sounds in "The Raven" create a particular mood? Which words seem especially evocative to you?
2. Characterize the speaker of the poem. What sort of personality does he reveal to you?
3. Explain how Poe's language produces suspense throughout the poem.

### CONNECTION TO ANOTHER SELECTION

1. Compare Poe's treatment of pain and suffering with Mary Oliver's in "The Poet with His Face in His Hands" (p. 35).

# CORNELIUS EADY (B. 1954)

## *The Supremes*                                               *1991*

We were born to be gray. We went to school,
Sat in rows, ate white bread,
Looked at the floor a lot. In the back
Of our small heads

A long scream. We did what we could,                              5
And all we could do was
Turn on each other. How the fat kids suffered!
Not even being jolly could save them.

And then there were the anal retentives,
The terrified brown-noses, the desperately                       10
Athletic or popular. This, of course,
Was training. At home

Our parents shook their heads and waited.
We learned of the industrial revolution,
The sectioning of the clock into pie slices.                     15
We drank cokes and twiddled our thumbs. In the
Back of our minds

A long scream. We snapped butts in the showers,
Froze out shy girls on the dance floor,
Pin-pointed flaws like radar.                                    20
Slowly we understood: this was to be the world.

We were born insurance salesmen and secretaries,
Housewives and short order cooks,
Stock room boys and repairmen,
And it wouldn't be a bad life, they promised,                    25
In a tone of voice that would force some of us
To reach in self-defense for wigs,
Lipstick,

Sequins.

### CONSIDERATIONS FOR CRITICAL THINKING AND WRITING

1. FIRST RESPONSE. What does the Internet tell you about the Supremes?
   Why is the title so crucial for this poem?

2. Explain how the meanings and mood of this poem would change if it
   ended with line 25.

3. How does the speaker's recollection of school experiences compare
   with your own?

### Connection to Another Selection

1. Discuss the speaker's memories of school in "The Supremes" and in Judy Page Heitzman's "The Schoolroom on the Second Floor of the Knitting Mill" (p. 113).

## Emily Dickinson (1830–1886)

### *To make a prairie it takes a clover and one bee*                                           *date unknown*

To make a prairie it takes a clover and one bee,
One clover, and a bee,
And revery.
The revery alone will do,
If bees are few.

### Considerations for Critical Thinking and Writing

1. FIRST RESPONSE. What word in the poem is the most crucial for an understanding of its subject matter?

2. What do you think this poem is about?

3. Is there any humor here?

# 2

# Writing about Poetry:
# From Inquiry to Final Paper

Many people, especially beginning writers, think that writing is mostly inspiration. The muse tosses down a lightning bolt and you write something good. I think writing is mostly perspiration. You go to your chair or desk, and you stay there.

— MICHAEL CHITWOOD

Derek Anderson.

## FROM READING TO WRITING

Writing about poetry can be a rigorous means of testing the validity of your own reading of a poem. Anyone who has been asked to write several pages about a fourteen-line poem knows how intellectually challenging this exercise is, because it means paying close attention to language. Such scrutiny of words, however, sensitizes you not only to the poet's use of language but also to your own use of language. At first you may feel intimidated by having to compose a paper that is longer than the poem you're writing about, but a careful reading will reveal that there's plenty to write about what the poem says and how it says it. Keep in mind that your job is not to produce a definitive reading of the poem — even Carl Sandburg once confessed that "I've written some poetry I don't understand myself." It is enough to develop an interesting thesis and to present it clearly and persuasively.

An interesting thesis will come to you if you read and reread, take notes, annotate the text, and generate ideas (for a discussion of this process, see Chapter 16, "Reading and the Writing Process"). Although it requires energy to read closely and to write convincingly about the charged language found in poetry, there is nothing mysterious about such reading and writing. This chapter provides a set of questions designed to sharpen

44

your reading and writing about poetry. Following these questions is a sample paper that offers a clear and well-developed thesis concerning Elizabeth Bishop's "Manners."

---

### Questions for Responsive Reading and Writing

The following questions can help you respond to important elements that reveal a poem's effects and meanings. The questions are general, so not all of them will necessarily be relevant to a particular poem. Many, however, should prove useful for thinking, talking, and writing about each poem in this collection. If you are uncertain about the meaning of a term used in a question, consult the Glossary of Literary Terms beginning on page 403.

Before addressing these questions, read the poem you are studying in its entirety. Don't worry about interpretation on a first reading; allow yourself the pleasure of enjoying whatever makes itself apparent to you. Then on subsequent readings, use the questions to understand and appreciate how the poem works.

1. Who is the speaker? Is it possible to determine the speaker's age, sex, sensibilities, level of awareness, and values?

2. Is the speaker addressing anyone in particular?

3. How do you respond to the speaker? Favorably? Negatively? What is the situation? Are there any special circumstances that inform what the speaker says?

4. Is there a specific setting of time and place?

5. Does reading the poem aloud help you understand it?

6. Does a paraphrase reveal the basic purpose of the poem?

7. What does the title emphasize?

8. Is the theme presented directly or indirectly?

9. Do any allusions enrich the poem's meaning?

10. How does the diction reveal meaning? Are any words repeated? Do any carry evocative connotative meanings? Are there any puns or other forms of verbal wit?

11. Are figures of speech used? How does the figurative language contribute to the poem's vividness and meaning?

12. Do any objects, persons, places, events, or actions have allegorical or symbolic meanings? What other details in the poem support your interpretation?

13. Is irony used? Are there any examples of situational irony, verbal irony, or dramatic irony? Is understatement or paradox used?

14. What is the tone of the poem? Is the tone consistent?

15. Does the poem use onomatopoeia, assonance, consonance, or alliteration? How do these sounds affect you?

16. What sounds are repeated? If there are rhymes, what is their effect? Do they seem forced or natural? Is there a rhyme scheme? Do the rhymes contribute to the poem's meaning?

17. Do the lines have a regular meter? What is the predominant meter? Are there significant variations? Does the rhythm seem appropriate for the poem's tone?

18. Does the poem's form — its overall structure — follow an established pattern? Do you think the form is a suitable vehicle for the poem's meaning and effects?

19. Is the language of the poem intense and concentrated? Do you think it warrants more than one or two close readings?

20. Did you enjoy the poem? What, specifically, pleased or displeased you about what was expressed and how it was expressed?

21. Is there a particular critical approach that seems especially appropriate for this poem? (See Chapter 15, "Critical Strategies for Reading.")

22. How might biographical information about the author help to determine the poem's central concerns?

23. How might historical information about the poem provide a useful context for interpretation?

24. To what extent do your own experiences, values, beliefs, and assumptions inform your interpretation?

25. What kinds of evidence from the poem are you focusing on to support your interpretation? Does your interpretation leave out any important elements that might undercut or qualify your interpretation?

26. Given that there are a variety of ways to interpret the poem, which one seems the most useful to you?

## Elizabeth Bishop (1911–1979)

### *Manners*                    1965

*for a Child of 1918*

My grandfather said to me
as we sat on the wagon seat,
"Be sure to remember to always
speak to everyone you meet."

© Bettmann/Corbis.

We met a stranger on foot.                                    5
My grandfather's whip tapped his hat.
"Good day, sir. Good day. A fine day."
And I said it and bowed where I sat.

Then we overtook a boy we knew
with his big pet crow on his shoulder.                         10
"Always offer everyone a ride;
don't forget that when you get older,"

my grandfather said. So Willy
climbed up with us, but the crow
gave a "Caw!" and flew off. I was worried.                    15
How would he know where to go?

But he flew a little way at a time
from fence post to fence post, ahead;
and when Willy whistled he answered.
"A fine bird," my grandfather said,                            20

"and he's well brought up. See, he answers
nicely when he's spoken to.
Man or beast, that's good manners.
Be sure that you both always do."

When automobiles went by,                                     25
the dust hid the people's faces,
but we shouted "Good day! Good day!
Fine day!" at the top of our voices.

When we came to Hustler Hill,
he said that the mare was tired,
so we all got down and walked,                                30
as our good manners required.

# A SAMPLE CLOSE READING

## *An Annotated Version of "Manners"*

The following annotations represent insights about the relationship of various elements at work in the poem gleaned only after several close readings. Don't expect to be able to produce these kinds of interpretive notes on a first reading because such perceptions will not be apparent until you've read the poem and then gone back to the beginning to discover how each word, line, and stanza contributes to the overall effect. Writing your responses in the margins of the page can be a useful means of recording your impressions as well as discovering new insights as you read the text closely.

## ELIZABETH BISHOP (1911–1979)

### *Manners*                                              1965

*for a Child of 1918*

My grandfather said to me
as we sat on the wagon seat,
"Be sure to remember to always
speak to everyone you meet."

We met a stranger on foot.
My grandfather's whip tapped his hat.          5
"Good day, sir. Good day. A fine day."
And I said it and bowed where I sat.

Then we overtook a boy we knew
with his big pet crow on his shoulder.          10
"Always offer everyone a ride;
don't forget that when you get older,"

my grandfather said. So Willy
climbed up with us, but the crow
gave a "Caw!" and flew off. I was worried.      15
How would he know where to go?

But he flew a little way at a time
from fence post to fence post, ahead;
and when Willy whistled he answered.
"A fine bird," my grandfather said,            20

"and he's well brought up. See, he answers
nicely when he's spoken to.
Man or beast, that's good manners.
Be sure that you both always do."

When automobiles went by,                       25
the dust hid the people's faces,
but we shouted "Good day! Good day!
Fine day!" at the top of our voices.

When we came to Hustler Hill,
he said that the mare was tired,               30
so we all got down and walked,
as our good manners required.

**Annotations (margin notes):**

Title refers to what is socially correct, polite, and/or decent behavior.

WWI ended in 1918 and denotes a shift in values and manners that often follows rapid social changes brought about by war.

Idea that values "always" transcend time is emphasized by the grandfather's urging: "don't forget."

"My grandfather," repeated four times in first five stanzas, reflects the child's affection and a sense of belonging in his world. The crow, however, worries the child and indicates an uncertain future.

Third time the grandfather says "always." This and the inverted syntax of line 24 call attention, again, to idea that good manners are forever important.

The horse, like the simple past it symbolizes, is weakened by the hustle of modern life, but even so, "our" good manners prevail, internalized from the grandfather's values.

Wagon seat suggests a simpler past — as does simple language and informal diction of the child speaker.

Grandfather seems kind, but he also carries a whip that reinforces his authoritative voice.

Predictable quatrains and *abcb* rhyme scheme throughout the poem take the worry out of where they — and the crow — are headed.

The modern symbolic automobile races by raising dust that obscures everyone's vision and forces them to shout. Rhymes in lines 26 and 28 are off (unlike all the other rhymes) just enough to suggest the dissonant future that will supersede the calm wagon ride.

# A SAMPLE STUDENT ANALYSIS

## *Memory in Elizabeth Bishop's "Manners"*

The following sample paper on Elizabeth Bishop's "Manners" was written in response to an assignment that called for a 750-word discussion of the ways in which at least five of the following elements work to develop and reinforce the poem's themes:

| | | |
|---|---|---|
| diction and tone | irony | form |
| images | sound and rhyme | speaker |
| figures of speech | rhythm and meter | setting and situation |
| symbols | | |

In her paper, Debra Epstein discusses the ways in which a number of these elements contribute to what she sees as a central theme of "Manners": the loss of a way of life that Bishop associates with the end of World War I. Not all of the elements of poetry are covered equally in Epstein's paper because some, such as the speaker and setting, are more important to her argument than others. Notice how rather than merely listing each of the elements, Epstein mentions them in her discussion as she needs to in order to develop the thesis that she clearly and succinctly expresses in her opening paragraph.

Epstein 1

Debra Epstein

Professor Brown

English 210

1 May 2015

Memory in Elizabeth Bishop's "Manners"

The subject of Elizabeth Bishop's "Manners" has to do with behaving well, but the theme of the poem has more to do with a way of life than with etiquette. The poem suggests that modern society has lost something important—a friendly openness, a generosity of spirit, a sense of decency and consideration—in its race toward progress. Although the narrative is simply told, Bishop enriches this poem about manners by developing an implicit theme through her subtle use of such elements of poetry as speaker, setting, rhyme, meter, symbol, and images.

> Thesis providing interpretation of poem.

> Statement of elements in poem to be discussed in paper.

The dedication suggests that the speaker is "a Child of 1918" who accompanies his or her grandfather on a wagon ride and who is urged to practice

**Summary of poem's narrative and introduction to discussion of elements.**

good manners by greeting people, offering everyone a ride, and speaking when spoken to by anyone. During the ride they say hello to a stranger, give a ride to a boy with a pet crow, shout greetings to a passing automobile, and get down from the wagon when they reach a hill because the horse is tired. They walk because "good manners required" (line 32) such consideration, even for a horse. This summary indicates what goes on in the poem but not its significance. That requires a closer look at some of the poem's elements.

**Analysis of speaker in poem.**

Given the speaker's simple language (there are no metaphors or similes and only a few words out of thirty-two lines are longer than two syllables), it seems likely that he or she is a fairly young child rather than an adult reminiscing. (It is interesting to note that Bishop herself, though not identical with the speaker, would have been seven in 1918.) Because the speaker is a young child who uses simple diction, Bishop has to show us the ride's significance indirectly rather than having the speaker explicitly state it.

**Analysis of poem's setting.**

The setting for the speaker's narrative is important because 1918 was the year World War I ended, and it marked the beginning of a new era of technology that was the result of rapid industrialization during the war. Horses and wagons would soon be put out to pasture. The grandfather's manners emphasize a time gone by; the child must be told to "remember" what the grandfather says because he or she will take that advice into a new and very different world.

**Analysis of rhyme scheme and meter.**

The grandfather's world of the horse and wagon is uncomplicated, and this is reflected in both the simple quatrains that move predictably along in an *abcb* rhyme scheme and the frequent anapestic meter (ăs wĕ sát ŏn thĕ wágŏn [2]) that pulls the lines rapidly and lightly. The one moment Bishop breaks the set rhyme scheme is in the seventh stanza when the automobile (the single four-syllable word in the poem) rushes by in a cloud of dust so that people cannot see or hear each other. The only off rhymes in the poem—"faces" (26) and "voices" (28)—are also in this stanza, which suggests that the automobile and

**Analysis of symbols.**

the people in it are somehow off or out of sync with what goes on in the other stanzas. The automobile is a symbol of a way of life in which people—their faces hidden—and manners take a back seat to speed and noise. The people in the car don't wave, don't offer a ride, and don't speak when spoken to.

**Analysis of images.**

Maybe the image of the crow's noisy cawing and flying from post to post is a foreshadowing that should prepare readers for the automobile. The speaker feels "worried" about the crow's apparent directionlessness: "How would he know where to go?" (16). However, neither the child nor the grandfather (nor the reader on a first reading) clearly sees the two worlds that Bishop contrasts in the final stanza.

"Hustler Hill" is the perfect name for what finally tires out the mare. There is no hurry for the grandfather and child, but there is for those people in the car and the postwar hustle and bustle they represent. The fast-paced future overtakes the tired symbol of the past in the poem. The pace slows as the wagon passengers get down to walk, but the reader recognizes that the grandfather's way has been lost to a world in which good manners are not required.

Conclusion supporting thesis on poem's theme.

## Work Cited

Bishop, Elizabeth. "Manners." *Thinking and Writing about Poetry*. Ed. Michael Meyer. Boston: Bedford/St. Martin's, 2016. 46–47. Print.

# 3

# Word Choice, Word Order, and Tone

I still feel that a poet has a duty to words, and that words can do wonderful things. And it's too bad to just let them lie there without doing anything with and for them.
— GWENDOLYN BROOKS

Granger, NYC.

## WORD CHOICE

### *Diction*

Like all other good writers, poets are keenly aware of *diction*, their choice of words. Poets, however, choose words especially carefully because the words in poems call attention to themselves. Characters, actions, settings, and symbols may appear in a poem, but in the foreground, before all else, is the poem's language. Also, poems are usually briefer than other forms of writing. A few inappropriate words in a 200-page novel (which would have about 100,000 words) create fewer problems than they would in a 100-word poem. Functioning in a compressed atmosphere, the words in a poem must convey meanings gracefully and economically. Readers therefore have to be alert to the ways in which those meanings are released.

Although poetic language is often more intensely charged than ordinary speech, the words used in poetry are not necessarily different from everyday speech. Inexperienced readers may sometimes assume that language must be high-flown and out of date to be included in a poem: instead of reading about a boy "enjoying a swim," they expect to read about a boy "disporting with pliant arm o'er a glassy wave." During the eighteenth century this kind of *poetic diction* — the use of elevated language rather than ordinary language — was highly valued in English poetry, but since the nineteenth century, poets have generally overridden the distinctions that were once made between words used in everyday speech and those used in poetry. Today all levels of diction can be found in poetry.

A poet, like any other writer, has several levels of diction from which to choose; they range from formal to middle to informal. **Formal diction** consists of a dignified, impersonal, and elevated use of language. Notice, for example, the formality of Thomas Hardy's description of the sunken luxury liner *Titanic* in this stanza from "The Convergence of the Twain" (the entire poem appears on p. 71):

> In a solitude of the sea
> Deep from human vanity,
> And the Pride of Life that planned her, stilly couches she.

There is nothing casual or relaxed about these lines. Hardy's use of "stilly," meaning "quietly" or "calmly," is purely literary; the word rarely, if ever, turns up in everyday English.

The language used in Sharon Olds's "Last Night" (p. 69) represents a less formal level of diction; the speaker uses a **middle diction** spoken by most educated people. Consider how Olds's speaker struggles the next day to comprehend her passion:

> Love? It was more like dragonflies
> in the sun, 100 degrees at noon,
> the ends of their abdomens stuck together, I
> close my eyes when I remember.

The words used to describe this encounter are common enough, yet it is precisely Olds's use of language that evokes the extraordinary nature of this couple's connection.

**Informal diction** is evident in Philip Larkin's "A Study of Reading Habits" (p. 21). The speaker's account of his early reading is presented **colloquially**, in a conversational manner that in this instance includes slang expressions not used by the culture at large:

> When getting my nose in a book
> Cured most things short of school,
> It was worth ruining my eyes
> To know I could still keep cool,
> And deal out the old right hook
> To dirty dogs twice my size.

This level of diction is clearly not that of Hardy's or Olds's speakers.

Poets may also draw on another form of informal diction, called **dialect**. Dialects are spoken by definable groups of people from a particular geographic region, economic group, or social class. New England dialects are often heard in Robert Frost's poems, for example. Gwendolyn Brooks uses a black dialect in "We Real Cool" (p. 77) to characterize a group of pool players. Another form of diction related to particular groups is *jargon*, a category of language defined by a trade or profession. Sociologists, photographers, carpenters, baseball players, and dentists, for example, all use words that are specific to their fields. Sally Croft offers an appetizing dish of cookbook jargon in "Home-Baked Bread" (p. 97).

Many levels of diction are available to poets. The variety of diction to be found in poetry is enormous, and that is how it should be. No language is foreign to poetry because it is possible to imagine any human voice as the speaker of a poem. When we say a poem is formal, informal, or somewhere in between, we are making a descriptive statement rather than an evaluative one. What matters in a poem is not only which words are used but how they are used.

## Denotations and Connotations

One important way that the meaning of a word is communicated in a poem is through sound: snakes *hiss*, saws *buzz*. This and other matters related to sound are discussed in Chapter 7. Individual words also convey meanings through denotations and connotations. *Denotations* are the literal, dictionary meanings of a word. For example, *bird* denotes a feathered animal with wings (other denotations for the same word include a shuttlecock, an airplane, or an odd person), but in addition to its denotative meanings, *bird* also carries *connotations* — associations and implications that go beyond a word's literal meanings. Connotations derive from how the word has been used and the associations people make with it. Therefore, the connotations of *bird* might include fragility, vulnerability, altitude, the sky, or freedom, depending on the context in which the word is used. Consider also how different the connotations are for the following types of birds: hawk, dove, penguin, pigeon, chicken, peacock, duck, crow, turkey, gull, owl, goose, coot, and vulture. These words have long been used to refer to types of people as well as birds. They are rich in connotative meanings.

Connotations derive their resonance from a person's experiences with a word. Those experiences may not always be the same, especially when the people having them are in different times and places. *Theater*, for instance, was once associated with depravity, disease, and sin, whereas today the word usually evokes some sense of high culture and perhaps visions of elegant opulence. In several ethnic communities in the United States many people would find *squid* appetizing, but elsewhere the word is likely to produce negative connotations. Readers must recognize, then, that words written in other times and places may have unexpected connotations. Annotations usually help in these matters, which is why it makes sense to pay attention to them when they are available.

Ordinarily, though, the language of poetry is accessible, even when the circumstances of the reader and the poet are different. Although connotative language may be used subtly, it mostly draws on associations experienced by many people. Poets rely on widely shared associations rather than on the idiosyncratic response that an individual might have to a word. Someone who has received a severe burn from a fireplace accident may associate the word *hearth* with intense pain instead of home and family life, but that reader must not allow a personal experience to undermine the response the poet intends to evoke. Connotative meanings are usually public meanings.

Perhaps this can be seen most clearly in advertising, where language is also used primarily to convey moods and feelings rather than information. For instance, three decades of increasing interest in nutrition and general fitness have created a collective consciousness that advertisers have capitalized on successfully. Knowing that we want to be slender or lean or slim (not *spare* or *scrawny* and certainly not *gaunt*), advertisers have created a new word to describe beers, wines, sodas, cheeses, canned fruits, and other products that tend to overload what used to be called sweatclothes and sneakers. The word is *lite*. The assumed denotative meaning of *lite* is "low in calories," but as close readers of ingredient labels know, some *lites* are heavier than regularly prepared products. There can be no doubt about the connotative meaning of *lite*, however. Whatever is *lite* cannot hurt you; less is more. Even the word is lighter than *light*; there is no unnecessary droopy *g* or plump *h*. *Lite* is a brilliantly manufactured use of connotation.

Connotative meanings are valuable because they allow poets to be economical and suggestive simultaneously. In this way emotions and attitudes are carefully woven into the texture of the poem's language. Read the following poem and pay close attention to the connotative meanings of its words.

## RANDALL JARRELL (1914–1965)

### *The Death of the Ball Turret Gunner*    1945

From my mother's sleep I fell into the State
And I hunched in its belly till my wet fur froze.
Six miles from earth, loosed from its dream of life,
I woke to black flak and the nightmare fighters.
When I died they washed me out of the turret with a hose.

The title of this poem establishes the setting and the speaker's situation. Like the setting of a short story, the setting of a poem is important when the time and place influence what happens. "The Death of the Ball Turret Gunner" is set in the midst of a war and, more specifically, in a ball turret — a Plexiglas sphere housing machine guns on the underside of a bomber. The speaker's situation obviously places him in extreme danger; indeed, his fate is announced in the title.

Although the poem is written in the first-person singular, its speaker is clearly not the poet. Jarrell uses a ***persona***, a speaker created by the poet. In this poem the persona is a disembodied voice that makes the gunner's story all the more powerful. What is his story? A paraphrase might read something like this:

> After I was born, I grew up to find myself at war, cramped into the turret of a bomber's belly some 31,000 feet above the ground. Below me were exploding shells from antiaircraft guns and attacking fighter planes. I was killed, but the bomber returned to base, where my remains were cleaned out of the turret so the next man could take my place.

This paraphrase is accurate, but its language is much less suggestive than the poem's. The first line of the poem has the speaker emerge from his "mother's sleep," the anesthetized sleep of her giving birth. The phrase also suggests the comfort, warmth, and security he knew as a child. This safety was left behind when he "fell," a verb that evokes the danger and involuntary movement associated with his subsequent "State" (*fell* also echoes, perhaps, the fall from innocence to experience related in the Bible).

Several dictionary definitions appear for the noun *state*; it can denote a territorial unit, the power and authority of a government, a person's social status, or a person's emotional or physical condition. The context provided by the rest of the poem makes clear that "State" has several denotative meanings here: because it is capitalized, it certainly refers to the violent world of a government at war, but it also refers to the gunner's vulnerable status as well as his physical and emotional condition. By having "State" carry more than one meaning, Jarrell has created an intentional ambiguity. *Ambiguity* allows for two or more simultaneous interpretations of a word, a phrase, an action, or a situation, all of which can be supported by the context of a work. Through his ambiguous use of "State," Jarrell connects the horrors of war not just to bombers and gunners but to the governments that control them.

Related to this ambiguity is the connotative meaning of "State" in the poem. The context demands that the word be read with a negative charge. The word is not used with patriotic pride but to suggest an anonymous, impersonal "State" that kills rather than nurtures the life in its "belly." The state's "belly" is a bomber, and the gunner is "hunched" like a fetus in the cramped turret, where, in contrast to the warmth of his mother's womb, everything is frozen, even the "wet fur" of his flight jacket (newborn infants have wet fur too). The gunner is not just 31,000 feet from the ground but "Six miles from earth." *Six miles* has roughly the same denotative meaning as 31,000 feet, but Jarrell knew that the connotative meaning of *six miles* makes the speaker's position seem even more remote and frightening.

When the gunner is born into the violent world of war, he finds himself waking up to a "nightmare" that is all too real. The poem's final line is grimly understated, but it hits the reader with the force of an exploding shell: what the State-bomber-turret gives birth to is a gruesome death that is merely one of an endless series. It may be tempting to reduce the theme of this poem to the idea that "war is hell," but Jarrell's target is more specific. He implicates the "State," which routinely executes such violence, and he does so without preaching or hysterical denunciations. Instead, his use of language conveys his theme subtly and powerfully.

## WORD ORDER

Meanings in poems are conveyed not only by denotations and connotations but also by the poet's arrangement of words into phrases, clauses, and sentences to achieve particular effects. The ordering of words into meaningful verbal patterns is called *syntax*. A poet can manipulate the syntax of a line to place emphasis on a word; this is especially apparent when a poet varies normal word order. In Emily Dickinson's "A narrow Fellow in the Grass" (p. 2), for example, the speaker says about the snake that "His notice sudden is." Ordinarily, that would be expressed as "his notice is sudden." By placing the verb *is* unexpectedly at the end of the line, Dickinson creates the sense of surprise we feel when we suddenly come upon a snake. Dickinson's inversion of the standard word order also makes the final sound of the line a hissing *is*.

## TONE

*Tone* is the writer's attitude toward the subject, the mood created by all the elements in the poem. Writing, like speech, can be characterized as serious or light, sad or happy, private or public, angry or affectionate, bitter or nostalgic, or by any other attitudes and feelings that human beings experience. In Jarrell's "The Death of the Ball Turret Gunner," the tone is clearly serious; the voice in the poem even sounds dead. Listen again to the persona's final words: "When I died they washed me out of the turret with a hose." The brutal, restrained matter-of-factness of this line is effective because the reader is called on to supply the appropriate anger and despair — a strategy that makes those emotions all the more convincing.

Consider how tone is used to convey meaning in the next poem, inspired by the poet's contemplation of mortality.

COLETTE INEZ (B. 1931)

### *Back When All Was Continuous Chuckles*                    *2004*

*after a line by Anselm Hollo°*

Doris and I were helpless on the Beeline Bus
laughing at what was it? "What did the moron
who killed his mother and father eat
at the orphan's picnic?" "Crow?" Har-har.

Anselm Hollo: Finnish poet (1934–2013) who taught creative writing in the United States.

The bus was grinding towards Hempstead,                                              5
past the cemetery whose stones Doris
and I found hilarious. Freaky ghouls and skeletons.
"What did the dead man say to the ghost?"

"I like the movie better than the book."
Even "I don't get it" was funny.                                                     10
The war was on, rationing, sirens.
Silly billies, we poked each other's arms

with balled fists, held hands and howled
at crabby ladies in funny hats, dusty feathers,
fake fruit. Doris' mom wore this headgear                                            15
before she got the big C which no one said out loud.

In a shadowy room her skin seemed gray
as moon dust on Smith Street, at Doris' house
where we tiptoed down the hall.
Sometimes we heard moans from the back room                                          20

and I helped wring out cloths while Doris
brought water in a glass held to her mother's lips.
But soon we were flipping through joke books
and writhing on the floor, war news shut off

back when we pretended all was continuous chuckles,                                  25
and we rode the bus past Greenfield's rise
where stones, trumpeting angels,
would bear names we later came to recognize.

### CONSIDERATIONS FOR CRITICAL THINKING AND WRITING

1. FIRST RESPONSE. Compare the difference between the title and its slightly revised version as it appears in line 25. How does that difference reveal the theme?

2. At what point does the tone of the poem shift from chuckles to something else?

3. What is the effect of the rhymes in lines 26 and 28? How do the rhymes serve to reinforce the poem's theme?

### CONNECTION TO ANOTHER SELECTION

1. Discuss the tone of this poem and that of Gwendolyn Brooks's "We Real Cool" (p. 77).

WHEN I WRITE "Although I usually wind up showing my poems to my best friend, sometimes I ask other people to be first-readers because I don't want to ask too much of my friend! I recently joined a poetry group. Their suggestions are useful, mostly in helping me see what I'm really trying to get at." — MARILYN NELSON

## MARILYN NELSON (B. 1946)

### *How I Discovered Poetry*                                1997

It was like soul-kissing, the way the words
filled my mouth as Mrs. Purdy read from her desk.
All the other kids zoned an hour ahead to 3:15,
but Mrs. Purdy and I wandered lonely as clouds borne
by a breeze off Mount Parnassus. She must have seen                5
the darkest eyes in the room brim: The next day
she gave me a poem she'd chosen especially for me
to read to the all except for me white class.
She smiled when she told me to read it, smiled harder,
said oh yes I could. She smiled harder and harder                 10
until I stood and opened my mouth to banjo playing
darkies, pickaninnies, disses and dats. When I finished
my classmates stared at the floor. We walked silent
to the buses, awed by the power of words.

### CONSIDERATIONS FOR CRITICAL THINKING AND WRITING

1. FIRST RESPONSE. Trace your response to Mrs. Purdy from the beginning to the end of the poem.

2. What do the references to William Wordsworth's poem "I Wandered Lonely as a Cloud" and Mount Parnassus (look these up) in lines 4 and 5 suggest to you about the speaker?

3. How do you interpret the tone of the final two lines?

### CONNECTION TO ANOTHER SELECTION

1. How does Nelson's early school experience compare with Judy Page Heitzman's in "The Schoolroom on the Second Floor of the Knitting Mill" (p. 113)?

The next work is a **dramatic monologue**, a type of poem in which a character — the speaker — addresses a silent audience in such a way as to reveal unintentionally some aspect of his or her temperament or personality. What tone is created by Machan's use of a persona?

## KATHARYN HOWD MACHAN (B. 1952)

### *Hazel Tells LaVerne*                    1976

WHEN I WRITE "When a poem begins to find its shape and form and voice inside you, let your heart and your head join to give it the best life you can: passion! imagery! music! And if it will let you, humor: ah, the world needs all it can get."

—KATHARYN HOWD MACHAN

last night
im cleanin out my
howard johnsons ladies room
when all of a sudden
up pops this frog                                                        5
musta come from the sewer
swimmin aroun an tryin ta
climb up the sida the bowl
so i goes ta flushm down
but sohelpmegod he starts talkin                                          10
bout a golden ball
an how i can be a princess
me a princess
well my mouth drops
all the way to the floor                                                  15
an he says
kiss me just kiss me
once on the nose
well i screams
ya little green pervert                                                   20
an i hitsm with my mop
an has ta flush
the toilet down three times
me
a princess                                                               25

### CONSIDERATIONS FOR CRITICAL THINKING AND WRITING

1. **FIRST RESPONSE.** What do you imagine the situation and setting are for this poem? Do you like this revision of the fairy tale "The Frog Prince"?

2. What creates the poem's humor? How does Hazel's use of language reveal her personality? Is her treatment of the frog consistent with her character?

3. Although it has no punctuation, this poem is easy to follow. How does the arrangement of the lines organize Hazel's speech for clarity and emphasis?

4. What is the theme? Is it conveyed through denotative or connotative language?

5. **CREATIVE RESPONSE.** Write what you think might be LaVerne's reply to Hazel. First, write LaVerne's response as a series of ordinary sentences, and then try editing and organizing them into poetic lines.

### CONNECTION TO ANOTHER SELECTION

1. Although Robert Browning's "My Last Duchess" (p. 139) is a more complex poem than Machan's, both use dramatic monologues to reveal character. How are the strategies in each poem similar?

# A SAMPLE STUDENT RESPONSE

Alex Georges

Professor Myerov

English 200

2 April 2015

Tone in Katharyn Howd Machan's "Hazel Tells LaVerne"

"Tone," Michael Meyer writes, "is the writer's attitude toward the subject, the mood created by all the elements in the poem" (70) and is used to convey meaning and character. In her dramatic monologue, "Hazel Tells LaVerne," the poet Katharyn Howd Machan reveals through the persona of Hazel—a funny, tough-talking, no-nonsense cleaning lady—a satirical revision of "The Frog Prince" fairy tale. Hazel's attitude toward the possibility of a fairy-tale romance is evident in her response to the frog prince. She has no use for him or his offers "bout a golden ball / an how i can be a princess" (lines 11-12). If Hazel is viewed by the reader as a princess, it is clear from her words and tone that she is far from a traditional one.

Machan's word choice and humorous tone also reveal much about Hazel's personality and circumstances. Through the use of slang, alternate spellings, and the omission of punctuation, we learn a great deal about the character:

> well i screams
>
> ya little green pervert
>
> an i hitsm with my mop
>
> an has ta flush
>
> the toilet down three times
>
> me
>
> a princess (19-25)

Listening to her speak, the reader understands that Hazel, a cleaner at Howard Johnson's, does not have an extensive education. She speaks in the colloquial, running words into one another and using phrases like "ya little green pervert" (20) and "i screams" (19). The lack of complete sentences, capital letters, and punctuation adds to her informal tone. Hazel's speech defines her social status, brings out details of her personality, and gives the reader her view of herself. She is accustomed to the thankless daily grind of work and will not allow herself even a moment's fantasy of becoming a princess. It is a notion that she has to flush away—literally, has "ta flush . . . down three times." She tells LaVerne that the very idea of such fantasy is absurd to her, as she states in the final lines: "me / a princess" (24-25).

Works Cited

Machan, Katharyn Howd. "Hazel Tells LaVerne." Meyer 60.

Meyer, Michael, ed. *Thinking and Writing about Poetry*. Boston: Bedford/St. Martin's, 2016. 57. Print.

## MARTÍN ESPADA (B. 1957)

### *Latin Night at the Pawnshop*    1987

*Chelsea, Massachusetts*
*Christmas, 1987*

The apparition of a salsa band
gleaming in the Liberty Loan
pawnshop window:

Golden trumpet,
silver trombone,
congas, maracas, tambourine,

all with price tags dangling
like the city morgue ticket
on a dead man's toe.

WHEN I WRITE "As a poet and a reader, I am most interested in the theme of justice. I am interested in poems that address justice vividly, concretely, specifically. Poets are, as Shelley put it, the 'unacknowledged legislators of the world.' We shouldn't leave justice to the lawyers and the politicians." —MARTÍN ESPADA

### CONSIDERATIONS FOR CRITICAL THINKING AND WRITING

1. FIRST RESPONSE. What is "Latin" about this night at the pawnshop?
2. What kind of tone is created by the poet's word choice and by the poem's rhythm?

3. Does it matter that this apparition occurs on Christmas night? Why or why not?

4. What do you think is the central point of this poem?

How do the speaker's attitude and tone change during the course of this next poem?

## Paul Laurence Dunbar (1872–1906)

### To a Captious Critic                                                     1903

Dear critic, who my lightness so deplores,
Would I might study to be prince of bores,
Right wisely would I rule that dull estate —
But, sir, I may not; till you abdicate.

### Considerations for Critical Thinking and Writing

1. FIRST RESPONSE. How do Dunbar's vocabulary and syntax signal the level of diction used in the poem?

2. Describe the speaker's tone. How does it characterize the speaker as well as the critic?

3. CREATIVE RESPONSE. Using "To a Captious Critic" as a model, try writing a four-line witty reply to someone in your own life — perhaps a roommate, coach, teacher, waiter, dentist, or anyone else who provokes a strong response in you.

## DICTION AND TONE IN FOUR LOVE POEMS

The first three of these love poems share the same basic situation and theme: a male speaker addresses a female (in the first poem it is a type of female) urging that love should not be delayed because time is short. This theme is as familiar in poetry as it is in life. In Latin this tradition is known as *carpe diem*, "seize the day." Notice how the poets' diction helps create a distinctive tone in each poem, even though the subject matter and central ideas are similar (although not identical) in all three.

## Robert Herrick (1591–1674)

### To the Virgins, to Make Much of Time                                    1648

Gather ye rose-buds while ye may,
    Old Time is still a-flying;
And this same flower that smiles today,
    Tomorrow will be dying.

The glorious lamp of heaven, the sun,
  The higher he's a-getting,
The sooner will his race be run,
  And nearer he's to setting.

That age is best which is the first,
  When youth and blood are warmer;
But being spent, the worse, and worst
  Times still succeed the former.

Then be not coy, but use your time,
  And while ye may, go marry;
For having lost but once your prime,
  You may for ever tarry.

Hulton Archive/Getty Images.

### Considerations for Critical Thinking and Writing

1. **FIRST RESPONSE.** Would there be any change in meaning if the title of this poem were "To Young Women, to Make Much of Time"? Do you think the poem can apply to young men too?

2. What do the virgins have in common with the flowers (lines 1–4) and the course of the day (5–8)?

3. How does the speaker develop his argument? What will happen to the virgins if they don't "marry"? Paraphrase the poem.

4. What is the tone of the speaker's advice?

The next poem was also written in the seventeenth century, but it includes some words that have changed in usage and meaning over the past three hundred years. The title of Andrew Marvell's "To His Coy Mistress" requires some explanation. "Mistress" does not refer to a married man's illicit lover but to a woman who is loved and courted — a sweetheart. Marvell uses "coy" to describe a woman who is reserved and shy rather than coquettish or flirtatious. Often such shifts in meanings over time are explained in the notes that accompany reprintings of poems. You should keep in mind, however, that it is helpful to have a reasonably thick dictionary available when you are reading poetry. The most thorough is the *Oxford English Dictionary (OED)*, which provides histories of words. The *OED* is a multivolume leviathan, but there are other useful unabridged dictionaries and desk dictionaries.

Knowing a word's original meaning can also enrich your understanding of why a contemporary poet chooses a particular word. In "Design" (p. 271), Robert Frost raises provocative questions about the nature of evil and the existence of God in his dark examination of a moth's death, all presented in unexpected images of whiteness. He ends the poem with a series of questions concerning what causes "death and blight," wondering if it is a "design of darkness to appall" or no design at all, a universe informed only by random meaninglessness. Frost's precise contemporary use of "appall" captures the sense of consternation and dismay that such a frightening contemplation of death might evoke, but a dictionary reveals some further relevant insights. The dictionary's additional information about the history of *appall* shows us why it is the perfect word to establish the overwhelming effect of the poem. The word comes from the Middle English *appallen*, meaning "to grow faint," and in Old French *apalir* means "to grow pale" or white. These meanings reinforce the powerful sense of death buried in the images of whiteness throughout the poem. Moreover, Frost's "appall" also echoes a funereal pall, or coffin, allowing the word to bear even more connotative weight. Knowing the origin of *appall* gives us the full heft of the poet's word choice.

Although some of the language in "To His Coy Mistress" requires annotations for the modern reader, this poem continues to serve as a powerful reminder that time is a formidable foe, even for lovers.

De Agostini Picture Library/Getty Images.

## Andrew Marvell (1621–1678)

### *To His Coy Mistress*     *1681*

Had we but world enough, and time,
This coyness, lady, were no crime.
We would sit down, and think which way
To walk, and pass our long love's day.
Thou by the Indian Ganges'° side
Shouldst rubies find; I by the tide
Of Humber° would complain.° I would     *write love songs*
Love you ten years before the Flood,
And you should, if you please, refuse
Till the conversion of the Jews.     10
My vegetable love should grow°
Vaster than empires, and more slow;
An hundred years should go to praise
Thine eyes and on thy forehead gaze,
Two hundred to adore each breast,     15
But thirty thousand to the rest:
An age at least to every part,
And the last age should show your heart.
For, lady, you deserve this state,

---

5 *Ganges:* A river in India sacred to the Hindus.     7 *Humber:* A river that flows through Marvell's native town, Hull.     11 *My vegetable love . . . grow:* A slow, unconscious growth.

Nor would I love at lower rate.                                          20
   But at my back I always hear
Time's wingèd chariot hurrying near;
And yonder all before us lie
Deserts of vast eternity.
Thy beauty shall no more be found,                                      25
Nor in thy marble vault shall sound
My echoing song; then worms shall try
That long preserved virginity,
And your quaint honor turn to dust,
And into ashes all my lust.                                             30
The grave's a fine and private place,
But none, I think, do there embrace.
   Now, therefore, while the youthful hue
Sits on thy skin like morning dew,
And while thy willing soul transpires°                *breathes forth*   35
At every pore with instant fires,
Now let us sport us while we may,
And now, like amorous birds of prey,
Rather at once our time devour
Than languish in his slow-chapped° power.              *slow-jawed*   40
Let us roll all our strength and all
Our sweetness up into one ball,
And tear our pleasures with rough strife
Thorough° the iron gates of life.                          *through*
Thus, though we cannot make our sun                                      45
Stand still, yet we will make him run.

## Considerations for Critical Thinking and Writing

1. FIRST RESPONSE. Do you think this *carpe diem* poem is hopelessly dated, or does it speak to our contemporary concerns?

2. This poem is divided into a three-part argument. Briefly summarize each section: if (lines 1–20), but (21–32), therefore (33–46).

3. What is the speaker's tone in lines 1–20? How much time would he spend adoring his mistress? Is he sincere? How does he expect his mistress to respond to these lines?

4. How does the speaker's tone change beginning with line 21? What is his view of time in lines 21–32? What does this description do to the lush and leisurely sense of time in lines 1–20? How do you think his mistress would react to lines 21–32?

5. In the final lines of Herrick's "To the Virgins, to Make Much of Time" (p. 63), the speaker urges the virgins to "go marry." What does Marvell's speaker urge in lines 33–46? How is the pace of these lines (notice the verbs) different from that of the first twenty lines of the poem?

6. This poem is sometimes read as a vigorous but simple celebration of flesh. Is there more to the theme than that?

The third in this series of *carpe diem* poems is a twenty-first-century work. The language of Ann Lauinger's "Marvell Noir" is more immediately accessible than that of Marvell's "To His Coy Mistress"; an ordinary dictionary will quickly identify any words unfamiliar to a reader. But the title might require a dictionary of biography for the reference to Marvell, as well as a dictionary of allusions to provide a succinct description that explains the reference to film noir. An **allusion** is a brief cultural reference to a person, a place, a thing, an event, or an idea in history or literature. Allusive words, like connotative words, are both suggestive and economical; poets use allusions to conjure up biblical authority, scenes from Shakespeare's plays, historic figures, wars, great love stories, and anything else that might serve to deepen and enrich their own work. The title of "Marvell Noir" makes two allusions that an ordinary dictionary may not explain, because it alludes to Marvell's most famous poem, "To His Coy Mistress," and to dark crime films (*noir* is "black" in French) of the 1940s that were often filmed in black and white featuring tough-talking, cynical heroes — such as those portrayed by Humphrey Bogart — and hardened, cold women — like the characters played by Joan Crawford. Lauinger assumes that her reader will understand the allusions.

Allusions imply reading and cultural experiences shared by the poet and the reader. Literate audiences once had more in common than they do today because more people had similar economic, social, and educational backgrounds. But a judicious use of specialized dictionaries, encyclopedias, and other reference tools can help you decipher allusions that grow out of this body of experience. As you read more, you'll be able to make connections based on your own experiences with literature. In a sense, allusions make available what other human beings have deemed worth remembering, and that is certainly an economical way of supplementing and enhancing your own experience.

Lauinger's version of the *carpe diem* theme follows. What strikes you as particularly modern about it?

## ANN LAUINGER (B. 1948)

### *Marvell Noir*                    *2005*

> WHEN I READ "As a writer, my best friends are some very dead poets. Reading them is what made me want to write, and re-reading them keeps me writing."   — ANN LAUINGER

Sweetheart, if we had the time,
A week in bed would be no crime.
I'd light your Camels, pour your Jack;
You'd do shiatsu on my back.
When you got up to scramble eggs,                5
I'd write a sonnet to your legs,
And you could watch my stubble grow.
Yes, gorgeous, we'd take it slow.
I'd hear the whole sad tale again:
A roadhouse band; you can't trust men;          10

He set you up; you had to eat,
And bitter with the bittersweet
Was what they dished you; Ginger lied;
You weren't there when Sanchez died;
You didn't know the pearls were fake . . .                           15
Aw, can it, sport! Make no mistake,
You're in it, doll, up to your eyeballs!
Tears? Please! You'll dilute our highballs,
And make that angel face a mess
For the nice Lieutenant. I confess                                   20
I'm nuts for you — but take the rap?
You must think I'm some other sap!
And, precious, I kind of wish I was.
Well, when they spring you, give a buzz;
Guess I'll get back to Archie's wife,                                25
And you'll get twenty-five to life.
You'll have time then, more than enough,
To reminisce about the stuff
That dreams are made of, and the men
You suckered. Sadly, in the pen                                      30
Your kind of talent goes to waste.
But Irish bars are more my taste
Than iron ones: stripes ain't my style.
You're going down; I promise I'll
Come visit every other year.                                        35
Now kiss me, sweet — the squad car's here.

### CONSIDERATIONS FOR CRITICAL THINKING AND WRITING

1. FIRST RESPONSE. How does Lauinger's poem evoke Marvell's *carpe diem* poem (p. 65) and the tough-guy tone of a "noir" narrative, a crime story or thriller that is especially dark?

2. Discuss the ways in which time is a central presence in the poem.

3. Explain the allusion to dreams in lines 28–29.

### CONNECTION TO ANOTHER SELECTION

1. Compare the speaker's voice in this poem with that of the speaker in "To His Coy Mistress" (p. 65). What significant similarities and differences do you find?

    This fourth love poem is a twentieth-century work in which the speaker's voice is a woman's. How does it sound different from the way the men speak in the previous three poems?

# SHARON OLDS (B. 1942)

## *Last Night*                                                    *1996*

The next day, I am almost afraid.
Love? It was more like dragonflies
in the sun, 100 degrees at noon,
the ends of their abdomens stuck together, I
close my eyes when I remember. I hardly                               5
knew myself, like something twisting and
twisting out of a chrysalis,
enormous, without language, all
head, all shut eyes, and the humming
like madness, the way they writhe away,                              10
and do not leave, back, back,
away, back. Did I know you? No kiss,
no tenderness — more like killing, death-grip
holding to life, genitals
like violent hands clasped tight                                     15
barely moving, more like being closed
in a great jaw and eaten, and the screaming
I groan to remember it, and when we started
to die, then I refuse to remember,
the way a drunkard forgets. After,                                   20
you held my hands extremely hard as my
body moved in shudders like the ferry when its
axle is loosed past engagement, you kept me
sealed exactly against you, our hairlines
wet as the arc of a gateway after                                    25
a cloudburst, you secured me in your arms till I slept —
that was love, and we woke in the morning
clasped, fragrant, buoyant, that was
the morning after love.

### CONSIDERATIONS FOR CRITICAL THINKING AND WRITING

1. **FIRST RESPONSE.** How is your response to this poem affected by the fact that the speaker is female? Explain why this is or isn't a *carpe diem* poem.

2. Comment on the descriptive passages of "Last Night." Which images seem especially vivid to you? How do they contribute to the poem's meaning?

3. Explain how the poem's tone changes from beginning to end.

### CONNECTIONS TO OTHER SELECTIONS

1. How does the speaker's description of intimacy compare with Herrick's and Marvell's?

2. Compare the speaker's voice in Olds's poem with the voice you imagine for the coy mistress in Marvell's poem.

3. CRITICAL STRATEGIES. Read the section on formalist criticism (pp. 329–31) in Chapter 15, "Critical Strategies for Reading," and compare the themes in Olds's poem and Philip Larkin's "A Study of Reading Habits" (p. 21) the way you think a feminist critic might analyze them.

## Perspective

GENE WEINGARTEN (B. 1951), DAN WEINGARTEN (B. 1984), AND DAVID CLARK (B. 1960)

### *Barney & Clyde*                                      *2012*

Barney and Clyde used with the permission of Gene Weingarten, Dan Weingarten, David Clark and the Washington Post Writers group. All rights reserved.

### CONSIDERATIONS FOR CRITICAL THINKING AND WRITING

1. Did you get the joke? Probably not, but how does a Google search help you?

2. Additional strips of *Barney & Clyde* can be found on the Internet, which provides information about the comic's characters as well as its writers and illustrator. How does that information serve to characterize the type of humor in the strip?

3. Choose a poem from Chapter 14, "A Collection of Poems," that is rich in allusions and use the Internet to explain their function in the poem.

# POEMS FOR FURTHER STUDY

## THOMAS HARDY (1840–1928)

### *The Convergence of the Twain*                    1912

*Lines on the Loss of the "Titanic"°*


### I

In a solitude of the sea
Deep from human vanity,
And the Pride of Life that planned her, stilly couches she.


### II

Steel chambers, late the pyres
Of her salamandrine fires,°                              5
Cold currents thrid,° and turn to rhythmic tidal lyres.    *thread*


### III

Over the mirrors meant
To glass the opulent
The sea-worm crawls — grotesque, slimed, dumb, indifferent.


### IV

Jewels in joy designed                                  10
To ravish the sensuous mind
Lie lightless, all their sparkles bleared and black and blind.


### V

Dim moon-eyed fishes near
Gaze at the gilded gear
And query: "What does this vaingloriousness down here?"      15


---

*"Titanic"*: A luxurious ocean liner, reputed to be unsinkable, which sank after hitting an iceberg on its maiden voyage in 1912. Only a third of the 2,200 passengers survived. 5 *salamandrine fires*: Salamanders were, according to legend, able to survive fire; hence the ship's fires burned even though under water.

## VI

Well: while was fashioning
This creature of cleaving wing,
The Immanent Will that stirs and urges everything

## VII

Prepared a sinister mate
For her — so gaily great —                                         20
A Shape of Ice, for the time far and dissociate.

## VIII

And as the smart ship grew
In stature, grace, and hue,
In shadowy silent distance grew the Iceberg too.

## IX

Alien they seemed to be:                                          25
No mortal eye could see
The intimate welding of their later history,

## X

Or sign that they were bent
By paths coincident
On being anon twin halves of one august event,                   30

## XI

Till the Spinner of the Years
Said "Now!" And each one hears,
And consummation comes, and jars two hemispheres.

### Considerations for Critical Thinking and Writing

1. FIRST RESPONSE. Describe a contemporary disaster comparable to the sinking of the *Titanic*. How was your response to it similar to or different from the speaker's response to the fate of the *Titanic*?

2. How do the words used to describe the ship in this poem reveal the speaker's attitude toward the *Titanic*?

3. The diction of the poem suggests that the *Titanic* and the iceberg participate in something like an arranged marriage. What specific words imply this?

4. Who or what causes the disaster? Does the speaker assign responsibility?

# DAVID R. SLAVITT (B. 1935)
## Titanic                                                           1983

Who does not love the *Titanic*?
If they sold passage tomorrow for that same crossing,
who would not buy?

To go down . . . We all go down, mostly
alone. But with crowds of people, friends, servants,                    5
well fed, with music, with lights! Ah!

And the world, shocked, mourns, as it ought to do
and almost never does. There will be the books and movies
to remind our grandchildren who we were
and how we died, and give them a good cry.                             10

Not so bad, after all. The cold
water is anesthetic and very quick.
The cries on all sides must be a comfort.

We all go: only a few, first-class.

### CONSIDERATIONS FOR CRITICAL THINKING AND WRITING

1. FIRST RESPONSE. What, according to the speaker in this poem, is so
   compelling about the *Titanic*? Do you agree?
2. Discuss the speaker's tone. Is "Titanic" merely a sarcastic poem?
3. What is the effect of the poem's final line? What emotions does it elicit?

### CONNECTIONS TO OTHER SELECTIONS

1. How does "Titanic" differ in its attitude toward opulence from "The
   Convergence of the Twain" (p. 71)?
2. Which poem, "Titanic" or "The Convergence of the Twain," is more
   emotionally satisfying to you? Explain why.
3. Compare the speakers' tones in "Titanic" and "The Convergence of the
   Twain."
4. CRITICAL STRATEGIES. Read the section on Marxist criticism (pp. 335–
   36) in Chapter 15, "Critical Strategies for Reading," and analyze the
   attitudes toward opulence that are manifested in the two poems.

## Joanne Diaz (b. 1972)

### *On My Father's Loss of Hearing*          2006

© Jason Reblando. Reprinted by permission of the photographer.

*I'd like to see more poems treat the deaf as*
*being abled differently, not lost or missing*
*something, weakened, deficient.*
                    *— from a listserv for the deaf*

Abled differently — so vague compared
with deaf, obtuse but true to history,
from deave: to deafen, stun, amaze with noise.
Perhaps that's what we've done — amazed
         him with
our sorrows and complaints, the stupid
         jabs,
the loneliness of boredom in the house,

our wants so foreign to his own. What else
is there but loss? He's lost the humor of
sarcastic jokes, the snarky dialogue
of British films eludes him, phone calls          10
cast him adrift in that cochlear maze
that thrums and bristles even now, when
it doesn't have to: an unnecessary kind
of elegance, the vestige of a sense

no longer obligated to transmit                   15
the crack of thawing ice that fills the yard's
wide dip in winter, or the scrape of his
dull rake in spring, its prongs' vibration thrilled
by grass and peat moss. Imagine his desires
released like saffron pistils in the wind;        20
mark their trace against the cords of wood

he spent the summer splitting. See his quiet
flicker like a film, a Super-8
projected on the wall, and all of us
there, laughing on the porch without a sound.     25
No noisome cruelty, no baffled rage,
no aging children sullen in their lack.
Love hurts much less in this serenity.

### Considerations for Critical Thinking and Writing

1. **FIRST RESPONSE.** Why does the speaker prefer the word *deaf* to the phrase "abled differently" as a means of describing her father? Which description do you prefer? Why?

2. Explain how sound and silence move through the poem from beginning to end.

3. Choose a single word from each stanza that strikes you as particularly effective, and explain why you think Diaz chose it over other possibilities.

4. What do you make of the poem's final line? How does it relate to the tone of the rest of the poem?

### CONNECTION TO ANOTHER SELECTION

1. Discuss the relationship between love and pain in "On My Father's Loss of Hearing" and in Theodore Roethke's "My Papa's Waltz" (p. 190).

## JOHN KEATS (1795–1821)

### Ode on a Grecian Urn                                                  1819

### I

Thou still unravished bride of quietness,
   Thou foster-child of silence and slow time,
Sylvan° historian, who canst thus express
   A flowery tale more sweetly than our rhyme:
What leaf-fringed legend haunts about thy shape                     5
   Of deities or mortals, or of both,
      In Tempe or the dales of Arcady?°
What men or gods are these? What maidens loath?
   What mad pursuit? What struggle to escape?
      What pipes and timbrels? What wild ecstasy?             10

### II

Heard melodies are sweet, but those unheard
   Are sweeter; therefore, ye soft pipes, play on;
Not to the sensual ear, but, more endeared,
   Pipe to the spirit ditties of no tone:
Fair youth, beneath the trees, thou canst not leave               15
   Thy song, nor ever can those trees be bare;
      Bold Lover, never, never canst thou kiss,
Though winning near the goal — yet, do not grieve;
   She cannot fade, though thou hast not thy bliss,
      For ever wilt thou love, and she be fair!                 20

3 *Sylvan:* Rustic. The urn is decorated with a forest scene.    7 *Tempe, Arcady:* Beautiful rural valleys in Greece.

## III

Ah, happy, happy boughs! that cannot shed
    Your leaves, nor ever bid the Spring adieu;
And, happy melodist, unwearièd,
    For ever piping songs for ever new;
More happy love! more happy, happy love!                       25
    For ever warm and still to be enjoyed,
        For ever panting, and for ever young;
All breathing human passion far above,
    That leaves a heart high-sorrowful and cloyed,
        A burning forehead, and a parching tongue.         30

## IV

Who are these coming to the sacrifice?
    To what green altar, O mysterious priest,
Lead'st thou that heifer lowing at the skies,
    And all her silken flanks with garlands drest?
What little town by river or sea shore,                        35
    Or mountain-built with peaceful citadel,
        Is emptied of this folk, this pious morn?
And, little town, thy streets for evermore
    Will silent be; and not a soul to tell
        Why thou art desolate, can e'er return.           40

## V

O Attic° shape! Fair attitude! with brede°
    Of marble men and maidens overwrought,
With forest branches and the trodden weed;
    Thou, silent form, dost tease us out of thought
As doth eternity: Cold Pastoral!                          45
    When old age shall this generation waste,
        Thou shalt remain, in midst of other woe
Than ours, a friend to man, to whom thou say'st,
    Beauty is truth, truth beauty — that is all
        Ye know on earth, and all ye need to know.         50

41 *Attic:* Possessing classic Athenian simplicity; *brede:* Design.

## CONSIDERATIONS FOR CRITICAL THINKING AND WRITING

1. FIRST RESPONSE. What does the speaker's diction reveal about his attitude toward the urn in this ode? Does his view develop or change?

2. How is the happiness in stanza 3 related to the assertion in lines 11–12 that "Heard melodies are sweet, but those unheard / Are sweeter"?

3. What is the difference between the world depicted on the urn and the speaker's world?

4. What do lines 49 and 50 suggest about the relation of art to life? Why is the urn described as a "Cold Pastoral" (line 45)?

5. Which world does the speaker seem to prefer, the urn's or his own?

6. Describe the overall tone of the poem.

## CONNECTIONS TO OTHER SELECTIONS

1. Write an essay comparing the view of time in this ode with that in Marvell's "To His Coy Mistress" (p. 65). Pay particular attention to the connotative language in each poem.

2. Compare the tone and attitude toward life in this ode with those in John Keats's "To Autumn" (p. 98).

## GWENDOLYN BROOKS (1917–2000)

### *We Real Cool*                                                    1960

*The Pool Players.*
*Seven at the Golden Shovel.*

We real cool. We
Left school. We

Lurk late. We
Strike straight. We

Sing sin. We
Thin gin. We

Jazz June. We
Die soon.

### CONSIDERATIONS FOR CRITICAL THINKING AND WRITING

1. FIRST RESPONSE. How does the speech of the pool players in this poem help to characterize them? What is the effect of the pronouns coming at the ends of the lines? How would the poem sound if the pronouns came at the beginnings of lines?

2. What is the author's attitude toward the players? Is there a change in tone in the last line?

3. How is the pool hall's name related to the rest of the poem and its theme?

## Joan Murray (b. 1945)
### We Old Dudes                2006

We old dudes. We
White shoes. We

Golf ball. We
Eat mall. We

Soak teeth. We
Palm Beach; We

Vote red. We
Soon dead.

### Considerations for Critical Thinking and Writing

1. **first response.** Consider the poem's humor. To what extent does it make a serious point?

2. What does the reference to Palm Beach tell you about these "old dudes"?

3. **creative response.** Write a poem similar in style that characterizes your life as a student.

### Connection to Another Selection

1. Compare the themes of "We Old Dudes" and Brooks's "We Real Cool." How do the two poems speak to each other?

## Alice Jones (b. 1949)
### The Larynx                1993

Under the epiglottic flap
the long-ringed tube sinks
its shaft down to the bronchial
   fork, divides from two
to four then infinite branches,
each ending finally in a clump
   of transparent sacs knit
with small vessels into a mesh
that sponge-like soaks up breath
   and gives it off with a push
from the diaphragm's muscular wall,
   forces wind out of the lungs'
wide tree, up through this organ's

5

10

single pipe, through the puzzle
box of gristle, where resonant                                    15
    plates of cartilage fold
    into shield, horns, bows,
    bound by odd half-spirals
of muscles that modulate air
as it rises through this empty place                              20
    at our core, where lip-like
folds stretch across the vestibule,
    small and tough, they flutter,
    bend like birds' wings finding
        just the right angle to stay                              25
airborne; here the cords arch
in the hollow of this ancient instrument,
curve and vibrate to make a song.

### CONSIDERATIONS FOR CRITICAL THINKING AND WRITING

1. FIRST RESPONSE. What is the effect of having this poem written as one long sentence? How does the length of the sentence contribute to the poem's meaning?

2. Make a list of words and phrases from the poem that strike you as scientific, and compare those with a list of words that seem poetic. How do they compete or complement each other in terms of how they affect your reading?

3. Comment on the final three lines. How would your interpretation of this poem change if it ended before the semicolon in line 26?

### CONNECTION TO ANOTHER SELECTION

1. Compare the diction and the ending in "The Larynx" with those of "The Foot" (p. 181), another poem by Jones.

## LOUIS SIMPSON (1923–2012)

### *In the Suburbs*                                             *1963*

There's no way out.
You were born to waste your life.
You were born to this middleclass life

As others before you
Were born to walk in procession
To the temple, singing.

1. FIRST RESPONSE. Is the title of this poem especially significant? What images does it conjure up for you?

2. What does the repetition in lines 2–3 suggest?

3. Discuss the possible connotative meanings of lines 5 and 6. Who are the "others before you"?

## GARRISON KEILLOR (B. 1942)

### *The Anthem*                                                                2006

*If famous poets had written "The Star-Spangled Banner"*

Whose flag this is I think I know
His house is being bombed now though
He will not see that I have come
To watch the twilight's ebbing glow.

My little horse must think it dumb,                                              5
The cannons' pandemonium,
The rockets bursting in the air,
The sound of bugle, fife, and drum.

He turns and shakes his derrière
To show me that he doesn't care                                                 10
Who takes this battle flag or why,
When in the redness of the glare

I see the banner flying high
Through the tumult in the sky
And, knowing all is now okay,                                                   15
We walk away, my horse and I.

The flag is lovely, hip hooray,
But I have things to do today,
Some here and others far away,
Before I stop to hit the hay.                                                   20
—*Robert Frost*

1. FIRST RESPONSE. Explain why a familiarity with both "The Star-Spangled Banner" and Frost's "Stopping by Woods on a Snowy Evening" (p. 271) is vital to an informed reading of Keillor's "Anthem."

2. Discuss the lines from each poem that Keillor appropriates for his own purposes.

3. What makes this poem humorous?

4. **CREATIVE RESPONSE.** "Anthem" is reprinted from an issue of the *Atlantic* (Jan.–Feb. 2006) in which Keillor also includes versions of "The Star-Spangled Banner" as if written by Emily Dickinson and by Billy Collins. (You might want to look those poems up.) Choose a poet whose style you find interesting and write a version of the anthem as if written by that poet.

# 4

# Images

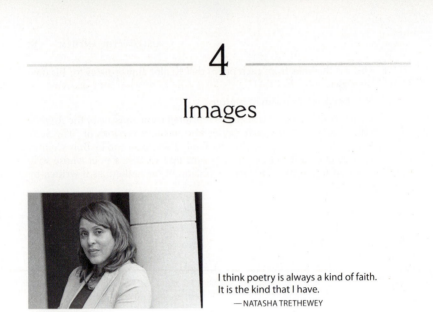

I think poetry is always a kind of faith.
It is the kind that I have.
— NATASHA TRETHEWEY

AP Photo/Rogelio V. Solis.

## POETRY'S APPEAL TO THE SENSES

A poet, to borrow a phrase from Henry James, is one on whom nothing is lost. Poets take in the world and give us impressions of what they experience through images. An *image* is language that addresses the senses. The most common images in poetry are visual; they provide verbal pictures of the poets' encounters — real or imagined — with the world. But poets also create images that appeal to our other senses. Li Ho arouses several senses in "A Beautiful Girl Combs Her Hair":

Awake at dawn
she's dreaming
by cool silk curtains

fragrance of spilling hair
half sandalwood, half aloes

windlass creaking at the well
singing jade

These vivid images deftly blend textures, fragrances, and sounds that tease out the sensuousness of the moment. Images give us the physical world to experience in our imaginations. Some poems, like the following one, are written to do just that; they make no comment about what they describe.

## WILLIAM CARLOS WILLIAMS  (1883–1963)

### *Poem*                                                           *1934*

As the cat
climbed over
the top of

the jamcloset
first the right                                                          5
forefoot

carefully
then the hind
stepped down

into the pit of                                                         10
the empty
flowerpot

   This poem defies paraphrase because it is all an image of agile movement. No statement is made about the movement; the title, "Poem" —really no title— signals Williams's refusal to comment on the movements. To impose a meaning on the poem, we'd probably have to knock over the flowerpot.

   We experience the image in Williams's "Poem" more clearly because of how the sentence is organized into lines and groups of lines, or stanzas. Consider how differently the sentence is read if it is arranged as prose:

   As the cat climbed over the top of the jamcloset, first the right forefoot
   carefully then the hind stepped down into the pit of the empty flowerpot.

The poem's line and stanza division transforms what is essentially an awkward prose sentence into a rhythmic verbal picture. Especially when the poem is read aloud, this line and stanza division allows us to feel the image we see. Even the lack of a period at the end suggests that the cat is only pausing.

   Images frequently do more than offer only sensory impressions, however. They also convey emotions and moods, as in the following poem's view of Civil War troops moving across a river.

## WALT WHITMAN (1819–1892)

## *Cavalry Crossing a Ford*                    *1865*

A line in long array where they wind betwixt green islands,
They take a serpentine course, their arms flash in the sun — hark to the
     musical clank,
Behold the silvery river, in it the splashing horses loitering stop to drink,
Behold the brown-faced men, each group, each person, a picture, the
     negligent rest on the saddles,
Some emerge on the opposite bank, others are just entering the
     ford — while,
Scarlet and blue and snowy white,
The guidon flags flutter gaily in the wind.

### CONSIDERATIONS FOR CRITICAL THINKING AND WRITING

1. FIRST RESPONSE. Do the colors and sounds establish the mood of this poem? What is the mood?

2. How would the poem's mood have been changed if Whitman had used "look" or "see" instead of "behold" (lines 3–4)?

3. Where is the speaker as he observes this troop movement?

4. Does "serpentine" in line 2 have an evil connotation in this poem? Explain your answer.

Whitman seems to capture momentarily all of the troop's actions, and through carefully chosen, suggestive details — really very few — he succeeds in making "each group, each person, a picture." Specific details, even when few are provided, give us the impression that we see the entire picture; it is as if those are the details we would remember if we had viewed the scene ourselves. Notice, too, that the movement of the "line in long array" is emphasized by the continuous winding syntax of the poem's lengthy lines.

Movement is also central to the next poem, in which action and motion are created through carefully chosen verbs.

## DAVID SOLWAY (B. 1941)

## *Windsurfing*                    *1993*

> WHEN I READ "The good poet always generates a sense of lexical surprise, an openness toward the unexpected, a feeling of novelty and delight."
> — DAVID SOLWAY

It rides upon the wrinkled hide
of water, like the upturned hull
of a small canoe or kayak
waiting to be righted — yet its law
is opposite to that of boats,
it floats upon its breastbone and

5

brings whatever spine there is to light.
A thin shaft is slotted into place.
Then a puffed right-angle of wind
pushes it forward, out into the bay,                                      10
where suddenly it glitters into speed,
tilts, knifes up, and for the moment's
nothing but a slim projectile
of cambered fiberglass,
peeling the crests.                                                      15

        The man's
clamped to the mast, taut as a guywire.
Part of the sleek apparatus
he controls, immaculate nerve
of balance, plunge and curvet,                                           20
he clinches all component movements
into single motion.
It bucks, stalls, shudders, yaws, and dips
its hissing sides beneath the surface
that sustains it, tensing                                                25
into muscle that nude ellipse
of lunging appetite and power.

And now the mechanism's wholly
dolphin, springing toward its prey
of spume and beaded sunlight,                                            30
tossing spray, and hits the vertex
of the wide, salt glare of distance,
and reverses.

        Back it comes through
a screen of particles,                                                   35
scalloped out of water, shimmer
and reflection, the wind snapping
and lashing it homeward,
shearing the curve of the wave,
breaking the spell of the caught breath                                 40
and articulate play of sinew, to enter
the haven of the breakwater
and settle in a rush of silence.

Now the crossing drifts
in the husk of its wake                                                  45
and nothing's the same again
as, gliding elegantly on a film of water,
the man guides
his brash, obedient legend
into shore.                                                             50

## Considerations for Critical Thinking and Writing

1. FIRST RESPONSE. Draw a circle around the verbs that seem especially effective in conveying a strong sense of motion, and explain why they are effective.

2. How is the man made to seem to be one with his board and sail?

3. How does the rhythm of the poem change beginning with line 45?

### Connection to Another Selection

1. Consider the effects of the images in "Windsurfing" and John Keats's "To Autumn" (p. 98). In an essay, explain how these images elicit the emotional responses they do.

"Windsurfing" is awash with images of speed, fluidity, and power. Even the calming aftermath of the breakwater is described as a "rush of silence," adding to the sense of motion that is detailed and expanded throughout the poem. The tone of the images and mood of the speaker are consistent in Solway's "Windsurfing." In Matthew Arnold's "Dover Beach," however, they shift as the theme is developed.

## Matthew Arnold (1822–1888)

### *Dover Beach*                                                         *1867*

The sea is calm tonight.
The tide is full, the moon lies fair
Upon the straits; — on the French coast the light
Gleams and is gone; the cliffs of England stand,
Glimmering and vast, out in the tranquil bay.                              5
Come to the window, sweet is the night-air!
Only, from the long line of spray
Where the sea meets the moon-blanched land,
Listen! you hear the grating roar
Of pebbles which the waves draw back, and fling,                          10
At their return, up the high strand,
Begin, and cease, and then again begin,
With tremulous cadence slow, and bring
The eternal note of sadness in.

Sophocles long ago                                                        15
Heard it on the Aegean, and it brought
Into his mind the turbid ebb and flow
Of human misery;° we

15–18 *Sophocles . . . misery:* In *Antigone* (lines 656–77), Sophocles likens the disasters that beset the house of Oedipus to a "mounting tide."

Find also in the sound a thought,
Hearing it by this distant northern sea.                              20

The Sea of Faith
Was once, too, at the full, and round earth's shore
Lay like the folds of a bright girdle furled.
But now I only hear
Its melancholy, long, withdrawing roar,                               25
Retreating, to the breath
Of the night-wind, down the vast edges drear
And naked shingles° of the world.                              *pebble beaches*

Ah, love, let us be true
To one another! for the world, which seems                            30
To lie before us like a land of dreams,
So various, so beautiful, so new,
Hath really neither joy, nor love, nor light,
Nor certitude, nor peace, nor help for pain;
And we are here as on a darkling plain                                35
Swept with confused alarms of struggle and flight,
Where ignorant armies clash by night.

## Considerations for Critical Thinking and Writing

1. FIRST RESPONSE. Discuss what you consider to be this poem's central point. How do the speaker's descriptions of the ocean work toward making that point?

2. Contrast the images in lines 4–8 and 9–13. How do they reveal the speaker's mood? To whom is he speaking?

3. What is the cause of the "sadness" in line 14? What is the speaker's response to the ebbing "Sea of Faith"? Is there anything to replace his sense of loss?

4. What details of the beach seem related to the ideas in the poem? How is the sea used differently in lines 1–14 and 21–28?

5. Describe the differences in tone between lines 1–8 and 35–37. What has caused the change?

6. CRITICAL STRATEGIES. Read the section on mythological strategies (pp. 339–42) in Chapter 15, "Critical Strategies for Reading," and discuss how you think a mythological critic might make use of the allusion to Sophocles in this poem.

## Connection to Another Selection

1. Explain how the images in Wilfred Owen's "Dulce et Decorum Est" (p. 95) develop further the ideas and sentiments suggested by Arnold's final line concerning "ignorant armies clash[ing] by night."

Consider the appetite for images displayed in the celebration of poetry in the following poem.

# Ruth Forman (b. 1968)

## *Poetry Should Ride the Bus*    *1993*

poetry should hopscotch in a polka dot dress
wheel cartwheels
n hold your hand
when you walk past the yellow crackhouse

poetry should wear bright red lipstick
n practice kisses in the mirror
for all the fine young men with fades
shootin craps around the corner

Christine Bennett.

poetry should dress in fine plum linen suits
n not be so educated that it don't stop in                    10
every now n then to sit on the porch
and talk about the comins and goins of the world

poetry should ride the bus
in a fat woman's Safeway bag
between the greens n chicken wings                             15
to be served with tuesday's dinner

poetry should drop by a sweet potato pie
ask about the grandchildren
n sit through a whole photo album
on a orange plastic covered lazy boy with no place to go      20

poetry should sing red revolution love songs
that massage your scalp
and bring hope to your blood
when you think you're too old to fight

yeah                                                          25
poetry should whisper electric blue magic
all the years of your life
never forgettin to look you in the soul
every one in a while
n smile                                                       30

### Considerations for Critical Thinking and Writing

1. **first response.** How do the images in each stanza reveal the speaker's attitude toward poetry? Do you agree with the poem's ideas about what poetry should do and be?

2. What does the poem's diction tell you about the speaker?

3. Discuss the tone of this poem and why you think it does or does not work.

CONNECTION TO ANOTHER SELECTION

1. How does Forman's speaker's view of poetry compare with that of the speaker in Billy Collins's "Introduction to Poetry" (p. 28)?

# POEMS FOR FURTHER STUDY

## AMY LOWELL (1874–1925)

### The Pond
*1919*

Cold, wet leaves
Floating on moss-colored water,
And the croaking of frogs —
Cracked bell-notes in the twilight.

CONSIDERATIONS FOR CRITICAL THINKING AND WRITING

1. FIRST RESPONSE. This poem is not a complete sentence. What is missing? Does it matter in terms of understanding what is described by the images?

2. What senses are stimulated by the images? Which sense seems to be the most dominant in the poem? Why?

3. CREATIVE RESPONSE. Is the title of the poem necessary to convey its meaning? Choose an appropriate alternate title and explain how it subtly suggests something different from "The Pond."

## H. D. (HILDA DOOLITTLE/1886–1961)

### Heat
*1916*

O wind, rend open the heat,
cut apart the heat,
rend it to tatters.

Fruit cannot drop
through this thick air —                                        5
fruit cannot fall into heat
that presses up and blunts
the points of pears
and rounds the grapes.

Cut the heat —                                                  10
plough through it,
turning it on either side
of your path.

## CONSIDERATIONS FOR CRITICAL THINKING AND WRITING

1. FIRST RESPONSE. Is this poem more about heat or fruit? Explain your answer.
2. What physical properties are associated with heat in this poem?
3. Explain the effect of the description of fruit in lines 4–9.
4. Why is the image of the cutting plow especially effective in lines 10–13?

## RUTH FAINLIGHT (B. 1931)

### Crocuses                                              2006

Pale, bare, tender stems rising
from the muddy winter-faded grass,

shivering petals the almost luminous
blue and mauve of bruises on the naked

bodies of men, women, children
herded into a forest clearing

before the shouted order, crack of gunfire,
final screams and prayers and moans.

## CONSIDERATIONS FOR CRITICAL THINKING AND WRITING

1. FIRST RESPONSE. Comment on Fainlight's choice of title. What effect does it have on your reading of the poem?
2. Trace your response to each image in the poem and describe the poem's tone as it moves from line to line.
3. CREATIVE RESPONSE. Try writing an eight-line poem in the style of Fainlight's based on images that gradually but radically shift in tone.

## MARY ROBINSON (1758–1800)

### London's Summer Morning                             1806

Who has not wak'd to list° the busy sounds            listen to
Of summer's morning, in the sultry smoke
Of noisy London? On the pavement hot
The sooty chimney-boy, with dingy face
And tatter'd covering, shrilly bawls his trade,              5
Rousing the sleepy housemaid. At the door
The milk-pail rattles, and the tinkling bell
Proclaims the dustman's office; while the street

Is lost in clouds impervious. Now begins
The din of hackney-coaches, waggons, carts;                          10
While tinmen's shops, and noisy trunk-makers,
Knife-grinders, coopers, squeaking cork-cutters,
Fruit-barrows, and the hunger-giving cries
Of vegetable venders, fill the air.
Now ev'ry shop displays its varied trade,                            15
And the fresh-sprinkled pavement cools the feet
Of early walkers. At the private door
The ruddy housemaid twirls the busy mop,
Annoying the smart 'prentice, or neat girl,
Tripping with band-box° lightly. Now the sun           *hat box*   20
Darts burning splendour on the glitt'ring pane,
Save where the canvas awning throws a shade
On the gay merchandize. Now, spruce and trim,
In shops (where beauty smiles with industry),
Sits the smart damsel; while the passenger                           25
Peeps thro' the window, watching ev'ry charm.
Now pastry dainties catch the eye minute
Of humming insects, while the limy snare
Waits to enthral them. Now the lamp-lighter
Mounts the tall ladder, nimbly vent'rous,                            30
To trim the half-fill'd lamp; while at his feet
The pot-boy° yells discordant! All along         *drink server*
The sultry pavement, the old-clothes-man cries
In tones monotonous, and side-long views
The area for his traffic: now the bag                                35
Is slily open'd, and the half-worn suit
(Sometimes the pilfer'd treasure of the base
Domestic spoiler), for one half its worth,
Sinks in the green abyss. The porter now
Bears his huge load along the burning way;                           40
And the poor poet wakes from busy dreams,
To paint the summer morning.

## CONSIDERATIONS FOR CRITICAL THINKING AND WRITING

1. **FIRST RESPONSE.** How effective is this picture of a London summer
   morning in 1806? Which images do you find particularly effective?

2. How does the end of the poem bring us full circle to its beginning?
   What effect does this structure have on your understanding of the
   poem?

3. **CREATIVE RESPONSE.** Try writing about the start of your own day — in
   the dormitory, at home, at the start of a class — using a series of images
   that provide a vivid sense of what happens and how you experience it.

### CONNECTION TO ANOTHER SELECTION

1. How does Robinson's description of London differ from William Blake's "London," the next poem? What would you say is the essential difference in purpose between the two poems?

## WILLIAM BLAKE (1757–1827)

## *London*                                                        *1794*

I wander through each chartered° street,                    *defined by law*
Near where the chartered Thames does flow,
And mark in every face I meet
Marks of weakness, marks of woe.

In every cry of every man,                                              5
In every Infant's cry of fear,
In every voice, in every ban,
The mind-forged manacles I hear.

How the Chimney-sweeper's cry
Every black'ning Church appalls;                                    10
And the hapless Soldier's sigh
Runs in blood down Palace walls.

But most through midnight streets I hear
How the youthful Harlot's curse
Blasts the new-born Infant's tear,                                  15
And blights with plagues the Marriage hearse.

### CONSIDERATIONS FOR CRITICAL THINKING AND WRITING

1. FIRST RESPONSE. What feelings do the visual images in this poem suggest to you?
2. What is the predominant sound heard in the poem?
3. What is the meaning of line 8? What is the cause of the problems that the speaker sees and hears in London? Does the speaker suggest additional causes?
4. The image in lines 11 and 12 cannot be read literally. Comment on its effectiveness.
5. How does Blake's use of denotative and connotative language enrich this poem's meaning?
6. An earlier version of Blake's last stanza appeared this way:

   But most the midnight harlot's curse
   From every dismal street I hear,
   Weaves around the marriage hearse
   And blasts the new-born infant's tear.

Examine carefully the differences between the two versions. How do Blake's revisions affect his picture of London life? Which version do you think is more effective? Why?

# A SAMPLE STUDENT RESPONSE

Anna Tamara

Professor Burton

English 211

30 March 2015

Imagery in William Blake's "London" and Mary Robinson's

"London's Summer Morning"

Both William Blake and Mary Robinson use strong imagery to examine and bring to life the city of London, yet each writer paints a very different picture. The images in both poems "[address] the senses," as Meyer writes (82). But while Blake's images depict a city weighed down by oppression and poverty, Robinson's images are lighter, happier, and, arguably, idealized. Both poems use powerful imagery in very different ways to establish theme.

In Blake's poem, oppression and social discontent are defined by the speaker, who sees "weakness" and "woe" (line 4) in the faces he meets; he hears cries of men and children and "mind-forged manacles" (8). And, through imagery, the poem makes a political statement:

> How the Chimney-sweeper's cry
>
> Every black'ning Church appalls;
>
> And the hapless Soldier's sigh
>
> Runs in blood down Palace walls. (9-12)

These images indicate the speaker's dark view of the religious and governmental institutions that he believes cause the city's suffering. The "black'ning Church" and bloody "Palace walls" can be seen to represent misused power and corruption, while the "manacles" are the rules and physical and psychological burdens that lead to societal ills. In Blake's view of London, children are sold into servitude (as chimney sweeps) and soldiers pay in blood.

Robinson's poem, on the other hand, offers the reader a pleasant view of a sunny London morning through a different series of images. The reader hears "the tinkling bell" (7) and sees a bright moment in which "the sun / Darts burning splendour on the glitt'ring pane" (20-21). Even the chimney-boy is shown in a rosy glow. Though he is described as having a "dingy face / And tatter'd covering," he wakes the "sleepy" house servant when he "shrilly bawls his trade" (4-6). In contrast to the chimney-sweep of Blake's "London," Robinson's boy is painted as a charming character who announces the morning amid a backdrop of happy workers. Also unlike Blake's London, Robinson's is a city of contentment in which a "ruddy housemaid twirls the busy mop" (18) . . .

## Works Cited

Blake, William. "London." Meyer 92.

Meyer, Michael, ed. *Thinking and Writing about Poetry*. Boston: Bedford/St. Martin's, 2016. 82. Print.

Robinson, Mary. "London's Summer Morning." Meyer 90–91.

## EMILY DICKINSON  (1830–1886)

### *Wild Nights — Wild Nights!*                    *c. 1861*

Wild Nights — Wild Nights!
Were I with thee
Wild Nights should be
Our luxury!

Futile — the Winds —                                     5
To a Heart in port —
Done with the Compass —
Done with the Chart!

Rowing in Eden —
Ah, the Sea!                                             10
Might I but moor — Tonight —
In Thee!

## CONSIDERATIONS FOR CRITICAL THINKING AND WRITING

1. FIRST RESPONSE. Thomas Wentworth Higginson, Dickinson's mentor, once said he was afraid that some "malignant" readers might "read into [a poem like this] more than that virgin recluse ever dreamed of putting there." What do you think?

2. Look up the meaning of *luxury* in a dictionary. Why does this word work especially well here?

3. Given the imagery of the final stanza, do you think the speaker is a man or a woman? Explain why.

## CONNECTION TO ANOTHER SELECTION

1. Write an essay that compares the voice, figures of speech, and theme of this poem with those of Margaret Atwood's "you fit into me" (p. 103).

## WILFRED OWEN (1893–1918)

### *Dulce et Decorum Est* 1920

Bent double, like old beggars under sacks,
Knock-kneed, coughing like hags, we cursed through sludge,
Till on the haunting flares we turned our backs,
And towards our distant rest began to trudge.

Men marched asleep. Many had lost their boots,                         5
But limped on, blood-shod. All went lame, all blind;
Drunk with fatigue; deaf even to the hoots
Of gas-shells dropping softly behind.

Gas! GAS! Quick, boys! — An ecstasy of fumbling,
Fitting the clumsy helmets just in time,                               10
But someone still was yelling out and stumbling
And flound'ring like a man in fire or lime. —
Dim through the misty panes and thick green light,
As under a green sea, I saw him drowning.

In all my dreams before my helpless sight                             15
He plunges at me, guttering, choking, drowning.

If in some smothering dreams, you too could pace
Behind the wagon that we flung him in,
And watch the white eyes writhing in his face,
His hanging face, like a devil's sick of sin,                         20
If you could hear, at every jolt, the blood
Come gargling from the froth-corrupted lungs

Obscene as cancer, bitter as the cud
Of vile, incurable sores on innocent tongues, —
My friend, you would not tell with such high zest                25
To children ardent for some desperate glory,
The old lie: *Dulce et decorum est*
*Pro patria mori.*

### CONSIDERATIONS FOR CRITICAL THINKING AND WRITING

1. FIRST RESPONSE. The Latin quotation in lines 28 and 29 is from Horace: "It is sweet and fitting to die for one's country." Owen served as a British soldier during World War I and was killed. Is this poem unpatriotic? What is its purpose?

2. Which images in the poem are most vivid? To which senses do they speak?

3. Describe the speaker's tone. What is his relationship to his audience?

4. How are the images of the soldiers in this poem different from the images that typically appear in recruiting posters?

## PATRICIA SMITH (B. 1955)

### What It's Like to Be a Black Girl (for Those of You Who Aren't)                1991

First of all, it's being 9 years old and
feeling like you're not finished, like your
edges are wild, like there's something,
everything, wrong. it's dropping food coloring
in your eyes to make them blue and suffering                5
their burn in silence. it's popping a bleached
white mophead over the kinks of your hair and
primping in front of the mirrors that deny your
reflection. it's finding a space between your
legs, a disturbance at your chest, and not knowing           10
what to do with the whistles. it's jumping
double dutch until your legs pop, it's sweat
and vaseline and bullets, it's growing tall and
wearing a lot of white, it's smelling blood in
your breakfast, it's learning to say fuck with                15
grace but learning to fuck without it, it's
flame and fists and life according to motown,
it's finally having a man reach out for you
then caving in
around his fingers.                                           20

#### CONSIDERATIONS FOR CRITICAL THINKING AND WRITING

1. FIRST RESPONSE. Describe the speaker's tone. What images in particular contribute to it? How do you account for the selected tone?

2. How does the speaker characterize her life? On which elements of it does she focus?

3. Discuss the poem's final image. What sort of emotions does it elicit in you?


## SALLY CROFT (B. 1935)

### *Home-Baked Bread*                                    *1981*

*Nothing gives a household a greater sense of stability and common comfort than the aroma of cooling bread. Begin, if you like, with a loaf of whole wheat, which requires neither sifting nor kneading, and go on from there to more cunning triumphs.*    — The Joy of Cooking

What is it she is not saying?
*Cunning triumphs.* It rings
of insinuation. Step into my kitchen,
I have prepared a cunning triumph
for you. Spices and herbs                                      5
sealed in this porcelain jar,

a treasure of my great-aunt
who sat up past midnight
in her Massachusetts bedroom
when the moon was dark. Come,                                 10
rest your feet. I'll make
you tea with honey and slices

of warm bread spread with peach butter.
I picked the fruit this morning
still fresh with dew. The fragrance                           15
is seductive? I hoped you would say that.
See how the heat rises
when the bread opens. Come,

we'll eat together, the small flakes
have scarcely any flavor. What cunning                        20
triumphs we can discover in my upstairs room
where peach trees breathe their sweetness
beside the open window and
sun lies like honey on the floor.

## CONSIDERATIONS FOR CRITICAL THINKING AND WRITING

1. FIRST RESPONSE. Why does the speaker in this poem seize on the phrase "cunning triumphs" from the *Joy of Cooking* excerpt?

2. Distinguish between the voice we hear in lines 1–3 and the second voice in lines 3–24. Who is the "you" in the poem?

3. Why is the word "insinuation" an especially appropriate choice in line 3?

4. How do the images in lines 20–24 bring together all the senses evoked in the preceding lines?

5. CREATIVE RESPONSE. Write a paragraph — or stanza — that describes the sensuous (and perhaps sensual) qualities of a food you enjoy.

## JOHN KEATS (1795–1821)

### *To Autumn*                                              *1819*

#### I

Season of mists and mellow fruitfulness,
    Close bosom-friend of the maturing sun;
Conspiring with him how to load and bless
    With fruit the vines that round the thatch-eves run;
To bend with apples the mossed cottage-trees,                      5
    And fill all fruit with ripeness to the core;
        To swell the gourd, and plump the hazel shells
    With a sweet kernel; to set budding more,
And still more, later flowers for the bees,
Until they think warm days will never cease,                       10
        For summer has o'er-brimmed their clammy cells.

#### II

Who hath not seen thee oft amid thy store?
    Sometimes whoever seeks abroad may find
Thee sitting careless on a granary floor,
    Thy hair soft-lifted by the winnowing wind;                   15
Or on a half-reaped furrow sound asleep,
    Drowsed with the fume of poppies, while thy hook°      *scythe*
        Spares the next swath and all its twinèd flowers:
And sometimes like a gleaner thou dost keep
    Steady thy laden head across a brook;                          20
    Or by a cider-press, with patient look,
        Thou watchest the last oozings hours by hours.

## III

Where are the songs of spring? Ay, where are they?
  Think not of them, thou hast thy music too —
While barred clouds bloom the soft-dying day,             25
  And touch the stubble-plains with rosy hue;
Then in a wailful choir the small gnats mourn
  Among the river swallows,° borne aloft        *willows*
    Or sinking as the light wind lives or dies;
And full-grown lambs loud bleat from hilly bourn;°    *territory*  30
  Hedge-crickets sing; and now with treble soft
  The redbreast whistles from a garden-croft,
    And gathering swallows twitter in the skies.

### Considerations for Critical Thinking and Writing

1. **FIRST RESPONSE.** How is autumn made to seem like a person in each stanza of this ode?
2. Which senses are most emphasized in each stanza?
3. How is the progression of time expressed in the ode?
4. How does the imagery convey tone? Which words have especially strong connotative values?
5. What is the speaker's view of death?

### Connection to Another Selection

1. Compare this poem's tone and perspective on death with those of Robert Frost's "After Apple-Picking" (p. 265).

## Dave Lucas (B. 1980)

### *November*        *2007*

October's brief, bright gush is over.
Leaf-lisp and fetch, their cold-tea smell
raked to the curb in copper- and shale-
stained piles, or the struck-match-sweet
    of sulfur

becoming smoke. The overcast
sky the same slight ambergris.
Hung across it, aghast surprise
of so many clotted, orphaned nests.

**WHEN I WRITE** "I admire and envy writers who can keep a structured writing schedule. The lines and poems I tend to keep are those written in time stolen from other responsibilities — so that the act of writing always feels subversive, even if I'm only subverting the laundry that needs to be done."
—DAVE LUCAS

## Considerations for Critical Thinking and Writing

1. **FIRST RESPONSE.** What overall impression does this poem convey about the month of November? How does it serve as a dramatic contrast to October?

2. Carefully examine the diction in each line to determine how the poem's images achieve their effects.

3. **CREATIVE RESPONSE.** Choose two consecutive months that offer striking climatic environmental changes in the region where you live and write a two-stanza poem that includes vivid diction and images.

## Connection to Another Selection

1. Consider the tone and theme of "November" and of John Keats's "To Autumn" (p. 98).

# 5

# Figures of Speech

© Bettmann/Corbis.

Like a piece of ice on a hot stove the
poem must ride on its own melting.
— ROBERT FROST

*Figures of speech* are broadly defined as a way of saying one thing in terms of something else. An overeager funeral director might, for example, be described as a vulture. Although figures of speech are indirect, they are designed to clarify, not obscure, our understanding of what they describe. Poets frequently use them because, as Emily Dickinson said, the poet's work is to "tell all the Truth but tell it slant" to capture the reader's interest and imagination. But figures of speech are not limited to poetry. Hearing them, reading them, or using them is as natural as using language itself.

Suppose that in the middle of a class discussion concerning the economic causes of World War II your history instructor introduces a series of statistics by saying, "Let's get down to brass tacks." Would anyone be likely to expect a display of brass tacks for students to examine? Of course not. To interpret the statement literally would be to wholly misunderstand the instructor's point that the time has come for a close look at the economic circumstances leading to the war. A literal response transforms the statement into the sort of hilariously bizarre material often found in a sketch by Woody Allen.

The class does not look for brass tacks because, in a nutshell, they understand that the instructor is speaking figuratively. They would understand, too, that in the preceding sentence "in a nutshell" refers to brevity and conciseness rather than to the covering of a kernel of a nut. Figurative language makes its way into our everyday speech and writing as well as into literature because it is a means of achieving color, vividness, and intensity.

Consider the difference, for example, between these two statements:

Literal: The diner strongly expressed anger at the waiter.
Figurative: The diner leaped from his table and roared at the waiter.

The second statement is more vivid because it creates a picture of ferocious anger by likening the diner to some kind of wild animal, such as a lion or tiger. By comparison, "strongly expressed anger" is neither especially strong nor especially expressive; it is flat. Not all figurative language avoids this kind of flatness, however. Figures of speech such as "getting down to brass tacks" and "in a nutshell" are clichés because they lack originality and freshness. Still, they suggest how these devices are commonly used to give language some color, even if that color is sometimes a bit faded.

There is nothing weak about William Shakespeare's use of figurative language in the following passage from *Macbeth*. Macbeth has just learned that his wife is dead, and he laments her loss as well as the course of his own life.

## WILLIAM SHAKESPEARE (1564–1616)

### *From* Macbeth *(Act V, Scene v)*                              *1605–1606*

Tomorrow, and tomorrow, and tomorrow
Creeps in this petty pace from day to day
To the last syllable of recorded time;
And all our yesterdays have lighted fools
The way to dusty death. Out, out, brief candle!                    5
Life's but a walking shadow, a poor player,
That struts and frets his hour upon the stage,
And then is heard no more. It is a tale
Told by an idiot, full of sound and fury,
Signifying nothing.                                                10

This passage might be summarized as "life has no meaning," but such a brief paraphrase does not take into account the figurative language that reveals the depth of Macbeth's despair and his view of the absolute meaninglessness of life. By comparing life to a "brief candle," Macbeth emphasizes the darkness and death that surround human beings. The light of life is too brief and unpredictable to be of any comfort. Indeed, life for Macbeth is a "walking shadow," futilely playing a role that is more farcical than dramatic, because life is, ultimately, a desperate story filled with pain and devoid of significance. What the figurative language provides, then, is the emotional force of Macbeth's assertion; his comparisons are disturbing because they are so apt.

The remainder of this chapter discusses some of the most important figures of speech used in poetry. A familiarity with them will help you to understand how poetry achieves its effects.

## SIMILE AND METAPHOR

The two most common figures of speech are simile and metaphor. Both compare things that are ordinarily considered unlike each other. A *simile* makes an explicit comparison between two things by using words such as *like, as, than, appears,* or *seems:* "A sip of Mrs. Cook's coffee is like a punch in the stomach." The force of the simile is created by the differences between the two things compared. There would be no simile if the comparison were stated this way: "Mrs. Cook's coffee is as strong as the cafeteria's coffee." This is a literal comparison because Mrs. Cook's coffee is compared with something like it, another kind of coffee. Consider how simile is used in this poem.

### MARGARET ATWOOD (B. 1939)

*you fit into me*    *1971*

you fit into me
like a hook into an eye

a fish hook
an open eye

© Sophie Bassouls/Corbis Sygma.

If you blinked on a second reading, you got the point of this poem because you recognized that the simile "like a hook into an eye" gives way to a play on words in the final two lines. There the hook and eye, no longer a pleasant domestic image of a clothing fastener or door latch that fits closely together, become a literal, sharp fishhook and a human eye. The wordplay qualifies the simile and drastically alters the tone of this poem by creating a strong and unpleasant surprise.

A *metaphor*, like a simile, makes a comparison between two unlike things, but it does so implicitly, without words such as *like* or *as:* "Mrs. Cook's coffee is a punch in the stomach." Metaphor asserts the identity of dissimilar things. Macbeth tells us that life *is* a "brief candle," life *is* "a walking shadow," life *is* "a poor player," life *is* "a tale / Told by an idiot." Metaphor transforms people, places, objects, and ideas into whatever the poet imagines them to be, and if metaphors are effective, the reader's experience, understanding, and appreciation of what is described are enhanced. Metaphors are frequently more demanding than similes because they are not signaled by particular words. They are both subtle and powerful.

Here is a poem about presentiment, a foreboding that something terrible is about to happen.

## EMILY DICKINSON (1830–1886)

## *Presentiment — is that long Shadow — on the lawn —*

ca. 1863

Presentiment — is that long Shadow — on the lawn —
Indicative that Suns go down —

The notice to the startled Grass
That Darkness — is about to pass —

The metaphors in this poem define the abstraction "Presentiment." The sense of foreboding that Dickinson expresses is identified with a particular moment — the moment when darkness is just about to envelop an otherwise tranquil, ordinary scene. The speaker projects that fear onto the "startled Grass" so that it seems any life must be frightened by the approaching "Shadow" and "Darkness" — two richly connotative words associated with death. The metaphors obliquely tell us ("tell it slant" was Dickinson's motto, remember) that presentiment is related to a fear of death, and, more important, the metaphors convey the feelings that attend that idea.

Some metaphors are more subtle than others because their comparison of terms is less explicit. Notice the difference between the following two metaphors, both of which describe a shaggy derelict refusing to leave the warmth of a hotel lobby: "He was a mule standing his ground" is a quite explicit comparison. The man is a mule; X is Y. But this metaphor is much more covert: "He brayed his refusal to leave." This second version is an ***implied metaphor*** because it does not explicitly identify the man with a mule. Instead it hints at or alludes to the mule. Braying is associated with mules and is especially appropriate in this context because of the mule's reputation for stubbornness. Implied metaphors can slip by readers, but they offer the alert reader the energy and resonance of carefully chosen, highly concentrated language.

Some poets write extended comparisons in which part or all of the poem consists of a series of related metaphors or similes. Extended metaphors are more common than extended similes. In "Catch" (p. 16), Robert Francis creates an ***extended metaphor*** that compares poetry to a game of catch. The entire poem is organized around this comparison. Because these comparisons are at work throughout the entire poem, they are called ***controlling metaphors***. Extended comparisons can serve as a poem's organizing principle; they are also a reminder that in good poems, metaphor and simile are not merely decorative but inseparable from what is expressed.

Notice the controlling metaphor in this poem, published posthumously by a woman whose contemporaries identified her more as a wife and mother than as a poet. Bradstreet's first volume of poetry, *The Tenth Muse*, was published by her brother-in-law in 1650 without her prior knowledge.

## ANNE BRADSTREET (CA. 1612–1672)

### *The Author to Her Book*                    *1678*

Thou ill-formed offspring of my feeble brain,
Who after birth did'st by my side remain,
Till snatched from thence by friends, less wise than true,
Who thee abroad exposed to public view;
Made thee in rags, halting, to the press to trudge,                    5
Where errors were not lessened, all may judge.
At thy return my blushing was not small,
My rambling brat (in print) should mother call;
I cast thee by as one unfit for light,
Thy visage was so irksome in my sight;                    10
Yet being mine own, at length affection would
Thy blemishes amend, if so I could:
I washed thy face, but more defects I saw,
And rubbing off a spot, still made a flaw.
I stretched thy joints to make thee even feet,                    15
Yet still thou run'st more hobbling than is meet;
In better dress to trim thee was my mind,
But nought save homespun cloth in the house I find.
In this array, 'mongst vulgars may'st thou roam;
In critics' hands beware thou dost not come;                    20
And take thy way where yet thou are not known.
If for thy Father asked, say thou had'st none;
And for thy Mother, she alas is poor,
Which caused her thus to send thee out of door.

The extended metaphor likening her book to a child came naturally
to Bradstreet and allowed her to regard her work both critically and affec-
tionately. Her conception of the book as her child creates just the right tone
of amusement, self-deprecation, and concern.

The controlling metaphor in the following poem is identified by the title.

## RICHARD WILBUR (B. 1921)

### *The Writer*                    *1976*

In her room at the prow of the house
Where light breaks, and the windows are tossed with linden,
My daughter is writing a story.

I pause in the stairwell, hearing
From her shut door a commotion of typewriter-keys                    5
Like a chain hauled over a gunwale.

Young as she is, the stuff
Of her life is a great cargo, and some of it heavy:
I wish her a lucky passage.

But now it is she who pauses,                                                   10
As if to reject my thought and its easy figure.
A stillness greatens, in which

The whole house seems to be thinking,
And then she is at it again with a bunched clamor
Of strokes, and again is silent.                                               15

I remember the dazed starling
Which was trapped in that very room, two years ago;
How we stole in, lifted a sash

And retreated, not to affright it;
And how for a helpless hour, through the crack of the door,                    20
We watched the sleek, wild, dark

And iridescent creature
Batter against the brilliance, drop like a glove
To the hard floor, or the desk-top,

And wait then, humped and bloody,                                              25
For the wits to try it again; and how our spirits
Rose when, suddenly sure,

It lifted off from a chair-back,
Beating a smooth course for the right window
And clearing the sill of the world.                                            30

It is always a matter, my darling,
Of life or death, as I had forgotten. I wish
What I wished you before, but harder.

### CONSIDERATIONS FOR CRITICAL THINKING AND WRITING

1. FIRST RESPONSE. How does the speaker reveal affection for the daughter? What makes it authentic rather than sentimental?

2. In what sense do you think lines 1–11 represent an "easy figure" to the speaker?

3. Describe the effect of Wilbur's second extended metaphor concerning the "dazed starling" (line 16). How does it convey the poem's major ideas?

## OTHER FIGURES

Perhaps the humblest figure of speech — if not one of the most familiar — is the pun. A *pun* is a play on words that relies on a word having more than one meaning or sounding like another word. For example, "A fad is in one era and out the other" is the sort of pun that produces obligatory groans. But most of us find pleasant and interesting surprises in puns. Here's one that has a slight edge to its humor.

## EDMUND CONTI (B. 1929)

### *Pragmatist*                                                    *1985*

Apocalypse soon
Coming our way
Ground zero at noon
Halve a nice day.

Grimly practical under the circumstances, the pragmatist divides the familiar cheerful cliché by half. As simple as this poem is, its tone is mixed because it makes us laugh and wince at the same time.

Puns can be used to achieve serious effects as well as humorous ones. Although we may have learned to underrate puns as figures of speech, it is a mistake to underestimate their power and the frequency with which they appear in poetry. A close examination, for example, of Henry Reed's "Naming of Parts" (p. 137), Robert Frost's "Design" (p. 271), or almost any lengthy passage from a Shakespeare play will confirm the value of puns.

**Synecdoche** is a figure of speech in which part of something is used to signify the whole: a neighbor is a "wagging tongue" (a gossip); a criminal is placed "behind bars" (in prison). Less typically, synecdoche refers to the whole used to signify the part: "Germany invaded Poland"; "Princeton won the fencing match." Clearly, certain individuals, not all of Germany or Princeton, participated in these activities. Another related figure of speech is **metonymy** in which something closely associated with a subject is substituted for it: "She preferred the silver screen [motion pictures] to reading." "At precisely ten o'clock the paper shufflers [office workers] stopped for coffee."

Synecdoche and metonymy may overlap and are therefore sometimes difficult to distinguish. Consider this description of a disapproving minister entering a noisy tavern: "As those pursed lips came through the swinging door, the atmosphere was suddenly soured." The pursed lips signal the presence of the minister and are therefore a synecdoche, but they additionally suggest an inhibiting sense of sin and guilt that makes the bar patrons feel uncomfortable. Hence the pursed lips are also a metonymy, as they are in this context so closely connected with religion. Although the distinction between synecdoche and metonymy can be useful, a figure of speech is usually labeled a metonymy when it overlaps categories.

Knowing the precise term for a figure of speech is, finally, less important than responding to its use in a poem. Consider how metonymy and synecdoche convey the tone and meaning of the following poem.

## Dylan Thomas (1914–1953)
### The Hand That Signed the Paper
1936

The hand that signed the paper felled a city;
Five sovereign fingers taxed the breath,
Doubled the globe of dead and halved a
    country;
These five kings did a king to death.

The mighty hand leads to a sloping shoulder,
The finger joints are cramped with chalk;
A goose's quill has put an end to murder
That put an end to talk.

© Hulton-Deutsch Collection/Corbis.

The hand that signed the treaty bred a fever,
And famine grew, and locusts came;
Great is the hand that holds dominion over
Man by a scribbled name.                                      10

The five kings count the dead but do not soften
The crusted wound nor stroke the brow;
A hand rules pity as a hand rules heaven;                     15
Hands have no tears to flow.

The "hand" in this poem is a synecdoche for a powerful ruler because it is a part of someone used to signify the entire person. The "goose's quill" is a metonymy that also refers to the power associated with the ruler's hand. By using these figures of speech, Thomas depersonalizes and ultimately dehumanizes the ruler. The final synecdoche tells us that "Hands have no tears to flow." It makes us see the political power behind the hand as remote and inhuman. How is the meaning of the poem enlarged when the speaker says, "A hand rules pity as a hand rules heaven"?

One of the ways writers energize the abstractions, ideas, objects, and animals that constitute their created worlds is through **personification**, the attribution of human characteristics to nonhuman things: temptation pursues the innocent; trees scream in the raging wind; mice conspire in the cupboard. We are not explicitly told that these things are people; instead, we are invited to see that they behave like people. Perhaps it is human vanity that makes personification a frequently used figure of speech. Whatever the reason, personification, a form of metaphor that connects the nonhuman with the human, makes the world understandable in human terms. Consider this concise example from William Blake's *The Marriage of Heaven and Hell,* a long poem that takes delight in attacking conventional morality: "Prudence is a rich ugly old maid courted by Incapacity." By personifying prudence, Blake transforms what is usually considered a virtue into a comic figure hardly worth emulating.

Often related to personification is another rhetorical figure called *apostrophe*, an address either to someone who is absent and therefore cannot hear the speaker or to something nonhuman that cannot comprehend. Apostrophe provides an opportunity for the speaker of a poem to think aloud, and often the thoughts expressed are in a formal tone. John Keats, for example, begins "Ode on a Grecian Urn" (p. 75) this way: "Thou still unravished bride of quietness." Apostrophe is frequently accompanied by intense emotion that is signaled by phrasing such as "O Life." In the right hands — such as Keats's — apostrophe can provide an intense and immediate voice in a poem, but when it is overdone or extravagant it can be ludicrous. Modern poets are more wary of apostrophe than their predecessors because apostrophizing strikes many self-conscious twenty-first-century sensibilities as too theatrical. Thus modern poets tend to avoid exaggerated situations in favor of less charged though equally meditative moments, as in this next poem, with its amusing, half-serious cosmic twist.

## JANICE TOWNLEY MOORE (B. 1939)

### *To a Wasp*                    1984

You must have chortled
finding that tiny hole
in the kitchen screen. Right
into my cheese cake batter
you dived,                                                  5
no chance to swim ashore,
no saving spoon,
the mixer whirring
your legs, wings, stinger,
churning you into such                                     10
delicious death.
Never mind the bright April day.
Did you not see
rising out of cumulus clouds
That fist aimed at both of us?                             15

**WHEN I WRITE** "I began writing poetry as a freshman in college. I wrote using poetic diction and sometimes rhyme. Then I discovered 'modern poetry.' Seeing what was published in literary magazines quickly changed my style."
— JANICE TOWNLEY MOORE

Moore's apostrophe "To a Wasp" is based on the simplest of domestic circumstances; there is almost nothing theatrical or exaggerated in the poem's tone until "That fist" in the last line, when exaggeration takes center stage. As a figure of speech, exaggeration is known as **overstatement** or **hyperbole** and adds emphasis without intending to be literally true: "The teenage boy ate everything in the house." Notice how the speaker of

Andrew Marvell's "To His Coy Mistress" (p. 65) exaggerates his devotion in the following overstatement:

> An hundred years should go to praise
> Thine eyes and on thy forehead gaze,
> Two hundred to adore each breast,
> But thirty thousand to the rest:

That comes to 30,500 years. What is expressed here is heightened emotion, not deception.

The speaker also uses the opposite figure of speech, **understatement**, which says less than is intended. In the next section he sums up why he cannot take 30,500 years to express his love:

> The grave's a fine and private place,
> But none, I think, do there embrace.

The speaker is correct, of course, but by deliberately understating — saying "I think" when he is actually certain — he makes his point, that death will overtake their love, all the more emphatic. Another powerful example of understatement appears in the final line of Randall Jarrell's "The Death of the Ball Turret Gunner" (p. 55), when the disembodied voice of the machine-gunner describes his death in a bomber: "When I died they washed me out of the turret with a hose."

*Paradox* is a statement that initially appears to be self-contradictory but that, on closer inspection, turns out to make sense: "The pen is mightier than the sword." In a fencing match, anyone would prefer the sword, but if the goal is to win the hearts and minds of people, the art of persuasion can be more compelling than swordplay. To resolve the paradox, it is necessary to discover the sense that underlies the statement. If we see that "pen" and "sword" are used as metonymies for writing and violence, then the paradox rings true. *Oxymoron* is a condensed form of paradox in which two contradictory words are used together. Combinations such as "sweet sorrow," "silent scream," "sad joy," and "cold fire" indicate the kinds of startling effects that oxymorons can produce. Paradox is useful in poetry because it arrests a reader's attention by its seemingly stubborn refusal to make sense, and once a reader has penetrated the paradox, it is difficult to resist a perception so well earned. Good paradoxes are knotty pleasures. Here is a simple but effective one.

## Tajana Kovics (b.1985)

### Text Message                                                   *2011*

Because I think you're nearly perfect,
I want to love you best:
And since absence makes the heart grow fonder,
We should see each other less.

As the title suggests, the medium is part of the implicit subtext in this quatrain. Consider how the very idea of romantic love is conveyed and built on separation rather than intimacy in this witty paradox.

The following poems are rich in figurative language. As you read and study them, notice how their figures of speech vivify situations, clarify ideas, intensify emotions, and engage your imagination. Although the terms for the various figures discussed in this chapter are useful for labeling the particular devices used in poetry, they should not be allowed to get in the way of your response to a poem. Don't worry about rounding up examples of figurative language. First relax and let the figures work their effects on you. Use the terms as a means of taking you further into poetry, and they will serve your reading well.


# POEMS FOR FURTHER STUDY

## GARY SNYDER (B. 1930)

### *How Poetry Comes to Me*                                    *1992*

It comes blundering over the
Boulders at night, it stays
Frightened outside the
Range of my campfire
I go to meet it at the
Edge of the light

#### CONSIDERATIONS FOR CRITICAL THINKING AND WRITING

1. FIRST RESPONSE. How does personification in this poem depict the creative process?

2. Why do you suppose Snyder makes each successive line shorter?

3. CREATIVE RESPONSE. How would eliminating the title change your understanding of the poem? Substitute another title that causes you to reinterpret it.

# A SAMPLE STUDENT RESPONSE

Jennifer Jackson

Professor Kahane

English 215

16 February 2015

Metaphor in Gary Snyder's "How Poetry Comes to Me"

"A metaphor," Michael Meyer writes, "makes a comparison between two unlike things . . . implicitly, without words such as *like* or *as*" (103). In his poem "How Poetry Comes to Me," Gary Snyder uses metaphor to compare poetic inspiration and creativity with a kind of wild creature.

In this work, poetry itself is both an ungraceful beast and a timid animal. It is something big and unwieldy, that "comes blundering over the / Boulders at night" (lines 1-2). The word "blunder" suggests that poetic inspiration moves clumsily, blindly—not knowing where it will go next—and somewhat dangerously. Yet it is hesitant and "stays / Frightened outside the / Range of [the] campfire" (2-4). According to Snyder's poem, the creature poetry comes only partway to meet the poet; the poet has to go to meet it on its terms, "at the / Edge of the light" (5-6). The metaphor of the poem as wild animal tells the reader that poetic inspiration is elusive and unpredictable. It must be sought out carefully or it will run back over the boulders, by the way it came. . . .

Works Cited

Meyer, Michael, ed. *Thinking and Writing about Poetry*. Boston: Bedford/St. Martin's, 2016. 103. Print.

Snyder, Gary. "How Poetry Comes to Me." Meyer 111.

## Ernest Slyman (b. 1946)

### Lightning Bugs

1988

In my backyard,
They burn peepholes in the night
And take snapshots of my house.

#### Considerations for Critical Thinking and Writing

1. **FIRST RESPONSE.** Explain why the title is essential to this poem.
2. What makes the description of the lightning bugs effective? How do the second and third lines complement each other?
3. **CREATIVE RESPONSE.** As Slyman has done, take a simple, common fact of nature and make it vivid by using a figure of speech to describe it.

---

**WHEN I WRITE** "Only on very rare occasions is a poem complete in a first draft. The first draft of a poem can sit for a long time waiting for its other half, or its meaning. Save everything you write, no matter how unhappy you are with it. You often won't see the beauty until later." — JUDY PAGE HEITZMAN

---

## Judy Page Heitzman (b. 1952)

### The Schoolroom on the Second Floor of the Knitting Mill

1991

While most of us copied letters out of books,
Mrs. Lawrence carved and cleaned her nails.
Now the red and buff cardinals at my back-room window
make me miss her, her room, her hallway,
even the chimney outside                                     5
that broke up the sky.

In my memory it is afternoon.
Sun streams in through the door
next to the fire escape where we are lined up
getting our coats on to go out to the playground,        10
the tether ball, its towering height, the swings.
She tells me to make sure the line
does not move up over the threshold.
That would be dangerous.
So I stand guard at the door.                            15
Somehow it happens
the way things seem to happen when we're not really looking,
or we are looking, just not the right way.
Kids crush up like cattle, pushing me over the line.

*Judy is not a good leader* is all Mrs. Lawrence says.                    20
She says it quietly. Still, everybody hears.
Her arms hang down like sausages.
I hear her every time I fail.

### CONSIDERATIONS FOR CRITICAL THINKING AND WRITING

1. FIRST RESPONSE. Does your impression of Mrs. Lawrence change from the beginning to the end of the poem? How so?

2. How can line 2 be read as an implied metaphor?

3. Discuss the use of similes in the poem. How do they contribute to the poem's meaning?

## WILLIAM WORDSWORTH  (1770–1850)

### *London, 1802*                                                   *1802*

Milton!° thou should'st be living at this hour:
England hath need of thee: she is a fen
Of stagnant waters: altar, sword, and pen,
Fireside, the heroic wealth of hall and bower,
Have forfeited their ancient English dower                            5
Of inward happiness. We are selfish men;
Oh! raise us up, return to us again;
And give us manners, virtue, freedom, power.
Thy soul was like a star, and dwelt apart:
Thou hadst a voice whose sound was like the sea:                     10
Pure as the naked heavens, majestic, free,
So didst thou travel on life's common way,
In cheerful godliness; and yet thy heart
The lowliest duties on herself did lay.

1 *Milton:* John Milton (1608–1674), poet, famous especially for his religious epic *Paradise Lost* and his defense of political freedom.

### CONSIDERATIONS FOR CRITICAL THINKING AND WRITING

1. FIRST RESPONSE. Describe the poem's tone. Is it nostalgic, angry, or something else?

2. Explain the metonymies in lines 3–6 of this poem. What is the speaker's assessment of England?

3. How would the effect of the poem be different if it were in the form of an address to Wordsworth's contemporaries rather than an apostrophe to Milton? What qualities does Wordsworth attribute to Milton by the use of figurative language?

4. CRITICAL STRATEGIES. Read the section on literary history criticism (pp. 334–35) in Chapter 15, "Critical Strategies for Reading," and use

the library to find out about the state of London in 1802. How does the poem reflect or refute the social values of its time?

## JIM STEVENS (B. 1922)

### *Schizophrenia*                                                                   *1992*

It was the house that suffered most.

It had begun with slamming doors, angry feet scuffing the carpets,
dishes slammed onto the table,
greasy stains spreading on the cloth.

Certain doors were locked at night,                                               5
feet stood for hours outside them,
dishes were left unwashed, the cloth
disappeared under a hardened crust.

The house came to miss the shouting voices,
the threats, the half-apologies, noisy                                            10
reconciliations, the sobbing that followed.

Then lines were drawn, borders established,
some rooms declared their loyalties,
keeping to themselves, keeping out the other.
The house divided against itself.                                                 15

Seeing cracking paint, broken windows,
the front door banging in the wind,
the roof tiles flying off, one by one,
the neighbors said it was a madhouse.

It was the house that suffered most.                                              20

#### CONSIDERATIONS FOR CRITICAL THINKING AND WRITING

1. FIRST RESPONSE. What is the effect of personifying the house in this poem?
2. How are the people who live in the house characterized? What does their behavior reveal about them? How does the house respond to them?
3. Comment on the title. If the title were missing, what, if anything, would be missing from the poem? Explain your answer.

## WALT WHITMAN (1819–1892)

### *A Noiseless Patient Spider*                     *1868*

A noiseless patient spider,
I mark'd where on a little promontory it stood isolated,
Mark'd how to explore the vacant vast surrounding,
It launch'd forth filament, filament, filament, out of itself,
Ever unreeling them, ever tirelessly speeding them.                     5

And you O my soul where you stand,
Surrounded, detached, in measureless oceans of space,
Ceaselessly musing, venturing, throwing, seeking
          the spheres to connect them,
Till the bridge you will need be form'd, till the ductile anchor hold,
Till the gossamer thread you fling catch somewhere, O my soul.          10

#### CONSIDERATIONS FOR CRITICAL THINKING AND WRITING

1. FIRST RESPONSE. Spiders are not usually regarded as pleasant creatures. Why does the speaker in this poem liken his soul to one? What similarities are there in the poem between spider and soul? Are there any significant differences?

2. How do the images of space relate to the connections made between the speaker's soul and the spider?

## JOHN DONNE (1572–1631)

### *A Valediction: Forbidding Mourning*                 *1611*

As virtuous men pass mildly away,
   And whisper to their souls to go,
While some of their sad friends do say,
   The breath goes now, and some say, no:

So let us melt, and make no noise,                     5
   No tear-floods, nor sigh-tempests move;
'Twere profanation of our joys
   To tell the laity our love.

Moving of th' earth° brings harms and fears,             *earthquakes*
   Men reckon what it did and meant,                   10
But trepidation of the spheres,°
   Though greater far, is innocent.

11 *trepidation of the spheres:* According to Ptolemaic astronomy, the planets sometimes moved violently, like earthquakes, but these movements were not felt by people on Earth.

Dull sublunary° lovers' love
    (Whose soul is sense) cannot admit
Absence, because it doth remove
    Those things which elemented° it.                 15

*composed*

But we by a love so much refined,
    That ourselves know not what it is,
Inter-assured of the mind,
    Care less, eyes, lips, and hands to miss.         20

Our two souls therefore, which are one,
    Though I must go, endure not yet
A breach, but an expansion,
    Like gold to airy thinness beat.

If they be two, they are two so               25
    As stiff twin compasses are two;
Thy soul the fixed foot, makes no show
    To move, but doth, if th' other do.

And though it in the center sit,
    Yet when the other far doth roam,
It leans, and hearkens after it,               30
    And grows erect, as that comes home.

Such wilt thou be to me, who must
    Like th' other foot, obliquely run;
Thy firmness makes my circle just,°
    And makes me end, where I begun.         35

13 *sublunary:* Under the moon; hence, mortal and subject to change.    35 *circle just:*
The circle is a traditional symbol of perfection.

## CONSIDERATIONS FOR CRITICAL THINKING AND WRITING

1. FIRST RESPONSE. A valediction is a farewell. Donne wrote this poem for his wife before leaving on a trip to France. What kind of "mourning" is the speaker forbidding?

2. Explain how the simile in lines 1–4 is related to the couple in lines 5–8. Who is described as dying?

3. How does the speaker contrast the couple's love to "sublunary lovers' love" (line 13)?

4. Explain the similes in lines 24 and 25–36.

## KAY RYAN (B. 1945)

### *Turtle*    2010

Who would be a turtle who could help it?
A barely mobile hard roll, a four-oared
    helmet,
she can ill afford the chances she must take
in rowing toward the grasses that she eats.
Her track is graceless, like dragging
a packing case places, and almost any
    slope
defeats her modest hopes. Even being
    practical,
she's often stuck up to the axle on her way
to something edible. With everything
    optimal,
she skirts the ditch which would convert
her shell into a serving dish. She lives
below luck-level, never imagining some lottery
will change her load of pottery to wings.
Her only levity is patience,
the sport of truly chastened things.

© Christopher Felver/Corbis.

### CONSIDERATIONS FOR CRITICAL THINKING AND WRITING

1. FIRST RESPONSE. Explain how the poem's figurative language captures what it means to be a turtle.

2. How does Ryan transform all the perceived disadvantages of being a turtle into something positive?

3. Discuss the paradox created by the diction in the final two lines.

### CONNECTION TO ANOTHER SELECTION

1. Compare Ryan's "Turtle" with Emily Dickinson's "A narrow Fellow in the Grass" (p. 2). How do the poems make you feel about the respective animal in each?

## RONALD WALLACE (B. 1945)

### *Building an Outhouse*    1991

Is not unlike building a poem: the pure
mathematics of shape; the music of hammer
and tenpenny nail, of floor joist, stud wall,
and sill; the cut wood's sweet smell.

WHEN I WRITE "I've always admired people who can make beautiful things — out of wood, or paint, or the movement of the human body, or the strings of a musical instrument. I have spent my life trying to make beautiful things out of words."
— RONALD WALLACE

If the Skil saw rear up in your unpracticed hand,                    5
cussing, hawking its chaw of dust,
and you're lost in the pounding particulars
of fly rafters, siding, hypotenuse, and load,
until nothing seems level or true
but the scorn of the tape's clucked tongue,                          10

let the nub of your plainspoken pencil prevail
and it's up! Functional. Tight as a sonnet.
It will last forever (or at least for awhile)
though the critics come sit on it, and sit on it.

## Considerations for Critical Thinking and Writing

1. FIRST RESPONSE. Explain how the poem's diction contributes to the extended simile. Why is the language of building especially appropriate here?

2. What is the effect of the repetition and sounds in the final line? How does that affect the poem's tone?

3. Consult the Glossary of Literary Terms (p. 403) for the definition of *sonnet*. To what extent does "Building an Outhouse" conform to a sonnet's structure?

# 6

# Symbol, Allegory, and Irony

© Barbara Savage Cheresh.

Poetry is serious business; literature is the apparatus through which the world tries to keep intact its important ideas and feelings.
—MARY OLIVER

## SYMBOL

A *symbol* is something that represents something else. An object, a person, a place, an event, or an action can suggest more than its literal meaning. A handshake between two world leaders might be simply a greeting, but if it is done ceremoniously before cameras, it could be a symbolic gesture signifying unity, issues resolved, and joint policies that will be followed. We live surrounded by symbols. When a $100,000 Mercedes-Benz comes roaring by in the fast lane, we get a quick glimpse of not only an expensive car but also an entire lifestyle that suggests opulence, broad lawns, executive offices, and power. One of the reasons some buyers are willing to spend roughly the cost of five Chevrolets for a single Mercedes-Benz is that they are aware of the car's symbolic value. A symbol is a vehicle for two things at once: it functions as itself, and it implies meanings beyond itself.

The meanings suggested by a symbol are determined by the context in which it appears. The Mercedes could symbolize very different things depending on where it was parked. Would an American political candidate be likely to appear in a Detroit blue-collar neighborhood with such a car? Probably not. Although a candidate might be able to afford the car, it would be an inappropriate symbol for someone seeking votes from all of the people. As a symbol, the German-built Mercedes would backfire if voters perceived it as representing an entity partially responsible for lay-offs of automobile workers or, worse, as a sign of decadence and corruption. Similarly, a huge portrait of Mao Tse-tung conveys different meanings to residents of Beijing than it would to farmers in Prairie Center, Illinois. Because symbols depend on contexts for their meaning, literary artists provide those contexts so that the reader has enough information to determine the probable range of meanings suggested by a symbol.

In the following poem, the speaker describes walking at night. How is the night used symbolically?

## Robert Frost (1874–1963)

### *Acquainted with the Night*                    *1928*

I have been one acquainted with the night.
I have walked out in rain — and back in rain.
I have outwalked the furthest city light.

I have looked down the saddest city lane.
I have passed by the watchman on his beat            5
And dropped my eyes, unwilling to explain.

I have stood still and stopped the sound of feet
When far away an interrupted cry
Came over houses from another street,

But not to call me back or say good-by;              10
And further still at an unearthly height
One luminary clock against the sky

Proclaimed the time was neither wrong nor right.
I have been one acquainted with the night.

In approaching this or any other poem, you should read for literal meanings first and then allow the elements of the poem to invite you to symbolic readings, if they are appropriate. Here the somber tone suggests that the lines have symbolic meaning, too. The flat matter-of-factness created by the repetition of "I have" (lines 1–5, 7, 14) understates the symbolic subject matter of the poem, which is, finally, more about the "night" located in the speaker's mind or soul than it is about walking away from a city and back again. The speaker is "acquainted with the night." The importance of this phrase is emphasized by Frost's title and by the fact that he begins and ends the poem with it. Poets frequently use this kind of repetition to alert readers to details that carry more than literal meanings.

The speaker in this poem has personal knowledge of the night but does not indicate specifically what the night means. To arrive at the potential meanings of the night in this context, it is necessary to look closely at its connotations, along with the images provided in the poem. The connotative meanings of night suggest, for example, darkness, death, and grief. By drawing on these connotations, Frost uses a *conventional symbol*— something that is recognized by many people to represent certain ideas. Roses conventionally symbolize love or beauty; laurels, fame; spring, growth; the moon, romance. Poets often use conventional symbols to convey tone and meaning.

Frost uses the night as a conventional symbol, but he also develops it into a *literary* or *contextual symbol* that goes beyond traditional, public meanings. A literary symbol cannot be summarized in a word or two. It tends to be as elusive as experience itself. The night cannot be reduced to or equated with darkness or death or grief, but it evokes those associations and more. Frost took what perhaps initially appears to be an overworked, conventional symbol and prevented it from becoming a cliché by deepening and extending its meaning.

The images in "Acquainted with the Night" lead to the poem's symbolic meaning. Unwilling, and perhaps unable, to explain explicitly to the watchman (and to the reader) what the night means, the speaker nevertheless conveys feelings about it. The brief images of darkness, rain, sad city lanes, the necessity for guards, the eerie sound of a distressing cry coming over rooftops, and the "luminary clock against the sky" proclaiming "the time was neither wrong nor right" all help to create a sense of anxiety in this tight-lipped speaker. Although we cannot know what unnamed personal experiences have acquainted the speaker with the night, the images suggest that whatever the night means, it is somehow associated with insomnia, loneliness, isolation, coldness, darkness, death, fear, and a sense of alienation from humanity and even time. Daylight—ordinary daytime thoughts and life itself—seems remote and unavailable in this poem. The night is literally the period from sunset to sunrise, but, more important, it is an internal state of being felt by the speaker and revealed through the images.

Frost used symbols rather than an expository essay that would explain the conditions that cause these feelings because most readers can provide their own list of sorrows and terrors that evoke similar emotions. Through symbol, the speaker's experience is compressed and simultaneously expanded by the personal darkness that each reader brings to the poem. The suggestive nature of symbols makes them valuable for poets and evocative for readers.

## ALLEGORY

Unlike expansive, suggestive symbols, *allegory* is a narration or description usually restricted to a single meaning because its events, actions, characters, settings, and objects represent specific abstractions or ideas. Although the elements in an allegory may be interesting in themselves, the emphasis tends to be on what they ultimately mean. Characters may be given names such as Hope, Pride, Youth, and Charity; they have few, if any, personal qualities beyond their abstract meanings. These personifications are a form of extended metaphor, but their meanings are severely restricted. They are not symbols because, for instance, the meaning of a character named Charity is precisely that virtue.

There is little or no room for broad speculation and exploration in allegories. If Frost had written "Acquainted with the Night" as an allegory, he might have named his speaker Loneliness and had him leave the City of Despair to walk the Streets of Emptiness, where Crime, Poverty, Fear, and other characters would define the nature of city life. The literal elements in an allegory tend to be deemphasized in favor of the message. Symbols, however, function both literally and symbolically, so that "Acquainted with the Night" is about both a walk and a sense that something is terribly wrong.

Allegory especially lends itself to **didactic poetry**, which is designed to teach an ethical, moral, or religious lesson. Many stories, poems, and plays are concerned with values, but didactic literature is specifically created to convey a message. "Acquainted with the Night" does not impart advice or offer guidance. If the poem argued that city life is self-destructive or sinful, it would be didactic; instead, it is a lyric poem that expresses the emotions and thoughts of a single speaker.

Although allegory is often enlisted in didactic causes because it can so readily communicate abstract ideas through physical representations, not all allegories teach a lesson. Here is a poem describing a haunted palace while also establishing a consistent pattern that reveals another meaning.

## Edgar Allan Poe (1809–1849)

### The Haunted Palace                             *1839*

#### I

In the greenest of our valleys,
   By good angels tenanted,
Once a fair and stately palace —
   Radiant palace — reared its head.
In the monarch Thought's dominion —          5
   It stood there!
Never seraph spread a pinion
   Over fabric half so fair.

#### II

Banners yellow, glorious, golden,
   On its roof did float and flow;          10

(This — all this — was in the olden
    Time long ago)
And every gentle air that dallied,
    In that sweet day,
Along the ramparts plumed and pallid,        15
    A wingèd odor went away.

### III

Wanderers in that happy valley
    Through two luminous windows saw
Spirits moving musically
    To a lute's well-tunèd law,        20
Round about a throne, where sitting
    (Porphyrogene!)°        *born to purple, royal*
In state his glory well befitting,
    The ruler of the realm was seen.

### IV

And all with pearl and ruby glowing        25
    Was the fair palace door,
Through which came flowing, flowing, flowing
    And sparkling evermore,
A troop of Echoes whose sweet duty
    Was but to sing,        30
In voices of surpassing beauty,
    The wit and wisdom of their king.

### V

But evil things, in robes of sorrow,
    Assailed the monarch's high estate;
(Ah, let us mourn, for never morrow        35
    Shall dawn upon him, desolate!)
And, round about his home, the glory
    That blushed and bloomed
Is but a dim-remembered story
    Of the old time entombed.        40

### VI

And travelers now within that valley,
    Through the red-litten windows see
Vast forms that move fantastically
    To a discordant melody;

While, like a rapid ghastly river,                                    45
    Through the pale door,
A hideous throng rush out forever,
    And laugh — but smile no more.

   On one level this poem describes how a once happy palace is desolated
by "evil things" (line 33). If the reader pays close attention to the diction,
however, an allegorical meaning becomes apparent on a second reading. A systematic pattern develops in the choice of words used to describe
the palace, so that it comes to stand for a human mind. The palace, banners, windows, door, echoes, and throng are equated with a person's head,
hair, eyes, mouth, voice, and laughter. That mind, once harmoniously
ordered, is overthrown by evil, haunting thoughts that lead to the mad
laughter in the poem's final lines. Once the general pattern is seen, the rest
of the details fall neatly into place to strengthen the parallels between the
surface description of a palace and the allegorical representation of a disor-
dered mind.
   Modern writers generally prefer symbol over allegory because they
tend to be more interested in opening up the potential meanings of an experience instead of transforming it into a closed pattern of meaning. Perhaps
the major difference is that while allegory may delight a reader's imagination, symbol challenges and enriches it.

## IRONY

Another important resource writers use to take readers beyond literal
meanings is **irony**, a technique that reveals a discrepancy between what
appears to be and what is actually true. Here is a classic example in which
appearances give way to the underlying reality.

EDWIN ARLINGTON ROBINSON  (1869–1935)

## *Richard Cory*                                    *1897*

Whenever Richard Cory went down town,
We people on the pavement looked at him:
He was a gentleman from sole to crown,
Clean favored, and imperially slim.

And he was always quietly arrayed,                                    5
And he was always human when he talked;
But still he fluttered pulses when he said,
"Good-morning," and he glittered when he walked.

And he was rich — yes, richer than a king —
And admirably schooled in every grace:                    10
In fine, we thought that he was everything
To make us wish that we were in his place.

So on we worked, and waited for the light,
And went without the meat, and cursed the bread;
And Richard Cory, one calm summer night,                  15
Went home and put a bullet through his head.

Richard Cory seems to have it all. Those less fortunate, the "people on the pavement," regard him as well-bred, handsome, tasteful, and richly endowed with both money and grace. Until the final line of the poem, the reader, like the speaker, is charmed by Cory's good fortune, so quietly expressed in his decent, easy manner. That final, shocking line, however, shatters the appearances of Cory's life and reveals him to have been a desperately unhappy man. While everyone else assumes that Cory represented "everything" to which they aspire, the reality is that he could escape his miserable life only as a suicide. This discrepancy between what appears to be true and what actually exists is known as *situational irony*: what happens is entirely different from what is expected. We are not told why Cory shoots himself; instead, the irony in the poem shocks us into the recognition that appearances do not always reflect realities.

Words are also sometimes intended to be taken at other than face value. *Verbal irony* is saying something different from what is meant. If after reading "Richard Cory," you said, "That rich gentleman sure was happy," your statement would be ironic. Your tone of voice would indicate that just the opposite was meant; hence verbal irony is usually easy to detect in spoken language. In literature, however, a reader can sometimes take literally what a writer intends ironically. The remedy for this kind of misreading is to pay close attention to the poem's context. There is no formula that can detect verbal irony, but contradictory actions and statements as well as the use of understatement and overstatement can often be signals that verbal irony is present.

# A SAMPLE STUDENT RESPONSE

Diaz 1

Cipriano Diaz
Professor Young
English 200
16 September 2015

Irony in Edwin Arlington Robinson's "Richard Cory"

In Edwin Arlington Robinson's poem "Richard Cory," appearances are not reality. The character Richard Cory, viewed by the townspeople as "richer than a king" (line 9) and "a gentleman from sole to crown" (3), is someone who inspires envy. The poem's speaker says, "we thought that he was everything / To make us wish that we were in his place" (11-12). However, the final shocking line of the poem creates a situational irony that emphasizes the difference between what seems—and what really is.

In lines 1 through 14, the speaker sets up a shining, princely image of Cory, associating him with such regal words as "imperially" (4), "crown" (3), and "king" (9). Cory is viewed by the townspeople from the "pavement" as if he is on a pedestal (2); far below him, those who must work and "[go] without the meat" (14) stand in stark contrast. Further, not only is Cory a gentleman, he is so good-looking that he "flutter[s] pulses" (7) of those around him when he speaks. He's a rich man who "glitter[s] when he walk[s]" (8). He is also a decent man who is "always human when he talk[s]" (6). However, this noble image of Cory is unexpectedly shattered "one calm summer night" (15) in the final couplet. What the speaker and townspeople believed Cory to be and aspired to imitate was merely an illusion. The irony is that what Cory seemed to be—a happy, satisfied man—is exactly what he was not. . . .

Diaz 3

Work Cited

Robinson, Edwin Arlington. "Richard Cory." *Thinking and Writing about Poetry*. Ed. Michael Meyer. Boston: Bedford/St. Martin's, 2016. 125–26. Print.

Consider how verbal irony is used in this poem.

## KENNETH FEARING (1902–1961)

### *AD*                                                1938

*Wanted:* Men;
Millions of men are *wanted at once* in a big new field;
*New, tremendous, thrilling, great.*
If you've ever been a figure in the chamber of horrors,
If you've ever escaped from a psychiatric ward,                5
If you thrill at the thought of throwing poison into wells, have heavenly
    visions of people, by the thousands, dying in flames —

*You are the very man we want*
We mean business and our business is *you*
*Wanted:* A race of brand-new men.

Apply: Middle Europe;                                         10
No skill needed;
No ambition required; no brains wanted and no character allowed;

*Take a permanent job in the coming profession*
Wages: *Death.*

This poem was written as Nazi troops stormed across Europe at the
start of World War II. The advertisement suggests on the surface that killing
is just an ordinary job, but the speaker indicates through understatement
that there is nothing ordinary about the "business" of this "*coming profession.*" Fearing uses verbal irony to indicate how casually and mindlessly
people are prepared to accept the horrors of war.

"AD" is a **satire**, an example of the literary art of ridiculing a folly or
vice in an effort to expose or correct it. The object of satire is usually some
human frailty; people, institutions, ideas, and things are all fair game for satirists. Fearing satirizes the insanity of a world mobilizing itself for war: his
irony reveals the speaker's knowledge that there is nothing "*New, tremendous, thrilling,* [or] *great*" about going off to kill and be killed. The implica-
tion of the poem is that no one should respond to advertisements for war.
The poem serves as a satiric corrective to those who would troop off armed
with unrealistic expectations: wage war, and the wages consist of death.

**Dramatic irony** is used when a writer allows a reader to know more
about a situation than a character does. This creates a discrepancy between
what a character says or thinks and what the reader knows to be true. Dramatic irony is often used to reveal character. In the following poem the
speaker delivers a public address that ironically tells us more about him
than it does about the patriotic holiday he is commemorating.

## E. E. Cummings (1894–1962)

### next to of course god america i

"next to of course god america i
love you land of the pilgrims' and so forth oh
say can you see by the dawn's early my
country 'tis of centuries come and go
and are no more what of it we should worry                          5
in every language even deafanddumb
thy sons acclaim your glorious name by gorry
by jingo by gee by gosh by gum
why talk of beauty what could be more beaut-
iful than these heroic happy dead                                  10
who rushed like lions to the roaring slaughter
they did not stop to think they died instead
then shall the voice of liberty be mute?"

He spoke. And drank rapidly a glass of water

This verbal debauch of chauvinistic clichés (notice the run-on phrases and lines) reveals that the speaker's relationship to God and country is not, as he claims, one of love. His public address suggests a hearty mindlessness that leads to "roaring slaughter" rather than to reverence or patriotism. Cummings allows the reader to see through the speaker's words to their dangerous emptiness. What the speaker means and what Cummings means are entirely different. Like Fearing's "AD," this poem is a satire that invites the reader's laughter and contempt in order to deflate the benighted attitudes expressed in it.

When a writer uses God, destiny, or fate to dash the hopes and expectations of a character or humankind in general, it is called **cosmic irony**. In "The Convergence of the Twain" (p. 71), for example, Thomas Hardy describes how "The Immanent Will" brought together the *Titanic* and a deadly iceberg. Technology and pride are no match for "the Spinner of the Years." Here's a painfully terse version of cosmic irony.

## Stephen Crane (1871–1900)

### A Man Said to the Universe

A man said to the universe:
"Sir, I exist!"
"However," replied the universe,
"The fact has not created in me
A sense of obligation."

Unlike in "The Convergence of the Twain," there is the slightest bit of humor in Crane's poem, but the joke is on us.

Irony is an important technique that allows a writer to distinguish between appearances and realities. In situational irony a discrepancy exists between what we expect to happen and what actually happens; in verbal irony a discrepancy exists between what is said and what is meant; in dramatic irony a discrepancy exists between what a character believes and what the reader knows to be true; and in cosmic irony a discrepancy exists between what a character aspires to and what universal forces provide. With each form of irony, we are invited to move beyond surface appearances and sentimental assumptions to see the complexity of experience. Irony is often used in literature to reveal a writer's perspective on matters that previously seemed settled.

# POEMS FOR FURTHER STUDY

## BOB HICOK (B. 1960)

### Making it in poetry    2004

The young teller
at the credit union
asked why so many
small checks
from universities?                                        5
Because I write
poems I said. Why
haven't I heard
of you? Because
I write poems                                             10
I said.

CONSIDERATIONS FOR CRITICAL THINKING AND WRITING

1. FIRST RESPONSE. Explain how the speaker's verbal irony is central to the poem's humor.
2. What sort of portrait of the poet-speaker emerges from this very brief poem?

# JANE KENYON  (1947–1995)

## *Surprise*                          *1996*

He suggests pancakes at the local diner,
followed by a walk in search of mayflowers,
while friends convene at the house
bearing casseroles and a cake, their cars
pulled close along the sandy shoulders
of the road, where tender ferns unfurl
in the ditches, and this year's budding leaves
push last year's spectral leaves from the tips
of the twigs of the ash trees. The gathering
itself is not what astounds her, but the casual      10
accomplishment with which he has lied.

Donald Hall.

### CONSIDERATIONS FOR CRITICAL THINKING AND WRITING

1. FIRST RESPONSE. Does it matter that this poem is set in the spring?
2. Consider the connotative meaning of "ash trees" in line 9. Why are they particularly appropriate?
3. Why do you suppose Kenyon uses "astounds" rather than "surprises" in line 10? Use a dictionary to help you determine the possible reasons for this choice.
4. Discuss the irony in the poem.

### CONNECTIONS TO OTHER SELECTIONS

1. Write an essay on the nature of the surprises in Kenyon's poem and in William Hathaway's "Oh, Oh" (p. 14). Include in your discussion a comparison of the tone and irony in each poem.
2. Compare and contrast in an essay the irony in this poem and in Denise Duhamel's "How It Will End" (p. 133).

# KEVIN PIERCE  (B. 1958)

## *Proof of Origin*                          *2005*

*NEWSWIRE — A U.S. judge ordered a Georgia school district to remove from textbooks stickers challenging the theory of evolution.*

Though close to their hearts is the version that starts
With Adam and Eve and no clothes,
What enables their grip as the stickers they strip
Is Darwinian thumbs that oppose.

### CONSIDERATIONS FOR CRITICAL THINKING AND WRITING

1. FIRST RESPONSE. How do the rhymes contribute to the humorous tone?
2. Discuss the levels of irony in the poem.
3. How do you read the title? Can it be explained in more than one way?
4. CREATIVE RESPONSE. Write a brief ironic poem on a topic of your choice using Pierce's style as a model.

## CARL SANDBURG (1878–1967)

### *Buttons*                                                        1905

I have been watching the war map slammed up for advertising in front of
    the newspaper office.
Buttons — red and yellow buttons — blue and black buttons — are shoved
    back and forth across the map.

A laughing young man, sunny with freckles,
Climbs a ladder, yells a joke to somebody in the crowd,
And then fixes a yellow button one inch west
And follows the yellow button with a black button one inch west.

(Ten thousand men and boys twist on their bodies in a red soak along a
    river edge,
Gasping of wounds, calling for water, some rattling death in their throats.)
Who would guess what it cost to move two buttons one inch on the war
    map here in front of the newspaper office where the freckle-faced
    young man is laughing to us?

### CONSIDERATIONS FOR CRITICAL THINKING AND WRITING

1. FIRST RESPONSE. Why is the date of this poem significant?
2. Discuss the symbolic meaning of the buttons and whether you think the symbolism is too spelled out or not.
3. What purpose does the "laughing young man, sunny with freckles" (line 3) serve in the poem?

### CONNECTION TO OTHER SELECTIONS

1. Discuss the symbolic treatment of war in this poem, Kenneth Fearing's "AD" (p. 128), and Henry Reed's "Naming of Parts" (p. 137).

# Denise Duhamel (b. 1961)

## *How It Will End*                                    *2009*

**When I Write** "I don't really believe in writer's block as I believe in writing. I believe in free associating and free writing until I get to an original idea, a line or word that will inspire me for a poem."  — DENISE DUHAMEL

We're walking on the boardwalk
but stop when we see a lifeguard and his
        girlfriend
fighting. We can't hear what they're saying,
but it is as good as a movie. We sit on a bench to find out
how it will end. I can tell by her body language                              5
he's done something really bad. She stands at the bottom
of the ramp that leads to his hut. He tries to walk halfway down
to meet her, but she keeps signaling *Don't come closer.*
My husband says, "Boy, he's sure in for it,"
and I say, "He deserves whatever's coming to him."                           10
My husband thinks the lifeguard's cheated, but I think
she's sick of him only working part-time
or maybe he forgot to put the rent in the mail.
The lifeguard tries to reach out
and she holds her hand like Diana Ross                                       15
when she performed "Stop in the Name of Love."
The red flag that slaps against his station means strong currents.
"She has to just get it out of her system,"
my husband laughs, but I'm not laughing.
I start to coach the girl to leave the no-good lifeguard,                    20
but my husband predicts she'll never leave.
I'm angry at him for seeing glee in their situation
and say, "That's your problem — you think every fight
is funny. You never take her seriously," and he says,
"You never even give the guy a chance and you're always
        nagging,                                                             25
so how can he tell the real issues from the nitpicking?"
and I say, "She doesn't nitpick!" and he says, "Oh really?
Maybe he should start recording her tirades," and I say
"Maybe he should help out more," and he says
"Maybe she should be more supportive," and I say                            30
"Do you mean supportive or do you mean support him?"
and my husband says that he's doing the best he can,
that's he's a lifeguard for Christ's sake, and I say
that her job is much harder, that she's a waitress
who works nights carrying heavy trays and is hit on all the time            35
by creepy tourists and he just sits there most days napping
and listening to "Power 96" and then ooh
he gets to be the big hero blowing his whistle
and running into the water to save beach bunnies who
        flatter him

and my husband says it's not as though she's Miss Innocence                    40
and what about the way she flirts, giving free refills
when her boss isn't looking or cutting extra large pieces of pie
to get bigger tips, oh no she wouldn't do that because she's
      a saint
and he's the devil, and I say, "I don't know why you can't
      just admit
he's a jerk," and my husband says, "I don't know why you
      can't admit                                                             45
she's a killjoy," and then out of the blue the couple is making up.
The red flag flutters, then hangs limp.
She has her arms around his neck and is crying into his shoulder.
He whisks her up into his hut. We look around, but no one is
      watching us.

### CONSIDERATIONS FOR CRITICAL THINKING AND WRITING

1. FIRST RESPONSE. Discuss how Duhamel creates the ironic situation in this boardwalk scene.

2. What is the significance of the red flag that appears in lines 17 and 47? Are there any other details that you think yield symbolic meanings?

3. Explain the embedded complexity of the end of the final line of the poem: "We look around, but no one is watching us."

### CONNECTION TO ANOTHER SELECTION

1. Compare the tensions that are exposed in this poem and in Jane Kenyon's "Surprise" (p. 131).

## JULIO MARZÁN (B. 1946)
### *Ethnic Poetry*               1994

The ethnic poet said: "The earth is maybe
a huge maraca / and the sun a trombone /
and life / is to move your ass / to slow beats."
The ethnic audience roasted a suckling pig.

The ethnic poet said: "Oh thank Goddy,
      Goddy /                                                                  5
I be me, my toenails curled downward /
deep, deep, deep into Mama earth."
The ethnic audience shook strands of sea shells.

The ethnic poet said: "The sun was created black /
so we should imagine light / and also dream /                                 10

> WHEN I WRITE "Words you are sure convey your truest feelings or thoughts may record only sentiment, not a line of poetry, while another arrangement, different words in another tone or rhythm, unlock and reveal what you really wanted to say." — JULIO MARZÁN

a walrus emerging from the broken ice."
The ethnic audience beat on sealskin drums.

The ethnic poet said: "Reproductive organs /
Eagles nesting California redwoods /
Shut up and listen to my ancestors."                                    15
The ethnic audience ate fried bread and honey.

The ethnic poet said: "Something there is that
doesn't love a wall / That sends
the frozen-ground-swell under it."
The ethnic audience deeply understood humanity.                         20

### Considerations for Critical Thinking and Writing

1. **FIRST RESPONSE.** What is the implicit definition of *ethnic poetry* in this poem?

2. The final stanza quotes lines from Robert Frost's "Mending Wall" (p. 260). Read the entire poem. Why do you think Marzán chooses these lines and this particular poem as one kind of ethnic poetry?

3. What is the poem's central irony? Pay particular attention to the final line. What is being satirized here?

4. **CRITICAL STRATEGIES.** Read the section on the literary canon (pp. 5–6) in the Introduction and discuss how the formation of the literary canon is related to the theme of "Ethnic Poetry."

### Connection to Another Selection

1. Write an essay that discusses the speakers' ideas about what poetry should be in "Ethnic Poetry" and in Ruth Forman's "Poetry Should Ride the Bus" (p. 88).

## Mark Halliday (b. 1949)

### *Graded Paper*                                                       *1991*

On the whole this is quite successful work:
your main argument about the poet's ambivalence —
how he loves the very things he attacks —
is mostly persuasive and always engaging.

At the same time,                                                        5
                    there are spots
where your thinking becomes, for me,
alarmingly opaque, and your syntax seems to jump
backwards through unnecessary hoops,
as on p. 2 where you speak of "precognitive awareness                    10

not yet disestablished by the shell that encrusts
each thing that a person actually says"
or at the top of p. 5 where your discussion of
"subverbal undertow miming the subversion of self-belief
woven counter to desire's outreach"                                      15
leaves me groping for firmer footholds.
(I'd have said it differently,
or rather, said something else.)
And when you say that women "could not fulfill themselves" (p. 6)
"in that era" (only forty years ago, after all!)                          20
are you so sure that the situation is so different today?
Also, how does Whitman bluff his way into
your penultimate paragraph? He is the *last* poet
I would have quoted in this context!
What plausible way of behaving                                            25
does the passage you quote represent? Don't you think
literature should ultimately reveal possibilities for *action*?

Please notice how I've repaired your use of semicolons.

And yet, despite what may seem my cranky response,
I do admire the freshness of                                              30
your thinking and your style; there is
a vitality here; your sentences thrust themselves forward
with a confidence as impressive as it is cheeky. . . .
You are not
        me, finally,                                                    35
and though this is an awkward problem, involving
the inescapable fact that you are so young, so young
it is also a delightful provocation.

(A−)

## CONSIDERATIONS FOR CRITICAL THINKING AND WRITING

1. FIRST RESPONSE. How do you characterize the grader of this paper based
   on the comments about the paper?

2. Is the speaker a man or a woman? What makes you think so? Does the
   gender of the speaker affect your reading of the poem? How?

3. Explain whether you think the teacher's comments on the paper are consistent with the grade awarded it. How do you account for the grade?

## CONNECTION TO ANOTHER SELECTION

1. Compare the ways in which Halliday reveals the speaker's character in this
   poem with the strategies used by Robert Browning in "My Last Duchess"
   (p. 139).

# CHARLES SIMIC (B. 1938)

## *The Storm*                                    *2008*

I'm going over to see what those weeds
By the stone wall are worried about.
Perhaps, they don't care for the way
The shadows creep across the lawn
In the silence of the afternoon.                                    5

The sky keeps being blue,
Though we hear no birds,
See no butterflies among the flowers
Or ants running over our feet.

Trees, you bend your branches ever so slightly                     10
In deference to something
About to make its entrance
Of which we know nothing,
Spellbound as we are by the deepening quiet,
The light just beginning to dim.                                    15

### CONSIDERATIONS FOR CRITICAL THINKING AND WRITING

1. FIRST RESPONSE. How does the diction of this poem invite more than
   just a literal reading about a storm?
2. How does Simic manipulate sound in the poem to help create its tone?
3. Describe how the images in each stanza advance the sense of the storm's
   progression.

### CONNECTION TO ANOTHER SELECTION

1. Write a comparative analysis of the themes of "The Storm" and Emily
   Dickinson's "Presentiment — is that long Shadow — on the lawn —"
   (p. 104).

# HENRY REED (1914–1986)

## *Naming of Parts*                              *1946*

Today we have naming of parts. Yesterday,
We had daily cleaning. And tomorrow morning,
We shall have what to do after firing. But today,
Today we have naming of parts. Japonica
Glistens like coral in all of the neighboring gardens,          5
      And today we have naming of parts.

This is the lower sling swivel. And this
Is the upper sling swivel, whose use you will see,
When you are given your slings. And this is the piling swivel,
Which in your case you have not got. The branches                    10
Hold in the gardens their silent, eloquent gestures,
   Which in our case we have not got.

This is the safety-catch, which is always released
With an easy flick of the thumb. And please do not let me
See anyone using his finger. You can do it quite easy              15
If you have any strength in your thumb. The blossoms
Are fragile and motionless, never letting anyone see
   Any of them using their finger.

And this you can see is the bolt. The purpose of this
Is to open the breech, as you see. We can slide it                    20
Rapidly backwards and forwards: we call this
Easing the spring. And rapidly backwards and forwards
The early bees are assaulting and fumbling the flowers:
   They call it easing the Spring.

They call it easing the Spring: it is perfectly easy              25
If you have any strength in your thumb: like the bolt,
And the breech, and the cocking-piece, and the point of balance,
Which in our case we have not got; and the almond-blossom
Silent in all of the gardens and the bees going backwards and forwards,
   For today we have naming of parts.                    30

### Considerations for Critical Thinking and Writing

1. FIRST RESPONSE. Characterize the two speakers in this poem. Identify the lines spoken by each. How do their respective lines differ in tone?

2. What is the effect of the last line of each stanza?

3. How do ambiguities and puns contribute to the poem's meaning?

4. What symbolic contrast is made between the rifle instruction and the gardens? How is this contrast ironic?

## Allen Braden (B. 1968)

### The Hemlock Tree                                                2000

Did I mention that last night an owl swept down
from her perch in the hemlock nearby
to devour a wild dove tamed by Safeway birdseed?
Of course I can reconstruct the scene for you
from knowing how this testimony                                        5
beyond the limits of your city implies the inevitable

circuit of hunger, from knowing how all life must
enter into a kind of covenant with nature
*for the living shall consume*
                                   *the flesh of the living*                    10
and from the delicate evidence at hand:
a wreath of down and drops of blood.
And right now you might be wondering
about the wisteria spiraling up that hemlock,
inching a bit higher with each passing year,                                     15
offering loveliness in powder-blue clusters
for a few weeks of May, and all the while killing
the tree with its gradual, constrictive, necessary beauty.

### Considerations for Critical Thinking and Writing

1. **FIRST RESPONSE.** Braden carefully chooses the flora and fauna for this poem. Explain why you think he makes these particular choices.

2. Describe the speaker's attitude toward nature.

3. Consider whether there is any humor in this poem. Is the tone consistent?

## Robert Browning (1812–1889)

### *My Last Duchess*    *1842*

*Ferrara°*

DEA/A. Dagli Orti/Da Agostino/Getty Images.

That's my last Duchess painted on the wall,
Looking as if she were alive. I call
That piece a wonder, now: Frà Pandolf's°
            hands
Worked busily a day, and there she stands.
Will't please you sit and look at her? I said
"Frà Pandolf" by design, for never read
Strangers like you that pictured countenance,
The depth and passion of its earnest glance,
But to myself they turned (since none puts by
The curtain I have drawn for you, but I)                                         10
And seemed as they would ask me, if they durst,
How such a glance came there; so, not the first
Are you to turn and ask thus. Sir, 'twas not
Her husband's presence only, called that spot

*Ferrara:*  In the sixteenth century, the duke of this Italian city arranged to marry a second time after the mysterious death of his very young first wife.    3 *Frà Pandolf:* A fictitious artist.

Of joy into the Duchess' cheek: perhaps                          15
Frà Pandolf chanced to say "Her mantle laps
Over my lady's wrist too much," or "Paint
Must never hope to reproduce the faint
Half-flush that dies along her throat": such stuff
Was courtesy, she thought, and cause enough           20
For calling up that spot of joy. She had
A heart — how shall I say? — too soon made glad,
Too easily impressed; she liked whate'er
She looked on, and her looks went everywhere.
Sir, 'twas all one! My favor at her breast,               25
The dropping of the daylight in the West,
The bough of cherries some officious fool
Broke in the orchard for her, the white mule
She rode with round the terrace — all and each
Would draw from her alike the approving speech,        30
Or blush, at least. She thanked men, — good! but thanked
Somehow — I know not how — as if she ranked
My gift of a nine-hundred-years-old name
With anybody's gift. Who'd stoop to blame
This sort of trifling? Even had you skill                   35
In speech — which I have not — to make your will
Quite clear to such an one, and say, "Just this
Or that in you disgusts me; here you miss,
Or there exceed the mark" — and if she let
Herself be lessoned so, nor plainly set                      40
Her wits to yours, forsooth, and made excuse,
— E'en then would be some stooping; and I choose
Never to stoop. Oh sir, she smiled, no doubt,
Whene'er I passed her; but who passed without
Much the same smile? This grew; I gave commands;       45
Then all smiles stopped together. There she stands
As if alive. Will't please you rise? We'll meet
The company below, then. I repeat,
The Count your master's known munificence
Is ample warrant that no just pretense                       50
Of mine for dowry will be disallowed;
Though his fair daughter's self, as I avowed
At starting, is my object. Nay, we'll go
Together down, sir. Notice Neptune, though,
Taming a sea-horse, thought a rarity,                        55
Which Claus of Innsbruck° cast in bronze for me!

---

56 *Claus of Innsbruck:* Also a fictitious artist.

## Considerations for Critical Thinking and Writing

1. FIRST RESPONSE. What do you think happened to the duchess?

2. To whom is the duke addressing his remarks about the duchess in this poem? What is ironic about the situation?

3. Why was the duke unhappy with his first wife? What does this reveal about him? What does the poem's title suggest about his attitude toward women in general?

4. What seems to be the visitor's response (lines 53–54) to the duke's account of his first wife?

## Connection to Another Selection

1. Write an essay describing the ways in which the speakers of "My Last Duchess" and Katharyn Howd Machan's "Hazel Tells LaVerne" (p. 60) inadvertently reveal themselves.

## WILLIAM BLAKE (1757–1827)

### The Chimney Sweeper                                1789

When my mother died I was very young,
And my father sold me while yet my tongue
Could scarcely cry "'weep! 'weep! 'weep! 'weep!"
So your chimneys I sweep, and in soot I sleep.

There's little Tom Dacre, who cried when his head,                    5
That curled like a lamb's back, was shaved: so I said
"Hush, Tom! never mind it, for when your head's bare
You know that the soot cannot spoil your white hair."

And so he was quiet, and that very night,
As Tom was a-sleeping, he had such a sight!                          10
That thousands of sweepers, Dick, Joe, Ned, and Jack,
Were all of them locked up in coffins of black.

And by came an Angel who had a bright key,
And he opened the coffins and set them all free;
Then down a green plain leaping, laughing, they run,                 15
And wash in a river, and shine in the sun.

Then naked and white, all their bags left behind,
They rise upon clouds and sport in the wind;
And the Angel told Tom, if he'd be a good boy,
He'd have God for his father, and never want joy.                    20

And so Tom awoke; and we rose in the dark,
And got with our bags and our brushes to work.
Though the morning was cold, Tom was happy and warm;
So if all do their duty they need not fear harm.

## CONSIDERATIONS FOR CRITICAL THINKING AND WRITING

1. FIRST RESPONSE. Discuss the validity of this statement: "'The Chimney Sweeper' is a sentimental poem about a shameful eighteenth-century social problem; such a treatment of child abuse cannot be taken seriously."

2. Characterize the speaker in this poem and describe his tone. Is his tone the same as the poet's? Consider especially lines 7, 8, and 24.

3. What is the symbolic value of the dream in lines 11–20?

4. Why is irony central to the meaning of this poem?

## WALT WHITMAN (1819–1892)

### *From* Song of Myself                                          *1881*

#### 6

A child said *What is the grass?* fetching it to me with full hands;
How could I answer the child? I do not know what it is any more than he.

I guess it must be the flag of my disposition, out of hopeful green stuff woven.

Or I guess it is the handkerchief of the Lord,
A scented gift and remembrancer designedly dropt,                          5
Bearing the owner's name someway in the corners, that we may see and
    remark, and say *Whose?*

Or I guess the grass is itself a child, the produced babe of the vegetation.

Or I guess it is a uniform hieroglyphic,
And it means, Sprouting alike in broad zones and narrow zones,
Growing among black folks as among white,                                  10
Kanuck, Tuckahoe, Congressman, Cuff,° I give them the same, I receive
    them the same.

And now it seems to me the beautiful uncut hair of graves.

Tenderly will I use you curling grass,
It may be you transpire from the breasts of young men,
It may be if I had known them I would have loved them,                     15
It may be you are from old people, or from offspring taken soon out of
    their mothers' laps,
And here you are the mothers' laps.

This grass is very dark to be from the white heads of old mothers,
Darker than the colorless beards of old men,
Dark to come from under the faint red roofs of mouths.                     20

---

11 *Kanuck . . . Cuff:* Kanuck, a French Canadian; Tuckahoe, a Virginian; Cuff, an African American.

O I perceive after all so many uttering tongues,
And I perceive they do not come from the roofs of mouths for nothing.

I wish I could translate the hints about the dead young men and women,
And the hints about old men and mothers, and the offspring taken soon
   out of their laps.

What do you think has become of the young and old men?                    25
And what do you think has become of the women and children?

They are alive and well somewhere,
The smallest sprout shows there is really no death,
And if ever there was it led forward life, and does not wait at the end to
   arrest it,
And ceas'd the moment life appear'd.                                       30

All goes onward and outward . . . and nothing collapses,
And to die is different from what any one supposed, and luckier.

### CONSIDERATIONS FOR CRITICAL THINKING AND WRITING

1. FIRST RESPONSE. What does the grass mean to the speaker? Describe the
   various symbolic possibilities offered in lines 1–11. What seems to be
   the most important symbolic meaning?

2. Describe the tone of lines 12–26. Explain why these lines are or aren't
   representative of the poem's entire tone.

3. How does the final line compare with your own view of death?

### CONNECTION TO ANOTHER SELECTION

1. Compare attitudes toward death in Whitman's poem and in Emily
   Dickinson's "The Bustle in a House" (p. 302).

## GARY SOTO (B. 1952)

### *Behind Grandma's House*          1985

At ten I wanted fame. I had a comb
And two Coke bottles, a tube of Bryl-creem.
I borrowed a dog, one with
Mismatched eyes and a happy tongue,
And wanted to prove I was tough
In the alley, kicking over trash cans,
A dull chime of tuna cans falling.
I hurled light bulbs like grenades
And men teachers held their heads,
Fingers of blood lengthening

Gary Soto.

On the ground. I flicked rocks at cats,
Their goofy faces spurred with foxtails.
I kicked fences. I shooed pigeons.
I broke a branch from a flowering peach
And frightened ants with a stream of spit.                    15
I said "*Chale*," "In your face," and "No way
Daddy-O" to an imaginary priest
Until grandma came into the alley,
Her apron flapping in a breeze,
Her hair mussed, and said, "Let me help you,"                 20
And punched me between the eyes.

### CONSIDERATIONS FOR CRITICAL THINKING AND WRITING

1. FIRST RESPONSE. What is the central irony of this poem?

2. How does the speaker characterize himself at ten?

3. Though the "grandma" appears only briefly, she seems, in a sense, fully characterized. How would you describe her? Why do you think she says, "Let me help you"?

### CONNECTION TO ANOTHER SELECTION

1. Write an essay comparing how the grandmother in "Behind Grandma's House" and the grandfather in Elizabeth Bishop's "Manners" (p. 46) are used to generate the poems' tones and themes.

# 7

# Sounds

In a poem the words should be as pleasing to the ear as the meaning is to the mind.

—MARIANNE MOORE

© Bettmann/Corbis.

## LISTENING TO POETRY

Poems yearn to be read aloud. Much of their energy, charm, and beauty come to life only when they are heard. Poets choose and arrange words for their sounds as well as for their meanings. Most poetry is best read with your lips, teeth, and tongue because they serve to articulate the effects that sound may have in a poem. When a voice is breathed into a good poem, there is pleasure in the reading, the saying, and the hearing.

The earliest poetry — before writing and painting — was chanted or sung. The rhythmic quality of such oral performances served two purposes: it helped the chanting bard remember the lines, and it entertained audiences with patterned sounds of language, which were sometimes accompanied by musical instruments. Poetry has always been closely related to music. Indeed, as the word suggests, lyric poetry evolved from songs. "Western Wind" (p. 24), an anonymous Middle English lyric, survived as song long before it was written down. Had Robert Frost lived in a nonliterate society, he probably would have sung some version — a very different version to be sure — of "Acquainted with the Night" (p. 121) instead of ly ring it down. Even though Eliot creates a speaking rather than a singing voice, the speaker's emotions thus implicitly heard in any careful reading of the poem.

Like lyrics, early narrative poems were originally part of an anonymous oral folk tradition. A **ballad** told a story that was sung from one generation to the next until it was finally transcribed. Since the eighteenth century, this narrative form has sometimes been imitated by poets who write **literary ballads**. John Keats's "La Belle Dame sans Merci" (p. 313) is, for example, a more complex and sophisticated nineteenth-century reflection of the original ballad traditions that developed in the fifteenth century and earlier. In considering poetry as sound, we should not forget that poetry traces its beginnings to song.

Of course, reading a ballad is not the same as hearing it. Like the lyrics of a song, many poems must be heard — or at least read with listening eyes — before they can be fully understood and enjoyed. The sounds of words are a universal source of music for human beings. This has been so from ancient tribes to bards to the two-year-old child in a bakery gleefully chanting "Cuppitycake, cuppitycake!"

Listen to the sound of this poem as you read it aloud. How do the words provide, in a sense, their own musical accompaniment?

## John Updike (1932–2009)

### Player Piano                                        1958

My stick fingers click with a snicker
And, chuckling, they knuckle the keys;
Light-footed, my steel feelers flicker
And pluck from these keys melodies.

My paper can caper; abandon                              5
Is broadcast by dint of my din,
And no man or band has a hand in
The tones I turn on from within.

At times I'm a jumble of rumbles,
At others I'm light like the moon,                       10
But never my numb plunker fumbles,
Misstrums me, or tries a new tune.

The speaker in this poem is a piano that can play automatically by means of a mechanism that depresses keys in response to signals on a perforated roll. Notice how the speaker's voice approximates the sounds of a piano. In each stanza a predominant sound emerges from the carefully chosen words. How is the sound of each stanza tuned to its sense?

## May Swenson (1919–1989)

### *A Nosty Fright*    1984

© Oscar White/Corbis.

The roldengod and the soneyhuckle,
the sack eyed blusan and the wistle theed
are all tangled with the oison pivy,
the fallen nine peedles and the
    wumbleteed.

A mipchunk caught in a wobceb tried
to hip and skide in a dandy sune
but a stobler put up a EEP KOFF sign.
Then the unfucky lellow met a phytoon

and was sept out to swea. He difted for drays
till a hassgropper flying happened to spot
the boolish feast all debraggled and wet,
covered with snears and tot.

Loonmight shone through the winey poods
where rushmooms grew among risted twoots.
Back blats flew betreen the twees                                15
and orned howls hounded their soots.

A kumkpin stood with tooked creeth
on the sindow will of a house
where a icked wold itch lived all alone
except for her stoombrick, a mitten and a kouse.                20

"Here we part," said hassgropper.
"Pere we hart," said mipchunk, too.
They purried away on opposite haths,
both scared of some "Bat!" or "Scoo!"

October was ending on a nosty fright                            25
with scroans and greeches and chanking clains,
with oblins and gelfs, coaths and urses,
skinning grulls and stoodblains.

Will it ever be morning, Nofember virst,
skue bly and the sappy hun, our friend?                         30
With light breaves of wall by the fayside?
I sope ho, so that this oem can pend.

At just the right moments Swenson transposes letters to create amusing
sound effects and wild wordplays. Although there is a story lurking in "A
Nosty Fright," any serious attempt to interpret its meaning is confronted
with "a EEP KOFF sign." Instead, we are invited to enjoy the delicious
sounds the poet has cooked up.

184   DICKINSON

Few poems read in round or complete. Most ideally, the texture
of a poem contribute to its meaning rather than be an attractive. Con

**EMILY DICKINSON** (1830–1886)

## A Bird came down the Walk —                              *ca. 1862*

A Bird came down the Walk —
He did not know I saw —
He bit an Angleworm in halves
And ate the fellow, raw,

And then he drank a Dew                                          5
From a convenient Grass —
And then hopped sidewise to the Wall
To let a Beetle pass —

He glanced with rapid eyes
That hurried all around —                                        10
They looked like frightened Beads, I thought —
He stirred his Velvet Head

Like one in danger, Cautious,
I offered him a Crumb
And he unrolled his feathers                                     15
And rowed him softer home —

Than Oars divide the Ocean,
Too silver for a seam —
Or Butterflies, off Banks of Noon
Leap, plashless as they swim.                                    20

This description of a bird offers a close look at how differently a bird
moves when it hops on the ground than when it flies in the air. On the
ground the bird moves quickly, awkwardly, and irregularly as it plucks up
a worm, washes it down with dew, and then hops aside to avoid a passing
beetle. The speaker recounts the bird's rapid, abrupt actions from a somewhat superior, amused perspective. By describing the bird in human terms
(as if, for example, it chose to eat the worm "raw"), the speaker is almost
condescending. But when the attempt to offer a crumb fails and the frightened bird flies off, the speaker is left looking up instead of down at the bird.

With that shift in perspective the tone shifts from amusement to awe
in response to the bird's graceful flight. The jerky movements of lines 1 to
13 give way to the smooth motion of lines 15 to 20. The pace of the first
three stanzas is fast and discontinuous. We tend to pause at the end of each
line, and this reinforces a sense of disconnected movements. In contrast,

the final six lines are to be read as a single sentence in one flowing move-ment, lubricated by various sounds.

Read again the description of the bird flying away. Several *o*-sounds contribute to the image of the serene, expansive, confident flight, just as the *s*-sounds serve as smooth transitions from one line to the next. Notice how these sounds are grouped in the following vertical columns:

| | | | | | |
|---|---|---|---|---|---|
| un*ro*lled | *softer* | T*oo* | *his* | Ocean | Banks |
| r*o*wed | Oars | N*oo*n | feather*s* | *s*ilver | plashle*ss* |
| h*o*me | Or | | *softer* | *s*eam | a*s* |
| Ocean | *o*ff | | Oar*s* | Butterflie*s* | *s*wim |

This blending of sounds (notice how "Leap, plashless" brings together the *p*- and *l*-sounds without a ripple) helps convey the bird's smooth grace in the air. Like a feathered oar, the bird moves seamlessly in its element.

The repetition of sounds in poetry is similar to the function of the tones and melodies that are repeated, with variations, in music. Just as the patterned sounds in music unify a work, so do the words in poems, which have been carefully chosen for the combinations of sounds they create. These sounds are produced in a number of ways.

The most direct way in which the sound of a word suggests its mean-ing is through **onomatopoeia**, which is the use of a word that resembles the sound it denotes: *quack, buzz, rattle, bang, squeak, bowwow, burp, choo-choo, ding-a-ling, sizzle.* The sound and sense of these words are closely related, but such words represent a very small percentage of the words avail-able to us. Poets usually employ more subtle means for echoing meanings.

Onomatopoeia can consist of more than just single words. In its broad-est meaning the term refers to lines or passages in which sounds help to convey meanings, as in these lines from Updike's "Player Piano":

My stick fingers click with a snicker
And, chuckling, they knuckle the keys.

The sharp, crisp sounds of these two lines approximate the sounds of a piano; the syllables seem to "click" against one another. Contrast Updike's rendition with the following lines:

My long fingers play with abandon
And, laughing, they cover the keys.

The original version is more interesting and alive because the sounds of the words are pleasurable and reinforce the meaning through a careful blending of consonants and vowels.

**Alliteration** is the repetition of the same consonant sounds at the beginnings of nearby words: "*d*escending *d*ewdrops," "*l*uscious *l*emons." Sometimes the term is also used to describe the consonant sounds within words: "tres*pass*er's re*pr*oach," "we*dd*ed la*d*y." Alliteration is based on sound rather than spelling. "*K*een" and "*c*ar" alliterate, but "*c*ar" does not alliterate with "*cite*." Rarely is heavy-handed alliteration effective. Used too self-consciously, it can be distracting instead of strengthening meaning or emphasizing a relation between words. Consider the relentless *h*'s in this line: "Horrendous horrors haunted Helen's happiness." Those *h*'s certainly suggest that Helen is being pursued, but they have a more comic than serious effect because they are overdone.

   *Assonance* is the repetition of the same vowel sound in nearby words: "asl*ee*p under a tr*ee*," "t*i*me and t*i*de," "h*au*nt" and "*aw*esome," "*ea*ch *e*vening." Both alliteration and assonance help to establish relations among words in a line or a series of lines. Whether the effect is **euphony** (lines that are musically pleasant to the ear and smooth, like the final lines of Dickinson's "A Bird came down the Walk—") or **cacophony** (lines that are discordant and difficult to pronounce, like the claim that "never my numb plunker fumbles" in Updike's "Player Piano"), the sounds of words in poetry can be as significant as the words' denotative or connotative meanings.

# A SAMPLE STUDENT RESPONSE

Lee 1

Ryan Lee

Professor McDonough

English 211

1 May 2015

Sound in Emily Dickinson's "A Bird came down the Walk—"

   In her poem "A Bird came down the Walk—" Emily Dickinson uses the sound and rhythm of each line to reflect the motion of a bird walking awkwardly—and then flying gracefully. Particularly when read aloud, the staccato phrases and stilted breaks in lines 1 through 14 create a sense of the bird's movement on land, quick and off-balanced, which helps bring the scene to life.

   The first three stanzas are structured to make the bird's movement consistent. The bird hops around, eating worms while keeping guard for any threats. Vulnerable on the ground, the bird is intensely aware of danger:

> He glanced with rapid eyes
>
> That hurried all around—
>
> They looked like frightened Beads, I thought—
>
> He stirred his Velvet Head (9-12)

In addition to choosing words that portray the bird as cautious—it "glanced with rapid eyes" (9) that resemble "frightened Beads" (11)—Dickinson chooses to end each line abruptly. This abrupt halting of sound allows the reader to experience the bird's fear more immediately, and the effect is similar to the missing of a beat or a breath.

These halting lines stand in contrast to the smoothness of the last six lines, during which the bird takes flight. The sounds in these lines are pleasingly soft, and rich in the "s" sound. The bird

> unrolled his feathers
> And rowed him softer home—
>
> Than Oars divide the Ocean,
> Too silver for a seam—(15-18). . . .

Work Cited

Dickinson, Emily. "A Bird came down the Walk —." *Thinking and Writing about Poetry*. Ed. Michael Meyer. Boston: Bedford/St. Martin's, 2016. 148. Print.

This next poem provides a feast of sounds. Read the poem aloud and try to determine the effects of its sounds.

## Anya Krugovoy Silver (b. 1968)

### French Toast                                                              *2010*

*Pain perdu*: lost bread. Thick slices sunk in milk,
fringed with crisp lace of browned egg and scattered sugar.
Like spongiest challah, dipped in foaming cream
and frothy egg, richness drenching every yeasted
crevice and bubble, that's how sodden with luck                          5
I felt when we fell in love. Now, at forty,
I remember that "lost bread" means bread that's gone
stale, leftover heels and crusts, too dry for simple
jam and butter. Still, week-old bread makes the best
French toast, soaks up milk as greedily as I turn                        10
toward you under goose down after ten years
of marriage, craving, still, that sweet white immersion.

### Considerations for Critical Thinking and Writing

1. **FIRST RESPONSE.** What types of sounds does Silver use throughout this poem? What categories can you place them in? What is the effect of these sounds?

2. Explain what you think the poem's theme is.

3. Write an essay that considers the speaker's love of French toast along with the speaker's appetite for words. How are the two blended in the poem?

4. **CREATIVE RESPONSE.** Try writing a poem that emphasizes sounds about a food you love.

# RHYME

Like alliteration and assonance, **rhyme** is a way of creating sound patterns. Rhyme, broadly defined, consists of two or more words or phrases that repeat the same sounds: *happy* and *snappy*. Rhyme words often have similar spellings, but that is not a requirement of rhyme; what matters is that the words sound alike: *vain* rhymes with *reign* as well as *rain*. Moreover, words may look alike but not rhyme at all. In **eye rhyme** the spellings are similar, but the pronunciations are not, as with *bough* and *cough,* or *brow* and *blow.*

Not all poems use rhyme. Many great poems have no rhymes, and many weak verses use rhyme as a substitute for poetry. These are especially apparent in commercial messages and greeting-card lines. At its worst, rhyme is merely a distracting decoration that can lead to dullness and predictability. But used skillfully, rhyme creates lines that are memorable and musical.

Here is a poem using rhyme that you might remember the next time you are in a restaurant.

## RICHARD ARMOUR (1906–1989)

### *Going to Extremes*                                    *1954*

Shake and shake
  The catsup bottle
None'll come —
  And then a lot'll.

The experience recounted in Armour's poem is common enough, but the rhyme's humor is special. The final line clicks the poem shut — an effect that is often achieved by the use of rhyme. That click provides a sense of a satisfying and fulfilled form. Rhymes have a number of uses: they can emphasize words, direct a reader's attention to relations between words, and provide an overall structure for a poem.

Rhyme is used in the following poem to imitate the sound of cascading water.

## ROBERT SOUTHEY (1774–1843)

### *From "The Cataract of Lodore"*                        *1820*

"How does the water

Come down at Lodore?"

.  .  .  .  .  .  .  .  .  .  .  .  .  .  .  .  .  .  .  .

From its sources which well
  In the tarn on the fell;
    From its fountains                                     5
    In the mountains,
  Its rills and its gills;
Through moss and through brake,
  It runs and it creeps
  For awhile, till it sleeps                               10
    In its own little lake.
  And thence at departing,
  Awakening and starting,
  It runs through the reeds
  And away it proceeds,                                    15
Through meadow and glade,
  In sun and in shade,
And through the wood-shelter,
  Among crags in its flurry,
    Helter-skelter,                                        20
    Hurry-scurry.
  Here it comes sparkling,

And there it lies darkling;
Now smoking and frothing
Its tumult and wrath in, 25
Till in this rapid race
On which it is bent,
It reaches the place
Of its steep descent.

The cataract strong 30
Then plunges along,
Striking and raging
As if a war waging
Its caverns and rocks among:
Rising and leaping, 35
Sinking and creeping,
Swelling and sweeping,
Showering and springing,
Flying and flinging,
Writhing and ringing, 40
Eddying and whisking,
Spouting and frisking,
Turning and twisting,
Around and around
With endless rebound! 45
Smiting and fighting,
A sight to delight in;
Confounding, astounding,
Dizzying and deafening the ear with its sound.
. . . . . . . . . . . . . . . . . . . . . . . .
Dividing and gliding and sliding, 50
And falling and brawling and sprawling,
And driving and riving and striving,
And sprinkling and twinkling and wrinkling,
And sounding and bounding and rounding,
And bubbling and troubling and doubling, 55
And grumbling and rumbling and tumbling,
And clattering and battering and shattering;
Retreating and beating and meeting and sheeting,
Delaying and straying and playing and spraying,
Advancing and prancing and glancing and dancing, 60
Recoiling, turmoiling and toiling and boiling,
And gleaming and streaming and steaming and beaming,
And rushing and flushing and brushing and gushing,
And flapping and rapping and clapping and slapping,
And curling and whirling and purling and twirling, 65
And thumping and plumping and bumping and jumping,

And dashing and flashing and splashing and clashing;
And so never ending, but always descending,
Sounds and motions forever and ever are blending,
All at once and all o'er, with a mighty uproar;                    70
And this way the water comes down at Lodore.

This deluge of rhymes consists of "Sounds and motions forever and ever . . . blending" (line 69). The pace quickens as the water creeps from its mountain source and then descends in rushing cataracts. As the speed of the water increases, so do the number of rhymes, until they run in fours: "dashing and flashing and splashing and clashing" (line 67). Most rhymes meander through poems instead of flooding them; nevertheless, Southey's use of rhyme suggests how sounds can flow with meanings. "The Cataract of Lodore" has been criticized, however, for overusing onomatopoeia. Some readers find the poem silly; others regard it as a brilliant example of sound effects. What do you think?

A variety of types of rhyme is available to poets. The most common form, **end rhyme**, comes at the ends of lines (lines 14–17).

It runs through the reeds
    And away it proceeds,
Through meadow and glade,
    In sun and in shade.

**Internal rhyme** places at least one of the rhymed words within the line, as in "Dividing and gliding and sliding" (line 50) or, more subtly, in the fourth and final words of "In mist or cloud, on mast or shroud."

The rhyming of single-syllable words such as *glade* and *shade* is known as **masculine rhyme**, as we see in these lines from A. E. Housman:

Loveliest of trees, the cherry now
Is hung with bloom along the bough.

Rhymes using words of more than one syllable are also called masculine when the same sound occurs in a final stressed syllable, as in *defend, contend; betray, away*. A **feminine rhyme** consists of a rhymed stressed syllable followed by one or more rhymed unstressed syllables, as in *butter, clutter; gratitude, attitude; quivering, shivering*. This rhyme is evident in John Millington Synge's verse:

Lord confound this surly sister,
Blight her brow and blotch and blister.

All of the examples so far have been **exact rhymes** because they share the same stressed vowel sounds as well as any sounds that follow the vowel. In **near rhyme** (also called **off rhyme**, **slant rhyme**, and **approximate rhyme**), the sounds are almost but not exactly alike. There are several kinds of near rhyme. One of the most common is **consonance,** an identical consonant sound preceded by a different vowel sound: *home, same; worth, breath; trophy, daffy.* Near rhyme can also be achieved by using different vowel sounds with identical consonant sounds: *sound, sand; kind, conned; fellow, fallow.* The dissonance of *blade* and *blood* in the following lines from Wilfred Owen helps to reinforce their grim tone:

> Let the boy try along this bayonet-blade
> How cold steel is, and keen with hunger of blood.

Near rhymes greatly broaden the possibility for musical effects in English, a language that, compared with Spanish or Italian, contains few exact rhymes. Do not assume, however, that a near rhyme represents a failed attempt at exact rhyme. Near rhymes allow a musical subtlety and variety and can avoid the sometimes overpowering jingling effects that exact rhymes may create.

These basic terms hardly exhaust the ways in which the sounds in poems can be labeled and discussed, but the terms can help you to describe how poets manipulate sounds for effect. Read "God's Grandeur" (p. 157) aloud and try to determine how the sounds of the lines contribute to their sense.

---

## Perspective

### DAVID LENSON (B. 1945)

## *On the Contemporary Use of Rhyme*                    1988

One impediment to a respectable return to rhyme is the popular survival of "functional" verse: greeting cards, pedagogical and mnemonic devices ("Thirty days hath September"), nursery rhymes, advertising jingles, and of course song lyrics. Pentameters, irregular rhymes, and free verse aren't much use in songwriting, where the meter has to be governed by the time signature of the music.

Far from universities, there has been a revival of rhymed couplets in rap music, in which, to the accompaniment of synthesizers, vocalists deliver lengthy first-person narratives in tetrameter. While most writing teachers would dismiss such lyrics as doggerel, the aim of the songs is really not so far from that of Alexander Pope: to use rhyme to sharpen social insight, in the hope that the world may be reordered.

From *The Chronicle of Higher Education,* February 24, 1988

#### CONSIDERATIONS FOR CRITICAL THINKING AND WRITING

1. Read some contemporary song lyrics from a wide range of groups or vocalists. Is Lenson correct in his assessment that irregular rhyme is not much use in songwriting?

2. Examine the rhymed couplets of some rap music. Discuss whether they are used "to sharpen social insight." What is the effect of using rhymes in rap music?

3. What is your own response to rhymed poetry? Do you like yours with or without? What do you think informs your preference?

# SOUND AND MEANING

## GERARD MANLEY HOPKINS (1844–1889)

### God's Grandeur                                             *1877*

The world is charged with the grandeur of God.
  It will flame out, like shining from shook foil;°       *shaken gold foil*
  It gathers to a greatness, like the ooze of oil
Crushed.° Why do men then now not reck his rod?°
Generations have trod, have trod, have trod;            5
  And all is seared with trade; bleared, smeared with toil;
  And wears man's smudge and shares man's smell: the soil
Is bare now, nor can foot feel, being shod.

And for all this, nature is never spent;
  There lives the dearest freshness deep down things;     10
And though the last lights off the black West went
  Oh, morning, at the brown brink eastward, springs —
Because the Holy Ghost over the bent
  World broods with warm breast and with ah! bright wings.

4 *Crushed:* Olives crushed in their oil; *reck his rod:* Obey God.

    The subject of this poem is announced in the title and the first line: "The world is charged with the grandeur of God." The poem is a celebration of the power and greatness of God's presence in the world, but the speaker is also perplexed and dismayed by people who refuse to recognize God's authority and grandeur as they are manifested in the creation. Instead of glorifying God, "men" have degraded the earth through meaningless toil and cut themselves off from the spiritual renewal inherent in the beauty of nature. The relentless demands of commerce and industry have blinded people to the earth's natural and spiritual resources. Despite this abuse and insensitivity to God's grandeur, however, "nature is never spent"; the morning light that "springs" in the east redeems the "black West" of the night and is a sign that the spirit of the Holy Ghost is ever present in the world. This summary of the poem sketches some of the thematic significance of the lines, but it does not do justice to how they are organized around the use of sound. Hopkins's poem, unlike Southey's "The Cataract of Lodore," uses sounds in a subtle and complex way.

In the opening line Hopkins uses alliteration—a device apparent in almost every line of the poem—to connect "God" to the "world," which is "charged" with his "grandeur." These consonants unify the line as well. The alliteration in lines 2 and 3 suggests a harmony in the creation: the *f*'s in "*f*lame" and "*f*oil," the *sh*'s in "*sh*ining" and "*sh*ook," the *g*'s in "*g*athers" and "*g*reatness," and the visual (not alliterative) similarities of "*ooze of oil*" emphasize a world that is held together by God's will.

That harmony is abruptly interrupted by the speaker's angry question in line 4: "Why do men then now not reck his rod?" The question is as painful to the speaker as it is difficult to pronounce. The arrangement of the alliteration ("*n*ow," "*n*ot"; "*r*eck," "*r*od"), the assonance ("n*o*t," "r*o*d"; "m*e*n," "th*e*n," "r*e*ck"), and the internal rhyme ("m*en*," "th*en*") contribute to the difficulty in saying the line—a difficulty associated with human behavior. That behavior is introduced in line 5 by the repetition of "have trod" to emphasize the repeated mistakes—sins—committed by human beings. The tone is dirgelike because humanity persists in its mistaken path rather than progressing. The speaker's horror at humanity is evident in the cacophonous sounds of lines 6 to 8. Here the alliteration of "*sm*eared," "*sm*udge," and "*sm*ell" along with the internal rhymes of "s*eared*," "bl*eared*," and "sm*eared*" echo the disgust with which the speaker views humanity's "toil" with the "soil," an end rhyme that calls attention to our mistaken equation of nature with production rather than with spirituality.

In contrast to this cacophony, the final six lines build toward the joyful recognition of the new possibilities that accompany the rising sun. This recognition leads to the euphonic description of the "H*o*ly Gh*o*st *o*ver" (notice the reassuring consistency of the assonance) the world. Traditionally represented as a dove, the Holy Ghost brings love and peace to the "*w*orld," and "*br*oods *w*ith *w*arm *br*east and *w*ith ah! *br*ight *w*ings." The effect of this alliteration is mellifluous: the sound bespeaks the harmony that prevails at the end of the poem resulting from the speaker's recognition that "nature is never spent" because God loves and protects the world.

The sounds of "God's Grandeur" enhance the poem's theme; more can be said about its sounds, but it is enough to point out here that for this poem, the sound strongly echoes the theme in nearly every line. Here are some more poems in which sound plays a significant role.

# POEMS FOR FURTHER STUDY

## DIANE LOCKWARD (B. 1953)

### *Linguini*                                2006

It was always linguini between us.
Linguini with white sauce, or
red sauce, sauce with basil snatched from
the garden, oregano rubbed between
our palms, a single bay leaf adrift amidst
plum tomatoes. Linguini with meatballs,
sausage, a side of brascioli. Like lovers
trying positions, we enjoyed it every way
we could — artichokes, mushrooms, little
neck clams, mussels, and calamari — linguini          10
twining and braiding us each to each.
Linguini knew of the kisses, the smooches,
the *molti baci*.° It was never spaghetti                 *many kisses*
between us, not cappellini, nor farfalle,
vermicelli, pappardelle, fettucini, perciatelli,          15
or even tagliarini. Linguini we stabbed, pitched,
and twirled on forks, spun round and round
on silver spoons. Long, smooth, and always
*al dente*. In dark trattorias, we broke crusty panera,
toasted each other — *La dolce vita!*° — and sipped    *The Sweet Life* 20
Amarone,° wrapped ourselves in linguini,                  *Italian wine*
briskly boiled, lightly oiled, salted, and lavished
with sauce. *Bellissimo, paradisio, belle gente!*°
Linguini witnessed our slurping, pulling, and
sucking, our unraveling and raveling, chins               25
glistening, napkins tucked like bibs in collars,
linguini stuck to lips, hips, and bellies, cheeks
flecked with *formaggio*° — parmesan, romano,              *cheese*
and shaved pecorino — strands of linguini flung
around our necks like two fine silk scarves.              30

23 *Bellissimo, paradisio, belle gente:* Beautiful, paradise, beautiful people.

## CONSIDERATIONS FOR CRITICAL THINKING AND WRITING

1. FIRST RESPONSE. Read this poem aloud. Which words and sounds do you think make this such an exuberant celebration of linguini?

2. Comment on the effect of the repetitions of sound in the poem.

3. Consider the poem's final image. What would be missing if the "two fine silk scarves" were omitted?

**CONNECTION TO ANOTHER SELECTION**

1. What similarities and differences do you find in the use of sound in "Linguini" and in Silver's "French Toast" (p. 152)?

**LEWIS CARROLL** (CHARLES LUTWIDGE DODGSON/1832–1898)

## *Jabberwocky*          1871

'Twas brillig, and the slithy toves
    Did gyre and gimble in the wabe:
All mimsy were the borogoves,
    And the mome raths outgrabe.

"Beware the Jabberwock, my son!           5
    The jaws that bite, the claws that catch!
Beware the Jubjub bird, and shun
    The frumious Bandersnatch!"

He took his vorpal sword in hand;
    Long time the manxome foe he sought —       10
So rested he by the Tumtum tree,
    And stood awhile in thought.

And, as in uffish thought he stood,
    The Jabberwock, with eyes of flame,
Came whiffling through the tulgey wood,       15
    And burbled as it came!

One, two! One, two! And through and through
    The vorpal blade went snicker-snack!
He left it dead, and with its head
    He went galumphing back.           20

"And hast thou slain the Jabberwock?
    Come to my arms, my beamish boy!
O frabjous day! Callooh, Callay!"
    He chortled in his joy.

'Twas brillig, and the slithy toves       25
    Did gyre and gimble in the wabe:
All mimsy were the borogoves,
    And the mome raths outgrabe.

**CONSIDERATIONS FOR CRITICAL THINKING AND WRITING**

1. FIRST RESPONSE. What happens in this poem? Does it have any meaning?
2. Not all of the words used in this poem appear in dictionaries. In *Through the Looking Glass,* Humpty Dumpty explains to Alice that "'slithy' means 'lithe and slimy.' 'Lithe' is the same as 'active.' You see it's

like a portmanteau — there are two meanings packed up into one word."
Are there any other portmanteau words in the poem?

3. Which words in the poem sound especially meaningful, even if they are
devoid of any denotative meanings?

### CONNECTION TO ANOTHER SELECTION

1. Compare Carroll's strategies for creating sound and meaning with those
used by Swenson in "A Nosty Fright" (p. 147).

## HARRYETTE MULLEN (B. 1953)

### Blah-Blah

2002

Ack-ack, aye-aye.
Baa baa, Baba, Bambam, Bebe, Berber, Bibi, blah-blah, Bobo,
        bonbon,
booboo, Bora Bora, Boutros Boutros, bye-bye.
Caca, cancan, Cece, cha-cha, chichi, choo-choo, chop chop,
        chow chow, Coco, cocoa,
come come, cuckoo.                                                    5
Dada, Dee Dee, Didi, dindin, dodo, doodoo, dumdum,
        Duran Duran.
Fifi, fifty-fifty, foofoo, froufrou.
Gaga, Gigi, glug-glug, go-go, goody-goody, googoo, grisgris.
Haha, harhar, hear hear, heehee, hey hey, hip-hip, hoho,
        Hsing-Hsing, hubba-hubba, humhum.
is is, It'sIts.                                                      10
JarJar, Jo Jo, juju.
Kiki, knock knock, Koko, Kumkum.
Lala, Lili, Ling-Ling looky-looky, Lulu.
Mahi mahi, mama, Mau Mau, Mei-Mei, Mimi, Momo, murmur,
        my my.
Na Na, No-no, now now.                                              15
Oh-oh, oink oink.
Pago Pago, Palau Palau, papa, pawpaw, peepee, Phen Fen,
        pooh-pooh, poopoo, pupu, putt-putt.
Rah-rah, ReRe.
Shih-Shih, Sing Sing, Sirhan Sirhan, Sen Sen, Sisi, so-so.
Tata, taki-taki, talky-talky, Tam Tam, Tartar, teetee, Tintin,      20
Tingi Tingi, tom-tom, toot toot, tsetse, tsk tsk, tutu,
        tumtum, tut tut.
Van Van, veve, vroom-vroom.
Wahwah, Walla Walla, weewee, win-win.
Yadda yadda, Yari Yari, yaya, ylang ylang, yo-yo, yuk-yuk, yum-yum.
Zizi, ZsaZsa, Zouzou, Zuzu.                                         25

## CONSIDERATIONS FOR CRITICAL THINKING AND WRITING

1. **FIRST RESPONSE.** The title probably makes sense to you, but does the rest of the poem? Why or why not?

2. Read the poem aloud, and describe the poem's sound effects.

3. **CREATIVE RESPONSE.** Write ten lines of your own alliterative string of words and read it aloud to hear what it sounds like.

## CONNECTION TO OTHER SELECTIONS

1. Compare Mullen's strategies for emphasizing sound in her poem with those of Swenson in "A Nosty Fright" (p. 147) and Carroll in "Jabberwocky" (p. 160).

## WILLIAM HEYEN (B. 1940)

### The Trains                                                                1984

Signed by Franz Paul Stangl, Commandant,
there is in Berlin a document,
an order of transmittal from Treblinka:

248 freight cars of clothing,
400,000 gold watches,                                                          5
25 freight cars of women's hair.

Some clothing was kept, some pulped for paper.
The finest watches were never melted down.
All the women's hair was used for mattresses, or dolls.

Would these words like to use some of that same paper?          10
One of those watches may pulse in your own wrist.
Does someone you know collect dolls, or sleep on human hair?

He is dead at last, Commandant Stangl of Treblinka,
but the camp's three syllables still sound like freight cars
straining around a curve, Treblinka,                                        15

Treblinka. Clothing, time in gold watches,
women's hair for mattresses and dolls' heads.
Treblinka. The trains from Treblinka.

## CONSIDERATIONS FOR CRITICAL THINKING AND WRITING

1. **FIRST RESPONSE.** How does the sound of the word *Treblinka* inform your understanding of the poem?

2. Why does the place name of Treblinka continue to resonate over time? To learn more about Treblinka, search the Web, perhaps starting at ushmm.org, the site of the United States Holocaust Memorial Museum.

3. Why do you suppose Heyen uses the word *in* instead of *on* in line 11?

4. Why is sound so important for establishing the tone of this poem? In what sense do "the camp's three syllables still sound like freight cars" (line 14)?

5. CRITICAL STRATEGIES. Read the section on reader-response strategies (pp. 342–44) in Chapter 15, "Critical Strategies for Reading." How does this poem make you feel? Why?

# JOHN DONNE (1572–1631)

## *Song*                                                                1633

Go and catch a falling star,
   Get with child a mandrake root,°
Tell me where all past years are,
   Or who cleft the Devil's foot,
Teach me to hear mermaids singing,                                          5
   Or to keep off envy's stinging,
        And find
        What wind
Serves to advance an honest mind.

If thou be'st borne to strange sights,                                      10
   Things invisible to see,
Ride ten thousand days and nights,
   Till age snow white hairs on thee,
Thou, when thou return'st, wilt tell me
   All strange wonders that befell thee,                            15
        And swear
        Nowhere
Lives a woman true, and fair.

If thou findst one, let me know,
   Such a pilgrimage were sweet —                                  20
Yet do not, I would not go,
   Though at next door we might meet;
Though she were true, when you met her,
   And last, till you write your letter,
        Yet she                                   25
        Will be
False, ere I come, to two or three.

2 *mandrake root:* This V-shaped root resembles the lower half of the human body.

## CONSIDERATIONS FOR CRITICAL THINKING AND WRITING

1. FIRST RESPONSE. What is the speaker's tone in this poem? What is his view of a woman's love? What does the speaker's use of hyperbole reveal about his emotional state?

2. Do you think Donne wants the speaker's argument to be taken seriously? Is there any humor in the poem?

3. Most of these lines end with masculine rhymes. What other kinds of rhymes are used for end rhymes?

## ALEXANDER POPE (1688–1774)

### *From* An Essay on Criticism                                    *1711*

But most by numbers° judge a poet's song;                          *versification*
And smooth or rough, with them, is right or wrong;
In the bright muse though thousand charms conspire,
Her voice is all these tuneful fools admire;
Who haunt Parnassus° but to please their ear,                          5
Not mend their minds; as some to church repair,
Not for the doctrine, but the music there.
These equal syllables alone require,
Though oft the ear the open vowels tire;
While expletives° their feeble aid do join;                         10
And ten low words oft creep in one dull line;
While they ring round the same unvaried chimes,
With sure returns of still expected rhymes;
Where'er you find "the cooling western breeze,"
In the next line, it "whispers through the trees":                  15
If crystal streams "with pleasing murmurs creep,"
The reader's threatened (not in vain) with "sleep":
Then, at the last and only couplet fraught
With some unmeaning thing they call a thought,
A needless Alexandrine° ends the song,                              20
That, like a wounded snake, drags its slow length along.
Leave such to tune their own dull rhymes, and know
What's roundly smooth, or languishingly slow;
And praise the easy vigor of a line,
Where Denham's strength, and Waller's° sweetness join.              25
True ease in writing comes from art, not chance,
As those move easiest who have learned to dance.
'Tis not enough no harshness gives offense,
The sound must seem an echo to the sense:
Soft is the strain when Zephyr° gently blows,                 *the west wind*   30
And the smooth stream in smoother numbers flows;
But when loud surges lash the sounding shore,

---

5 *Parnassus:* A Greek mountain sacred to the Muses.    10 *expletives:* Unnecessary words used to fill a line, as the *do* in this line.    20 *Alexandrine:* A twelve-syllable line, as line 21.    25 *Denham's . . . Waller's:* Sir John Denham (1615–1669) and Edmund Waller (1606–1687) were poets who used heroic couplets.

The hoarse, rough verse should like the torrent roar:
When Ajax° strives some rock's vast weight to throw,
The line too labors, and the words move slow;                    35
Not so, when swift Camilla° scours the plain,
Flies o'er th' unbending corn, and skims along the main.

34 *Ajax:* A Greek warrior famous for his strength in the Trojan War.    36 *Camilla:* A
goddess famous for her delicate speed.

### CONSIDERATIONS FOR CRITICAL THINKING AND WRITING

1. FIRST RESPONSE. In these lines Pope describes some faults he finds in
   poems and illustrates those faults within the lines that describe them. How
   do the sounds in lines 4, 9, 10, 11, and 21 illustrate what they describe?

2. What is the objection to the "expected rhymes" in lines 12–17? How do
   they differ from Pope's end rhymes?

3. Some lines discuss how to write successful poetry. How do lines 23, 24,
   32–33, 35, 36, and 37 illustrate what they describe?

4. Do you agree that in a good poem, "The sound must seem an echo to
   the sense" (line 29)?


## WILFRED OWEN (1893–1918)

### *Anthem for Doomed Youth*                                    *1917*

What passing-bells for these who die as cattle?
Only the monstrous anger of the guns.
Only the stuttering rifles' rapid rattle
Can patter out their hasty orisons.
No mockeries now for them; no prayers nor bells,                 5
Nor any voice of mourning save the choirs, —
The shrill, demented choirs of wailing shells;
And bugles calling for them from sad shires.
What candles may be held to speed them all?
Not in the hands of boys, but in their eyes                      10
Shall shine the holy glimmers of good-byes.
The pallor of girls' brows shall be their pall;
Their flowers the tenderness of patient minds,
And each slow dusk a drawing-down of blinds


### CONSIDERATIONS FOR CRITICAL THINKING AND WRITING

1. FIRST RESPONSE. Why is the date of this poem relevant to an appreciation of it?

2. Discuss the effects of Owen's use of alliteration.

3. How do the images and tone shift in lines 9–14 compared to lines 1–8?

### CONNECTION TO ANOTHER SELECTION

1. Compare the themes of this poem and Kenneth Fearing's "AD" (p. 128).

## PAUL HUMPHREY (1915–2001)

### *Blow*                                                                1983

Her skirt was lofted by the gale;
When I, with gesture deft,
Essayed to stay her frisky sail
She luffed, and laughed, and left.

### CONSIDERATIONS FOR CRITICAL THINKING AND WRITING

1. FIRST RESPONSE. How do alliteration and assonance contribute to the euphonic effects in this poem?

2. What is the poem's controlling metaphor? Why is it especially appropriate?

3. Explain the ambiguity of the title.

## HELEN CHASIN (B. 1938)

### *The Word* Plum                                                      1968

The word *plum* is delicious

pout and push, luxury of
self-love, and savoring murmur
full in the mouth and falling
like fruit                                                                  5

taut skin
pierced, bitten, provoked into
juice, and tart flesh

question
and reply, lip and tongue                                                   10
of pleasure.

### CONSIDERATIONS FOR CRITICAL THINKING AND WRITING

1. FIRST RESPONSE. What is the effect of the repetitions of the alliteration and assonance throughout the poem? How does it contribute to the poem's meaning?

2. Which sounds in the poem are like the sounds one makes while eating a plum?

3. Discuss the title. Explain whether you think this poem is more about the word *plum* or about the plum itself. Can the two be separated in the poem?

**WHEN I READ** "I like poems that don't tell me how the writer feels; they tell me how the world looks to someone who feels that way. They make sense by engaging the senses, and so they become an experience. The reader is not merely an audience but a participant." — RICHARD WAKEFIELD

## RICHARD WAKEFIELD (B. 1952)

### *The Bell Rope*                                                      *2005*

In Sunday school the boy who learned a psalm
by heart would get to sound the steeple bell
and send its tolling through the sabbath calm
to call the saved and not-so-saved as well.
For lack of practice all the lines are lost —                           5
something about how angels' hands would bear
me up to God — but on one Pentecost
they won me passage up the steeple stair.
I leapt and grabbed the rope up high to ride
it down, I touched the floor, the rope went slack,                      10
the bell was silent. Then, beatified,
I rose, uplifted as the rope pulled back.
I leapt and fell again; again it took
me up, but still the bell withheld its word —
until at last the church foundation shook                               15
in bass approval, felt as much as heard,
and after I let go the bell tolled long
and loud as if repaying me for each
unanswered pull with heaven-rending song
a year of Sunday school could never teach                               20
and that these forty years can not obscure.
Some nights when sleep won't come I think of how
just once there came an answer, clear and sure.
If I could find that rope I'd grasp it now.

#### CONSIDERATIONS FOR CRITICAL THINKING AND WRITING

1. **FIRST RESPONSE.** Describe the rhyme scheme and then read the poem aloud. How does Wakefield manage to avoid making this heavily rhymed poem sound clichéd or sing-songy?

2. Comment on the appropriateness of Wakefield's choice of diction and how it relates to the poem's images.

3. Explain how sound becomes, in a sense, the theme of the poem.

CONNECTION TO ANOTHER SELECTION

1. Compare the images and themes of "The Bell Rope" with those in Robert Frost's "Birches" (p. 266).

JOHN KEATS (1795–1821)

## Ode to a Nightingale                                      *1819*

### I

My heart aches, and a drowsy numbness pains
  My sense, as though of hemlock° I had drunk,                    *a poison*
Or emptied some dull opiate to the drains
  One minute past, and Lethe-wards° had sunk:
'Tis not through envy of thy happy lot,                                 5
  But being too happy in thine happiness —
    That thou, light-wingèd Dryad° of the trees,          *wood nymph*
      In some melodious plot
  Of beechen green, and shadows numberless,
    Singest of summer in full-throated ease.                      10

### II

O, for a draught of vintage! that hath been
  Cooled a long age in the deep-delved earth,
Tasting of Flora° and the country green,                       *goddess of flowers*
  Dance, and Provençal song,° and sunburnt mirth!
O for a beaker full of the warm South,                                 15
  Full of the true, the blushful Hippocrene,°
    With beaded bubbles winking at the brim,
      And purple-stainèd mouth;
  That I might drink, and leave the world unseen,
    And with thee fade away into the forest dim.                  20

### III

Fade far away, dissolve, and quite forget
  What thou among the leaves hast never known,
The weariness, the fever, and the fret
  Here, where men sit and hear each other groan;
Where palsy shakes a few, sad, last gray hairs,                        25
  Where youth grows pale, and specter-thin, and dies,
    Where but to think is to be full of sorrow

---

4 *Lethe-wards:* Toward Lethe, the river of forgetfulness in the Hades of Greek mythology.    14 *Provençal song:* The medieval troubadours of Provence, France, were known for their singing.    16 *Hippocrene:* The fountain of the Muses in Greek mythology.

And leaden-eyed despairs,
Where Beauty cannot keep her lustrous eyes;
Or new Love pine at them beyond tomorrow.                    30

### IV

Away! away! for I will fly to thee,
Not charioted by Bacchus and his pards,°
But on the viewless wings of Poesy,
Though the dull brain perplexes and retards:
Already with thee! tender is the night,                      35
And haply the Queen-Moon is on her throne,
Clustered around by all her starry Fays;
But here there is no light,
Save what from heaven is with the breezes blown
Through verdurous glooms and winding mossy ways.             40

### V

I cannot see what flowers are at my feet,
Nor what soft incense hangs upon the boughs,
But, in embalmèd° darkness, guess each sweet          *perfumed*
Wherewith the seasonable month endows
The grass, the thicket, and the fruit-tree wild;             45
What hawthorn, and the pastoral eglantine;
Fast fading violets covered up in leaves;
And mid-May's eldest child,
The coming musk-rose, full of dewy wine,
The murmurous haunt of flies on summer eves.                 50

### VI

Darkling° I listen; and for many a time               *in the dark*
I have been half in love with easeful Death,
Called him soft names in many a musèd rhyme,
To take into the air my quiet breath;
Now more than ever seems it rich to die,                     55
To cease upon the midnight with no pain,
While thou art pouring forth thy soul abroad
In such an ecstasy!
Still wouldst thou sing, and I have ears in vain —
To thy high requiem become a sod.                            60

### VII

Thou wast not born for death, immortal Bird!
No hungry generations tread thee down;
The voice I hear this passing night was heard

32 *Bacchus and his pards:* The Greek god of wine traveled in a chariot drawn by leopards.

In ancient days by emperor and clown:
Perhaps the selfsame song that found a path                    65
  Through the sad heart of Ruth,° when, sick for home,
    She stood in tears amid the alien corn:
      The same that oft-times hath
  Charmed magic casements, opening on the foam
    Of perilous seas, in faery lands forlorn.                  70

### VIII

Forlorn! the very word is like a bell
  To toll me back from thee to my sole self!
Adieu! the fancy cannot cheat so well
  As she is famed to do, deceiving elf.
Adieu! adieu! thy plaintive anthem fades                       75
  Past the near meadows, over the still stream,
    Up the hill side; and now 'tis buried deep
      In the next valley-glades:
  Was it a vision, or a waking dream?
    Fled is that music: — Do I wake or sleep?                  80

66  *Ruth:*  A young widow in the Bible (see the Book of Ruth).

### CONSIDERATIONS FOR CRITICAL THINKING AND WRITING

1. FIRST RESPONSE. Why does the speaker in this ode want to leave his world for the nightingale's? What might the nightingale symbolize?

2. How does the speaker attempt to escape his world? Is he successful?

3. What changes the speaker's view of death at the end of stanza VI?

4. What does the allusion to Ruth (line 66) contribute to the ode's meaning?

5. In which lines is the imagery especially sensuous? How does this effect add to the conflict presented?

6. What calls the speaker back to himself at the end of stanza VII and the beginning of stanza VIII?

7. Choose a stanza and explain how sound is related to its meaning.

8. How regular is the stanza form of this ode?

## MICHAEL CHITWOOD (B. 1958)

### Men Throwing Bricks                                        2007

The one on the ground lofts two at a time
with just the right lift for them to finish
their rise as the one on the scaffold turns
to accept them like a gift and place them

on the growing stack. They chime slightly
on the catch. You'd have to do this daily,
morning and afternoon, not to marvel.

### Considerations for Critical Thinking and Writing

1. FIRST RESPONSE. Explain the title's ironic surprise.
2. Discuss the sounds in the poem. How does it "chime"?
3. Why is "marvel" a better choice to describe the men throwing bricks than the phrase "be impressed"?

# 8

# Patterns of Rhythm

I would define, in brief, the Poetry of words as the Rhythmical Creation of Beauty. Its sole arbiter is Taste.

— EDGAR ALLAN POE

Library of Congress
Reproduction Number:
LC-USZ62-104482.

The rhythms of everyday life surround us in regularly recurring movements and sounds. As you read these words, your heart pulsates while somewhere else a clock ticks, a cradle rocks, a drum beats, a dancer sways, a foghorn blasts, a wave recedes, or a child skips. We may tend to overlook rhythm because it is so tightly woven into the fabric of our experience, but it is there nonetheless, one of the conditions of life. Rhythm is also one of the conditions of speech because the voice alternately rises and falls as words are stressed or unstressed and as the pace quickens or slackens. In poetry *rhythm* refers to the recurrence of stressed and unstressed sounds. Depending on how the sounds are arranged, this can result in a pace that is fast or slow, choppy or smooth.

## SOME PRINCIPLES OF METER

Poets use rhythm to create pleasurable sound patterns and to reinforce meanings. "Rhythm," Edith Sitwell once observed, "might be described as, to the world of sound, what light is to the world of sight. It shapes and gives new meaning." Prose can use rhythm effectively too, but prose that does so tends to be an exception. The following exceptional lines are from a speech by Winston Churchill to the House of Commons after Allied forces lost a great battle to German forces at Dunkirk during World War II:

> We shall not flag or fail. We shall go on to the end. We shall fight in France, we shall fight on the seas and oceans, we shall fight with growing confidence and growing strength in the air, we shall defend our island, whatever the cost may be, we shall fight on the beaches, we shall fight on the landing grounds, we shall fight in the fields and in the streets, we shall fight in the hills; we shall never surrender.

The stressed repetition of "we shall" bespeaks the resolute singleness of purpose that Churchill had to convey to the British people if they were to win the war. Repetition is also one of the devices used in poetry to create rhythmic effects. In the following excerpt from "Song of the Open Road," Walt Whitman urges the pleasures of limitless freedom on his reader:

> Allons!° the road is before us!                                          *Let's go!*
> It is safe — I have tried it — my own feet have tried it well — be not detain'd!
> Let the paper remain on the desk unwritten, and the book on the
>           shelf unopen'd!
> Let the tools remain in the workshop! Let the money remain unearn'd!
> Let the school stand! mind not the cry of the teacher!                    5
> Let the preacher preach in his pulpit! Let the lawyer plead in the
>           court, and the judge expound the law.
>
> Camerado,° I give you my hand!                                           *friend*
> I give you my love more precious than money,
> I give you myself before preaching or law;
> Will you give me yourself? will you come travel with me?                  10
> Shall we stick by each other as long as we live?

These rhythmic lines quickly move away from conventional values to the open road of shared experiences. Their recurring sounds are created not by rhyme or alliteration and assonance (see Chapter 7) but by the repetition of words and phrases.

Although the repetition of words and phrases can be an effective means of creating rhythm in poetry, the more typical method consists of patterns of accented or unaccented syllables. Words contain syllables that are either stressed or unstressed. A **stress** (or **accent**) places more emphasis on one syllable than on another. We say "*syl*lable" not "syl*la*ble," "*em*phasis" not "em*pha*sis." We routinely stress syllables when we speak: "*Is* she con*tent* with the *con*tents of the *yel*low *pack*age?" To distinguish between two people we might say "Is *she* content . . . ?" In this way stress can be used to emphasize a particular word in a sentence. Poets often arrange words so that the desired meaning is suggested by the rhythm; hence emphasis is controlled by the poet rather than left entirely to the reader.

When a rhythmic pattern of stresses recurs in a poem, the result is **meter**. Taken together, all the metrical elements in a poem make up what is called the poem's **prosody**. **Scansion** consists of measuring the stresses in a line to determine its metrical pattern. Several methods can be used to mark lines. One widely used system uses ´ for a stressed syllable and ˘ for an unstressed syllable. In a sense, the stress mark represents the equivalent of tapping one's foot to a beat:

> Híckŏrÿ, díckŏrÿ, dóck,
>
> The móuse răn úp the clóck.
>
> The clóck strŭck óne,
>
> Ănd dówn hĕ rún,
>
> Híckŏrÿ, díckŏrÿ, dóck.

In the first two lines and the final line of this familiar nursery rhyme, we hear three stressed syllables. In lines 3 and 4, where the meter changes for variety, we hear just two stressed syllables. The combination of stresses provides the pleasure of the rhythm we hear.

To hear the rhythms of "Hickory, dickory, dock" does not require a formal study of meter. Nevertheless, an awareness of the basic kinds of meter that appear in English poetry can enhance your understanding of how a poem achieves its effects. Understanding the sound effects of a poem and having a vocabulary with which to discuss those effects can intensify your pleasure in poetry. Although the study of meter can be extremely technical, the terms used to describe the basic meters of English poetry are relatively easy to comprehend.

The *foot* is the metrical unit by which a line of poetry is measured. A foot usually consists of one stressed and one or two unstressed syllables. A vertical line is used to separate the feet: "The clóck | strŭck óne" consists of two feet. A foot of poetry can be arranged in a variety of patterns; here are five of the chief ones:

| Foot | Pattern | Example |
|------|---------|---------|
| iamb | ˘ ´ | ăwáy |
| trochee | ´ ˘ | Lóvelÿ |
| anapest | ˘ ˘ ´ | ŭndĕrstánd |
| dactyl | ´ ˘ ˘ | déspĕratĕ |
| spondee | ´ ´ | déad sét |

The most common lines in English poetry contain meters based on iambic feet. However, even lines that are predominantly iambic will often include variations to create particular effects. Other important patterns include trochaic, anapestic, and dactylic feet. The spondee is not a sustained meter but occurs for variety or emphasis.

*Iambic*
> Whăt képt | hĭs eyés | frŏm gív | ĭng báck | thĕ gáze

*Trochaic*
> Hé wăs | loúdĕr | thán thĕ | préachĕr

*Anapestic*
> Ĭ ăm callĕd | tŏ thĕ frónt | ŏf thĕ roóm

*Dactylic*
> Síng ĭt ăll | mérrĭlў

These meters have different rhythms and can create different effects. Iambic and anapestic are known as **rising meters** because they move from unstressed to stressed sounds, while trochaic and dactylic are known as **falling meters**. Anapests and dactyls tend to move more lightly and rapidly than iambs or trochees. Although no single kind of meter can be considered always better than another for a given subject, it is possible to determine whether the meter of a specific poem is appropriate for its subject. A serious poem about a tragic death would most likely not be well served by lilting rhythms. Keep in mind, too, that though one or another of these four basic meters might constitute the predominant rhythm of a poem, variations can occur within lines to change the pace or call attention to a particular word.

A **line** is measured by the number of feet it contains. Here, for example, is an iambic line with three feet: "Ĭf shé | shŏuld wríte | ă nóte." These are the names for line lengths:

monometer: one foot        pentameter: five feet

dimeter: two feet          hexameter: six feet

trimeter: three feet       heptameter: seven feet

tetrameter: four feet      octameter: eight feet

By combining the name of a line length with the name of a foot, we can describe the metrical qualities of a line concisely. Consider, for example, the pattern of feet and length of this line:

I didn't want the boy to hit the dog.

The iambic rhythm of this line falls into five feet; hence it is called **iambic pentameter**. Iambic is the most common pattern in English poetry because its rhythm appears so naturally in English speech and writing. Unrhymed iambic pentameter is called **blank verse**; Shakespeare's plays are built on such lines.

Less common than the iamb, trochee, anapest, or dactyl is the **spondee**, a two-syllable foot in which both syllables are stressed (′′). Note the effect of the spondaic foot at the beginning of this line:

> Déad sét | ăgaínst | thĕ plán | hĕ wént | ăwáy.

Spondees can slow a rhythm and provide variety and emphasis, particularly in iambic and trochaic lines. Also less common is a *pyrrhic* foot which consists of two unstressed syllables, as in Shakespeare's "A horse! A horse! My kingdŏm fŏr a horse!" Pyrrhic feet are typically variants for iambic verse rather than predominant patterns in lines. A line that ends with a stressed syllable is said to have a *masculine ending*, whereas a line that ends with an extra unstressed syllable is said to have a *feminine ending*. Consider, for example, these two lines from Timothy Steele's "Waiting for the Storm" (the entire poem appears on p. 178):

feminine: Thĕ sánd | ăt my fĕet | grŏw cóld | er̆,

masculine: Thĕ damp | aír chíll | and spréad.

The effects of English meters are easily seen in the following lines by Samuel Taylor Coleridge, in which the rhythm of each line illustrates the meter described in it:

Trochee trips from long to short;
From long to long in solemn sort
Slow Spondee stalks; strong foot yet ill able
Ever to come up with Dactylic trisyllable.
Iambics march from short to long —
With a leap and a bound the swift Anapests throng.

The speed of a line is also affected by the number of pauses in it. A pause within a line is called a *caesura* and is indicated by a double vertical line (‖). A caesura can occur anywhere within a line and need not be indicated by punctuation:

Camerado, ‖ I give you my hand!
I give you my love ‖ more precious than money.

A slight pause occurs within each of these lines and at its end. Both kinds of pauses contribute to the lines' rhythm.

When a line has a pause at its end, it is called an *end-stopped line*. Such pauses reflect normal speech patterns and are often marked by punctuation. A line that ends without a pause and continues into the next line for its meaning is called a *run-on line*. Running over from one line to another is also called *enjambment*. The first and eighth lines of the following poem are run-on lines; the rest are end-stopped.

## WILLIAM WORDSWORTH (1770–1850)

### My Heart Leaps Up                                                          1807

My heart leaps up when I behold
    A rainbow in the sky:
So was it when my life began;
So is it now I am a man;

So be it when I shall grow old,
  Or let me die!
The child is father of the Man;
And I could wish my days to be
Bound each to each by natural piety.

Run-on lines have a different rhythm from end-stopped lines. Lines 3 and 4 and lines 8 and 9 are iambic, but the effect of their two rhythms is very different when we read these lines aloud. The enjambment of lines 8 and 9 reinforces their meaning; just as the "days" are bound together, so are the lines.

The rhythm of a poem can be affected by several devices: the kind and number of stresses within lines, the length of lines, and the kinds of pauses that appear within lines or at their ends. In addition, as we saw in Chapter 7, the sound of a poem is affected by alliteration, assonance, rhyme, and consonance. These sounds help to create rhythms by controlling our pronunciations, as in the following lines by Alexander Pope (the entire poem appears on p. 164):

Soft is the strain when Zephyr gently blows,
And the smooth stream in smoother numbers flows;
But when loud surges lash the sounding shore,
The hoarse, rough verse should like the torrent roar.

These lines are effective because their rhythm and sound work with their meaning.

---

### Suggestions for Scanning a Poem

These suggestions should help you in talking about a poem's meter.

1. After reading the poem through, read it aloud and mark the stressed syllables in each line. Then mark the unstressed syllables.

2. From your markings, identify what kind of foot is dominant (iambic, trochaic, dactylic, or anapestic) and divide the lines into feet, keeping in mind that the vertical line marking a foot may come in the middle of a word as well as at its beginning or end.

3. Determine the number of feet in each line. Remember that there may be variations; some lines may be shorter or longer than the predominant meter. What is important is the overall pattern. Do not assume that variations represent the poet's inability to fulfill the overall pattern. Notice the effects of variations and whether they emphasize words and phrases or disrupt your expectation for some other purpose.

4. Listen for pauses within lines and mark the caesuras; many times there will be no punctuation to indicate them.

5. Recognize that scansion does not always yield a definitive measurement of a line. Even experienced readers may differ over the scansion of a given line. What is important is not a precise description of the line but an awareness of how a poem's rhythms contribute to its effects.

The following poem demonstrates how you can use an understanding of meter and rhythm to gain a greater appreciation for what a poem is saying.

## TIMOTHY STEELE (B. 1948)

### *Waiting for the Storm* 1986

Bréeze sént | ă wr̆ink | lĭng dárk | nĕss
Ácróss | thĕ b̆ay. || Ĭ knélt
B̆enéath | ăn úp | tur̆ned b́oat,
Ănd, m̆o | mĕnt b̆y m̆o | mĕnt, félt

Thĕ sánd | ăt m̆y féet | grŏw cóld | ér,
Thĕ dam̆p | áir chíll | ănd spr̆ead.
Thĕn thĕ | fir̆st ráin | dróps sóund | ĕd
Ŏn thĕ húll | ăbóve | m̆y héad.

The predominant meter of this poem is iambic trimeter, but there is plenty of variation as the storm rapidly approaches and finally begins to pelt the sheltered speaker. The emphatic spondee ("Breeze sent") pushes the darkness quickly across the bay, while the caesura at the end of the sentence in line 2 creates a pause that sets up a feeling of suspense and expectation that is measured in the ticking rhythm of line 4, a run-on line that brings us into the chilly sand and air of the second stanza. Perhaps the most impressive sound effect used in the poem appears in the second syllable of "sounded" in line 7. That "ed" precedes the sound of the poem's final word, "head," just as if it were the first drop of rain hitting the hull above the speaker. The visual, tactile, and auditory images make "Waiting for the Storm" an intense sensory experience.

# A SAMPLE STUDENT RESPONSE

Marco Pacini

Professor Fierstein

English 201

2 February 2015

The Rhythm of Anticipation in Timothy Steele's

"Waiting for the Storm"

In his poem "Waiting for the Storm," Timothy Steele uses run-on lines, or enjambment, to create a feeling of anticipation. Every line ends unfinished or is a continuation of the previous line, so we must read on to gain completion. This open-ended rhythm mirrors the waiting experienced by the speaker of the poem.

Nearly every line of the poem leaves the reader in suspense:

> I knelt
> Beneath an upturned boat,
> And, moment by moment, felt
>
> The sand at my feet grow colder,
> The damp air chill and spread. (2-6)

Action is interrupted at every line break. We have to wait to find out where the speaker knelt and what was felt, since information is given in small increments. So, like the speaker, we must take in the details of the storm little by little, "moment by moment" (4). Even when the first drops of rain hit the hull, the poem ends before we can see or feel the storm's full force, and we are left waiting, in a continuous state of anticipation. . . .

Work Cited

Steele, Timothy. "Waiting for the Storm." *Thinking and Writing about Poetry.* Ed. Michael Meyer. Boston: Bedford/St. Martin's, 2016. 178. Print.

This next poem also reinforces meanings through its use of meter and rhythm.

## WILLIAM BUTLER YEATS  (1865–1939)
### *That the Night Come*                                                    1912

She líved | in stórm | and strífe,

Her soúl | had súch | desiré

For whát | proud déath | may bríng

That ít | could nót | endúre

The cóm | mon goód | of lífe,                                               5

But líved | as 'twére | a kíng

That packed | his már | riage dáy

With bán | neret | and pén | non,

Trúmpet | and ket | tledrum,

And the | outrág | eous cán | non,                                          10

To bun | dle time | awáy

That the | night come.

Scansion reveals that the predominant meter here is iambic trimeter: each line contains three stressed and unstressed syllables that form a regular, predictable rhythm through line 7. That rhythm is disrupted, however, when the speaker compares the woman's longing for what death brings to a king's eager anticipation of his wedding night. The king packs the day with noisy fanfares and celebrations to fill up time and distract himself. Unable to accept "The common good of life," the woman fills her days with "storm and strife." In a determined effort "To bundle time away," she, like the king, impatiently awaits the night.

Lines 8–10 break the regular pattern established in the first seven lines. The extra unstressed syllable in lines 8 and 10 along with the trochaic feet in lines 9 ("Trúmpet") and 10 ("And the") interrupt the basic iambic trimeter and parallel the woman's and the king's frenetic activity. These lines thus echo the inability of the woman and king to "endure" regular or normal time. The last line is the most irregular in the poem. The final two accented syllables sound like the deep resonant beats of a kettledrum or a cannon firing. The words "night come" dramatically remind us that what the woman anticipates is not a lover but the mysterious finality of death. The meter serves, then, in both its regularity and variations to reinforce the poem's meaning and tone.

The following poems are especially rich in their rhythms and sounds. As you read and study them, notice how patterns of rhythm and the sounds of words reinforce meanings and contribute to the poems' effects. And, perhaps most important, read the poems aloud so that you can hear them.

## POEMS FOR FURTHER STUDY

### WILLIAM TROWBRIDGE (B. 1941)

### *Drumming behind You in the High School Band*    *1989*

Rehearsing in street clothes after school,
we measured off the football field
in the spice and chill of early fall.
Through roll-off, counterpoint, and turn,
by the grunt and pop of blocking drill,                                5
I marked the cadence of switching hips
no martial air could ever hold.
How left was left, how right was right!
We had a rhythm all our own
and made them march to it, slowing "The Stars                        10
and Stripes Forever" as the sun stretched
our shadows toward the rising moon
and my heart kept stepping on my heels.

#### CONSIDERATIONS FOR CRITICAL THINKING AND WRITING

1. FIRST RESPONSE. Describe the various "cadences" of this poem.
2. How are the rhythms of the lines related to their meaning?
3. Using the images from the poem to make your point, discuss whether the speaker is simply an ogling cad or something else.

### ALICE JONES (B. 1949)

### *The Foot*    *1993*

Our improbable support, erected
on the osseous architecture
of the calcaneus, talus, cuboid,
navicular, cuneiforms, metatarsals,
phalanges, a plethora of hinges,                                      5

all strung together by gliding
tendons, covered by the pearly
plantar fascia, then fat-padded
to form the sole, humble surface
of our contact with earth.                                          10

Here the body's broadest tendon
anchors the heel's fleshy base,
the finely wrinkled skin stretches
forward across the capillaried arch,
to the ball, a balance point.                                           15

A wide web of flexor tendons
and branched veins maps the dorsum,
fades into the stub-laden bone
splay, the stuffed sausage sacks
of toes, each with a tuft                                               20

of proximal hairs to introduce
the distal nail, whose useless
curve remembers an ancestor,
the vanished creature's wild
and necessary claw.                                                    25

### Considerations for Critical Thinking and Writing

1. FIRST RESPONSE. What is the effect of the diction? What sort of tone is
   established by the use of anatomical terms? How do the terms affect the
   rhythm?

2. Jones has described the form of "The Foot" as "five stubby stanzas."
   Explain why the lines of this poem may or may not warrant this description of the stanzas.

3. CRITICAL STRATEGIES. Read the section on formalist strategies (pp. 329–31)
   in Chapter 15, "Critical Strategies for Reading." Describe the effect of the
   final stanza. How would your reading be affected if the poem ended after
   the comma in the middle of line 22?

## A. E. HOUSMAN (1859–1936)

### *When I was one-and-twenty*                          *1896*

When I was one-and-twenty
    I heard a wise man say,
"Give crowns and pounds and guineas
    But not your heart away;
Give pearls away and rubies                                             5
    But keep your fancy free,"
But I was one-and-twenty,
    No use to talk to me.

When I was one-and-twenty
    I heard him say again,                                             10
"The heart out of the bosom
    Was never given in vain;

'Tis paid with sighs a plenty
      And sold for endless rue."
And I am two-and-twenty,                                           15
      And oh, 'tis true, 'tis true.

### Considerations for Critical Thinking and Writing

1. FIRST RESPONSE. How does the basic metrical pattern affect your understanding of the speaker?

2. How do lines 1–8 parallel lines 9–16 in their use of rhyme and metaphor? Are there any significant differences between the stanzas?

3. What do you think has happened to change the speaker's attitude
   toward love?

4. Explain why you agree or disagree with the advice given by the "wise
   man."

5. What is the effect of the repetition in line 16?

## Christopher Merrill (b. 1957)

### *A Boy Juggling a Soccer Ball*                              *1994*

      after practice: right foot
to left foot, stepping forward and back,
      to right foot and left foot,
and left foot up to his thigh, holding
      it on his thigh as he twists                                 5
around in a circle, until it rolls
      down the inside of his leg,
like a tickle of sweat, not catching
      and tapping on the soft
side of his foot, and juggling                                    10
      once, twice, three times,
hopping on one foot like a jump-roper
      in the gym, now trapping
and holding the ball in midair,
      balancing it on the instep                                   15
of his weak left foot, stepping forward
      and forward and back, then
lifting it overhead until it hangs there;
      and squaring off his body,
he keeps the ball aloft with a nudge                              20
      of his neck, heading it
from side to side, softer and softer,

like a dying refrain,
until the ball, slowing, balances
    itself on his hairline,                                            25
the hot sun and sweat filling his eyes
    as he jiggles this way
and that, then flicking it up gently,
    hunching his shoulders
and tilting his head back, he traps it                                 30
    in the hollow of his neck,
and bending at the waist, sees his shadow,
    his dangling T-shirt, the bent
blades of brown grass in summer heat;
    and relaxing, the ball slipping                                    35
down his back . . . and missing his foot.

He wheels around, he marches
over the ball, as if it were a rock
    he stumbled into, and pressing
his left foot against it, he pushes it                                 40
    against the inside of his right
until it pops into the air, is heeled
    over his head — the rainbow! —
and settles on his extended thigh before
    rolling over his knee and down                                     45
his shin, so he can juggle it again
    from his left foot to his right foot
— and right foot to left foot to thigh —
    as he wanders, on the last day
of summer, around the empty field.                                     50

## Considerations for Critical Thinking and Writing

1. **FIRST RESPONSE.** Read this poem aloud. How do its sounds and rhythms capture the soccer player's actions?

2. Comment on the effect of the poem's final lines.

3. How might this poem double as a description of writing a poem?

4. **CREATIVE RESPONSE.** Write a poem that captures the movement and rhythms of a sport — or another activity — for which you feel a passion.

## Connection to Another Selection

1. Compare the imagery in Merrill's poem with that in David Solway's "Windsurfing" (p. 84). How do the images contribute to the convincing description of each sport?

## Robert Herrick (1591–1674)

### *Delight in Disorder*

1648

A sweet disorder in the dress
Kindles in clothes a wantonness.
A lawn° about the shoulders thrown                    *linen scarf*
Into a fine distraction;
An erring lace, which here and there                          5
Enthralls the crimson stomacher,
A cuff neglectful, and thereby
Ribbons to flow confusedly;
A winning wave, deserving note,
In the tempestuous petticoat;                                10
A careless shoestring, in whose tie
I see a wild civility;
Do more bewitch me than when art
Is too precise in every part.

#### Considerations for Critical Thinking and Writing

1. FIRST RESPONSE. Why does the speaker in this poem value "disorder" so highly? How do the poem's organization and rhythmic order relate to its theme? Are they "precise in every part" (line 14)?

2. Which words in the poem indicate disorder? Which words indicate the speaker's response to that disorder? What are the connotative meanings of each set of words? Why are they appropriate? What do they suggest about the woman and the speaker?

3. Write a short essay in which you agree or disagree with the speaker's views on dress.

## Ben Jonson (1573–1637)

### *Still to Be Neat*

1609

Still° to be neat, still to be dressed,                    *continually*
As you were going to a feast;
Still to be powdered, still perfumed;
Lady, it is to be presumed,
Though art's hid causes are not found,                         5
All is not sweet, all is not sound.

Give me a look, give me a face
That makes simplicity a grace;
Robes loosely flowing, hair as free;
Such sweet neglect more taketh me                             10

Then all th' adulteries of art.
They strike mine eyes, but not my heart.

CONSIDERATIONS FOR CRITICAL THINKING AND WRITING

1. FIRST RESPONSE. What are the speaker's reservations about the lady in the first stanza? What do you think "sweet" means in line 6?

2. What does the speaker want from the lady in the second stanza? How has the meaning of "sweet" shifted from line 6 to line 10? What other words in the poem are especially charged with connotative meanings?

3. How do the rhythms of Jonson's lines help to reinforce meanings? Pay particular attention to lines 6 and 12.

CONNECTIONS TO OTHER SELECTIONS

1. Write an essay comparing the themes of "Still to Be Neat" and Herrick's preceding poem, "Delight in Disorder." How do the speakers make similar points but from different perspectives?

2. How does the rhythm of "Still to Be Neat" compare with that of "Delight in Disorder"? Which do you find more effective? Explain why.

## WILLIAM BLAKE (1757–1827)

### *The Lamb*                        *1789*

Hulton Archive/Getty Images.

Little Lamb, who made thee?
  Dost thou know who made thee?
Gave thee life, and bid thee feed
By the stream and o'er the mead;
Gave thee clothing of delight,
Softest clothing, wooly, bright;
Gave thee such a tender voice,
Making all the vales rejoice?
  Little Lamb, who made thee?
  Dost thou know who made thee?

Little Lamb, I'll tell thee,
  Little Lamb, I'll tell thee:
He is callèd by thy name,
For he calls himself a Lamb.
He is meek, and he is mild;                    15
He became a little child.
I a child, and thou a lamb,
We are callèd by his name.
  Little Lamb, God bless thee!
  Little Lamb, God bless thee!                 20

### Considerations for Critical Thinking and Writing

1. FIRST RESPONSE. This poem is from Blake's *Songs of Innocence*. Describe its tone. How do the meter, rhyme, and repetition help to characterize the speaker's voice?

2. Why is it significant that the animal addressed by the speaker is a lamb? What symbolic value would be lost if the animal were, for example, a doe?

3. How does the second stanza answer the question raised in the first? What is the speaker's view of the creation?

## WILLIAM BLAKE (1757–1827)

### *The Tyger*                                                                              *1794*

Tyger! Tyger! burning bright
In the forests of the night,
What immortal hand or eye
Could frame thy fearful symmetry?

In what distant deeps or skies                                              5
Burnt the fire of thine eyes?
On what wings dare he aspire?
What the hand dare seize the fire?

And what shoulder, and what art,
Could twist the sinews of thy heart?                                       10
And when thy heart began to beat,
What dread hand? and what dread feet?

What the hammer? what the chain?
In what furnace was thy brain?
What the anvil? what dread grasp                                           15
Dare its deadly terrors clasp?

When the stars threw down their spears,
And watered heaven with their tears,
Did he smile his work to see?
Did he who made the Lamb make thee?                                        20

Tyger! Tyger! burning bright
In the forests of the night,
What immortal hand or eye
Dare frame thy fearful symmetry?

### Considerations for Critical Thinking and Writing

1. FIRST RESPONSE. This poem from Blake's *Songs of Experience* is often paired with "The Lamb." Describe the poem's tone. Is the speaker's voice the same here as in "The Lamb"? Which words are repeated, and how do they contribute to the tone?

2. What is revealed about the nature of the tiger by the words used to describe its creation? What do you think the tiger symbolizes?

3. Unlike in "The Lamb," more than one question is raised in "The Tyger." What are these questions? Are they answered?

4. Compare the rhythms in "The Lamb" and "The Tyger." Each basically uses a seven-syllable line, but the effects are very different. Why?

5. Using these two poems as the basis of your discussion, describe what distinguishes innocence from experience.


CARL SANDBURG (1878–1967)

## *Chicago*                                                                1916

Hog Butcher for the World,
Tool Maker, Stacker of Wheat,
Player with Railroads and the Nation's Freight Handler;
Stormy, husky, brawling,
City of the Big Shoulders:                                                    5

They tell me you are wicked and I believe them, for I have seen your painted
    women under the gas lamps luring the farm boys.
And they tell me you are crooked and I answer: Yes, it is true I have seen the
    gunman kill and go free to kill again.
And they tell me you are brutal and my reply is: On the faces of women and
    children I have seen the marks of wanton hunger.
And having answered so I turn once more to those who sneer at this my
    city, and I give them back the sneer and say to them:
Come and show me another city with lifted head singing so proud to be
    alive and coarse and strong and cunning.                                  10
Flinging magnetic curses amid the toil of piling job on job, here is a tall bold
    slugger set vivid against the little soft cities;
Fierce as a dog with tongue lapping for action, cunning as a savage pitted
    against the wilderness,
    Bareheaded,
    Shoveling,
    Wrecking,                                                                 15
    Planning,
    Building, breaking, rebuilding,
Under the smoke, dust all over his mouth, laughing with white teeth,
Under the terrible burden of destiny laughing as a young man laughs,
Laughing even as an ignorant fighter laughs who has never lost a battle,     20
Bragging and laughing that under his wrist is the pulse, and under his ribs
    the heart of the people,
    Laughing!

Laughing the stormy, husky, brawling laughter of Youth, half-naked,
     sweating, proud to be Hog Butcher, Tool Maker, Stacker of Wheat,
     Player with Railroads and Freight Handler to the Nation.

### CONSIDERATIONS FOR CRITICAL THINKING AND WRITING

1. FIRST RESPONSE. Sandburg's personification of Chicago creates a strong
   identity for the city. Explain why you find the city attractive or not.

2. How do the length and rhythm of lines 1 to 5 compare with those of the
   final lines?

3. CREATIVE RESPONSE. Using "Chicago" as a model for style, try writing a
   tribute or condemnation about a place that you know well. Make an effort
   to use vivid images and stylistic techniques that capture its rhythms.

### CONNECTION TO ANOTHER SELECTION

1. Compare "Chicago" with William Blake's "London" (p. 92) in style and theme.

## JOHN MALONEY (B. 1947)

## *Good!*                                                              *1999*

The ball goes up off glass and rebounded
down the court, outlet flung to the quick guard
like clicking seconds: he dribbles, hounded
by hands, calls the play, stops short, looking hard
for a slant opening, fakes it twice, passes                              5
into the center — he lobs to the small
forward, top of the key, a pick: asses
crash (the pick-and-roll), he cuts, bumps, the ball
reaches him as he turns, dribbles, sends it
back to the baseline, forward back to him,                              10
jump — and in midair, twisting, he bends it
over a tangle of arms — SHOOTS, the rim
rattles as it jerks against the back joints,
and into the net, trippingly drop two points.

### CONSIDERATIONS FOR CRITICAL THINKING AND WRITING

1. FIRST RESPONSE. Comment on the effects of the lines' rhythms.

2. Notice the precise pattern of rhyme. How is that related to the action in
   the poem?

### CONNECTION TO ANOTHER SELECTION

1. Compare the diction and tone in "Good!" and in Christopher Merrill's
   "A Boy Juggling a Soccer Ball" (p. 183).

## THEODORE ROETHKE (1908–1963)

### *My Papa's Waltz*        *1948*

The whiskey on your breath
Could make a small boy dizzy;
But I hung on like death:
Such waltzing was not easy.

We romped until the pans       5
Slid from the kitchen shelf;
My mother's countenance
Could not unfrown itself.

The hand that held my wrist
Was battered on one knuckle;       10
At every step you missed
My right ear scraped a buckle.

You beat time on my head
With a palm caked hard by dirt,
Then waltzed me off to bed       15
Still clinging to your shirt.

### CONSIDERATIONS FOR CRITICAL THINKING AND WRITING

1. FIRST RESPONSE. What details characterize the father in this poem? How does the speaker's choice of words reveal his feeling about his father? Is the remembering speaker still a boy?

2. Characterize the rhythm of the poem. Does it move "like death" (line 3), or is it more like a waltz? Is the rhythm regular throughout the poem? What is its effect?

3. Comment on the appropriateness of the title. Why do you suppose Roethke didn't use "My Father's Waltz"?

## Perspective

## LOUISE BOGAN (1897–1970)

### *On Formal Poetry*        *1953*

What is formal poetry? It is poetry written in form. And what is *form*? The elements of form, so far as poetry is concerned, are meter and rhyme. Are these elements merely mold and ornaments that have been impressed upon poetry from without? Are they indeed restrictions which bind and fetter language and the thought and emotion behind, under, within language in a repressive way? Are they arbitrary rules which have lost all validity since they have been broken to good purpose by "experimental poets," ancient and modern? Does the breaking up of form, or its total elimination, always result in an increase of power and of effect; and is any return to form a sort of relinquishment of freedom, or retreat to old fogeyism?

From *A Poet's Alphabet*

### Considerations for Critical Thinking and Writing

1. Choose one of the questions Bogan raises and write an essay in response to it using two or three poems from this chapter to illustrate your answer.

2. CREATIVE RESPONSE. Try writing a poem in meter and rhyme. Does the experience make your writing feel limited or not?

# 9

# Poetic Forms

© William Hathaway.

Writing a poem is like repacking a small suitcase for a long trip over and over. The balance of want and need.

—WILLIAM HATHAWAY

Poems come in a variety of shapes. Although the best poems always have their own unique qualities, many of them also conform to traditional patterns. Frequently the *form* of a poem—its overall structure or shape—follows an already established design. A poem that can be categorized by the patterns of its lines, meter, rhymes, and stanzas is considered a *fixed form* because it follows a prescribed model such as a sonnet. However, poems written in a fixed form do not always fit models precisely; writers sometimes work variations on traditional forms to create innovative effects.

Not all poets are content with variations on traditional forms. Some prefer to create their own structures and shapes. Poems that do not conform to established patterns of meter, rhyme, and stanza are called *free verse* or *open form* poetry. (See Chapter 10 for further discussion of open forms.) This kind of poetry creates its own ordering principles through the careful arrangement of words and phrases in line lengths that embody rhythms appropriate to the meaning. Modern and contemporary poets in particular have learned to use the blank space on the page as a significant functional element (for a vivid example, see E. E. Cummings's "l(a" p. 23). Good poetry of this kind is structured in ways that can be as demanding, interesting, and satisfying as fixed forms. Open and fixed forms represent different poetic styles, but they are identical in the sense that both use language in concentrated ways to convey meanings, experiences, emotions, and effects.

## SOME COMMON POETIC FORMS

A familiarity with some of the most frequently used fixed forms of poetry is useful because it allows for a better understanding of how a poem works. Classifying patterns allows us to talk about the effects of established rhythm and rhyme and to recognize how significant variations from them affect the pace and meaning of the lines. An awareness of form also allows us to anticipate how a poem is likely to proceed. As we shall see, a sonnet creates a different set of expectations in a reader from those of, say, a limerick. A reader isn't likely to find in limericks the kind of serious themes that often make their way into sonnets. The discussion that follows identifies some of the important poetic forms frequently encountered in English poetry.

The shape of a fixed-form poem is often determined by the way in which the lines are organized into stanzas. A *stanza* consists of a grouping of lines, set off by a space, that usually has a set pattern of meter and rhyme. This pattern is ordinarily repeated in other stanzas throughout the poem. What is usual is not obligatory, however; some poems may use a different pattern for each stanza, somewhat like paragraphs in prose.

Traditionally, though, stanzas do share a common **rhyme scheme**, the pattern of end rhymes. We can map out rhyme schemes by noting patterns of rhyme with lowercase letters: the first rhyme sound is designated *a*, the second becomes *b*, the third *c*, and so on. Using this system, we can describe the rhyme scheme in the following poem this way: *aabb, ccdd, eeff.*

## A. E. HOUSMAN (1859–1936)
### *Loveliest of trees, the cherry now*                    1896

| | |
|---|---|
| Loveliest of trees, the cherry now | *a* |
| Is hung with bloom along the bough, | *a* |
| And stands about the woodland ride | *b* |
| Wearing white for Eastertide. | *b* |
| | |
| Now, of my threescore years and ten, | *c* |
| Twenty will not come again, | *c* |
| And take from seventy springs a score, | *d* |
| It only leaves me fifty more. | *d* |
| | |
| And since to look at things in bloom | *e* |
| Fifty springs are little room, | *e* |
| About the woodlands I will go | *f* |
| To see the cherry hung with snow. | *f* |

5

10

### CONSIDERATIONS FOR CRITICAL THINKING AND WRITING

1. FIRST RESPONSE. What is the speaker's attitude in this poem toward time and life?

2. Why is spring an appropriate season for the setting rather than, say, winter?

3. Paraphrase each stanza. How do the images in each reinforce the poem's themes?

4. Lines 1 and 12 are not intended to rhyme, but they are close. What is the effect of the near rhyme of "now" and "snow"? How does the rhyme enhance the theme?

Poets often create their own stanzaic patterns; hence there is an infinite number of kinds of stanzas. One way of talking about stanzaic forms is to describe a given stanza by how many lines it contains.

A *couplet* consists of two lines that usually rhyme and have the same meter; couplets are frequently not separated from each other by space on the page. A *heroic couplet* consists of rhymed iambic pentameter. Here is an example from Alexander Pope's "Essay on Criticism":

| | |
|---|---|
| One science only will one genius fit; | *a* |
| So vast is art, so narrow human wit: | *a* |
| Not only bounded to peculiar arts, | *b* |
| But oft in those confined to single parts. | *b* |

A *tercet* is a three-line stanza. When all three lines rhyme, they are called a *triplet*. Two triplets make up this captivating poem.

## ROBERT HERRICK (1591–1674)

## *Upon Julia's Clothes*                                            *1648*

| | |
|---|---|
| Whenas in silks my Julia goes, | *a* |
| Then, then, methinks, how sweetly flows | *a* |
| That liquefaction of her clothes. | *a* |
| | |
| Next, when I cast mine eyes, and see | *b* |
| That brave vibration, each way free, | *b* |
| O, how that glittering taketh me! | *b* |

### CONSIDERATIONS FOR CRITICAL THINKING AND WRITING

1. FIRST RESPONSE. What purpose does alliteration serve in this poem?

2. Comment on the effect of the meter. How is it related to the speaker's description of Julia's clothes?

3. Look up the word *brave* in the *Oxford English Dictionary*. Which of its meanings is appropriate to describe Julia's movement? Some readers

interpret lines 4–6 to mean that Julia has no clothes on. What do you think?

### CONNECTION TO ANOTHER SELECTION

1. Compare the tone of this poem with that of Paul Humphrey's "Blow" (p. 166). Are the situations and speakers similar? Is there any difference in tone between these two poems?

**Terza rima** consists of an interlocking three-line rhyme scheme: *aba, bcb, cdc, ded,* and so on. Dante's *Divine Comedy* uses this pattern, as does Robert Frost's "Acquainted with the Night" (p. 121) and Percy Bysshe Shelley's "Ode to the West Wind" (p. 214).

A **quatrain**, or four-line stanza, is the most common stanzaic form in the English language and can have various meters and rhyme schemes (if any). The most common rhyme schemes are *aabb, abba, aaba,* and *abcb.* This last pattern is especially characteristic of the popular **ballad stanza**, which consists of alternating eight- and six-syllable lines. Samuel Taylor Coleridge adopted this pattern in "The Rime of the Ancient Mariner"; here is one representative stanza:

All in a hot and copper sky
The bloody Sun, at noon,
Right up above the mast did stand,
No bigger than the Moon.

There are a number of longer stanzaic forms, and the list of types of stanzas could be extended considerably, but knowing these three most basic patterns should prove helpful to you in talking about the form of a great many poems. In addition to stanzaic forms, there are fixed forms that characterize entire poems. Lyric poems can be, for example, sonnets, villanelles, sestinas, or epigrams.

## Sonnet

The **sonnet** has been a popular literary form in English since the sixteenth century, when it was adopted from the Italian *sonnetto*, meaning "little song." A sonnet consists of fourteen lines, usually written in iambic pentameter. Because the sonnet has been such a favorite form, writers have experimented with many variations on its essential structure. Nevertheless, there are two basic types of sonnets: the Italian and the English.

The **Italian sonnet** (also known as the **Petrarchan sonnet**, from the fourteenth-century Italian poet Petrarch) divides into two parts. The first eight lines (the **octave**) typically rhyme *abbaabba*. The final six lines (the **sestet**) may vary; common patterns are *cdecde, cdcdcd,* and *cdccdc*. Very often the octave presents a situation, an attitude, or a problem that the sestet comments upon or resolves, as in John Keats's "On First Looking into Chapman's Homer."

## John Keats (1795–1821)

### On First Looking into Chapman's Homer°    *1816*

Much have I traveled in the realms of gold,
    And many goodly states and
        kingdoms seen;
    Round many western islands have I
        been
Which bards in fealty to Apollo° hold.
Oft of one wide expanse had I been told
    That deep-browed Homer ruled as
        his demesne;
    Yet did I never breathe its pure

Time Life Pictures/Getty Images.

        serene°                                                           *atmosphere*
Till I heard Chapman speak out loud and bold:
Then felt I like some watcher of the skies
    When a new planet swims into his ken;                               10
Or like stout Cortez° when with eagle eyes
    He stared at the Pacific — and all his men
Looked at each other with a wild surmise —
    Silent, upon a peak in Darien.

*Chapman's Homer:* Before reading George Chapman's (ca. 1560–1634) poetic Elizabethan translations of Homer's *Iliad* and *Odyssey*, Keats had known only stilted and pedestrian eighteenth-century translations.    4 *Apollo:* Greek god of poetry.    11 *Cortez:* Vasco Núñez de Balboa, not Hernando Cortés, was the first European to sight the Pacific from Darien, a peak in Panama.

### Considerations for Critical Thinking and Writing

1. **first response.** How do the images shift from the octave to the sestet? How does the tone change? Does the meaning change as well?

2. What is the controlling metaphor of this poem?

3. What is it that the speaker discovers?

4. How does the rhythm of the lines change between the octave and the sestet? How does that change reflect the tones of both the octave and the sestet?

5. Does Keats's mistake concerning Cortés and Balboa affect your reading of the poem? Explain why or why not.

The Italian sonnet pattern is also used in the next sonnet, but notice that the thematic break between octave and sestet comes within line 9 rather than between lines 8 and 9. This unconventional break helps to reinforce the speaker's impatience with the conventional attitudes he describes.

# William Wordsworth (1770–1850)

## *The World Is Too Much with Us*                                   *1807*

The world is too much with us; late and soon,
Getting and spending, we lay waste our powers;
Little we see in Nature that is ours;
We have given our hearts away, a sordid boon!
This Sea that bares her bosom to the moon;                          5
The winds that will be howling at all hours,
And are up-gathered now like sleeping flowers;
For this, for everything, we are out of tune;
It moves us not. — Great God! I'd rather be
A Pagan suckled in a creed outworn;                                 10
So might I, standing on this pleasant lea,
Have glimpses that would make me less forlorn;
Have sight of Proteus rising from the sea;
Or hear old Triton blow his wreathèd horn.

### Considerations for Critical Thinking and Writing

1. **first response.** What is the speaker's complaint in this sonnet? How do the conditions described affect him?

2. Look up "Proteus" and "Triton." What do these mythological allusions contribute to the sonnet's tone?

3. What is the effect of the personification of the sea and wind in the octave?

### Connection to Another Selection

1. Compare the theme of this sonnet with that of Gerard Manley Hopkins's "God's Grandeur" (p. 157).

The **English sonnet**, more commonly known as the **Shakespearean sonnet**, is organized into three quatrains and a couplet, which typically rhyme *abab cdcd efef gg*. This rhyme scheme is more suited to English poetry because English has fewer rhyming words than Italian. English sonnets, because of their four-part organization, also have more flexibility about where thematic breaks can occur. Frequently, however, the most pronounced break or turn comes with the concluding couplet.

In the following Shakespearean sonnet, the three quatrains compare the speaker's loved one to a summer's day and explain why the loved one is even more lovely. The couplet bestows eternal beauty and love upon both the loved one and the sonnet.

## WILLIAM SHAKESPEARE (1564–1616)

### *Shall I compare thee to a summer's day?*    *1609*

Shall I compare thee to a summer's day?
Thou art more lovely and more temperate:
Rough winds do shake the darling buds of May,
And summer's lease hath all too short a date.
Sometime too hot the eye of heaven shines,                              5
And often is his gold complexion dimmed;
And every fair from fair sometime declines,
By chance, or nature's changing course, untrimmed.
But thy eternal summer shall not fade,
Nor lose possession of that fair thou ow'st°                *possess*   10
Nor shall death brag thou wand'rest in his shade,
When in eternal lines to time thou grow'st.
    So long as men can breathe or eyes can see,
    So long lives this, and this gives life to thee.

#### CONSIDERATIONS FOR CRITICAL THINKING AND WRITING

1. FIRST RESPONSE. Describe the shift in tone and subject matter that begins in line 9.
2. Why is the speaker's loved one more lovely than a summer's day? What qualities does he admire in the loved one?
3. What does the couplet say about the relation between art and love?
4. Which syllables are stressed in the final line? How do these syllables relate to the line's meaning?

Sonnets have been the vehicles for all kinds of subjects, including love, death, politics, and cosmic questions. Although most sonnets tend to treat their subjects seriously, this fixed form does not mean a fixed expression; humor is also possible in it. Compare this next Shakespearean sonnet with "Shall I compare thee to a summer's day?" They are, finally, both love poems, but their tones are markedly different.

## WILLIAM SHAKESPEARE (1564–1616)

### *My mistress' eyes are nothing like the sun*    *1609*

My mistress' eyes are nothing like the sun;
Coral is far more red than her lips' red;
If snow be white, why then her breasts are dun;
If hairs be wires, black wires grow on her head.
I have seen roses damasked red and white,                               5
But no such roses see I in her cheeks;
And in some perfumes is there more delight
Than in the breath that from my mistress reeks.

I love to hear her speak, yet well I know
That music hath a far more pleasing sound;                    10
I grant I never saw a goddess go:
My mistress, when she walks, treads on the ground.
    And yet, by heaven, I think my love as rare
    As any she,° belied with false compare.                    *lady*

### CONSIDERATIONS FOR CRITICAL THINKING AND WRITING

1. FIRST RESPONSE.  What does "mistress" mean in this sonnet? Write a description of this particular mistress based on the images used in the sonnet.

2. What sort of person is the speaker? Does he truly love the woman he describes?

3. In what sense are this sonnet and "Shall I compare thee to a summer's day?" about poetry as well as love?

## EDNA ST. VINCENT MILLAY  (1892–1950)

### *I will put Chaos into fourteen lines*          1954

I will put Chaos into fourteen lines
And keep him there; and let him thence escape
If he be lucky; let him twist, and ape
Flood, fire, and demon — his adroit designs
Will strain to nothing in the strict confines
Of this sweet Order, where, in pious rape,
I hold his essence and amorphous shape,
Till he with Order mingles and combines.
Past are the hours, the years, of our duress,
His arrogance, our awful servitude:                    10
I have him. He is nothing more nor less
Than something simple not yet understood;
I shall not even force him to confess;
Or answer. I will only make him good.

© Corbis.

### CONSIDERATIONS FOR CRITICAL THINKING AND WRITING

1. FIRST RESPONSE.  Does the poem contain "Chaos"? If so, how? If not, why not?

2. What properties of a sonnet does this poem possess?

3. What do you think is meant by the phrase "pious rape" in line 6?

4. What is the effect of the personification in the poem?

### CONNECTION TO ANOTHER SELECTION

1. Compare the theme of this poem with that of Robert Frost's "Design" (p. 271).

# A SAMPLE STUDENT RESPONSE

Alexia Sykes
Professor Jones
English 211
1 March 2015

The Fixed Form in Edna St. Vincent Millay's

"I will put Chaos into fourteen lines"

In her poem "I will put Chaos into fourteen lines," Edna St. Vincent Millay does exactly what her title promises. Though the poem is of a fixed form, using patterns in meter, rhyme, line, and stanza, a sense of chaos is created through a complex structure, only to be calmed in the last six lines by a simpler rhyme scheme.

The first octave of the poem is structured *abbaabba,* a structure commonly found in sonnets. Although this is a fixed structure, the rhyme scheme is so complex that a chaotic tone is established:

> Flood, fire, and demon — his adroit designs
>
> Will strain to nothing in the strict confines
>
> Of this sweet Order, where, in pious rape,
>
> I hold his essence and amorphous shape,
>
> Till he with Order mingles and combines. (lines 4-8)

Rhyming couplets are fired at the reader and the seemingly haphazard pattern gives the impression that there is little or no structure at all, particularly on a first reading. It is difficult to determine the framework of the poem, and the absence of a decipherable structure creates in the reader a feeling of randomness, the same disorder mentioned by the speaker. It is not until the end of the poem that relief is provided. The final six lines contain a much simpler, more repetitive structure: *cdcdcd*. This rhyme scheme provides stability and consistency. The pattern is simple and predictable; order is restored. Chaos has been tamed and made "good" (14) by the poem's form. . . .

Work Cited

Millay, Edna St. Vincent. "I will put Chaos into fourteen lines." *Thinking and Writing about Poetry*. Ed. Michael Meyer. Boston: Bedford/St. Martin's, 2016. 199. Print.

## Sherman Alexie (b. 1966)

### *The Facebook Sonnet*                    *2011*

Welcome to the endless high-school
Reunion. Welcome to past friends
And lovers, however kind or cruel.
Let's undervalue and unmend

The present. Why can't we pretend                    5
Every stage of life is the same?
Let's exhume, resume, and extend
Childhood. Let's all play the games

That occupy the young. Let fame
And shame intertwine. Let one's search                    10
For God become public domain.
Let church.com become our church.

Let's sign up, sign in, and confess
Here at the altar of loneliness.

#### Considerations for Critical Thinking and Writing

1. FIRST RESPONSE. Why does a fixed form rather than an open form seem especially appropriate for the themes of this poem?
2. What type of sonnet is this?
3. How might Facebook be regarded as the "altar of loneliness" (line 14)? Explain why you agree or disagree with the speaker's assessment.

## Mark Jarman (b. 1952)

### *Unholy Sonnet*                    *1993*

After the praying, after the hymn-singing,
After the sermon's trenchant commentary
On the world's ills, which make ours secondary,
After communion, after the hand-wringing,
And after peace descends upon us, bringing                    5
Our eyes up to regard the sanctuary
And how the light swords through it, and how, scary
In their sheer numbers, motes of dust ride, clinging—
There is, as doctors say about some pain,
Discomfort knowing that despite your prayers,                    10
Your listening and rejoicing, your small part
In this communal stab at coming clean,
There is one stubborn remnant of your cares
Intact. There is still murder in your heart.

### Considerations for Critical Thinking and Writing

1. FIRST RESPONSE. Describe the rhyme scheme and structure of this sonnet. Explain why it is an English or Italian sonnet.

2. What are the effects of the use of "after" in lines 1, 2, 4, and 5 and "there" in lines 9, 13, and 14?

3. In what sense might this poem be summed up as a "communal stab" (line 12)? Discuss the accuracy of this assessment.

4. CREATIVE RESPONSE. Try writing a reply to the theme of Jarman's poem using the same sonnet form that he uses.

### Connection to Another Selection

1. Jarman has said that his "Unholy Sonnets" (there are about twenty of them) are modeled after John Donne's *Holy Sonnets* but that he does not share the same Christian assumptions about faith and mercy that inform Donne's sonnets. Instead, Jarman says, he "work[s] against any assumption or shared expression of faith, to write a devotional poetry against the grain." Keeping this statement in mind, write an essay comparing and contrasting the tone and theme of Jarman's sonnet with those of John Donne's "Death Be Not Proud" (p. 239).

## WILLIAM BAER (B. 1948)

### *Letter of Resignation*                                   2008

Dear [blank]: After much deliberation,
without qualm, scruple, or further delay,
I hereby tender my formal resignation
as your lover and future fiancé.
The job provides too little satisfaction:                          5
too many hours of unneeded duress,
a paucity of productive interaction,
uncertain working conditions, and endless stress.
Pay-wise, I'm undervalued and disenchanted:
advancement's slow, the bonus is routine,                          10
my "on-call" overtime is taken for granted,
and benefits are few and far between.
This document, I'm hopeful, underscores
my deep regret. I'm very truly yours. . . .

### Considerations for Critical Thinking and Writing

1. FIRST RESPONSE. Comment on the appropriateness of the poem's diction.

2. How is this English sonnet structured? Describe the effects of the meters.

3. Discuss the effect of the ironic tone in the final line.

<small>**CONNECTION TO ANOTHER SELECTION**</small>

1. Compare the form and content of "Letter of Resignation" and Billie Bolton's "Memorandum" (p. 235).

**R. S. GWYNN** (B. 1948)

## *Shakespearean Sonnet*                                    *2010*

*With a first line taken from the tv listings*

A man is haunted by his father's ghost.
Boy meets girl while feuding families fight.
A Scottish king is murdered by his host.
Two couples get lost on a summer night.
A hunchback murders all who block his way.                    5
A ruler's rivals plot against his life.
A fat man and a prince make rebels pay.
A noble Moor has doubts about his wife.
An English king decides to conquer France.
A duke learns that his best friend is a she.                 10
A forest sets the scene for this romance.
An old man and his daughters disagree.
A Roman leader makes a big mistake.
A sexy queen is bitten by a snake.

<small>**CONSIDERATIONS FOR CRITICAL THINKING AND WRITING**</small>

1. FIRST RESPONSE. How many Shakespearean plays can you identify from the fourteen encapsulated plots that make up this poem?

2. Discuss the significance of the title.

3. CREATIVE RESPONSE. Try your hand at creating a poem — a sonnet or another form — in whole or in part from TV listings.

## *Villanelle*

The *villanelle* is a fixed form consisting of nineteen lines of any length divided into six stanzas: five tercets and a concluding quatrain. The first and third lines of the initial tercet rhyme; these rhymes are repeated in each subsequent tercet (*aba*) and in the final two lines of the quatrain (*abaa*). Moreover, line 1 appears in its entirety as lines 6, 12, and 18, while line 3 appears as lines 9, 15, and 19. This form may seem to risk monotony, but in competent hands a villanelle can create haunting echoes, as in Dylan Thomas's "Do Not Go Gentle into That Good Night."

## Dylan Thomas (1914–1953)

### Do Not Go Gentle into That Good Night                              1952

Do not go gentle into that good night,
Old age should burn and rave at close of day;
Rage, rage against the dying of the light.

Though wise men at their end know dark is right,
Because their words had forked no lightning they                       5
Do not go gentle into that good night.

Good men, the last wave by, crying how bright
Their frail deeds might have danced in a green bay,
Rage, rage against the dying of the light.

Wild men who caught and sang the sun in flight,                       10
And learn, too late, they grieved it on its way,
Do not go gentle into that good night.

Grave men, near death, who see with blinding sight
Blind eyes could blaze like meteors and be gay,
Rage, rage against the dying of the light.                            15

And you, my father, there on the sad height,
Curse, bless, me now with your fierce tears, I pray.
Do not go gentle into that good night.
Rage, rage against the dying of the light.

#### Considerations for Critical Thinking and Writing

1. FIRST RESPONSE. How does Thomas vary the meanings of the poem's two refrains: "Do not go gentle into that good night" and "Rage, rage against the dying of the light"?
2. Thomas's father was close to death when this poem was written. How does the tone contribute to the poem's theme?
3. How is "good" used in line 1?
4. Characterize the men who are "wise" (line 4), "Good" (7), "Wild" (10), and "Grave" (13).
5. What do figures of speech contribute to this poem?
6. Discuss this villanelle's sound effects.

## Edwin Arlington Robinson (1869–1935)

### The House on the Hill                                               1894

They are all gone away,
  The House is shut and still,
There is nothing more to say.

Through broken walls and gray
   The winds blow bleak and shrill:                    5
They are all gone away.

Nor is there one to-day
   To speak them good or ill:
There is nothing more to say.

Why is it then we stray                                        10
   Around the sunken sill?
They are all gone away,

And our poor fancy-play
   For them is wasted skill:
There is nothing more to say.                                  15

There is ruin and decay
   In the House on the Hill:
They are all gone away,
There is nothing more to say.

### Considerations for Critical Thinking and Writing

1. FIRST RESPONSE. What connotations does "on the hill" suggest to you?
2. Is this poem about a house or something else?

### Connection to Another Selection

1. Compare the images and themes of "The House on the Hill" with Edgar Allan Poe's "The Haunted Palace" (p. 123).

## Sestina

Although the **sestina** usually does not rhyme, it is perhaps an even more demanding fixed form than the villanelle. A sestina consists of thirty-nine lines of any length divided into six six-line stanzas and a three-line concluding stanza called an **envoy**. The difficulty lies in repeating the six words at the ends of the first stanza's lines at the ends of the lines in the other five six-line stanzas as well. Those words must also appear in the final three lines, where they often resonate important themes. The sestina originated in the Middle Ages, but contemporary poets continue to find it a fascinating and challenging form.

## Algernon Charles Swinburne (1837–1909)
### Sestina                                                    1872

I saw my soul at rest upon a day
As a bird sleeping in the nest of night,
Among soft leaves that give the starlight way

To touch its wings but not its eyes with light;
So that it knew as one in visions may,                                  5
And knew not as men waking, of delight.

This was the measure of my soul's delight;
It had no power of joy to fly by day,
Nor part in the large lordship of the light;
But in a secret moon-beholden way                                      10
Had all its will of dreams and pleasant night,
And all the love and life that sleepers may.

But such life's triumph as men waking may
It might not have to feed its faint delight
Between the stars by night and sun by day,                             15
Shut up with green leaves and a little light;
Because its way was as a lost star's way,
A world's not wholly known of day or night.

All loves and dreams and sounds and gleams of night
Made it all music that such minstrels may,                             20
And all they had they gave it of delight;
But in the full face of the fire of day
What place shall be for any starry light,
What part of heaven in all the wide sun's way?

Yet the soul woke not, sleeping by the way,                            25
Watched as a nursling of the large-eyed night,
And sought no strength nor knowledge of the day,
Nor closer touch conclusive of delight,
Nor mightier joy nor truer than dreamers may,
Nor more of song than they, nor more of light.                         30

For who sleeps once and sees the secret light
Whereby sleep shows the soul a fairer way
Between the rise and rest of day and night,
Shall care no more to fare as all men may,
But be his place of pain or of delight,                                35
There shall he dwell, beholding night as day.

Song, have thy day and take thy fill of light
Before the night be fallen across thy way;
Sing while he may, man hath no long delight.

### Considerations for Critical Thinking and Writing

1. **FIRST RESPONSE.** How are the six end words — "day," "night," "way," "light," "may," and "delight" — central to the sestina's meaning?

2. Number the end words of the first stanza 1, 2, 3, 4, 5, and 6, and then use those numbers for the corresponding end words in the remaining five stanzas to see how the pattern of the line-end words is worked out in this sestina. Also locate the six end words in the envoy.

3. Underline the images that seem especially vivid to you. What effects do they create? What is the tone of the sestina?

4. CRITICAL STRATEGIES. Read the section on psychological strategies (pp. 333–34) in Chapter 15, "Critical Strategies for Reading." Write a brief essay explaining why you think a poet might derive pleasure from writing in a fixed form such as a villanelle or sestina. Can you think of similar activities outside the field of writing in which discipline and restraint give pleasure? How might this reflect an author's personal psychology?

## FLORENCE CASSEN MAYERS (B. 1940)

### All-American Sestina                                    1996

One nation, indivisible
two-car garage
three strikes you're out
four-minute mile
five-cent cigar                                                5
six-string guitar

six-pack Bud
one-day sale
five-year warranty
two-way street                                                10
fourscore and seven years ago
three cheers

three-star restaurant
sixty-
four-dollar question                                          15
one-night stand
two-pound lobster
five-star general

five-course meal
three sheets to the wind                                       20
two bits
six-shooter
one-armed bandit
four-poster

four-wheel drive                                               25
five-and-dime
hole in one
three-alarm fire
sweet sixteen
two-wheeler                                                    30

two-tone Chevy
four rms, hi flr, w/vu
six-footer
high five
three-ring circus                                                      35
one-room schoolhouse

two thumbs up, five-karat diamond
Fourth of July, three-piece suit
six feet under, one-horse town

### CONSIDERATIONS FOR CRITICAL THINKING AND WRITING

1. FIRST RESPONSE. Discuss the significance of the title; what is "All-American" about this sestina?

2. How is the structure of this poem different from that of a conventional sestina? (What structural requirement does Mayers add for this sestina?)

3. Do you think important themes are raised by this poem, as is traditional for a sestina? If so, what are they? If not, what is being played with by using this convention?

### CONNECTION TO ANOTHER SELECTION

1. Describe and compare the strategy used to create meaning in "All-American Sestina" with that used by E. E. Cummings in "next to of course god america i" (p. 129).

## Epigram

An *epigram* is a brief, pointed, and witty poem. Although most rhyme and often are written in couplets, epigrams take no prescribed form. Instead, they are typically polished bits of compressed irony, satire, or paradox. Here is an epigram that defines itself.

### SAMUEL TAYLOR COLERIDGE (1772–1834)

## What Is an Epigram?                                                 1802

What is an epigram? A dwarfish whole;
Its body brevity, and wit its soul.

These additional examples by A. R. Ammons, David McCord, and Paul Laurence Dunbar satisfy Coleridge's definition.

# A. R. AMMONS (1926–2001)

## Coward                                                         1975

Bravery runs in my family.

# DAVID McCORD (1897–1997)

## Epitaph on a Waiter                                            1954

By and by
God caught his eye.

# PAUL LAURENCE DUNBAR (1872–1906)

## Theology                                  1896

There is a heaven, for ever, day by day,
The upward longing of my soul doth tell
    me so.
There is a hell, I'm quite as sure; for pray,
If there were not, where would my
    neighbors go?

© Corbis.

### CONSIDERATIONS FOR CRITICAL THINKING AND WRITING

1. FIRST RESPONSE. In what sense is each of these epigrams, as Coleridge puts it, a "dwarfish whole"?

2. Explain which of these epigrams, in addition to being witty, makes a serious point.

3. CREATIVE RESPONSE. Try writing a few epigrams that say something memorable about whatever you choose to focus on.

## Limerick

The **limerick** is always light and humorous. Its usual form consists of five predominantly anapestic lines rhyming *aabba*; lines 1, 2, and 5 contain three feet, while lines 3 and 4 contain two. Limericks have delighted everyone from schoolchildren to sophisticated adults, and they range in subject matter from the simply innocent and silly to the satiric or obscene. The sexual humor helps to explain why so many limericks are written anonymously. Here is one that is more concerned with physics than physiology.

## ARTHUR HENRY REGINALD BUTLER (1874–1944)

### *There was a young lady named Bright*                    1923

There was a young lady named Bright,
Whose speed was far faster than light,
    She set out one day,
    In a relative way,
And returned home the previous night.

This next one is a particularly clever definition of a limerick.

## LAURENCE PERRINE (1915–1995)

### *The limerick's never averse*                    1982

The limerick's never averse
To expressing itself in a terse
    Economical style,
    And yet, all the while,
The limerick's *always* a verse.

### CONSIDERATIONS FOR CRITICAL THINKING AND WRITING

1. FIRST RESPONSE. How does this limerick differ from others you know? How is it similar?

2. Scan Perrine's limerick. How do the lines measure up to the traditional fixed metrical pattern?

3. CREATIVE RESPONSE. Try writing a limerick. Use the following basic pattern.

    ⌣ ⌣ ′    ⌣ ⌣ ′    ⌣ ⌣ ′

    ⌣ ⌣ ′    ⌣ ⌣ ′    ⌣ ⌣ ′

          ⌣ ⌣ ′    ⌣ ⌣ ′

          ⌣ ⌣ ′    ⌣ ⌣ ′

    ⌣ ⌣ ′    ⌣ ⌣ ′    ⌣ ⌣ ′

You might begin with a friend's name or the name of your school or town. Your instructor is, of course, fair game, too, provided your tact matches your wit.

## Haiku

Another brief fixed poetic form, borrowed from the Japanese, is the **haiku**. A haiku is usually described as consisting of seventeen syllables organized into three unrhymed lines of five, seven, and five syllables. Owing to language difference, however, English translations of haiku are often only approximated, because a Japanese haiku exists in time (Japanese syllables have duration). The number of syllables in our sense is not as significant as the duration in Japanese. These poems typically present an intense emotion or vivid image of nature, which, in the Japanese, are also designed to lead to a spiritual insight.

### MATSUO BASHŌ (1644–1694)
#### *Under cherry trees*    *date unknown*

Under cherry trees
Soup, the salad, fish and all . . .
Seasoned with petals.

### CAROLYN KIZER (1925–2014)
#### *After Bashō*    *1984*

Tentatively, you
slip onstage this evening,
pallid, famous moon.

### SONIA SANCHEZ (B. 1934)
#### *c'mon man hold me*    *1998*

c'mon man hold me
touch me before time love me
from behind your eyes.

#### CONSIDERATIONS FOR CRITICAL THINKING AND WRITING

1. FIRST RESPONSE. What different emotions do these three haiku evoke?
2. What differences and similarities are there between the effects of a haiku and those of an epigram?
3. CREATIVE RESPONSE. Compose a haiku. Try to make it as allusive and suggestive as possible.

## *Elegy*

An elegy in classical Greek and Roman literature was written in alternating hexameter and pentameter lines. Since the seventeenth century, however, the term *elegy* has been used to describe a lyric poem written to commemorate someone who is dead. The word is also used to refer to a serious meditative poem produced to express the speaker's melancholy thoughts. Elegies no longer conform to a fixed pattern of lines and stanzas, but their characteristic subject is related to death and their tone is mournfully contemplative.

## BEN JONSON (1573–1637)

### On My First Son                                          1603

Farewell, thou child of my right hand,° and joy.
My sin was too much hope of thee, loved boy;
Seven years thou wert lent to me, and I thee pay,
Exacted by thy fate, on the just day.°                        *his birthday*
Oh, could I lose all father° now. For why                     *fatherhood*   5
Will man lament the state he should envy? —
To have so soon 'scaped world's and flesh's rage,
And, if no other misery, yet age.
Rest in soft peace, and asked, say, "Here doth lie
Ben Jonson his best piece of poetry,"                                       10
For whose sake henceforth all his vows be such
As what he loves may never like too much.

1  *child of my right hand:*  This phrase translates the Hebrew name "Benjamin," Jonson's son.

### CONSIDERATIONS FOR CRITICAL THINKING AND WRITING

1. FIRST RESPONSE. Describe the tone of this elegy. What makes it so emotionally convincing?

2. In what sense is Jonson's son "his best piece of poetry" (line 10)?

3. Interpret the final two lines. Do they seem consistent with the rest of the poem? Why or why not?

## BRENDAN GALVIN (B. 1938)

### An Evel Knievel° Elegy                                     2008

We have all felt our parachutes
malfunctioning at a job interview
or cocktail party, with bystanders
reading the freefall on our faces,
and some of us have imagined                                                5
how it must have felt for you
above the Snake River Canyon

*Evel Knievel* (1938–2007): American motorcycle stunt performer whose daredevil jumps over lines of vehicles, canyons, and rivers were nationally televised in the 1960s and 1970s.

or the fountains outside Caesar's
Palace, though a mental bungee
reversed our flops before we were                                    10
converted to sacks of poker chips and spent
a month or more in a coma. You were
our star-spangled Icarus,° Evel,
while we dressed off the rack
for working lives among the common                                   15
asps and vipers, never jumping
the rattlers in what you and
the networks considered a sport.
Stunts, Evel. We loved their heights
and distances from our gray quotidian                                20
so much we bought the kids three
hundred million dollars' worth
of your wheels and getups. You were
our airborne Elvis, and rode
your rocket-powered bike through fire.                               25
Which we admired, though some,
annealing or annulled, knew that
they stand in fire all their lives,
and turned away, and didn't applaud,
and would not suffer the loss                                        30
of your departure.

13 *Icarus:* In Greek mythology, a character who fell to the earth and died after refusing
to heed his father's advice about not flying too close to the sun on manufactured wings of
wax and feathers that melted from the heat.

### Considerations for Critical Thinking and Writing

1. **FIRST RESPONSE.** To what extent is this poem a meditation on popular culture as well as an elegy for Evel Knievel?

2. Discuss Galvin's use of metaphor to characterize Knievel. Choose three metaphors that seem especially vivid to you and explain why.

3. Discuss the thematic significance of lines 26 to 31. How would you read the poem differently if it ended in the middle of line 26?

## Ode

An **ode** is characterized by a serious topic and formal tone, but no pre-scribed formal pattern describes all odes. In some odes the pattern of each stanza is repeated throughout, while in others each stanza introduces a new pattern. Odes are lengthy lyrics that often include lofty emotions conveyed by a dignified style. Typical topics include truth, art, freedom, justice, and the meaning of life. Frequently such lyrics tend to be more public than private, and their speakers often use apostrophe.

## Percy Bysshe Shelley (1792–1822)

# Ode to the West Wind                                        1820

### I

O wild West Wind, thou breath of Autumn's being,
Thou, from whose unseen presence the leaves dead
Are driven, like ghosts from an enchanter fleeing,

Yellow, and black, and pale, and hectic red,
Pestilence-stricken multitudes: O thou,                               5
Who chariotest to their dark wintry bed

The wingèd seeds, where they lie cold and low,
Each like a corpse within its grave, until
Thine azure sister of the Spring shall blow

Her clarion o'er the dreaming earth, and fill                        10
(Driving sweet buds like flocks to feed in air)
With living hues and odors plain and hill:

Wild Spirit, which art moving everywhere;
Destroyer and preserver; hear, oh, hear!

### II

Thou on whose stream, mid the steep sky's commotion,                 15
Loose clouds like earth's decaying leaves are shed,
Shook from the tangled boughs of Heaven and Ocean,

Angels° of rain and lightning: there are spread          *messengers*
On the blue surface of thine airy surge,
Like the bright hair uplifted from the head                          20

Of some fierce Maenad,° even from the dim verge
Of the horizon to the zenith's height,
The locks of the approaching storm. Thou dirge

Of the dying year, to which this closing night
Will be the dome of a vast sepulcher,                                25
Vaulted with all thy congregated might

Of vapors, from whose solid atmosphere
Black rain, and fire, and hail will burst: oh, hear!

### III

Thou who didst waken from his summer dreams
The blue Mediterranean, where he lay,                                30
Lulled by the coil of his crystálline streams,

21 *Maenad:* In Greek mythology, a frenzied worshipper of Dionysus, god of wine and
fertility.

Beside a pumice isle in Baiae's bay,°
And saw in sleep old palaces and towers
Quivering within the wave's intenser day,

All overgrown with azure moss and flowers                    35
So sweet, the sense faints picturing them! Thou
For whose path the Atlantic's level powers

Cleave themselves into chasms, while far below
The sea-blooms and the oozy woods which wear
The sapless foliage of the ocean, know                        40

Thy voice, and suddenly grow gray with fear,
And tremble and despoil themselves: oh, hear!

### IV

If I were a dead leaf thou mightest bear;
If I were a swift cloud to fly with thee;
A wave to pant beneath thy power, and share                   45

The impulse of thy strength, only less free
Than thou, O uncontrollable! If even
I were as in my boyhood, and could be

The comrade by thy wanderings over Heaven,
As then, when to outstrip thy skyey speed                     50
Scarce seemed a vision; I would ne'er have striven

As thus with thee in prayer in my sore need.
Oh, lift me as a wave, a leaf, a cloud!
I fall upon the thorns of life! I bleed!

A heavy weight of hours has chained and bowed                 55
One too like thee: tameless, and swift, and proud.

### V

Make me thy lyre,° even as the forest is:
What if my leaves are falling like its own!
The tumult of thy mighty harmonies

Will take from both a deep, autumnal tone,                    60
Sweet though in sadness. Be thou, Spirit fierce,
My spirit! Be thou me, impetuous one!

---

32 *Baiae's bay:*  A bay in the Mediterranean Sea.    57 *Make me thy lyre:*  Sound is produced on an Aeolian lyre, or wind harp, by wind blowing across its strings.

Drive my dead thoughts over the universe
Like withered leaves to quicken a new birth!
And, by the incantation of this verse,                                    65

Scatter, as from an unextinguished hearth
Ashes and sparks, my words among mankind!
Be through my lips to unawakened earth

The trumpet of a prophecy! O Wind,
If Winter comes, can Spring be far behind?                                70

### CONSIDERATIONS FOR CRITICAL THINKING AND WRITING

1. **FIRST RESPONSE.** Write a summary of each of this ode's five sections.
2. What is the speaker's situation? What is his "sore need" (line 52)? What does the speaker ask of the wind in lines 57–70?
3. What does the wind signify in this ode? How is it used symbolically?
4. Determine the meter and rhyme of the first five stanzas. How do these elements contribute to the ode's movement? Is this pattern continued in the other four sections?

## *Parody*

A *parody* is a humorous imitation of another, usually serious, work. It can take any fixed or open form because parodists imitate the tone, language, and shape of the original. While a parody may be teasingly close to a work's style, it typically deflates the subject matter to make the original seem absurd. Parody can be used as a kind of literary criticism to expose the defects in a work, but it is also very often an affectionate acknowledgment that a well-known work has become both institutionalized in our culture and fair game for some fun. Read Robert Frost's "The Road Not Taken" (p. 256) and then study this parody.

### BLANCHE FARLEY (B. 1937)

### *The Lover Not Taken*                    *1984*

Committed to one, she wanted both
And, mulling it over, long she stood,
Alone on the road, loath
To leave, wanting to hide in the undergrowth.
This new guy, smooth as a yellow wood

Really turned her on. She liked his hair,
His smile. But the other, Jack, had a claim
On her already and she had to admit, he did wear

**WHEN I WRITE** "Keep your work, even if it is unfinished or not to your liking. It can be revised or even rewritten in another form. Maybe the original idea is what will prove valuable. Most importantly, despite all else going on in your life, despite rejection or feelings of discouragement, keep writing." —BLANCHE FARLEY

Well. In fact, to be perfectly fair,
He understood her. His long, lithe frame                                    10

Beside hers in the evening tenderly lay.
Still, if this blond guy dropped by someday,
Couldn't way just lead on to way?
No. For if way led on and Jack
Found out, she doubted if he would ever come back.                          15

Oh, she turned with a sigh.
Somewhere ages and ages hence,
She might be telling this. "And I —"
She would say, "stood faithfully by."
But by then who would know the difference?                                  20

With that in mind, she took the fast way home,
The road by the pond, and phoned the blond.

### CONSIDERATIONS FOR CRITICAL THINKING AND WRITING

1. **FIRST RESPONSE.** To what degree does this poem duplicate Frost's style? How does it differ?

2. Does this parody seem successful to you? Explain what you think makes a successful parody.

3. **CREATIVE RESPONSE.** Choose a poet whose work you know reasonably well or would like to know better and determine what is characteristic about his or her style. Then choose a poem to parody. It's probably best to attempt a short poem or a section of a long work. If you have difficulty selecting an author, you might consider Herrick, Blake, Keats, Dickinson, Whitman, Hughes, or Frost, as a number of their works are included in this book.

## Picture Poem

By arranging lines into particular shapes, poets can sometimes organize typography into **picture poems** of what they describe. Words have been arranged into all kinds of shapes, from apples to light bulbs. Notice how the shape of this next poem embodies its meaning.

> **WHEN I WRITE** "I've shared my poems with a friend, who's also a poet, for decades now. He marks them up and gives them back; I do the same for him. You need a sympathetic critic who is not you, to help make your poetry as strong and clear as possible to readers who are not you." — MICHAEL MCFEE

## MICHAEL McFEE  (B. 1954)

### *In Medias Res°*                                          *1985*

His waist
like the plot
thickens, wedding
pants now breathtaking,
belt no longer the cinch                                          5
it once was, belly's cambium
expanding to match each birthday,
his body a wad of anonymous tissue
swung in the same centrifuge of years
that separates a house from its foundation,                       10
undermining sidewalks grim with joggers
and loose-filled graves and families
and stars collapsing on themselves,
no preservation society capable
of plugging entropy's dike,                                       15
under his zipper's sneer
a belly hibernation-
soft, ready for
the kill.

*In Medias Res:*  A Latin term for a story that begins "in the middle of things."

### CONSIDERATIONS FOR CRITICAL THINKING AND WRITING

1. **FIRST RESPONSE.** Explain how the title is related to this poem's shape and meaning.
2. Identify the puns. How do they work in the poem?
3. What is "cambium" (line 6)? Why is the phrase "belly's cambium" especially appropriate?
4. What is the tone of this poem? Is it consistent throughout?

# 10

## Open Form

Christine Bennett.

I'm not very good at communicating verbally. I'm somebody who listens more than talks. I like to listen and absorb. But when I need to connect with people and I need to reach out, I write.

— RUTH FORMAN

Many poems, especially those written in the past century, are composed of lines that cannot be scanned for a fixed or predominant meter. Moreover, very often these poems do not rhyme. Known as *free verse* (from the French, *vers libre*), such lines can derive their rhythmic qualities from the repetition of words, phrases, or grammatical structures; the arrangement of words on the printed page; or some other means. In recent years the term *open form* has been used in place of *free verse* to avoid the erroneous suggestion that this kind of poetry lacks all discipline and shape.

Although the following poem does not use measurable meters, it does have rhythm.

## WALT WHITMAN (1819–1892)

### From "I Sing the Body Electric"    *1855*

© Lebrecht Authors/Lebrecht Music & Arts/
Lebrecht Music & Arts/Corbis.

O my body! I dare not desert the likes of
    you in other men and women, nor
    the likes of the parts of you,
I believe the likes of you are to stand or
    fall with the likes of the soul, (and
    that they are the soul,)
I believe the likes of you shall stand or fall
    with my poems, and that they are
    my poems.
Man's, woman's, child's, youth's, wife's,
    husband's, mother's, father's, young
    man's, young woman's poems.
Head, neck, hair, ears, drop and tympan
    of the ears.                                                        5
Eyes, eye-fringes, iris of the eye, eyebrows, and the waking or sleeping of
    the lids,
Mouth, tongue, lips, teeth, roof of the mouth, jaws, and the jaw-hinges,
Nose, nostrils of the nose, and the partition,
Cheeks, temples, forehead, chin, throat, back of the neck, neck-slue,
Strong shoulders, manly beard, scapula, hind-shoulders, and the ample
    side-round of the chest,                                          10
Upper-arm, armpit, elbow-socket, lower-arm, arm-sinews, arm-bones,
Wrist and wrist-joints, hand, palm, knuckles, thumb, forefinger, finger-
    joints, finger-nails,
Broad breast-front, curling hair of the breast, breast-bone, breast-side,
Ribs, belly, backbone, joints of the backbone,
Hips, hip-sockets, hip-strength, inward and outward round, man-balls,
    man-root,                                                             15
Strong set of thighs, well carrying the trunk above,
Leg-fibers, knee, knee-pan, upper-leg, under-leg,
Ankles, instep, foot-ball, toes, toe-joints, the heel;
All attitudes, all the shapeliness, all the belongings of my or your body or of
    any one's body, male or female,
The lung-sponges, the stomach-sac, the bowels sweet and clean,          20
The brain in its folds inside the skull-frame,
Sympathies, heart-valves, palate-valves, sexuality, maternity,
Womanhood, and all that is a woman, and the man that comes from
    woman,
The womb, the teats, nipples, breast-milk, tears, laughter, weeping,
    love-looks, love-perturbations and risings,
The voice, articulation, language, whispering, shouting aloud,          25

Food, drink, pulse, digestion, sweat, sleep, walking, swimming,
Poise on the hips, leaping, reclining, embracing, arm-curving and
    tightening,
The continual changes of the flex of the mouth, and around the eyes,
The skin, the sunburnt shade, freckles, hair,
The curious sympathy one feels when feeling with the hand the naked
    meat of the body,                                                         30
The circling rivers the breath, and breathing it in and out,
The beauty of the waist, and thence of the hips, and thence downward
    toward the knees,
The thin red jellies within you or within me, the bones and the marrow
    in the bones,
The exquisite realization of health;
O I say these are not the parts and poems of the body only,
    but of the soul,                                                          35
O I say now these are the soul!

### CONSIDERATIONS FOR CRITICAL THINKING AND WRITING

1. FIRST RESPONSE. What informs this speaker's attitude toward the human
   body?

2. Read the poem aloud. Is it simply a tedious enumeration of body parts,
   or do the lines achieve some kind of rhythmic cadence?

## Perspective

## WALT WHITMAN (1819–1892)

## *On Rhyme and Meter*                                                1855

The poetic quality is not marshaled in rhyme or uniformity or abstract
addresses to things nor in melancholy complaints or good precepts, but is
the life of these and much else and is in the soul. The profit of rhyme is that
it drops seeds of a sweeter and more luxuriant rhyme, and of uniformity
that it conveys itself into its own roots in the ground out of sight. The rhyme
and uniformity of perfect poems show the free growth of metrical laws and
bud from them as unerringly and loosely as lilacs or roses on a bush, and
take shapes as compact as the shapes of chestnuts and oranges and mel-
ons and pears, and shed the perfume impalpable to form. The fluency and
ornaments of the finest poems or music or orations or recitations are not
independent but dependent. All beauty comes from beautiful blood and a
beautiful brain. If the greatnesses are in conjunction in a man or woman it
is enough . . . the fact will prevail through the universe . . . but the gaggery
and gilt of a million years will not prevail. Who troubles himself about his
ornaments or fluency is lost.

From the preface to the 1855 edition of *Leaves of Grass*

## Considerations for Critical Thinking and Writing

1. According to Whitman, what determines the shape of a poem?
2. Why does Whitman prefer open forms over fixed forms such as the sonnet?
3. Is Whitman's poetry devoid of any structure or shape? Choose one of his poems (listed in the index) to illustrate your answer.

# A SAMPLE STUDENT RESPONSE

Bloom 1

Avery Bloom

Professor Rios

English 212

7 October 2015

The Power of Walt Whitman's Open Form Poem

"I Sing the Body Electric"

Walt Whitman's "I Sing the Body Electric" is an ode to the human body. The poem is open form, without rhymes or consistent meter, and instead relies almost entirely on the use of language and the structure of lists to affect the reader. The result is a thorough inventory of parts of the body that illustrates the beauty of the human form and its intimate connection to the soul.

At times, Whitman lists the parts of the body with almost complete objectivity, making it difficult to understand the poem's purpose. The poem initially appears to do little more than recite the names of body parts: "Head, neck, hair, ears, drop and tympan of the ears" (line 5); "Mouth, tongue, lips, teeth, roof of the mouth, jaws, and the jaw-hinges" (7). There are no end rhymes, but the exhaustive and detailed list of body parts — from the brain to the "thin red jellies . . . , the bones and the marrow in the bones" (33) — offers language that has a certain rhythm. The language and rhythm of the list create a visual image full of energy and momentum that builds, emphasizing the body's functions and movements. As Michael Meyer writes, open form poems "rely on an intense use of language to establish rhythms and relations between meaning and form. [They] use the arrangement of words and phrases . . . to create unique forms" (page 223). No doubt Whitman chose the open form for this work—relying on his "intense use of language" and the rhythm of the list—because it allowed a basic structure that held together but did not restrain, and a full freedom and range of motion to create a poem that is alive with movement and electricity. . . .

### Works Cited

Meyer, Michael, ed. *Thinking and Writing about Poetry*. Boston: Bedford/St. Martin's, 2016. 223. Print.

Whitman, Walt. "From 'I Sing the Body Electric.'" Meyer 220–21.

Open form poetry is sometimes regarded as formless because it is unlike the strict fixed forms of a sonnet, villanelle, or sestina. But even though open form poems may not employ traditional meters and rhymes, they still rely on an intense use of language to establish rhythms and relations between meaning and form. Open form poems use the arrangement of words and phrases on the printed page, pauses, line lengths, and other means to create unique forms that express their particular meaning and tone.

The excerpt from Whitman's "I Sing the Body Electric" demonstrates how rhythmic cadences can be aligned with meaning, but there is one kind of open form poetry that doesn't even look like poetry on a page. A ***prose poem*** is printed as prose and represents, perhaps, the most clear opposite of fixed forms. Here are two brief examples.

## Louis Jenkins (b. 1942)

### *The Prose Poem*                                                2000

The prose poem is not a real poem, of course. One of the major differences is that the prose poet is simply too lazy or too stupid to break the poem into lines. But all writing, even the prose poem, involves a certain amount of skill, just the way throwing a wad of paper, say, into a wastebasket at a distance of twenty feet, requires a certain skill, a skill that, though it may improve hand-eye coordination, does not lead necessarily to an ability to play basketball. Still, it takes practice and thus gives one a way to pass the time, chucking one paper after another at the basket, while the teacher drones on about the poetry of Tennyson.

#### Considerations for Critical Thinking and Writing

1. FIRST RESPONSE. What is the effect of this prose poem? Does it have a theme?
2. What, if anything, is poetic in this work?
3. Arrange the lines so that they look like poetry on a page. What determines where you break the lines?

## David Shumate (b. 1950)

### *Shooting the Horse*                                             2004

I unlatch the stall door, step inside, and stroke the silky neck of the old mare like a lover about to leave. I take an ear in hand, fold it over, and run my fingers across her muzzle. I coax her head up so I can blow into those nostrils. All part of the routine we taught each other long ago. I turn a half turn, pull a pistol from my coat, raise it to that long brow with the white blaze and place it between her sleepy eyes. I clear my throat. A sound much louder than it should be. I squeeze the trigger and the horse's feet fly out from under her as gravity gives way to a force even more austere, which we have named mercy.

#### Considerations for Critical Thinking and Writing

1. FIRST RESPONSE. Describe the range of emotions that this poem produces for you.
2. Think of other words that could be substituted for *mercy* in the final line. How does your choice change the tone and theme of the poem?
3. Rearrange the poem so that its words, phrases, and sentences are set up to use the white space on the page to convey tone and meaning. Which version do you prefer? Why?

# RICHARD HAGUE (B. 1947)
## *Directions for Resisting the SAT*    *1996*

WHEN I READ "In an increasingly distracting and distracted world, poems are countercultural. They can pay attention — to public and private life, to the world of nature and rituals and things, in ways akin to prayer, or to precise and pointed cursing — like magic spells. They name what ails us." —RICHARD HAGUE

Do not believe in October or May
or in any Saturday morning with pencils.
Do not observe the rules of gravity,
commas, history.
Lie about numbers.
Blame your successes,
every one of them,
on rotten luck.
Resign all clubs and committees.
Go down with the ship — any ship.                    10
Speak nothing like English.
Desire to live whole,
like an oyster or snail,
and follow no directions.
Listen to no one.                                    15

Make your marks on everything.

Much of the poetry published today is written in open form; however, many poets continue to take pleasure in the requirements imposed by fixed forms. Some write both fixed form and open form poetry. Each kind offers rewards to careful readers as well. Here are several more open form poems that establish their own unique patterns.

# ELLEN BASS (B. 1947)
## *Gate C22*    *2002*

WHEN I WRITE "The hardest part of writing 'Gate C22' was the opening — locating the people in concise and natural syntax. I wrote the first three lines over and over. They were the foundation and until I could get them, I couldn't go on with the poem." —ELLEN BASS

At gate C22 in the Portland airport
a man in a broad-band leather hat kissed
a woman arriving from Orange County.
They kissed and kissed and kissed. Long after
the other passengers clicked the handles of
        their carry-ons                              5
and wheeled briskly toward short-term parking,
the couple stood there, arms wrapped around each other
like he'd just staggered off the boat at Ellis Island,
like she'd been released at last from ICU, snapped
out of a coma, survived bone cancer, made it down        10
from Annapurna° in only the clothes she was wearing.

11 *Annapurna:* A mountain in the Himalayas.

Neither of them was young. His beard was gray.
She carried a few extra pounds you could imagine
her saying she had to lose. But they kissed lavish
kisses like the ocean in the early morning,                    15
the way it gathers and swells, sucking
each rock under, swallowing it
again and again. We were all watching —
passengers waiting for the delayed flight
to San Jose, the stewardesses, the pilots,                     20
the aproned woman icing Cinnabons, the man selling
sunglasses. We couldn't look away. We could
taste the kisses crushed in our mouths.

But the best part was his face. When he drew back
and looked at her, his smile soft with wonder, almost          25
as though he were a mother still open from giving birth,
as your mother must have looked at you, no matter
what happened after — if she beat you or left you or
you're lonely now — you once lay there, the vernix
not yet wiped off, and someone gazed at you                    30
as if you were the first sunrise seen from the earth.
The whole wing of the airport hushed,
all of us trying to slip into that woman's middle-aged body,
her plaid Bermuda shorts, sleeveless blouse, glasses,
little gold hoop earrings, tilting our heads up.               35

### CONSIDERATIONS FOR CRITICAL THINKING AND WRITING

1. FIRST RESPONSE.  What is it that is so riveting about this kiss?
2. Explain how each stanza increases the sense of wonder in the speaker.
3. Discuss Bass's use of similes as a means of creating tone.

### CONNECTION TO ANOTHER SELECTION

1. Compare the poet's use of setting to establish theme in "Gate C22" and in George Eliot's "In a London Drawingroom" (p. 303).

## NATASHA TRETHEWEY (B. 1966)

### On Captivity                                              2007

*Being all Stripped as Naked as We were Born, and endeavoring to hide our Nakedness, these Cannaballs took [our] Books, and tearing out the Leaves would give each of us a Leaf to cover us . . .*

— *Jonathan Dickinson, 1699*

At the hands now
        of their captors, those
                they've named *savages,*
        do they say the word itself
savagely — hissing

AP Photo/Rogelio V. Solis.

that first letter,
        the serpent's image,
                releasing
        thought into speech?
For them now,                                                    10

everything is flesh
        as if their thoughts, made
                suddenly corporeal,
        reveal even more
their nakedness —                                               15

the shame of it:
        their bodies rendered
                plain as the natives' —
        homely and pale,
their ordinary sex,                                             20

the secret illicit hairs
        that do not (cannot)
                cover enough.
        This is how they are brought,
naked as newborns,                                             25

to knowledge. Adam and Eve
        in the New World,
                they have only the Bible
        to cover them. Think of it:
a woman holding before her                                     30

the torn leaves of *Genesis,*
        and a man covering himself
                with the Good Book's
        frontispiece — his own name
inscribed on the page.                                          35

### Considerations for Critical Thinking and Writing

1. **FIRST RESPONSE.** Trethewey has written about the sources of her epigraph: "Because the conquerors made use of the written word to claim land [in North America] inhabited by native people, I found the detail of settlers forced to cover themselves with torn pages from books a compelling irony" (*The Best American Poetry 2008,* p. 182). How does this comment contribute to the central irony in the poem?

2. Discuss Trethewey's use of alliteration in lines 1 to 9.

3. In what sense are the captors "brought, / naked as newborns, / to knowledge" (lines 24–26)?

# GARY GILDNER (B. 1938)

## *First Practice*                                                    1984

After the doctor checked to see
we weren't ruptured,
the man with the short cigar took us
under the grade school,
where we went in case of attack                               5
or storm, and said
he was Clifford Hill, he was
a man who believed dogs
ate dogs, he had once killed
for his country, and if                                      10
there were any girls present
for them to leave now.
                          No one
left. OK, he said, he said I take
that to mean you are hungry                                  15
men who hate to lose as much
as I do. OK. Then
he made two lines of us
facing each other,
and across the way, he said,                                 20
is the man you hate most
in the world,
and if we are to win
that title I want to see how.
But I don't want to see                                      25
any marks when you're dressed,
he said. He said, *Now.*

### CONSIDERATIONS FOR CRITICAL THINKING AND WRITING

1. FIRST RESPONSE. Do you recognize this coach? How does he compare with sports coaches you have known?

2. Comment on the significance of Clifford Hill's name.

3. Locate examples of irony in the poem and explain how they contribute to the theme.

4. Discuss the effect of line spacing in line 13.

### CONNECTION TO ANOTHER SELECTION

1. Write an essay comparing the coach in this poem and the teacher in Judy Page Heitzman's "The Schoolroom on the Second Floor of the Knitting Mill" (p. 113).

## JULIO MARZÁN (B. 1946)

### *The Translator at the Reception for Latin American Writers*                     *1997*

Air-conditioned introductions,
then breezy Spanish conversation
fan his curiosity to know
what country I come from.
"Puerto Rico and the Bronx."                                              5

Spectacled downward eyes
translate disappointment
like a poison mushroom
puffed in his thoughts as if,
after investing a sizable                                                10
intellectual budget, transporting
a huge cast and camera crew
to film on location
Mayan pyramid grandeur,
indigenes whose ancient gods                                             15
and comet-tail plumage
inspire a glorious epic
of revolution across a continent,
he received a lurid script
for a social documentary                                                 20
rife with dreary streets
and pathetic human interest,
meager in the profits of high culture.

Understandably he turns,
catches up with the hostess,                                             25
praising the uncommon quality
of her offerings of cheese.

### CONSIDERATIONS FOR CRITICAL THINKING AND WRITING

1. FIRST RESPONSE. What is the speaker's attitude toward the person he meets at the reception? What lines in particular lead you to that conclusion?

2. Why is that person so disappointed about the answer, "Puerto Rico and the Bronx" (line 5)?

3. Explain lines 6 to 23. How do they reveal both the speaker and the person encountered at the reception?

4. Why is the setting of this poem significant?

# ROBERT MORGAN (B. 1944)

## *Overalls*                                                                      *1990*

Even the biggest man will look
babylike in overalls, bib
up to his neck holding the trousers
high on his belly, with no chafing
at the waist, no bulging over                                               5
the belt. But it's the pockets on
the chest that are most interesting,
buttons and snaps like medals, badges,
flaps open with careless ease, thin
sheath for the pencil, little pockets                                      10
and pouches and the main zipper
compartment like a wallet over
the heart and the slit where the watch
goes, an eye where the chain is caught.
Every bit of surface is taken                                               15
up with patches, denim mesas
and envelopes, a many-level
cloth topography. And below,
the loops for hammers and pliers
like holsters for going armed                                               20
and armored yet free-handed
into the field another day
for labor's playful war with time.

### CONSIDERATIONS FOR CRITICAL THINKING AND WRITING

1. FIRST RESPONSE. How does the poem's last line announce its theme?

2. Why is it that the "pockets on / the chest . . . are most interesting" (lines 6–7) to the speaker?

3. Describe the way images of childhood and adulthood, along with work and war, are interwoven in Morgan's treatment of overalls.

## KEVIN YOUNG (B. 1970)
### *Eddie Priest's Barbershop & Notary*

1995

© Tod Martens.

*Closed Mondays*

*is* music is    *men*
off early from work    is waiting
for the chance at the chair
while the eagle claws holes
in your pockets    keeping
time    by the turning
of rusty fans    steel flowers with
cold breezes    is having nothing
better to do    than guess at the years
of hair    matted beneath the soiled caps
of drunks    the pain of running
a fisted comb through stubborn
knots    is the dark dirty low
down blues    the tender heads
of sons fresh from cornrows    all                              15
wonder at losing    half their height
is a mother gathering hair    for good
luck    for a soft wig    is the round
difficulty of ears    the peach
faced boys asking Eddie                                         20
to cut in parts and arrows
wanting to have their names read
for just a few days    and among thin
jazz    is the quick brush of a done
head    the black flood around                                 25
your feet    grandfathers
stopping their games of ivory
dominoes    just before they read the bone
yard    is winking widowers announcing
*cut it clean off   I'm through courting*                      30
*and hair only gets in the way*    is the final
spin of the chair    a reflection of
a reflection    that sting of wintergreen
tonic    on the neck of a sleeping snow
haired man    when you realize it is                           35
your turn    you are next

### CONSIDERATIONS FOR CRITICAL THINKING AND WRITING

1. FIRST RESPONSE. What does the speaker think and feel about the
   barbershop?

2. What is the effect of using extra word space as a substitute for conventional punctuation?

3. What do you think comes "next" in the last line?

## ANONYMOUS

### The Frog                                    *date unknown*

What a wonderful bird the frog are!
When he stand he sit almost;
When he hop he fly almost.
He ain't got no sense hardly;
He ain't got no tail hardly either.
When he sit, he sit on what he ain't got almost.

#### CONSIDERATIONS FOR CRITICAL THINKING AND WRITING

1. FIRST RESPONSE. How is the poem a description of the speaker as well as of a frog?

2. Though this poem is ungrammatical, it does have a patterned structure. How does the pattern of sentences create a formal structure?

## TATO LAVIERA (1951–2013)

### AmeRícan                                    *1985*

we gave birth to a new generation,
AmeRícan, broader than lost gold
never touched, hidden inside the
puerto rican mountains.

we gave birth to a new generation,                    5
AmeRícan, it includes everything
imaginable you-name-it-we-got-it
society.

we gave birth to a new generation,
AmeRícan salutes all folklores,                    10
european, indian, black, spanish,
and anything else compatible:

AmeRícan,    singing to composer pedro flores'° palm
             trees high up in the universal sky!

AmeRícan,    sweet soft spanish danzas gypsies                    15

---

13 *pedro flores:* Puerto Rican composer of popular romantic songs.

|  | moving lyrics la *española*° cascabelling | *Spanish* |
|---|---|---|
|  | presence always singing at our side! | |

AmeRícan,    beating jíbaro° modern troubadours
             crying guitars romantic continental
             bolero love songs!                                          20

AmeRícan,    across forth and across back
             back across and forth back
             forth across and back and forth
             our trips are walking bridges!

             it all dissolved into itself, the attempt              25
             was truly made, the attempt was truly
             absorbed, digested, we spit out
             the poison, we spit out the malice,
             we stand, affirmative in action,
             to reproduce a broader answer to the                   30
             marginality that gobbled us up abruptly!

AmeRícan,    walking plena-rhythms° in new york,
             strutting beautifully alert, alive,
             many turning eyes wondering,
             admiring!                                              35

AmeRícan,    defining myself my own way any way many
             ways Am e Rícan, with the big R and the
             accent on the í!

AmeRícan,    like the soul gliding talk of gospel
             boogie music!                                          40

AmeRícan,    speaking new words in spanglish tenements,
             fast tongue moving street corner *"que*
             *corta"*° talk being invented at the insistence     *that cuts*
             of a smile!

AmeRícan,    abounding inside so many ethnic english          45
             people, and out of humanity, we blend
             and mix all that is good!

AmeRícan,    integrating in new york and defining our
             own *destino,*° our own way of life,                *destiny*

AmeRícan,    defining the new america, humane america,          50
             admired america, loved america, harmonious
             america, the world in peace, our energies
             collectively invested to find other civili-
             zations, to touch God, further and further,
             to dwell in the spirit of divinity!                  55

18 *jíbaro:* A particular style of music played by Puerto Rican mountain farmers.    32 *plena-rhythms:* African–Puerto Rican folklore, music, and dance.

AmeRícan,    yes, for now, for i love this, my second
             land, and i dream to take the accent from
             the altercation, and be proud to call
             myself american, in the u.s. sense of the
             word, AmeRícan, America!                                    60

### CONSIDERATIONS FOR CRITICAL THINKING AND WRITING

1. FIRST RESPONSE. How does the arrangement of lines communicate a
   sense of energy and vitality?
2. How does the speaker portray Puerto Ricans living in the United States?
3. How does the poet describe the United States?

## KARL SHAPIRO (1913–2000)

### *Lower the Standard*                                                 1964

Lower the standard: that's my motto. Somebody is always putting the food
out of reach. We're tired of falling off ladders. Who says a child
can't paint? A pro is somebody who does it for money. Lower the
standards. Let's all play poetry. Down with ideals, flags, convention
buttons, morals, the scrambled eggs on the admiral's hat. I'm talking
sense. Lower the standards. Sabotage the stylistic approach. Let weeds
grow in the subdivision. Putty up the incisions in the library façade,
those names that frighten grade-school teachers, those names whose
U's are cut like V's. Burn the *Syntopicon* and *The Harvard Classics*.
Lower the standard on classics, battleships, Russian ballet, national
anthems (but they're low enough). Break through to the bottom. Be
natural as an American abroad who knows no language, not even
American. Keelhaul the poets in the vestry chairs. Renovate the Abbey
of cold-storage dreamers. Get off the Culture Wagon. Learn how to
walk the way you want. Slump your shoulders, stick your belly out,
arms all over the table. How many generations will this take? Don't
think about it, just make a start. (You have made a start.) Don't break
anything you can step around, *but don't pick it up.* The law of gravity
is the law of art. You first, poetry second, the good, the beautiful, the
true come last. As the lad said: We must love one another or die.

### CONSIDERATIONS FOR CRITICAL THINKING AND WRITING

1. FIRST RESPONSE. What is Shapiro satirizing in this poem?
2. What are the *Syntopicon* and *The Harvard Classics*? How do they reflect
   the speaker's tastes?
3. Write an essay that describes your sense of contemporary standards
   now that nearly fifty years have passed since this poem was published.

# BILLIE BOLTON (B. 1950)

## *Memorandum*                2004

TO:    My Boyfriend from Hell
FR:    Me
RE:    Shit I Never Want to Hear Another Word
       About as Long as I Live

**1. Your Addled Thoughts.** Anything about your ongoing interest in Lucy Liu's legs, Shania Twain's bellybutton, or Reese Witherspoon's whatever; your must-see TV dramas, your fantasy baseball addiction, or your addictions

Used by permission, Billie Bolton.

period. Anything about going anywhere with you at any time including, but not limited to: Sam's Club, Big Lots, Waffle House, church fish fries, local snake round-ups or Amvet turkey shoots, unless you promise to be the turkey.

**2. Your Wireless Connection.** Anything about your stage-four cell phone habit; the dames who have your cell phone number and why; who's on your speed-dial list or who left a voice mail message; anything about cell phone rebates, late fees, roaming charges, contracts or dropping your cell phone in the john by accident, even if you flush it and walk away.

**3. Your Adolescent Only Child.** Anything about his bed-wetting or fire-setting habits; his gang affiliation, court dates or swastika tattoo; anything about his tantrums, seizures or deep psychological need for video games and fruit roll-ups; anything about his pathological grudge against mankind or his particular beef against me.

**4. Your Significant Others (female).** Anything about the redneck redhead you banged in high school, the long-haired potheads you balled in your hippie days, the white trash airhead you married or the blue-haired battle-ax who pats you on the rump and pays for your dinner. Anything about your devotion to your long-suffering mother, your loopy sisters, or even the Blessed Virgin.

### CONSIDERATIONS FOR CRITICAL THINKING AND WRITING

1. FIRST RESPONSE. What makes this a poem rather than simply a memo?
2. How does the speaker's diction and choice of details reveal her own personality?
3. CREATIVE RESPONSE. Using Bolton's style, tone, and form as inspiration, write a reply from the boyfriend's point of view.

## *Found Poem*

This next selection is a *found poem*, unintentional verse discovered in a nonpoetic context, such as a conversation, news story, or an advertisement. Found poems are playful reminders that the words in poems are very often the language we use every day. Whether such found language should be regarded as a poem is an issue left for you to consider.

## DONALD JUSTICE (1925–2004)

### *Order in the Streets*                                              *1969*

(*From instructions printed on a child's toy, Christmas 1968, as reported in the* New York Times)

1. 2. 3.
Switch on.

Jeep rushes
to the scene
of riot                                                                        5

Jeep goes
in all directions
by mystery action.

Jeep stops periodically
to turn hood over                                                              10

machine gun appears
with realistic
shooting noise.

After putting down riot,
jeep goes                                                                      15
back to the headquarters.

### CONSIDERATIONS FOR CRITICAL THINKING AND WRITING

1. **FIRST RESPONSE.** What is the effect of arranging these instructions in discrete lines? How are the language and meaning enhanced by this arrangement?

2. How does this poem connect upon the many riots that occurred throughout the United States during the late sixties?

3. **CREATIVE RESPONSE.** Look for phrases or sentences in ads, textbooks, labels, or directions — in anything that might inadvertently contain provocative material that would be revealed by arranging the words in verse lines. You may even discover some patterns of rhyme and rhythm. After arranging the lines, explain why you organized them as you did.

# 11

# Combining the Elements of Poetry: A Writing Process

In poetry you have a form looking for a subject and a subject looking for a form. When they come together successfully you have a poem.

— W. H. AUDEN

© Bettmann/Corbis.

## THE ELEMENTS TOGETHER

The elements of poetry that you have studied in the first ten chapters of this book offer a vocabulary and a series of perspectives that open up avenues of inquiry into a poem. As you have learned, there are many potential routes that you can take. By asking questions about the speaker, diction, figurative language, sounds, rhythm, tone, or theme, you clarify your understanding while simultaneously sensitizing yourself to elements and issues especially relevant to the poem under consideration. This process of careful, informed reading allows you to see how the various elements of the poem reinforce its meanings.

A poem's elements do not exist in isolation, however. They work together to create a complete experience for the reader. Knowing how the elements combine helps you understand the poem's structure and to appreciate it as a whole. Robert Herrick's "Delight in Disorder" (p. 185), for example, is more easily understood (and the humor of the poem is better appreciated) when meter and rhyme are considered together with the poem's meaning. Musing about how he is more charmed by a naturally disheveled appearance than by those that seem contrived, the speaker lists several attributes of dishevelment and concludes that they

> Do more bewitch me than when art
> Is too precise in every part.

Noticing how the couplet's precise and sing-songy rhythm combines with the solid, obvious, and final rhyme of *art / part* helps in understanding what the speaker means by "too precise," as the lines are a little too precise themselves. Noticing this, you may even want to chart how rhythm and rhyme work together throughout the early (more disheveled) lines of the poem. Finding a pattern in the ways the elements work together throughout the poem will help you understand how the poem works.

## MAPPING THE POEM

When you write about a poem, you are, in some ways, providing a guide for a place that might otherwise seem unfamiliar and remote. Put simply, writing enables you to chart a work so that you can comfortably move around in it to discuss or write about what interests you. Your paper represents a record and a map of your intellectual journey through the poem, pointing out the things worth noting and your impressions about them. Your role as writer is to offer insights into the challenges, pleasures, and discoveries that the poem harbors. These insights are a kind of sightseeing, as you navigate the various elements of the poem to make some overall point about it.

This chapter shows you how one student, Rose Bostwick, moves through the stages of writing about how a poem's elements combine for a final effect. Included here are Rose's annotated version of the poem, her first response, her informal outline, and the final draft of an explication of John Donne's "Death Be Not Proud." A detailed explanation of what is implicit in a poem, an *explication* requires a line-by-line examination of the poem. (For more on explication, see page 362 in Chapter 16, "Reading and the Writing Process.") After reviewing the elements of poetry covered in the preceding chapters, Rose read the poem (which follows) several times, paying careful attention to diction, figurative language, irony, symbol, rhythm, sound, and so on. Her final paper is more concerned with the overall effect of the combination of elements than with a line-by-line breakdown, and her annotated version of the poem details her attention to that task. As you read and reread "Death Be Not Proud," keep notes on how *you* think the elements of this poem work together and to what overall effect.

# John Donne (1572–1631)

John Donne, now regarded as a major poet of the early seventeenth century, wrote love poems at the beginning of his career but shifted to religious themes after converting from Catholicism to Anglicanism in the early 1590s. Although trained in law, he was also ordained a priest and became dean of St. Paul's Cathedral in London in 1621. The following poem, from "Holy Sonnets," reflects both his religious faith and his ability to create elegant arguments in verse.

Universal Images Group/Getty Images.

## *Death Be Not Proud*    1611

Death be not proud, though some have callèd thee
Mighty and dreadful, for thou art not so;
For those whom thou think'st thou dost overthrow
Die not, poor Death, nor yet canst thou kill me.
From rest and sleep, which but thy pictures° be,                    *images*   5
Much pleasure; then from thee much more must flow,
And soonest our best men with thee do go,
Rest of their bones, and soul's delivery.°                    *deliverance*
Thou art slave to Fate, Chance, kings, and desperate men,
And dost with Poison, War, and Sickness dwell;                    10
And poppy or charms can make us sleep as well,
And better than thy stroke; why swell'st° thou then?    *swell with pride*
One short sleep past, we wake eternally
And death shall be no more; Death, thou shalt die.

### Considerations for Critical Thinking and Writing

1. **first response.** Why doesn't the speaker fear death? Explain why you find the argument convincing or not.

2. How does the speaker compare death with rest and sleep in lines 5 to 8? What is the point of this comparison?

3. Discuss the poem's rhythm by examining the breaks and end-stopped lines. How does the poem's rhythm contribute to its meaning?

4. What are the signs that this poem is structured as a sonnet?

# ASKING QUESTIONS ABOUT THE ELEMENTS

After reading a poem, use the Questions for Responsive Reading and Writing (p. 45) to help you think, talk, and write about any poem. Before you do, though, be sure that you have read the poem several times without worrying actively about interpretation. With poetry, as with all other literature, it's important to allow yourself the pleasure of enjoying whatever makes itself apparent to you. On subsequent readings, use the questions to understand and appreciate how the poem works; remember to keep in mind that not all questions will necessarily be relevant to a particular poem. A good starting point is to ask yourself what elements are exemplified in the parts of the poem that especially interest you. Then ask the Questions for Responsive Reading and Writing that relate to those elements. Finally, as you begin to get a sense of what elements are important to the poem and how those elements fit together, it often helps to put your impressions on paper.

# A SAMPLE CLOSE READING

## An Annotated Version of "Death Be Not Proud"

As she read the poem closely several times, Rose annotated it with impressions and ideas that would lead to insights on which her analysis would be built. Her close examination of the poem's elements allowed her to understand how its parts contribute to its overall effect; her annotations provide a useful map of her thinking.

Speaker scolds Death.

### Death Be Not Proud                    1611

In formal diction, speaker personifies and rebukes Death for undeserved pride.

Most lines are iambic pentameter, but first two begin with stressed syllables for emphasis.

Death be not proud, though some have callèd
        thee
Mighty and dreadful, for thou art not so;
For those whom thou think'st thou dost
        overthrow
Die not, poor Death, nor yet canst thou
        kill me.
From rest and sleep, which but thy
        pictures° be,                         *images*   5
Much pleasure; then from thee much more
        must flow,
And soonest our best men with thee do go,
Rest of their bones, and soul's
        delivery.°                            *deliverance*

Death cannot kill speaker, who even taunts Death.

Death is only like sleep rather than something eternal.

Thou art slave to Fate, Chance, kings, and
    desperate men,
And dost with Poison, War, and Sickness
    dwell;                                                          10
And poppy or charms can make us sleep
    as well,
And better than thy stroke; why
    swell'st° thou then?          *swell with pride*
One short sleep past, we wake eternally
And death shall be no more; Death, thou
    shalt die.

*[Left annotation:]* Argument in the couplet climaxes with allusion to humanity's resurrection and death of Death itself. In addition to Christianity, does sonnet form finally control Death too?

*[Right annotation, top:]* Each quatrain (4-line stanza) develops the argument that Death is ultimately weak and cannot be justly proud or rightly feared, building toward the conclusion of final two lines.

*[Right annotation, bottom:]* Rather than a power, Death is a slave to other forces.

# A SAMPLE FIRST RESPONSE

After Rose carefully read "Death Be Not Proud" and had a sense of how the elements work, she took the first step toward a formal explication by writing informally about the relevant elements and addressing the question *Why doesn't the speaker fear death? Explain why you find the argument convincing or not.* Note that at this point, she was not as concerned with textual evidence and detail as she would need to be in her final paper.

I've read the poem "Death Be Not Proud" by John Donne a few times now, and I have a sense of how it works. The poem is a sonnet, and each of the three quatrains presents a piece of the argument that Death should not be proud, because it is not really all-powerful, and may even be a source of pleasure. As a reader, I resist this seeming paradox at first, but I know it must be a trick, a riddle of some sort that the poem will proceed to untangle. I think one of the reasons the poem comes off as such a powerful statement is that Donne at first seems to be playful and paradoxical in his characterizations of Death. He's almost teasing Death. But beneath the teasing tone you feel the strong foundation of the real reason Death should not be proud—Donne's faith in the immortality of the soul. The poem begins to feel more solemn as it progresses, as the hints at the idea of immortality become more clearly articulated.

Donne utilizes two literary conventions to increase the effect of this poem: he uses the convention of personifying death, so that he can address it directly, and he uses the metaphor of death as a kind of sleep. These two things determine the tone and the progression from playful to solemn in the poem.

The last clause of the poem (line 14) plays with the paradoxical-seeming character of what he's been declaring. Ironically, it seems the only thing susceptible to death is death itself. Or, when death becomes powerless is when it only has power over itself.

# ORGANIZING YOUR THOUGHTS

Showing in a paper how different elements of a particular poem work together is often quite challenging. While you may have a clear intuitive sense of what elements are important to the poem and how they complement one another, it is important to organize your thoughts in such a way as to make the relationships clear to your audience. The simplest way is to go line by line, but that can quickly become rote for writer and reader. Because you will want to organize your paper in the way that best serves your thesis, it may help to write an informal outline that charts how you think the argument moves. You may find, for example, that the argument is not persuasive if you start with the final lines and go back to the beginning of the poem or passage. However you decide to organize your argument, keep in mind that a single idea, or thesis, will have to run throughout the entire paper.

# A SAMPLE INFORMAL OUTLINE

In her informal outline (following), Rose discovers that her argument works best if she begins at the beginning. Note that, though her later paper concerns itself with how several elements of poetry contribute to the poem's theme and message, her informal outline concerns itself much more with what that message is and how it develops as the poem progresses. She will fill in the details later.

_Thesis:_ From the very first word, addressing "Death" directly, Donne uses the literary conventions of personifying death and comparing it to sleep to begin an argument that Death should not be proud of its might or dreadfulness. But these two elements of his argument come to be seen as the superficial points when the true reason for death's powerlessness becomes clear. The Christian belief in the immortality of the soul is the reason for death's powerlessness and likeness to sleep.

_Body of essay:_ Show how argument proceeds by quatrains from playful address to Death, and statement that Death is much like sleep, its "picture," to statement that Death is "slave" to other forces (and so should not be proud of being the mightiest), to the couplet, which articulates clearly the idea of immortality and gives the final paradox, "Death, thou shalt die."

_Conclusion:_ Donne's faith in the immortality of the soul enables him to "prove" in this argument that Death is truly like its metaphorical representation, sleep. Faith allows him to derive a source for this conventional trope, and it allows him to state his truth in paradoxes. He relies on the conventional idea that death is an end, and a conqueror, and the only all-powerful force, to make the paradoxes that lend his argument the force of mystery — the mystery of faith.

# THE ELEMENTS AND THEME

As you create an informal outline, your understanding of the poem will grow, change, and finally, solidify. You will develop a much clearer sense of what the poem's elements combine to create, and you will have chosen a scheme for organizing your argument. The next step before drafting is to determine the paper's thesis, which will not only keep your paper focused but will also help you center your thoughts. For papers that discuss how the elements of poetry come together, the thesis is a single and concise statement of what the elements combine to create — the idea around which all the elements revolve. In the earlier discussion of Robert Herrick's "Delight in Disorder," for example, the two elements, rhythm and rhyme, work together to create the speaker's self-directed irony. To state this as a thesis, we might say that by making his own rhythm and rhyme "too precise," Herrick's speaker is making fun of himself while complimenting a certain type of woman. (You may ask yourself if he's doing a little flirting.)

Once you understand how all of the elements of the poem fit together and have articulated your understanding in the thesis statement, the next step is to flesh out your argument. By including quotations from the poem to illustrate the points you will be making, you will better explain exactly how each element relates to the others and, more specifically, to your thesis, and you will have created a finished paper that helps readers navigate the poem's geography.

# A SAMPLE EXPLICATION

## *The Use of Conventional Metaphors for Death in John Donne's "Death Be Not Proud"*

In Rose's final draft, she focuses on the use of metaphor in "Death Be Not Proud." Her essay provides a coherent reading that relates each line of the poem to the speaker's intense awareness of death. Although the essay discusses each stanza in order, the introductory paragraph provides a brief overview explaining how the poem's metaphor and arguments contribute to its total meaning. In addition, Rose does not hesitate to discuss a line out of sequence when it can be usefully connected to another phrase. She also works quotations into her sentences to support her points. When she adds something to a quotation to clarify it, she encloses her words in brackets so that they will not be mistaken for the poet's, and she uses a slash to indicate line divisions: "soonest . . . with thee do go, / [for] Rest of their bones, and soul's delivery." Finally, Rose is sure to cite the line numbers for any direct quotations from the poem. As you read through her final draft, remember that the word *explication* comes from the Latin *explicare*, "to unfold." How successful do you think Rose is at unfolding this poem to reveal how its elements — here ranging from metaphor, structure, meter, personification, paradox, and irony to theme — contribute to its meaning?

Rose Bostwick

English 101

Professor Hart

24 February 2015

The Use of Conventional Metaphors for Death

in John Donne's "Death Be Not Proud"

In the sonnet that begins "Death be not proud . . ." John Donne argues

that death is not "mighty and dreadful" but is more like its metaphorical

representation, sleep. Death, Donne puts forth, is even a source of pleasure

and rest. The poet builds this argument on two foundations. One is made up of

the metaphors and literary conventions for death: death is compared with sleep

and is often personified so that it can be addressed directly. The poem is an

address to death that at first seems paradoxical and somewhat playful, but which

then rises in all the emotion of faith as it reveals the second foundation of the

argument—the Christian belief in the immortality of the soul. Seen against the

backdrop of this belief, death loses its powerful threat and is seen as only a

metaphorical sleep, or rest.

> Thesis providing interpretation of the poem's use of metaphor and how it contributes to the poem's central argument.

The poem is an ironic argument that proceeds according to the structure

of the sonnet form. Each quatrain contains a new development or aspect of the

argument, and the final couplet serves as a conclusion. The metrical scheme is

mainly iambic pentameter, but in several places in the poem, the stress pattern

is altered for emphasis. For example, the first foot of the poem is inverted, so

that "Death," the first word, receives the stress. This announces to us right away

that Death is being personified and addressed. This inversion also serves to

begin the poem energetically and forcefully. The second line behaves in the same

way. The first syllable of "Mighty" receives the stress, emphasizing the meaning

of the word and its assumed relation to Death.

> Discussion of how form and meter contribute to the poem's central argument.

This first quatrain offers the first paradox and sets up the argument that

death has been conventionally personified with the wrong attributes, might and

dreadfulness. The poet tells death not to be proud, "though some have callèd

the / Mighty and dreadful," because, he says, death is "not so" (lines 1–2).

Donne will turn this conventional characterization of death on its head with the

paradox of the third and fourth lines: he says the people overthrown by death

(as if by a conqueror) "Die not, poor death, nor yet canst thou kill me." These

lines establish the paradox of death not being able to cause death.

> Discussion of how personification contributes to the poem's central argument.

Bostwick 2

The next quatrain will not begin to answer the question of why this paradox is so, but will posit another slight paradox—the idea of death as pleasurable. In lines 5–8, Donne uses the literary convention of describing death as a metaphorical sleep, or rest, to construct the argument that death must give pleasure: "From rest and sleep, which but thy pictures be, / Much pleasure; then from thee much more must flow" (5–6). At this point, the argument seems almost playful, but is carefully hinting at the solemnity of the deeper foundation of the belief in immortality. The metaphor of sleep for death includes the idea of waking; one doesn't sleep forever. The next two lines put forth the idea that death is pleasurable enough to be desired by "our best men" who "soonest . . . with thee do go, / [for] Rest of their bones, and soul's delivery" (7–8). This last line comes closer to announcing the true reason for death's powerlessness and pleasure: it is the way to the "soul's delivery" from the body and life on earth, and implicitly, into another, better realm.

A new reason for death's powerlessness arises in the next four lines. The poet says to death:

> Thou art slave to Fate, Chance, kings, and desperate men,
>
> And dost with Poison, War, and Sickness dwell;
>
> And poppy or charms can make us sleep as well,
>
> And better than thy stroke; why swell'st thou then? (9–12)

Donne argues here that there are forces more powerful than death that actually control it. Fate and chance determine when death occurs, and to whom it comes. Kings, with the powers of law and war, can summon death and throw it on whom they wish. And desperate men, murderers or suicides, can also summon death with the strength of their emotions. In lines 11 and 12, Donne again uses the metaphor of death as a kind of sleep, but says that drugs or "charms" give one a better sleep than death. And he asks playfully why death should be so proud, after all these illustrations of its weakness have been given: "why swell'st thou then?" (12).

Finally, with the last couplet, Donne reveals the true, deeper reason behind his argument that death should not be proud of its power. These lines also offer an explanation of the metaphor for death of sleep, or rest: "One short sleep past, we wake eternally / And death shall be no more; Death, thou shalt die" (13–14). After death, the soul lives on, according to Christian theology and belief. In the Christian heaven, where the soul is immortal, death will no longer exist, and

---

*Discussion of how metaphor of sleep and idea of immortality support the poem's central argument.*

*Discussion of how language and tone contribute to the poem's central argument.*

*Discussion of function of religious faith in the poem and how word order and meter create emphasis.*

so this last paradox, "Death, thou shalt die," becomes true. Again in this line, a significant inversion of metrical stress occurs. "Death," in the second clause, receives the stress, recalling the first line, emphasizing that it is an address and

**Conclusion supporting thesis in context of poet's beliefs.**

giving the clause a forceful sense of finality. His belief in the immortality of the soul enables Donne to "prove" in this argument that death is in actuality like its metaphorical representation, sleep. His faith allows him to derive a source for this conventional metaphor and to "disprove" the metaphor of death as an all-powerful conqueror. His Christian beliefs also allow him to state his truth in paradoxes, the mysteries that are justified by the mystery of faith.

## Work Cited

Donne, John. "Death Be Not Proud." *Thinking and Writing about Poetry.* Ed.
Michael Meyer. Boston: Bedford/St. Martin's, 2016. 239. Print.

Before you begin writing your own paper on poetry, review the Suggestions for Approaching Poetry (pp. 26–27) and Chapter 2, "Writing about Poetry," particularly the Questions for Responsive Reading and Writing (pp. 45–46). These suggestions and questions will help you focus and sharpen your critical thinking and writing. You'll also find help in Chapter 16, "Reading and the Writing Process," which offers a systematic overview of choosing a topic, developing a thesis, and organizing various types of assignments. If you use outside sources for the paper, be sure to acknowledge them adequately by using the conventional documentation procedures detailed in Chapter 17, "The Literary Research Paper."

# Approaches
# to Poetry

# 12

# A Study of Robert Frost

Courtesy of Rauner Special Collections
Library, Dartmouth College. Used by
permission of the Estate of Robert Lee
Frost.

A poem ... begins as a lump in the throat,
a sense of wrong, a home-sickness, a love-
sickness. ... It finds the thought and the
thought finds the words.
— ROBERT FROST

Every poem is doubtlessly affected by the personal history of its composer,
but Robert Frost's poems are especially known for their reflection of New
England life. Although the poems included in this chapter evoke the landscapes of Frost's life and work, the depth and range of those landscapes are
far more complicated than his popular reputation typically acknowledges.
He was an enormously private man and a much more subtle poet than
many of his readers have expected him to be. His poems warrant careful,
close readings. As you explore his poetry, you may find useful the following

Questions for Writing about an Author in Depth as a means of stimulating your thinking about his life and work.

---

## Questions for Writing about an Author in Depth

As you read multiple works by the same author, you're likely to be struck by the similarities and differences in those selections. You'll begin to recognize situations, events, characters, issues, perspectives, styles, and strategies — even recurring words or phrases — that provide a kind of signature, making the poems in some way identifiable with that particular writer.

The following questions can help you respond to multiple works by the same author. They should help you listen to how a writer's works can speak to one another and to you. Additional useful questions can be found in other chapters of this book. See Chapter 2, "Writing about Poetry," and Arguing about Literature (p. 353) in Chapter 16, "Reading and the Writing Process."

1. What topics reappear in the writer's work? What seem to be the major concerns of the author?

2. Does the author have a definable worldview that can be discerned from work to work? Is, for example, the writer liberal, conservative, apolitical, or religious?

3. What social values come through in the author's work? Does he or she seem to identify with a particular group or social class?

4. Is there a consistent voice or point of view from work to work? Is it a persona or the author's actual self?

5. How much of the author's own life experiences and historical moment make their way into the works?

6. Does the author experiment with style from work to work, or are the works mostly consistent with one another?

7. Can the author's work be identified with a literary tradition, such as *carpe diem* poetry, that aligns his or her work with that of other writers?

8. What is distinctive about the author's writing? Is the language innovative? Are the themes challenging? Are the voices conventional? Is the tone characteristic?

9. Could you identify another work by the same author without a name being attached to it? What are the distinctive features that allow you to do so?

10. Do any of the writer's works seem *not* to be by that writer? Why?

11. What other writers are most like this author in style and content? Why?

12. Has the writer's work evolved over time? Are there significant changes or developments? Are there new ideas and styles, or do the works remain largely the same?

13. How would you characterize the author's writing habits? Is it possible to anticipate what goes on in different works, or are you surprised by their content or style?

14. Can difficult or ambiguous passages in a work be resolved by referring to a similar passage in another work?

15. What does the writer say about his or her own work? Do you trust the teller or the tale? Which do you think is more reliable?

## A BRIEF BIOGRAPHY

Few poets have enjoyed the popular success that Robert Frost (1874–1963) achieved during his lifetime, and no other twentieth-century American poet has had his or her work as widely read and honored. Frost is as much associated with New England as the stone walls that help define its landscape; his reputation, however, transcends regional boundaries. Although he was named poet laureate of Vermont only two years before his death, he was

Robert Frost at age eighteen (1892), the year he graduated from high school. "Education," Frost once said, "is the ability to listen to almost anything without losing your temper or your self-confidence."

Courtesy of Rauner Special Collections Library, Dartmouth College. Used by permission of the Estate of Robert Lee Frost.

Robert Frost at age forty-seven (1921) at Stone Cottage in Shaftsbury, Vermont. Frost wrote, "I would have written of me on my stone: / I had a lover's quarrel with the world." Courtesy of Rauner Special Collections Library, Dartmouth College. Used by permission of the Estate of Robert Lee Frost.

Robert Frost at his writing desk in Franconia, New Hampshire, 1915. "I have never started a poem whose end I knew," Frost said, "writing a poem is discovering."
Amherst College Archives and Special Collections. Used by permission of the Estate of Robert Lee Frost.

for many years the nation's unofficial poet laureate. Frost collected honors the way some people pick up burrs on country walks. Among his awards were four Pulitzer Prizes, the Bollingen Prize, a Congressional Medal, and dozens of honorary degrees. Perhaps his most moving appearance was his recitation of "The Gift Outright" for millions of Americans at the inauguration of John F. Kennedy in 1961.

Frost's recognition as a poet is especially remarkable because his career as a writer did not attract any significant attention until he was nearly forty years old. He taught himself to write while he labored at odd jobs, taught school, or farmed.

Frost's early identity seems very remote from the New England soil. Although his parents were descended from generations of New Englanders, he was born in San Francisco and was named Robert Lee Frost after the Confederate general. After his father died in 1885, his mother moved the family back to Massachusetts to live with relatives. Frost graduated from high school sharing valedictorian honors with the classmate who would become his wife three years later. Between high school and marriage, he attended Dartmouth College for a few months and then taught. His teaching prompted him to enroll at Harvard in 1897, but after less than two years he withdrew without a degree (though Harvard would eventually award him an honorary doctorate in 1937, four years after Dartmouth conferred its honorary degree on him). For the next decade, Frost read and wrote poems when he was not chicken farming or teaching. In 1912, he sold his farm and moved his family to England, where he hoped to find the audience that his poetry did not have in America.

Three years in England made it possible for Frost to return home as a poet. His first two volumes of poetry, *A Boy's Will* (1913) and *North of Boston* (1914), were published in England. During the next twenty years, honors and awards were conferred on collections such as *Mountain Interval* (1916), *New Hampshire* (1923), *West-Running Brook* (1928), and *A Further Range* (1936). These are the volumes on which most of Frost's popular and critical reputation rests. Later collections include *A Witness Tree* (1942), *A Masque of Reason* (1945), *Steeple Bush* (1947), *A Masque of Mercy* (1947), *Complete Poems* (1949), and *In the Clearing* (1962). In addition to publishing his works, Frost endeared himself to audiences throughout the country by presenting his poetry almost as conversations. He also taught at a number of schools, including Amherst College, the University of Michigan, Harvard University, Dartmouth College, and Middlebury College.

Frost's countless poetry readings generated wide audiences eager to claim him as their poet. The image he cultivated resembled closely what the public likes to think a poet should be. Frost was seen as a lovable, wise old man; his simple wisdom and cracker-barrel sayings appeared comforting and homey. From this Yankee rustic, audiences learned that "There's a lot yet that isn't understood" or "We love the things we love for what they are" or "Good fences make good neighbors."

In a sense, Frost packaged himself for public consumption. "I am . . . my own salesman," he said. When asked direct questions about the meanings of his poems, he often winked or scratched his head to give the impression that the customer was always right. To be sure, there is a simplicity in Frost's language, but that simplicity does not fully reflect the depth of the man, the complexity of his themes, or the richness of his art.

The folksy optimist behind the public lectern did not reveal his private troubles to his audiences, although he did address those problems at his writing desk. Frost suffered from professional jealousies, anger, and depression. His family life was especially painful. Three of his four children died: a son at the age of four, a daughter in her late twenties from tuberculosis, and another son by suicide. His marriage was filled with tension. Although Frost's work is landscaped with sunlight, snow, birches, birds, blueberries, and squirrels, it is important to recognize that he was also intimately "acquainted with the night," a phrase that serves as the haunting title of one of his poems (see p. 121).

As a corrective to Frost's popular reputation, one critic, Lionel Trilling, described the world Frost creates in his poems as a "terrifying universe," characterized by loneliness, anguish, frustration, doubts, disappointment, and despair. To point this out is not to annihilate the pleasantness and even good-natured cheerfulness that can be enjoyed in Frost's poetry, but it is to say that Frost is not so one-dimensional as he is sometimes assumed to be. Frost's poetry requires readers who are alert and willing to penetrate the simplicity of its language to see the elusive and ambiguous meanings that lie below the surface.

# AN INTRODUCTION TO HIS WORK

Frost's treatment of nature helps explain the various levels of meaning in his poetry. The familiar natural world his poems evoke is sharply detailed. We hear icy branches clicking against themselves, we see the snow-white trunks of birches, we feel the smarting pain of a twig lashing across a face. The aspects of the natural world Frost describes are designated to give pleasure, but they are also frequently calculated to provoke thought. His use of nature tends to be symbolic. Complex meanings are derived from simple facts, such as a spider killing a moth or the difference between fire and ice (see "Design," p. 271, and "Fire and Ice," p. 270). Although Frost's strategy is to talk about particular events and individual experiences, his poems evoke universal issues.

Frost's poetry has strong regional roots and is "versed in country things," but it flourishes in any receptive imagination because, in the final analysis, it is concerned with human beings. Frost's New England landscapes are the occasion rather than the ultimate focus of his poems. Like the rural voices he creates in his poems, Frost typically approaches his themes indirectly. He explained the reason for this in a talk titled "Education by Poetry":

> Poetry provides the one permissible way of saying one thing and meaning another. People say, "Why don't you say what you mean?" We never do that, do we, being all of us too much poets. We like to talk in parables and in hints and in indirections — whether from diffidence or some other instinct.

The result is that the settings, characters, and situations that make up the subject matter of Frost's poems are vehicles for his perceptions about life.

In "Stopping by Woods on a Snowy Evening" (p. 271), for example, Frost uses the kind of familiar New England details that constitute his poetry for more than descriptive purposes. He shapes them into a meditation on the tension we sometimes feel between life's responsibilities and the "lovely, dark and deep" attraction that death offers. When the speaker's horse "gives his harness bells a shake," we are reminded that we are confronting a universal theme as well as a quiet moment of natural beauty.

Among the major concerns that appear in Frost's poetry are the fragility of life, the consequences of rejecting or accepting the conditions of one's life, the passion of inconsolable grief, the difficulty of sustaining intimacy, the fear of loneliness and isolation, the inevitability of change, the tensions between the individual and society, and the place of tradition and custom.

Whatever theme is encountered in a poem by Frost, a reader is likely to agree with him that "the initial delight is in the surprise of remembering something I didn't know." To achieve that fresh sense of discovery, Frost allowed himself to follow his instincts; his poetry

> inclines to the impulse, it assumes direction with the first line laid down, it runs a course of lucky events, and ends in a clarification of life — not necessarily a great clarification, such as sects and cults are founded on, but in a momentary stay against confusion.

This description from "On the Figure a Poem Makes" (see p. 274 for the complete essay), Frost's brief introduction to *Complete Poems,* may sound as if his poetry is formless and merely "lucky," but his poems tend to be more conventional than experimental: "The artist in me," as he put the matter in one of his poems, "cries out for design."

From Frost's perspective, "free verse is like playing tennis with the net down." He exercised his own freedom in meeting the challenges of rhyme and meter. His use of fixed forms such as couplets, tercets, quatrains, blank verse, and sonnets was not slavish because he enjoyed working them into the natural English speech patterns — especially the rhythms, idioms, and tones of speakers living north of Boston — that give voice to his themes. Frost often liked to use "Stopping by Woods on a Snowy Evening" as an example of his graceful way of making conventions appear natural and inevitable. He explored "the old ways to be new."

Frost's eye for strong, telling details was matched by his ear for natural speech rhythms. His flexible use of what he called "iambic and loose iambic" enabled him to create moving lyric poems that reveal the personal thoughts of a speaker and dramatic poems that convincingly characterize people caught in intense emotional situations. The language in his poems appears to be little more than a transcription of casual and even rambling speech, but it is in actuality Frost's poetic creation, carefully crafted to reveal the joys and sorrows that are woven into people's daily lives. What is missing from Frost's poems is artificiality, not art. Consider this poem.

## ROBERT FROST

### *The Road Not Taken*                                                1916

Two roads diverged in a yellow wood,
And sorry I could not travel both
And be one traveler, long I stood
And looked down one as far as I could
To where it bent in the undergrowth;                                      5

Then took the other, as just as fair,
And having perhaps the better claim,
Because it was grassy and wanted wear;
Though as for that the passing there
Had worn them really about the same,                                     10

And both that morning equally lay
In leaves no step had trodden black.
Oh, I kept the first for another day!
Yet knowing how way leads on to way,
I doubted if I should ever come back.                                    15

I shall be telling this with a sigh
Somewhere ages and ages hence:

Two roads diverged in a wood, and I —
I took the one less traveled by,
And that has made all the difference.                        20

    This poem intrigues readers because it is at once so simple and so deeply resonant. Recalling a walk in the woods, the speaker describes how he came to a fork in the road, which forced him to choose one path over another. Though "sorry" that he "could not travel both," he made a choice after carefully weighing his two options. This, essentially, is what happens in the poem; there is no other action. However, the incident is charged with symbolic significance by the speaker's reflections on the necessity and consequences of his decision.

    The final stanza indicates that the choice concerns more than simply walking down a road, for the speaker says that choosing the "less traveled" path has affected his entire life — that "that has made all the difference." Frost draws on a familiar enough metaphor when he compares life to a journey, but he is also calling attention to a less commonly noted problem: despite our expectations, aspirations, appetites, hopes, and desires, we can't have it all. Making one choice precludes another. It is impossible to determine what particular decision the speaker refers to: perhaps he had to choose a college, a career, a spouse; perhaps he was confronted with mutually exclusive ideas, beliefs, or values. There is no way to know because Frost wisely creates a symbolic choice and implicitly invites us to supply our own circumstances.

    The speaker's reflections about his choice are as central to an understanding of the poem as the choice itself; indeed, they may be more central. He describes the road taken as "having perhaps the better claim, / Because it was grassy and wanted wear"; he prefers the "less traveled" path. This seems to be an expression of individualism, which would account for "the difference" his choice made in his life. But Frost complicates matters by having the speaker also acknowledge that there was no significant difference between the two roads; one was "just as fair" as the other; each was "worn . . . really about the same"; and "both that morning equally lay / In leaves no step had trodden black."

    The speaker imagines that in the future, "ages and ages hence," he will recount his choice with "a sigh" that will satisfactorily explain the course of his life, but Frost seems to be having a little fun here by showing us how the speaker will embellish his past decision to make it appear more dramatic. What we hear is someone trying to convince himself that the choice he made significantly changed his life. When he recalls what happened in the "yellow wood," a color that gives a glow to that irretrievable moment when his life seemed to be on verge of a momentous change, he appears more concerned with the path he did not choose than with the one he took. Frost shrewdly titles the poem to suggest the speaker's sense of loss at not being able to "travel both" roads. When the speaker's reflections about his choice are examined, the poem reveals his nostalgia instead of affirming his decision to travel a self-reliant path in life.

The rhymed stanzas of "The Road Not Taken" follow a pattern established in the first five lines (*abaab*). This rhyme scheme reflects, perhaps, the speaker's efforts to shape his life into a pleasing and coherent form. The natural speech rhythms Frost uses allow him to integrate the rhymes unobtrusively, but there is a slight shift in lines 19 and 20, when the speaker asserts self-consciously that the "less traveled" road — which we already know to be basically the same as the other road — "made all the difference." Unlike all of the other rhymes in the poem, "difference" does not rhyme precisely with "hence." The emphasis that must be placed on "differ*ence*" to make it rhyme perfectly with "hence" may suggest that the speaker is trying just a little too hard to pattern his life on his earlier choice in the woods.

Perhaps the best way to begin reading Frost's poetry is to accept the invitation he placed at the beginning of many volumes of his poems. "The Pasture" means what it says, of course; it is about taking care of some farm chores, but it is also a means of "saying one thing in terms of another."

## ROBERT FROST

### *The Pasture*                                                      1913

I'm going out to clean the pasture spring;
I'll only stop to rake the leaves away
(And wait to watch the water clear, I may):
I shan't be gone long. — You come too.

I'm going out to fetch the little calf
That's standing by the mother. It's so young
It totters when she licks it with her tongue.
I sha'n't be gone long. — You come too.

"The Pasture" is a simple but irresistible songlike invitation to the pleasure of looking at the world through the eyes of a poet.

## Chronology

| 1874 | Born on March 26 in San Francisco. |
| 1885 | Father dies and family moves to Lawrence, Massachusetts. |
| 1892 | Graduates from Lawrence High School. |
| 1893–94 | Studies at Dartmouth College. |
| 1895 | Marries his high school sweetheart, Elinor White. |
| 1897–99 | Studies at Harvard College. |
| 1900 | Moves to a farm in West Derry, New Hampshire. |

| 1912 | Moves to England, where he farms and writes. |
| 1913 | *A Boy's Will* is published in London. |
| 1914 | *North of Boston* is published in London. |
| 1915 | Moves to a farm near Franconia, New Hampshire. |
| 1916 | Elected to National Institute of Letters. |
| 1917–20 | Teaches at Amherst College. |
| 1919 | Moves to South Shaftsbury, Vermont. |
| 1921–23 | Teaches at the University of Michigan. |
| 1923 | *Selected Poems* and *New Hampshire* are published; the latter is awarded a Pulitzer Prize. |
| 1928 | *West-Running Brook* is published. |
| 1930 | *Collected Poems* is published. |
| 1936 | *A Further Range* is published; teaches at Harvard. |
| 1938 | Wife dies. |
| 1939–42 | Teaches at Harvard. |
| 1942 | *A Witness Tree,* which is awarded a Pulitzer Prize, is published. |
| 1943–49 | Teaches at Dartmouth. |
| 1945 | *A Masque of Reason* is published. |
| 1947 | *Steeple Bush* and *A Masque of Mercy* are published. |
| 1949 | *Complete Poems* (enlarged) is published. |
| 1961 | Reads "The Gift Outright" at President John F. Kennedy's inauguration. |
| 1963 | Dies on January 29 in Boston. |

# Robert Frost

## *Mowing*                                                             *1913*

There was never a sound beside the wood but one,
And that was my long scythe whispering to the ground.
What was it it whispered? I knew not well myself;
Perhaps it was something about the heat of the sun,
Something, perhaps, about the lack of sound —                          5
And that was why it whispered and did not speak.
It was no dream of the gift of idle hours,
Or easy gold at the hand of fay or elf:
Anything more than the truth would have seemed too weak

To the earnest love that laid the swale in rows,                    10
Not without feeble-pointed spikes of flowers
(Pale orchises), and scared a bright green snake.
The fact is the sweetest dream that labour knows.
My long scythe whispered and left the hay to make.

### CONSIDERATIONS FOR CRITICAL THINKING AND WRITING

1.  FIRST RESPONSE. Describe the tone of "Mowing." How does reading the
    poem aloud affect your understanding of it?
2.  Discuss the image of the scythe. Do you think it has any symbolic value?
    Explain why or why not.
3.  Paraphrase the poem. What do you think its theme is?
4.  Describe the type of sonnet Frost uses in "Mowing."

## ROBERT FROST

### *Mending Wall*                                                  *1914*

Something there is that doesn't love a wall,
That sends the frozen-ground-swell under it,
And spills the upper boulders in the sun;
And makes gaps even two can pass abreast.
The work of hunters is another thing:                               5
I have come after them and made repair
Where they have left not one stone on a stone,
But they would have the rabbit out of hiding,
To please the yelping dogs. The gaps I mean,
No one has seen them made or heard them made,                       10
But at spring mending-time we find them there.
I let my neighbor know beyond the hill;
And on a day we meet to walk the line
And set the wall between us once again.
We keep the wall between us as we go.                               15
To each the boulders that have fallen to each.
And some are loaves and some so nearly balls
We have to use a spell to make them balance:
"Stay where you are until our backs are turned!"
We wear our fingers rough with handling them.                      20
Oh, just another kind of outdoor game,
One on a side. It comes to little more:
There where it is we do not need the wall:
He is all pine and I am apple orchard.
My apple trees will never get across                               25
And eat the cones under his pines, I tell him.

He only says, "Good fences make good neighbors."
Spring is the mischief in me, and I wonder
If I could put a notion in his head:
"*Why* do they make good neighbors? Isn't it                                30
Where there are cows? But here there are no cows.
Before I built a wall I'd ask to know
What I was walling in or walling out,
And to whom I was like to give offense.
Something there is that doesn't love a wall,                                 35
That wants it down." I could say "Elves" to him,
But it's not elves exactly, and I'd rather
He said it for himself. I see him there
Bringing a stone grasped firmly by the top
In each hand, like an old-stone savage armed.                               40
He moves in darkness as it seems to me,
Not of woods only and the shade of trees.
He will not go behind his father's saying,
And he likes having thought of it so well
He says again, "Good fences make good neighbors."                           45

## CONSIDERATIONS FOR CRITICAL THINKING AND WRITING

1. FIRST RESPONSE. What might the "Something" be that "doesn't love a wall" (line 1)? Why does the speaker remind his neighbor each spring that the wall needs to be repaired? Is it ironic that the *speaker* initiates the mending? Is there anything good about the wall?

2. How do the speaker and his neighbor differ in sensibilities? What is suggested about the neighbor in lines 41 and 42?

3. The neighbor likes the saying "Good fences make good neighbors" so well that he repeats it (lines 27, 45). Does the speaker also say something twice? What else suggests that the speaker's attitude toward the wall is not necessarily Frost's?

4. Although the speaker's language is colloquial, what is poetic about the sounds and rhythms he uses?

5. This poem was first published in 1914; Frost read it to an audience when he visited Russia in 1962. What do these facts suggest about the symbolic value of "Mending Wall"?

## CONNECTION TO ANTHER SELECTION

1. How do you think the neighbor in this poem would respond to Emily Dickinson's idea of imagination in "To make a prairie it takes a clover and one bee" (p. 43)?

## ROBERT FROST

### *Home Burial*                                                 1914

He saw her from the bottom of the stairs
Before she saw him. She was starting down,
Looking back over her shoulder at some fear.
She took a doubtful step and then undid it
To raise herself and look again. He spoke                          5
Advancing toward her: "What is it you see
From up there always — for I want to know."
She turned and sank upon her skirts at that,
And her face changed from terrified to dull.
He said to gain time: "What is it you see,"                       10
Mounting until she cowered under him.
"I will find out now — you must tell me, dear."
She, in her place, refused him any help
With the least stiffening of her neck and silence.
She let him look, sure that he wouldn't see,                      15
Blind creature; and awhile he didn't see.
But at last he murmured, "Oh," and again, "Oh."

"What is it — what?" she said.

                              "Just that I see."

"You don't," she challenged. "Tell me what it is."                20

"The wonder is I didn't see at once.
I never noticed it from here before.
I must be wonted° to it — that's the reason.          *accustomed*
The little graveyard where my people are!
So small the window frames the whole of it.                       25
Not so much larger than a bedroom, is it?
There are three stones of slate and one of marble,
Broad-shouldered little slabs there in the sunlight
On the sidehill. We haven't to mind *those*.
But I understand: it is not the stones,                           30
But the child's mound —"

                    "Don't, don't, don't, don't," she cried.

She withdrew, shrinking from beneath his arm
That rested on the banister, and slid downstairs;
And turned on him with such a daunting look,                      35
He said twice over before he knew himself:
"Can't a man speak of his own child he's lost?"

"Not you! — Oh, where's my hat? Oh, I don't need it!
I must get out of here. I must get air.
I don't know rightly whether any man can."                        40

"Amy! Don't go to someone else this time.
Listen to me. I won't come down the stairs."
He sat and fixed his chin between his fists.
"There's something I should like to ask you, dear."

"You don't know how to ask it." 45

                              "Help me, then."
Her fingers moved the latch for all reply.

"My words are nearly always an offense.
I don't know how to speak of anything
So as to please you. But I might be taught, 50
I should suppose. I can't say I see how.
A man must partly give up being a man
With women-folk. We could have some arrangement
By which I'd bind myself to keep hands off
Anything special you're a-mind to name. 55
Though I don't like such things 'twixt those that love.
Two that don't love can't live together without them.
But two that do can't live together with them."
She moved the latch a little. "Don't — don't go.
Don't carry it to someone else this time. 60
Tell me about it if it's something human.
Let me into your grief. I'm not so much
Unlike other folks as your standing there
Apart would make me out. Give me my chance.
I do think, though, you overdo it a little. 65
What was it brought you up to think it the thing
To take your mother-loss of a first child
So inconsolably — in the face of love.
You'd think his memory might be satisfied —"

"There you go sneering now!" 70

                              "I'm not, I'm not!

You make me angry. I'll come down to you.
God, what a woman! And it's come to this,
A man can't speak of his own child that's dead."

"You can't because you don't know how to speak. 75
If you had any feelings, you that dug
With your own hand — how could you? — his little grave;
I saw you from that very window there,
Making the gravel leap and leap in air,
Leap up, like that, like that, and land so lightly 80
And roll back down the mound beside the hole.
I thought, Who is that man? I didn't know you.
And I crept down the stairs and up the stairs

To look again, and still your spade kept lifting.
Then you came in. I heard your rumbling voice                    85
Out in the kitchen, and I don't know why,
But I went near to see with my own eyes.
You could sit there with the stains on your shoes
Of the fresh earth from your own baby's grave
And talk about your everyday concerns.                           90
You had stood the spade up against the wall
Outside there in the entry, for I saw it."

"I shall laugh the worst laugh I ever laughed.
I'm cursed. God, if I don't believe I'm cursed."

"I can repeat the very words you were saying.                    95
'Three foggy mornings and one rainy day
Will rot the best birch fence a man can build.'
Think of it, talk like that at such a time!
What had how long it takes a birch to rot
To do with what was in the darkened parlor                       100
You *couldn't* care! The nearest friends can go
With anyone to death, comes so far short
They might as well not try to go at all.
No, from the time when one is sick to death,
One is alone, and he dies more alone.                            105
Friends make pretense of following to the grave.
But before one is in it, their minds are turned
And making the best of their way back to life
And living people, and things they understand.
But the world's evil. I won't have grief so                      110
If I can change it. Oh, I won't, I won't!"

"There, you have said it all and you feel better.
You won't go now. You're crying. Close the door.
The heart's gone out of it: why keep it up.
Amy! There's someone coming down the road!"                      115

"*You* — oh, you think the talk is all. I must go —
Somewhere out of this house. How can I make you —"

"If — you — do!" She was opening the door wider.
"Where do you mean to go? First tell me that.
I'll follow and bring you back by force. I *will!* —"           120

## CONSIDERATIONS FOR CRITICAL THINKING AND WRITING

1. FIRST RESPONSE. This poem tells a story of a relationship. Is the husband
   insensitive and indifferent to his wife's grief? Characterize the wife. Has
   Frost invited us to sympathize with one character more than with the other?

2. How has the burial of the child within sight of the stairway window
   affected the relationship of the couple in this poem? Is the child's grave
   a symptom or a cause of the conflict between them?

3. What is the effect of splitting the iambic pentameter pattern in lines 18 and 19, 31 and 32, 45 and 46, and 70 and 71?

4. Is the conflict resolved at the conclusion of the poem? Do you think the husband and wife will overcome their differences?

## ROBERT FROST

### *After Apple-Picking*        *1914*

My long two-pointed ladder's sticking through a tree
Toward heaven still,
And there's a barrel that I didn't fill
Beside it, and there may be two or three
Apples I didn't pick upon some bough.      5
But I am done with apple-picking now.
Essence of winter sleep is on the night,
The scent of apples: I am drowsing off.
I cannot rub the strangeness from my sight
I got from looking through a pane of glass      10
I skimmed this morning from the drinking trough
And held against the world of hoary grass.
It melted, and I let it fall and break.
But I was well
Upon my way to sleep before it fell,      15
And I could tell
What form my dreaming was about to take.
Magnified apples appear and disappear,
Stem end and blossom end,
And every fleck of russet showing clear.      20
My instep arch not only keeps the ache,
It keeps the pressure of a ladder-round.
I feel the ladder sway as the boughs bend.
And I keep hearing from the cellar bin
The rumbling sound      25
Of load on load of apples coming in.
For I have had too much
Of apple-picking: I am overtired
Of the great harvest I myself desired.
There were ten thousand thousand fruit to touch,      30
Cherish in hand, lift down, and not let fall.
For all
That struck the earth,
No matter if not bruised or spiked with stubble,
Went surely to the cider-apple heap      35
As of no worth.
One can see what will trouble
This sleep of mine, whatever sleep it is.

Were he not gone,
The woodchuck could say whether it's like his                    40
Long sleep, as I describe its coming on,
Or just some human sleep.

### CONSIDERATIONS FOR CRITICAL THINKING AND WRITING

1. FIRST RESPONSE. How does this poem illustrate Frost's view that "poetry provides the one permissible way of saying one thing and meaning another"? When do you first sense that the detailed description of apple picking is being used that way?

2. What comes after apple picking? What does the speaker worry about in the dream beginning in line 18?

3. Why do you suppose Frost uses apples rather than, say, pears or squash?

## ROBERT FROST

## *Birches*                                                      *1916*

When I see birches bend to left and right
Across the lines of straighter darker trees,
I like to think some boy's been swinging them.
But swinging doesn't bend them down to stay
As ice-storms do. Often you must have seen them                  5
Loaded with ice a sunny winter morning
After a rain. They click upon themselves
As the breeze rises, and turn many-colored
As the stir cracks and crazes their enamel.
Soon the sun's warmth makes them shed crystal shells             10
Shattering and avalanching on the snow-crust —
Such heaps of broken glass to sweep away
You'd think the inner dome of heaven had fallen.
They are dragged to the withered bracken by the load,
And they seem not to break; though once they are bowed           15
So low for long, they never right themselves:
You may see their trunks arching in the woods
Years afterwards, trailing their leaves on the ground
Like girls on hands and knees that throw their hair
Before them over their heads to dry in the sun.                  20
But I was going to say when Truth broke in
With all her matter-of-fact about the ice-storm,
I should prefer to have some boy bend them
As he went out and in to fetch the cows —
Some boy too far from town to learn baseball,                    25
Whose only play was what he found himself,
Summer or winter, and could play alone.

One by one he subdued his father's trees
By riding them down over and over again
Until he took the stiffness out of them,                                30
And not one but hung limp, not one was left
For him to conquer. He learned all there was
To learn about not launching out too soon
And so not carrying the tree away
Clear to the ground. He always kept his poise                           35
To the top branches, climbing carefully
With the same pains you use to fill a cup
Up to the brim, and even above the brim.
Then he flung outward, feet first, with a swish,
Kicking his way down through the air to the ground.                     40
So was I once myself a swinger of birches.
And so I dream of going back to be.
It's when I'm weary of considerations,
And life is too much like a pathless wood
Where your face burns and tickles with the cobwebs                      45
Broken across it, and one eye is weeping
From a twig's having lashed across it open.
I'd like to get away from earth awhile
And then come back to it and begin over.
May no fate willfully misunderstand me                                  50
And half grant what I wish and snatch me away
Not to return. Earth's the right place for love:
I don't know where it's likely to go better.
I'd like to go by climbing a birch tree,
And climb black branches up a snow-white trunk,                         55
*Toward* heaven, till the tree could bear no more,
But dipped its top and set me down again.
That would be good both going and coming back.
One could do worse than be a swinger of birches.

## Considerations for Critical Thinking and Writing

1. FIRST RESPONSE. What do you think the swinging of birches symbolizes?

2. Why does the speaker in this poem prefer the birches to have been bent by boys instead of ice storms?

3. How is "Earth" (line 52) described in the poem? Why does the speaker choose it over "heaven" (line 56)?

4. How might the effect of this poem be changed if it were written in heroic couplets instead of blank verse?

5. CRITICAL STRATEGIES. Read the section on reader-response strategies (pp. 342–44) in Chapter 15, "Critical Strategies for Reading." Trace your response to this poem over three successive careful readings. How does your understanding of the poem change or develop?

## ROBERT FROST

### *"Out, Out —"*°                                                  *1916*

The buzz-saw snarled and rattled in the yard
And made dust and dropped stove-length sticks of wood,
Sweet-scented stuff when the breeze drew across it.
And from there those that lifted eyes could count
Five mountain ranges one behind the other                        5
Under the sunset far into Vermont.
And the saw snarled and rattled, snarled and rattled,
As it ran light, or had to bear a load.
And nothing happened: day was all but done.
Call it a day, I wish they might have said                       10
To please the boy by giving him the half hour
That a boy counts so much when saved from work.
His sister stood beside them in her apron
To tell them "Supper." At the word, the saw,
As if to prove saws knew what supper meant,                      15
Leaped out at the boy's hand, or seemed to leap —
He must have given the hand. However it was,
Neither refused the meeting. But the hand!
The boy's first outcry was a rueful laugh,
As he swung toward them holding up the hand                      20
Half in appeal, but half as if to keep
The life from spilling. Then the boy saw all —
Since he was old enough to know, big boy
Doing a man's work, though a child at heart —
He saw all spoiled. "Don't let him cut my hand off —            25
The doctor, when he comes. Don't let him, sister!"
So. But the hand was gone already.
The doctor put him in the dark of ether.
He lay and puffed his lips out with his breath.
And then — the watcher at his pulse took fright.                 30
No one believed. They listened at his heart.
Little — less — nothing! — and that ended it.
No more to build on there. And they, since they
Were not the one dead, turned to their affairs.

*"Out, Out —":* From Act V, scene v, of Shakespeare's *Macbeth.*

### CONSIDERATIONS FOR CRITICAL THINKING AND WRITING

1. FIRST RESPONSE. This narrative poem is about the accidental death of a
   Vermont boy. What is the purpose of the story? Some readers have
   argued that the final lines reveal the speaker's callousness and indiffer-
   ence. What do you think?

2. How does Frost's allusion to *Macbeth* contribute to the meaning of this poem? Does the speaker seem to agree with the view of life expressed in Macbeth's lines?

3. CRITICAL STRATEGIES. Read the section on Marxist criticism (pp. 335–36) in Chapter 15, "Critical Strategies for Reading." How do you think a Marxist critic would interpret the family and events described in this poem?

## CONNECTIONS TO OTHER SELECTIONS

1. What are the similarities and differences in theme between this poem and Frost's "Dust of Snow" (p. 270)?

2. Write an essay comparing how grief is handled by the boy's family in this poem and by the couple in "Home Burial" (p. 262).

3. Compare the tone and theme of "'Out, Out—'" with those of Stephen Crane's "A Man Said to the Universe" (p. 129).

## ROBERT FROST

### *The Oven Bird*                                               1916

There is a singer everyone has heard,
Loud, a mid-summer and a mid-wood bird,
Who makes the solid tree trunks sound again.
He says that leaves are old and that for flowers
Mid-summer is to spring as one to ten.                                    5
He says the early petal-fall is past
When pear and cherry bloom went down in showers
On sunny days a moment overcast;
And comes that other fall we name the fall.
He says the highway dust is over all.                                    10
The bird would cease and be as other birds
But that he knows in singing not to sing.
The question that he frames in all but words
Is what to make of a diminished thing.

### CONSIDERATIONS FOR CRITICAL THINKING AND WRITING

1. FIRST RESPONSE. What kind of sonnet is this poem? What is the relationship between the octave and the sestet?

2. The ovenbird is a warbler that makes its domed nest on the ground. What kinds of observations does the speaker have it make about spring, summer, and fall?

3. The final two lines invite symbolic readings. What do you make of them?

4. CRITICAL STRATEGIES. Read the section on critical thinking (pp. 327–29) in Chapter 15, "Critical Strategies for Reading," and then research critical commentary on this poem. Write an essay describing the range of interpretations that you find. Which interpretation do you think is the most convincing? Why?

# Robert Frost

## *Fire and Ice*                                                    *1923*

Some say the world will end in fire,
Some say in ice.
From what I've tasted of desire
I hold with those who favor fire.
But if it had to perish twice,
I think I know enough of hate
To say that for destruction ice
Is also great
And would suffice.

### Considerations for Critical Thinking and Writing

1. **FIRST RESPONSE.** What characteristics of human behavior does the
   speaker associate with fire and with ice?

2. What theories about the end of the world are alluded to in lines 1 and 2?

3. How does the speaker's use of understatement and rhyme affect the
   tone of this poem?

# Robert Frost

## *Dust of Snow*                                                    *1923*

The way a crow
Shook down on me
The dust of snow
From a hemlock tree

Has given my heart
A change of mood
And saved some part
Of a day I had rued.

### Considerations for Critical Thinking and Writing

1. **FIRST RESPONSE.** Explain why you are inclined to read this poem literally or symbolically.

2. What connotations are evoked by Frost's diction?

3. How would you describe the speaker's relation to nature?

### Connection to Another Selection

1. Compare the themes in "Dust of Snow" and in Mary Oliver's "The Poet
   with His Face in His Hands" (p. 35).

### ROBERT FROST

## *Stopping by Woods on a Snowy Evening*    *1923*

Whose woods these are I think I know.
His house is in the village, though;
He will not see me stopping here
To watch his woods fill up with snow.

My little horse must think it queer    5
To stop without a farmhouse near
Between the woods and frozen lake
The darkest evening of the year.

He gives his harness bells a shake
To ask if there is some mistake.    10
The only other sound's the sweep
Of easy wind and downy flake.

The woods are lovely, dark and deep,
But I have promises to keep,
And miles to go before I sleep,    15
And miles to go before I sleep.

#### CONSIDERATIONS FOR CRITICAL THINKING AND WRITING

1. FIRST RESPONSE. What is the significance of the setting in this poem? How is tone conveyed by the images?

2. What does the speaker find appealing about the woods? What is the purpose of the horse in the poem?

3. Although the last two lines are identical, they are not read at the same speed. Why the difference? What is achieved by the repetition?

4. What is the poem's rhyme scheme? What is the effect of the rhyme in the final stanza?

#### CONNECTION TO ANOTHER SELECTION

1. What do you think Frost might have to say about "A Parodic Interpretation of 'Stopping by Woods on a Snowy Evening'" by Herbert R. Coursen Jr. (p. 277)?

### ROBERT FROST

## *Design*    *1936*

I found a dimpled spider, fat and white,
On a white heal-all,° holding up a moth
Like a white piece of rigid satin cloth —

---

2 *heal-all:* A common flower, usually blue, once used for medicinal purposes.

Assorted characters of death and blight
Mixed ready to begin the morning right,                    5
Like the ingredients of a witches' broth —
A snow-drop spider, a flower like a froth,
And dead wings carried like a paper kite.

What had the flower to do with being white,
The wayside blue and innocent heal-all?                   10
What brought the kindred spider to that height,
Then steered the white moth thither in the night?
What but design of darkness to appall? —
If design govern in a thing so small.

### CONSIDERATIONS FOR CRITICAL THINKING AND WRITING

1. FIRST RESPONSE. What kinds of speculations are raised in the poem's final two lines? Consider the meaning of the title. Is there more than one way to read it?

2. How does the division of the octave and sestet in this sonnet serve to organize the speaker's thoughts and feelings? What is the predominant rhyme? How does that rhyme relate to the poem's meaning?

3. Which words seem especially rich in connotative meanings? Explain how they function in the sonnet.

### CONNECTIONS TO OTHER SELECTIONS

1. Compare the ironic tone of "Design" with the tone of William Hathaway's "Oh, Oh" (p. 14). What would you have to change in Hathaway's poem to make it more like Frost's?

2. In an essay discuss Frost's view of God in this poem and Emily Dickinson's perspective in "I know that He exists" (p. 301).

3. Compare "Design" with "In White," Frost's early version of it (following).

## Perspectives on Robert Frost

### ROBERT FROST

## *"In White": An Early Version of "Design"*          *1912*

A dented spider like a snow drop white
On a white Heal-all, holding up a moth
Like a white piece of lifeless satin cloth —
Saw ever curious eye so strange a sight? —
Portent in little, assorted death and blight        5
Like the ingredients of a witches' broth? —
The beady spider, the flower like a froth,

And the moth carried like a paper kite.
What had that flower to do with being white,
The blue prunella every child's delight.    10
What brought the kindred spider to that height?
(Make we no thesis of the miller's° plight.)    *miller moth*
What but design of darkness and of night?
Design, design! Do I use the word aright?

### CONSIDERATIONS FOR CRITICAL THINKING AND WRITING

1. Read "In White" and "Design" (p. 271) aloud. Which version sounds better to you? Why?

2. Compare these versions line for line, paying particular attention to word choice. List the differences and try to explain why you think Frost revised the lines.

3. How does the change in titles reflect a shift in emphasis in the poem?

## ROBERT FROST

## *On the Living Part of a Poem*    1914

The living part of a poem is the intonation entangled somehow in the syntax, idiom, and meaning of a sentence. It is only there for those who have heard it previously in conversation. . . . It is the most volatile and at the same time important part of poetry. It goes and the language becomes dead language, the poetry dead poetry. With it go the accents, the stresses, the delays that are not the property of vowels and syllables but that are shifted at will with the sense. Vowels have length there is no denying. But the accent of sense supersedes all other accent, overrides it and sweeps it away. I will find you the word *come* variously used in various passages, a whole, half, third, fourth, fifth, and sixth note. It is as long as the sense makes it. When men no longer know the intonations on which we string our words they will fall back on what I may call the absolute length of our syllables, which is the length we would give them in passages that meant nothing. . . . I say you can't read a single good sentence with the salt in it unless you have previously heard it spoken. Neither can you with the help of all the characters and diacritical marks pronounce a single word unless you have previously heard it actually pronounced. Words exist in the mouth not books.

From a letter to Sidney Cox in *A Swinger of Birches:*
*A Portrait of Robert Frost*

### CONSIDERATIONS FOR CRITICAL THINKING AND WRITING

1. FIRST RESPONSE. Why does Frost place so much emphasis on hearing poetry spoken?

2. Choose a passage from "Home Burial" (p. 262) or "After Apple-Picking" (p. 265) and read it aloud. How does Frost's description of his emphasis

on intonation help explain the effects he achieves in the passage you have
selected?

3. Do you think it is true that all poetry must be heard? Do "[w]ords exist
in the mouth not books"?

## Amy Lowell (1874–1925)

### On Frost's Realistic Technique                                    1915

I have said that Mr. Frost's work is almost photographic. The qualification
was unnecessary, it is photographic. The pictures, the characters, are reproduced directly from life, they are burnt into his mind as though it were a
sensitive plate. He gives out what has been put in unchanged by any personal mental process. His imagination is bounded by what he has seen, he
is confined within the limits of his experience (or at least what might have
been his experience) and bent all one way like the windblown trees of New
England hillsides.

From a review of *North of Boston, The New Republic,* February 20, 1915

#### Considerations for Critical Thinking and Writing

1. Consider the "photographic" qualities of Frost's poetry by discussing
particular passages that strike you as having been "reproduced directly
from life."

2. Write an essay that supports or refutes Lowell's assertion that "[Frost] gives
out what has been put in unchanged by any personal mental process."

## Robert Frost

### On the Figure a Poem Makes                                        1939

Abstraction is an old story with the philosophers, but it has been like a new
toy in the hands of the artists of our day. Why can't we have any one quality of
poetry we choose by itself? We can have in thought. Then it will go hard if
we can't in practice. Our lives for it.

Granted no one but a humanist much cares how sound a poem is if it is
only *a* sound. The sound is the gold in the ore. Then we will have the sound
out alone and dispense with the inessential. We do till we make the discovery that the object in writing poetry is to make all poems sound as different
as possible from each other, and the resources for that of vowels, consonants,
punctuation, syntax, words, sentences, meter are not enough. We need the
help of context — meaning — subject matter. That is the greatest help towards
variety. All that can be done with words is soon told. So also with meters —
particularly in our language where there are virtually but two, strict iambic
and loose iambic. The ancients with many were still poor if they depended
on meters for all tune. It is painful to watch our sprung-rhythmists straining

at the point of omitting one short from a foot for relief from monotony. The possibilities for tune from the dramatic tones of meaning struck across the rigidity of a limited meter are endless. And we are back in poetry as merely one more art of having something to say, sound or unsound. Probably better if sound, because deeper and from wider experience.

Then there is this wildness whereof it is spoken. Granted again that it has an equal claim with sound to being a poem's better half. If it is a wild tune, it is a poem. Our problem then is, as modern abstractionists, to have the wildness pure; to be wild with nothing to be wild about. We bring up as aberrationists, giving way to undirected associations and kicking ourselves from one chance suggestion to another in all directions as of a hot afternoon in the life of a grasshopper. Theme alone can steady us down. Just as the first mystery was how a poem could have a tune in such a straightness as meter, so the second mystery is how a poem can have wildness and at the same time a subject that shall be fulfilled.

It should be of the pleasure of a poem itself to tell how it can. The figure a poem makes. It begins in delight and ends in wisdom. The figure is the same as for love. No one can really hold that the ecstasy should be static and stand still in one place. It begins in delight, it inclines to the impulse, it assumes direction with the first line laid down, it runs a course of lucky events, and ends in a clarification of life — not necessarily a great clarification, such as sects and cults are founded on, but in a momentary stay against confusion. It has denouement. It has an outcome that though unforeseen was predestined from the first image of the original mood — and indeed from the very mood. It is but a trick poem and no poem at all if the best of it was thought of first and saved for the last. It finds its own name as it goes and discovers the best waiting for it in some final phrase at once wise and sad — the happy-sad blend of the drinking song.

No tears in the writer, no tears in the reader. No surprise for the writer, no surprise for the reader. For me the initial delight is in the surprise of remembering something I didn't know I knew. I am in a place, in a situation, as if I had materialized from cloud or risen out of the ground. There is a glad recognition of the long lost and the rest follows. Step by step the wonder of unexpected supply keeps going. The impressions most useful to my purpose seem always those I was unaware of and so made no note of at the time when taken, and the conclusion is come to that like giants we are always hurling experience ahead of us to pave the future with against the day when we may want to strike a line of purpose across it for somewhere. The line will have the more charm for not being mechanically straight. We enjoy the straight crookedness of a good walking stick. Modern instruments of precision are being used to make things crooked as if by eye and hand in the old days.

I tell how there may be a better wildness of logic than of inconsequence. But the logic is backward, in retrospect, after the act. It must be more felt than seen ahead like prophecy. It must be a revelation, or a series of revelations, as much for the poet as for the reader. For it to be that there must have been the greatest freedom of the material to move about in it and to establish relations in it regardless of time and space, previous relation, and everything but affinity. We prate of freedom. We call our schools free because we are not free to stay away from them till we are sixteen years of age. I have given up my democratic prejudices and now willingly set the lower classes free to be completely taken care of by the upper classes. Political freedom is nothing to me. I bestow it right and left. All I would keep for myself is the freedom of my material — the condition of body and mind now and then to summons aptly from the vast chaos of all I have lived through.

Scholars and artists thrown together are often annoyed at the puzzle of where they differ. Both work for knowledge; but I suspect they differ most importantly in the way their knowledge is come by. Scholars get theirs with conscientious thoroughness along projected lines of logic; poets theirs cavalierly and as it happens in and out of books. They stick to nothing deliberately, but let what will stick to them like burrs where they walk in the fields. No acquirement is on assignment, or even self-assignment. Knowledge of the second kind is much more available in the wild free ways of wit and art. A school boy may be defined as one who can tell you what he knows in the order in which he learned it. The artist must value himself as he snatches a thing from some previous order in time and space into a new order with not so much as a ligature clinging to it of the old place where it was organic.

More than once I should have lost my soul to radicalism if it had been the originality it was mistaken for by its young converts. Originality and initiative are what I ask for my country. For myself the originality need be no more than the freshness of a poem run in the way I have described: from delight to wisdom. The figure is the same as for love. Like a piece of ice on a hot stove the poem must ride on its own melting. A poem may be worked over once it is in being, but may not be worried into being. Its most precious quality will remain its having run itself and carried away the poet with it. Read it a hundred times: it will forever keep its freshness as a metal keeps its fragrance. It can never lose its sense of a meaning that once unfolded by surprise as it went.

From Complete Poems of Robert Frost

## CONSIDERATIONS FOR CRITICAL THINKING AND WRITING

1. Frost places a high premium on sound in his poetry because it "is the gold in the ore." Choose one of Frost's poems in this book and explain the effects of its sounds and how they contribute to its meaning.

2. Discuss Frost's explanation of how his poems are written. In what sense is the process both spontaneous and "predestined"?

3. What do you think Frost means when he says he's given up his "democratic prejudices"? Why is "political freedom" nothing to him?

4. Write an essay that examines in more detail the ways scholars and artists "come by" knowledge.

5. Explain what you think Frost means when he writes, "Like a piece of ice on a hot stove the poem must ride on its own melting."

Robert Frost

## *On the Way to Read a Poem* 1951

The way to read a poem in prose or verse is in the light of all the other poems ever written. We may begin anywhere. We *duff* into our first. We read that imperfectly (thoroughness with it would be fatal), but the better to read the second. We read the second the better to read the third, the third the better to read the fourth, the fourth better to read the fifth, the fifth the better to read the first again, or the second if it so happens. For poems are not meant to be read in course any more than they are to be made a study of. I once made a resolve never to put any book to any use it wasn't intended for by its author. Improvement will not be a progression but a widening circulation. Our instinct is to settle down like a revolving dog and make ourselves at home among the poems, completely at our ease as to how they should be taken. The same people will be apt to take poems right as know how to take a hint when there is one and not to take a hint when none is intended. Theirs is the ultimate refinement.

From "Poetry and School," *Atlantic Monthly,* June 1951

### Considerations for Critical Thinking and Writing

1. Given your own experience, how good is Frost's advice about reading in general and his poems in particular?

2. In what sense is a good reader like a "revolving dog" and a person who knows "how to take a hint"?

3. Frost elsewhere in this piece writes, "One of the dangers of college to anyone who wants to stay a human reader (that is to say a humanist) is that he will become a specialist and lose his sensitive fear of landing on the lovely too hard. (With beak and talon.)" Write an essay in response to this concern. Do you agree with Frost's distinction between a "human reader" and a "specialist"?

## Herbert R. Coursen Jr. (1932–2011)

## *A Parodic Interpretation of "Stopping by Woods on a Snowy Evening"* 1962

Much ink has spilled on many pages in exegesis of this little poem. Actually, critical jottings have only obscured what has lain beneath critical noses all these years. To say that the poem means merely that a man stops one night to observe a snowfall, or that the poem contrasts the mundane desire for creature comfort with the sweep of aesthetic appreciation, or that it renders worldly responsibilities paramount, or that it reveals the speaker's latent death-wish is to miss the point rather badly. Lacking has been that mind simple enough to see what is *really* there. . . .

The "darkest evening of the year" in New England is December 21st, a date near that on which the western world celebrates Christmas. It may be that December 21st *is* the date of the poem, or (and with poets this seems more likely) that this is the closest the poet can come to Christmas without giving it all away. Who has "promises to keep" at or near this date, and who must traverse much territory to fulfill these promises? Yes, and who but St. Nick would know the location of *each* home? Only he would know who had "just settled down for a long winter's nap" (the poem's third line — "He will not see me stopping here" — is clearly a veiled allusion) and would not be out inspecting his acreage this night. The unusual phrase "fill up with snow," in the poem's fourth line, is a transfer of Santa's occupational preoccupation to the countryside; he is mulling the filling of countless stockings hung above countless fireplaces by countless careful children. "Harness bells," of course, allude to "Sleighing Song," a popular Christmas tune of the time the poem was written in which the refrain "Jingle Bells! Jingle Bells!" appears; thus again are we put on the Christmas track. The "little horse," like the date, is another attempt at poetic obfuscation. Although the "rein-reindeer" ambiguity has been eliminated from the poem's final version,[1] probably because too obvious, we may speculate that the animal is really a reindeer disguised as a horse by the poet's desire for obscurity, a desire which we must concede has been fulfilled up to now.

The animal is clearly concerned, like the faithful Rudolph — another possible allusion (post facto, hence unconscious) — lest his master fail to complete his mission. Seeing no farmhouse in the second quatrain, but pulling a load of presents, no wonder the little beast wonders! It takes him a full two quatrains to rouse his driver to remember all the empty stockings which hang ahead. And Santa does so reluctantly at that, poor soul, as he ponders the myriad farmhouses and villages which spread between him and his own "winter's nap." The modern St. Nick, lonely and overworked, tosses no "Happy Christmas to all and to all a good night!" into the precipitation. He merely shrugs his shoulders and resignedly plods away.

From "The Ghost of Christmas Past: 'Stopping by Woods on a Snowy Evening,'" *College English*, December 1962

[1] The original draft contained the following line: "That bid me give the reins a shake" (Stageberg-Anderson, *Poetry as Experience* [New York, 1952], p. 457). [Coursen's note.]

### Considerations for Critical Thinking and Writing

1. Is this critical spoof at all credible? Does the interpretation hold any water? Is the evidence reasonable? Why or why not? Which of the poem's details are accounted for and which are ignored?

2. Choose a Frost poem and try writing a parodic interpretation of it.

3. What criteria do you use to distinguish between a sensible interpretation of a poem and an absurd one?

## Two Complementary Critical Readings

RICHARD POIRIER (1925–2009)

## *On Emotional Suffocation in "Home Burial"*   *1977*

Frost's poetry recurrently dramatizes the discovery that the sharing of a "home" can produce imaginations of uncontrollable threat inside or outside. "Home" can become the source of those fears from which it is supposed to protect us; it can become the habitation of that death whose anguish it is supposed to ameliorate. And this brings us to one of Frost's greatest poetic dramatizations of the theme, "Home Burial." [T]he pressure is shared by a husband and wife, but . . . the role of the husband is ambiguous. Though he does his best to comprehend the wife's difficulties, he is only partly able to do so. The very title of the poem means something about the couple as well as about the dead child buried in back of the house. It is as if "home" were a burial plot for all of them.

The opening lines of Frost's dramatic narratives are usually wonderfully deft in suggesting the metaphoric nature of "home," the human opportunities or imperatives which certain details represent for a husband or a wife. . . . [I]n "Home Burial," the couple are trapped inside the house, which is described as a kind of prison, or perhaps more aptly, a mental hospital. Even the wife's glance out the window can suggest to the husband the desperation she feels within the confines of what has always been his family's "home"; it looks directly on the family graveyard which now holds the body of their recently dead child: [lines 1–30 of "Home Burial" are quoted here].

The remarkable achievement here is that the husband and wife have become so nearly inarticulate in their animosities that the feelings have been transferred to a vision of household arrangements and to their own bodily movements. They and the house conspire together to create an aura of suffocation. . . . Frost's special genius is in the placement of words. The first line poses the husband as a kind of spy; the opening of the second line suggests a habituated wariness on her part, but from that point to line 5 we are shifted back to his glimpse of her as she moves obsessively again, as yet unaware of being watched, to the window. Suggestions of alienation, secretiveness, male intimidation ("advancing toward her") within a situation of mutual distrust, a miasmic fear inside as well as outside the house — we are made to sense this before anyone speaks. Initially the fault seems to lie mostly with the husband. But as soon as she catches him watching her, and as soon as he begins to talk, it is the grim mutuality of their dilemma and the shared responsibilities for it that sustain the dramatic intelligence and power of the poem.

*From Robert Frost: The Work of Knowing*

### CONSIDERATIONS FOR CRITICAL THINKING AND WRITING

1. According to Poirier, how can the couple's home be regarded as a kind of "mental hospital"? Compare Poirier's view with Katherine Kearns's

description in the following perspective on the house as a "marital asylum."

2. Explain why you agree or disagree that the husband's behavior is a form of "male intimidation."

3. Write an essay that discusses the "grim mutuality" of the couple's "dilemma."

## KATHERINE KEARNS (B. 1949)

## *On the Symbolic Setting of "Home Burial"*    1987

"Home Burial" may be used to clarify Frost's intimate relationships between sex, death, and madness. The physical iconography is familiar — a stairwell, a window, a doorway, and a grave — elements which Frost reiterates throughout his poetry. The marriage in "Home Burial" has been destroyed by the death of a first and only son. The wife is in the process of leaving the house, crossing the threshold from marital asylum into freedom. The house is suffocating her. Her window view of the graveyard is not enough and is, in fact, a maddening reminder that she could not enter the earth with her son. With its transparent barrier, the window is a mockery of a widened vision throughout Frost's poetry and seems to incite escape rather than quelling it; in "Home Burial" the woman can "see" through the window and into the grave in a way her husband cannot, and the fear is driving her down the steps toward the door — "She was starting down — / Looking back over her shoulder at some fear" — even before she sees her husband. He threatens to follow his wife and bring her back by force, as if he is the cause of her leaving, but his gesture will be futile because it is based on the mistaken assumption that she is escaping him. Pathetically, he is merely an obstacle toward which she reacts at first dully and then with angry impatience. He is an inanimate part of the embattled household, her real impetus for movement comes from the grave.

The house itself, reduced symbolically and literally to a womblike passageway between the bedroom and the threshold, is a correlative for the sexual tension generated by the man's insistence on his marital rights. He offers to "give up being a man" by binding himself "to keep hands off," but their marriage is already sexually damaged and empty. The man and woman move in an intricate dance, she coming downward and then retracing a step, he "Mounting until she cower[s] under him," she "shrinking from beneath his arm" to slide downstairs. Randall Jarrell examines the image of the woman sinking into "a modest, compact, feminine bundle" upon her skirts;[1] it might be further observed that this childlike posture is also very much a gesture of sexual denial, body bent, knees drawn up protectively

---

[1] "Robert Frost's 'Home Burial,'" in *The Moment of Poetry,* ed. Don Cameron Allen (Baltimore: Johns Hopkins UP, 1962), p. 104.

against the breasts, all encompassed by voluminous skirts. The two are in profound imbalance, and Frost makes the wife's speech and movements the poetic equivalent of stumbling and resistance; her lines are frequently eleven syllables, and often are punctuated by spondees whose forceful but awkward slowness embodies the woman's vacillations "from terrified to dull," and from frozen and silent immobility to anger. Her egress from the house will be symbolic verification of her husband's impotence, and if she leaves it and does not come back, the house will rot as the best birch fence will rot. Unfilled, without a woman with child, it will fall into itself, an image that recurs throughout Frost's poetry. Thus the child's grave predicts the dissolution of household, . . . almost a literal "home burial."

From "'The Place Is the Asylum': Women and Nature in Robert Frost's Poetry," *American Literature*, May 1987

## Considerations for Critical Thinking and Writing

1. How does Kearns's discussion of the stairwell, window, doorway, and grave shed light on your reading of "Home Burial"?

2. Discuss whether Kearns sympathizes more with the wife or the husband. Which character do you feel more sympathetic toward? Do you think Frost sides with one or the other? Explain your response.

3. Write an essay in which you agree or disagree with Kearns's assessment that "the wife is in the process of . . . crossing the threshold from marital asylum into freedom."

## Suggested Topics for Longer Papers

1. Research Frost's popular reputation and compare that with recent biographical accounts of his personal life. How does knowledge of his personal life affect your reading of his poetry?

2. Frost has been described as a cheerful poet of New England who creates pleasant images of the region as well as a poet who creates a troubling, frightening world bordered by anxiety, anguish, doubts, and darkness. How do the poems in this chapter support both of these readings of Frost's poetry?

# 13

## A THEMATIC CASE STUDY
# Humor and Satire

I think like a poet, and behave
like a poet. Occasionally
I need to sit in the corner
for bad behavior.
—GARY SOTO

Gary Soto.

Poetry can be a hoot. There are plenty of poets who leave you smiling, grinning, chuckling, and laughing out loud because they use language that is witty, surprising, teasing, or satirical. Occasionally, their subject matter is unexpectedly mundane. There's a poem in this chapter, for example, titled "Suburban" (p. 283), that reflects on a fastidious neighbor who complains about an errant dog wandering into her yard. Although this topic might seem to warrant a short leash, John Ciardi's treatment deftly shapes this unlikely material into a memorable satiric theme.

Sadly, however, poetry is too often burdened with a reputation for only being formal and serious, and readers sometimes show their deference by feeling intimidated and humbled in its earnest, weighty presence. After all, poetry frequently concerns itself with matters of great consequence: its themes contemplate subjects such as God and immortality, love and death, war and peace, injustice and outrage, racism and societal ills, deprivation and disease, alienation and angst, totalitarianism and terrorism, as well as a host of other tragic grievances and agonies that humanity might suffer. For readers of *The Onion*, a popular online satirical newspaper, this prevailing grim reputation is humorously framed in a bogus story about National Poetry Month, celebrated each April to increase an awareness of the value of poetry in American life. The brief article (April 27, 2005) quotes a speaker at a fund-raising meeting of the "American Poetry Prevention Society" who cautions that "we must stop this scourge before more lives are exposed to poetry." He warns that "young people, particularly morose high-school and college students, are very susceptible to this terrible affliction." *The Onion's* satire peels away the erroneous assumption that sorrow and tears are the only appropriate responses to a poetry "infection."

Poetry — at least in its clichéd popular form — is nearly always morosely dressed in black and rarely smiles. This severe image of somber profundity unfortunately tailors our expectations so that we assume that serious poetry cannot be playful and even downright funny or, putting the issue another way, that humorous poetry cannot be thoughtful and significant. The poems in this chapter demonstrate that serious poems can be funny and that comic poems can be thoughtful. Their humor, sometimes subtle, occasionally even savage, will serve to remind you that laughter engenders thought as well as pleasure.

## JOHN CIARDI (1916–1986)

### *Suburban*                                                    *1978*

Yesterday Mrs. Friar phoned. "Mr. Ciardi,
   how do you do?" she said. "I am sorry to say
this isn't exactly a social call. The fact is
   your dog has just deposited — forgive me —
a large repulsive object in my petunias."                            5

I thought to ask, "Have you checked the rectal grooving
   for a positive I.D.?" My dog, as it happened,
was in Vermont with my son, who had gone fishing —
   if that's what one does with a girl, two cases of beer,
and a borrowed camper. I guessed I'd get no trout.                  10

But why lose out on organic gold for a wise crack?
   "Yes, Mrs. Friar," I said, "I understand."
"Most kind of you," she said. "Not at all," I said.
   I went with a spade. She pointed, looking away.
"I always have loved dogs," she said, "but really!"                 15

I scooped it up and bowed. "The animal of it.
   I hope this hasn't upset you, Mrs. Friar."
"Not really," she said, "but really!" I bore the turd
   across the line to my own petunias
and buried it till the glorious resurrection                        20

when even these suburbs shall give up their dead.

## CONSIDERATIONS FOR CRITICAL THINKING AND WRITING

1. **FIRST RESPONSE.** How does the speaker transform Mrs. Friar into a symbolic figure of the suburbs?

2. Why do you suppose Ciardi focuses on this particular incident to make a comment on the suburbs? What is the speaker's attitude toward suburban life?

3. **CREATIVE RESPONSE.** Write a one-paragraph physical description of Mrs. Friar that captures her character.

## CONNECTION TO ANOTHER SELECTION

1. Compare the speakers' voices in "Suburban" and in John Updike's "Dog's Death" (p. 12).

## HARRYETTE MULLEN (B. 1953)

### *Dim Lady*                                    2002

My honeybunch's peepers are nothing like neon. Today's special at Red Lobster is redder than her kisser. If Liquid Paper is white, her racks are institutional beige. If her mop were Slinkys, dishwater Slinkys would grow on her noggin. I have seen tablecloths in Shakey's Pizza Parlors, red and white, but no such picnic colors do I see in her mug. And in some minty-fresh mouthwashes there is more sweetness than in the garlic breeze my main squeeze wheezes. I love to hear her rap, yet I'm aware that Muzak has a hipper beat. I don't know any Marilyn Monroes. My ball and chain is plain from head to toe. And yet, by gosh, my scrumptious Twinkie has as much sex appeal for me as any lanky model or platinum movie idol who's hyped beyond belief.

© Judy Natal, 2014, www.judynatal.com.

## CONSIDERATIONS FOR CRITICAL THINKING AND WRITING

1. **FIRST RESPONSE.** How does the poem's diction reveal the speaker as well as the "Lady"?

2. Why do you suppose Mullen chose to write a prose poem rather than a sonnet to praise the "Lady"?

CONNECTION TO ANOTHER SELECTION

1. Compare line for line "Dim Lady" with William Shakespeare's "My mistress' eyes are nothing like the sun" (p. 198). Which tribute do you prefer, the original parody of a love poem or the modern version?

# RONALD WALLACE (B. 1945)

## *In a Rut*                                          *2002*

She dogs me while
I try to take a catnap.
Of course, I'm playing possum but
I can feel her watching me,
eagle-eyed, like a hawk.                                                  5
She snakes over to my side
of the bed, and continues to
badger me. I may be a rat, but
I won't let her get my goat.
I refuse to make an                                                     10
ass of myself, no matter
how mulish I feel.
I'm trying to make a
bee-line for sleep, but
*You're a turkey!* she says, and                                          15
I'm thinking she's no
spring chicken. She *is* a busy beaver,
though, always trying to ferret
things out. She's a bit batty,
in fact, a bit cuckoo, but                                               20
*What's your beef, now?* I say.
*Get your head out*
*of the sand,* she replies. *What*
*are you — a man, or a mouse?*
That's a lot of bull, I think;                                           25
she can be a real bear.
*Don't horse around, now,* she says.
*You know you can't weasel out of it!*
She's having a whale of a time,
thinking she's got me skunked, thinking                                  30
that she's out-foxed me.
But I know she's just crying wolf,
and I won't be cowed. Feeling
my oats now, I merely look sheepish;
I give her the hang-dog look;                                            35
I give her the lion's share.

I give her something to crow about.
*Oh, lovey-dove,* I intone.
We're all odd ducks, strange
birds; this won't be my swan-                                    40
song, after all. She's in hog-
heaven now, ready to pig-out.
*Oh, my stallion,* she says, *Oh,*
*my lambkin! You are*
*a real animal, you know!*                                       45

### CONSIDERATIONS FOR CRITICAL THINKING AND WRITING

1. **FIRST RESPONSE.** Explain whether or not Wallace's orchestration of over-used phrases redeems them from being simply clichés.

2. How does the title contribute to your understanding of the poem's plot?

3. **CREATIVE RESPONSE.** Choose a set of familiar related expressions from sports, school, politics, religion, or whatever comes naturally to you, and write your own version of a poem that imitates Wallace's playful use of clichés.

### CONNECTION TO ANOTHER SELECTION

1. Compare Wallace's organizing strategy in this poem and E. E. Cummings's technique in "next to of course god america i" (p. 129).

## E. E. CUMMINGS  (1894–1962)

### *may i feel said he*                                         1935

may i feel said he
(i'll squeal said she
just once said he)
it's fun said she

(may i touch said he                                            5
how much said she
a lot said he)
why not said she

(let's go said he
not too far said she                                            10
what's too far said he
where you are said she)

may i stay said he
(which way said she
like this said he                                               15
if you kiss said she

may i move said he
is it love said she)
if you're willing said he
(but you're killing said she                                         20

but it's life said he
but your wife said she
now said he)
ow said she

(tiptop said he                                                     25
don't stop said she
oh no said he)
go slow said she

(cccome?said he
ummm said she)                                                      30
you're divine!said he
(you are Mine said she)

### CONSIDERATIONS FOR CRITICAL THINKING AND WRITING

1. FIRST RESPONSE. Describe the nature of the conflict between "he" and
   "she." With whom do you think Cummings wants us to identify more?
   What in the poem leads you to that conclusion?

2. How does Cummings's use of language create a humorous as well as a
   tense situation?

3. CREATIVE RESPONSE. Give "he" the last word by writing one additional
   stanza in Cummings's style.

### CONNECTION TO ANOTHER SELECTION

1. Discuss the views of marriage as they are presented in "may I feel said he"
   and in Anne Bradstreet's "To My Dear and Loving Husband" (p. 297).

## PETER SCHMITT (B. 1958)

### *Friends with Numbers*                                          1995

*If you make friends with numbers,*
*you don't need any other friends.*
  *— Shakuntala Devi, math genius*

They are not hard to get to know:
6 and 9 keep changing their minds,
8 cuts the most graceful figure
but sleeps for an eternity,
and 7, lucky 7, takes                                               5

an arrow to his heart always.
5, halfway to somewhere, only
wants to patch his unicycle
tire, and 4, who'd like to stand for
something solid, has never had                    10
two feet on the ground, yet flutters
gamely in the breeze like a flag.
3, for all his literary
accomplishments and pretensions
to immortality, is still                          15
(I can tell you) not half the man
8 is asleep or awake. 1,
little 1. I know him better
than all the others, these numbers
who are all my friends. Only 2,                   20
that strange smallest prime, can I count
as just a passing acquaintance.
Divisible by only 1
and herself, she seems on the verge,
yet, of always coming apart.                      25
And though she eludes me, swanlike,
though I'd love to know her better,
still I am fine, there are others,
many, I have friends in numbers.

### Considerations for Critical Thinking and Writing

1. **FIRST RESPONSE.** How does the personification of numbers create characters in the poem?

2. Explain how the speaker's use of language helps to characterize him.

3. Discuss the various ways in which the single digits are transformed into individual visual images.

### Connection to Another Selection

1. Discuss the originality — the fresh and unusual approach to their respective subject matter — in Schmitt's poem and in May Swenson's "A Nosty Fright" (p. 147). What makes these poems so interesting?

MARTÍN ESPADA  (B. 1957)

## The Community College Revises Its Curriculum in Response to Changing Demographics    2000

*SPA 100 Conversational Spanish*
*2 credits*

The course
is especially concerned
with giving police
the ability
to express themselves
tersely
in matters of interest
to them

### CONSIDERATIONS FOR CRITICAL THINKING AND WRITING

1. FIRST RESPONSE. What sort of political comment do you think Espada makes in this poem?
2. Would this be a poem without the title? Explain your answer.
3. CREATIVE RESPONSE. Choose a course description from your school's catalog and organize the catalog copy into poetic lines. Provide your poem with a title that offers a provocative commentary about it.

### CONNECTION TO ANOTHER SELECTION

1. Compare the themes in Espada's poem and in Donald Justice's "Order in the Streets" (p. 236).

DENISE DUHAMEL  (B. 1961)

## The Language Police    2006

*After Diane Ravitch's* The Language Police

The busybody (banned as sexist, demeaning to older women) who lives next door called my daughter a tomboy (banned as sexist) when she climbed the jungle (banned; replaced with "rain forest") gym. Then she had the nerve to call her an egghead and a bookworm (both banned as offensive; replaced with "intellectual") because she read fairy (banned because suggests homosexuality; replace with "elf") tales.

I'm tired of the Language Police turning a deaf ear (banned as handicapism) to my complaints. I'm no Pollyanna (banned as sexist) and will not accept any lame (banned as offensive; replace with "walks with a cane") excuses at this time.

If Alanis Morissette can play God (banned) in *Dogma* (banned as ethno-centric; replace with "Doctrine" or "Belief"), why can't my daughter play stickball (banned as regional or ethnic bias) on boy's night out (banned as sexist)? Why can't she build a snowman (banned, replace with "snow per-son") without that fanatic (banned as ethnocentric; replace with "believer," "follower," or "adherent") next door telling her she's going to hell (banned; replaced with "heck" or "darn")?

Do you really think this is what the Founding Fathers (banned as sexist; replace with "the Founders" or "the Framers") had in mind? That we can't even enjoy our Devil (banned)-ed ham sandwiches in peace? I say put a stop to this cult (banned as ethnocentric) of PC old wives' tales (banned as sexist; replace with "folk wisdom") and extremist (banned as ethnocen-tric; replace with "believer," "follower," or "adherent") conservative duffers (banned as demeaning to older men).

As an heiress (banned as sexist; replace with "heir") to the first amend-ment, I feel that only a heretic (use with caution when comparing religions) would try to stop American vernacular from flourishing in all its inspira-tional (banned as patronizing when referring to a person with disabilities) splendor.

### CONSIDERATIONS FOR CRITICAL THINKING AND WRITING

1. FIRST RESPONSE. Duhamel has explained that she was inspired to write this prose poem after reading a list of words banned as "politi-cally incorrect" in Diane Ravitch's study of editorial censorship, *The Language Police: How Pressure Groups Restrict What Students Learn.* She found this abuse of language both "horrifying and hilarious" (*The Best of American Poetry 2007,* p. 132). What do you think?

2. What is the speaker's basic argument against the "Language Police"?

3. CREATIVE RESPONSE. Write a stanza of your own that adds to the list.

### CONNECTION TO ANOTHER SELECTION

1. Compare the attitudes expressed toward politically charged language in this poem and in E. E. Cummings's "next to of course god america i" (p. 129).

## GARY SOTO (B. 1952)

### *Mexicans Begin Jogging*                    1995

At the factory I worked
In the fleck of rubber, under the press
Of an oven yellow with flame,
Until the border patrol opened
Their vans and my boss waved for us to run.                    5

"Over the fence, Soto," he shouted,
And I shouted that I was American.
"No time for lies," he said, and pressed
A dollar in my palm, hurrying me
Through the back door.                                         10

Since I was on his time, I ran
And became the wag to a short tail of Mexicans —
Ran past the amazed crowds that lined
The street and blurred like photographs, in rain.
I ran from that industrial road to the soft                   15
Houses where people paled at the turn of an autumn sky.
What could I do but yell *vivas*
To baseball, milkshakes, and those sociologists
Who would clock me
As I jog into the next century                                 20
On the power of a great, silly grin.

### CONSIDERATIONS FOR CRITICAL THINKING AND WRITING

1. **FIRST RESPONSE.** What ironies are present in this poem?

2. Soto was born and raised in Fresno, California. How does this fact affect your reading of the first stanza?

3. In what different ways does the speaker become "the wag" (line 12) in this poem? (You may want to look up the word to consider all possible meanings.)

4. Explain lines 17–21. What serious point is being made in these humorous lines?

### CONNECTION TO ANOTHER SELECTION

1. Compare the speaker's tone toward America in this poem and in Tato Laviera's "AmeRícan (p. 232).

> **WHEN I READ** "My advice is to read a lot of poetry; to begin with the contemporary and get an ear for contemporary poetic speech; then read your way gradually into the past. Form a strong attachment to a poet whose work you love, and immerse yourself in the work. Then find another." —TONY HOAGLAND

## TONY HOAGLAND (B. 1953)

### *America*                                                 2003

Then one of the students with blue hair and a tongue stud
Says that America is for him a maximum-security prison

Whose walls are made of RadioShacks and Burger Kings, and MTV episodes
Where you can't tell the show from the commercials,

And as I consider how to express how full of shit I think he is,                    5
He says that even when he's driving to the mall in his Isuzu

Trooper with a gang of his friends, letting rap music pour over them
Like a boiling Jacuzzi full of ballpeen hammers, even then he feels

Buried alive, captured and suffocated in the folds
Of the thick satin quilt of America                                               10

And I wonder if this is a legitimate category of pain,
Or whether he is just spin doctoring a better grade,

And then I remember that when I stabbed my father in the dream
      last night,
It was not blood but money

That gushed out of him, bright green hundred-dollar bills               15
Spilling from his wounds, and — this is the weird part —,

He gasped, "Thank god — those Ben Franklins were
Clogging up my heart —

And so I perish happily,
Freed from that which kept me from my liberty" —                       20

Which is when I knew it was a dream, since my dad
Would never speak in rhymed couplets,

And I look at the student with his acne and cell phone and phony
      ghetto clothes
And I think, "I am asleep in America too,

And I don't know how to wake myself either,"                              25
And I remember what Marx said near the end of his life:

"I was listening to the cries of the past,
When I should have been listening to the cries of the future."

But how could he have imagined 100 channels of 24-hour cable
Or what kind of nightmare it might be                                        30

When each day you watch rivers of bright merchandise run past you
And you are floating in your pleasure boat upon this river

Even while others are drowning underneath you
And you see their faces twisting in the surface of the waters

And yet it seems to be your own hand                                         35
Which turns the volume higher?


## CONSIDERATIONS FOR CRITICAL THINKING AND WRITING

1. **FIRST RESPONSE.** This poem consists of two sentences. How do they differ
   in tone and meaning?

2. Discuss the humor embedded in this serious poem.

3. To what extent does this poem reflect your own views about American life?

### CONNECTION TO ANOTHER SELECTION

1. Compare the perspective offered in "America" with that in Tato Laviera's "AmeRícan" (p. 232).

## THOMAS R. MOORE  (B. 1941)

### At the Berkeley Free Speech Café                                            2010

The students are seated,
one to a table,
at tables for two,
ears wired,
laptops humming,                                                                  5
cell phones buzzing,
fingers texting,
iPods thumping,
toes drumming,
email flashing,                                                                  10
lattés cooling,
textbooks open,
reading for an exam
in Issues in Contemporary Culture 102.

### CONSIDERATIONS FOR CRITICAL THINKING AND WRITING

1. FIRST RESPONSE. Discuss the appropriateness of the poem's title and the title of the course.

2. How do the sounds help establish tone?

### CONNECTION TO ANOTHER SELECTION

1. Write an essay comparing the treatment of undergraduate life in this poem and in the following poem by X. J. Kennedy.

## X. J. KENNEDY  (B. 1929)

### On a Young Man's Remaining
### an Undergraduate for Twelve Years                                           2006

Sweet scent of pot, the mellow smell of beer,
    Frat-house debates on sex, on God's existence
Lasting all night, vacations thrice a year,
    Pliant coeds who put up no resistance

Are all life is. Who'd give a damn for earning,                          5
  Who'd struggle by degrees to lofty places
When he can loll, adrift in endless learning,
  In a warm sea of academic stasis?

He's famous now: the everlasting kid.
  After conducting an investigation,                                    10
Two deans resigned, to do just what he did.
  They couldn't fault his ratiocination.

### CONSIDERATIONS FOR CRITICAL THINKING AND WRITING

1. FIRST RESPONSE. Comment on the description of undergraduate life in the first stanza and the effect of the enjambment in lines 4 and 5.

2. Discuss the sound effects in stanza three. How are they related to sense?

3. Why is "ratiocination" (line 12) just the right word in this context?

4. CREATIVE RESPONSE. Write a poem using Kennedy's stanzas and rhyme scheme as a model that reflects your own sense of undergraduate life.

## JIM TILLEY (B. 1950)

### Hello, Old Man                                                    2014

"Hello, old man," a voice called out as I
passed by the Kenter Canyon Charter School.
I paused and chuckled. "Hello back," I said
to the girl on the playground swing, knowing
it might be fifty years before she'd understand.          5
Unrestrained in expressing what they see,
the young are often right. She'd seen white hair.
But for me that day striding up the canyon's
steep hill, four miles into my morning walk,
old age was only a state of mind —                        10
or almost so. Right before the school,
I'd detoured onto a quiet side street
and climbed among some bushes, having spent
the last mile looking for a place a pee.

### CONSIDERATIONS FOR CRITICAL THINKING AND WRITING

1. FIRST RESPONSE. How does the man's choice of details to describe his encounter with the girl reveal what he thinks about getting older?

2. How would you read this poem differently if it had concluded at the end of line 10?

3. Why do you think the poet places the girl on a swing rather than on some other kind of playground equipment?

## CONNECTION TO ANOTHER SELECTION

1. Compare Tilley's treatment of youth and age with X. J. Kennedy's perspective in "On a Young Man's Remaining an Undergraduate for Twelve Years" (p. 293).

# 14

## A Collection of Poems

Now the role of poetry is not simply to hold understanding in place but to help create and hold a realm of experience. Poetry has become a kind of tool for knowing the world in a particular way.

—JANE HIRSHFIELD

---

### W. H. AUDEN (1907–1973)

#### *The Unknown Citizen*                                   *1940*

*(To JS/07/M/378
This Marble Monument
Is Erected by the State)*

He was found by the Bureau of Statistics to be
One against whom there was no official complaint,
And all the reports on his conduct agree
That, in the modern sense of an old-fashioned word, he was a saint,
For in everything he did he served the Greater Community.          5
Except for the War till the day he retired
He worked in a factory and never got fired,
But satisfied his employers, Fudge Motors Inc.
Yet he wasn't a scab or odd in his views,
For his Union reports that he paid his dues,                      10
(Our report on his Union shows it was sound)
And our Social Psychology workers found
That he was popular with his mates and liked a drink.

The Press are convinced that he bought a paper every day
And that his reactions to advertisements were normal in every way.    15
Policies taken out in his name prove that he was fully insured,
And his Health-card shows he was once in hospital but left it cured.
Both Producers Research and High-Grade Living declare
He was fully sensible to the advantages of the Installment Plan
And had everything necessary to the Modern Man,    20
A phonograph, radio, car and a frigidaire.
Our researchers into Public Opinion are content
That he held the proper opinions for the time of year;
When there was peace, he was for peace; when there was war, he went.
He was married and added five children to the population,    25
Which our Eugenist says was the right number for a parent of his
    generation,
And our teachers report that he never interfered with their education.
Was he free? Was he happy? The question is absurd:
Had anything been wrong, we should certainly have heard.

## WILLIAM BLAKE (1757–1827)

### The Garden of Love                                           *1794*

I went to the Garden of Love,
And saw what I never had seen:
A Chapel was built in the midst,
Where I used to play on the green.

And the gates of this Chapel were shut,    5
And "Thou shalt not" writ over the door;
So I turned to the Garden of Love
That so many sweet flowers bore;

And I saw it was filled with graves,
And tomb-stones where flowers should be;    10
And Priests in black gowns were walking their rounds,
And binding with briars my joys and desires.

## ANNE BRADSTREET (CA. 1612–1672)

### To My Dear and Loving Husband                               *1678*

If ever two were one, then surely we.
If ever man were loved by wife, then thee;
If ever wife was happy in a man,
Compare with me, ye women, if you can.
I prize thy love more than whole mines of gold    5

Or all the riches that the East doth hold.
My love is such that rivers cannot quench,
Nor ought but love from thee, give recompense.
Thy love is such I can no way repay,
The heavens reward thee manifold, I pray.                     10
Then while we live, in love let's so persevere
That when we live no more, we may live ever.

## ELIZABETH BARRETT BROWNING (1806–1861)

### When our two souls stand up erect and strong          1850

When our two souls stand up erect and strong,
Face to face, silent, drawing nigh and nigher,
Until the lengthening wings break into fire
At either curvèd point — what bitter wrong
Can the earth do to us, that we should not long           5
Be here contented? Think. In mounting higher,
The angels would press on us and aspire
To drop some golden orb of perfect song
Into our deep, dear silence. Let us stay
Rather on earth, Belovèd, — where the unfit             10
Contrarious moods of men recoil away
And isolate pure spirits, and permit
A place to stand and love in for a day,
With darkness and the death-hour rounding it.

## ROBERT BURNS (1759–1796)

### A Red, Red Rose          1799

O my luve's like a red, red rose
That's newly sprung in June;
O my luve's like the melodie
That's sweetly played in tune.

As fair art thou, my bonny lass,                         5
So deep in luve am I;
And I will luve thee still my dear,
Till a' the seas gang° dry —                             *go*

Till a' the seas gang dry, my dear,
And the rocks melt wi' the sun:                          10
O I will luve thee still, my dear,
While the sands o' life shall run.

And fare thee weel, my only luve,
And fare thee weel awhile!

And I will come again, my luve,                                          15
Though it were a thousand mile.

## GEORGE GORDON, LORD BYRON  (1788–1824)

### She Walks in Beauty                                          *1814*

*From Hebrew Melodies*

### I

She walks in Beauty, like the night
    Of cloudless climes and starry skies;
And all that's best of dark and bright
    Meet in her aspect and her eyes:
Thus mellowed to that tender light                                          5
    Which Heaven to gaudy day denies.

### II

One shade the more, one ray the less,
    Had half impaired the nameless grace
Which waves in every raven tress,
    Or softly lightens o'er her face;                                          10
Where thoughts serenely sweet express,
    How pure, how dear their dwelling-place.

### III

And on that cheek, and o'er that brow,
    So soft, so calm, yet eloquent,
The smiles that win, the tints that glow,                                          15
    But tell of days in goodness spent,
A mind at peace with all below,
    A heart whose love is innocent!

## SAMUEL TAYLOR COLERIDGE  (1772–1834)

### Kubla Khan: or, a Vision in a Dream°                                          *1798*

In Xanadu did Kubla Khan°
    A stately pleasure-dome decree:
Where Alph, the sacred river, ran

---

*Vision in a Dream:* This poem came to Coleridge in an opium-induced dream, but he was interrupted by a visitor while writing it down. He was later unable to remember the rest of the poem.  1 *Kubla Khan:* The historical Kublai Khan (1216–1294, grandson of Genghis Khan) was the founder of the Mongol dynasty in China.

Through caverns measureless to man
    Down to a sunless sea.                                                5

So twice five miles of fertile ground
With walls and towers were girdled round:
And here were gardens bright with sinuous rills
Where blossomed many an incense-bearing tree;
And there were forests ancient as the hills,                                       10
Enfolding sunny spots of greenery.

But oh! that deep romantic chasm which slanted
Down the green hill athwart a cedarn cover!°
A savage place! as holy and enchanted
As e'er beneath a waning moon was haunted                                          15
By woman wailing for her demon-lover!
And from this chasm, with ceaseless turmoil seething,
As if this earth in fast thick pants were breathing,
A mighty fountain momently was forced,
Amid whose swift half-intermitted burst                                            20
Huge fragments vaulted like rebounding hail,
Of chaffy grain beneath the thresher's flail:
And 'mid these dancing rocks at once and ever
It flung up momently the sacred river.
Five miles meandering with a mazy motion                                           25
Through wood and dale the sacred river ran,
Then reached the caverns measureless to man,
And sank in tumult to a lifeless ocean:
And 'mid this tumult Kubla heard from far
Ancestral voices prophesying war!                                                  30
    The shadow of the dome of pleasure
      Floated midway on the waves;
      Where was heard the mingled measure
      From the fountain and the caves.
It was a miracle of rare device,                                                   35
A sunny pleasure-dome with caves of ice!
    A damsel with a dulcimer
    In a vision once I saw:
    It was an Abyssinian maid,
    And on her dulcimer she played,                                        40
    Singing of Mount Abora.
    Could I revive within me
    Her symphony and song,
    To such a deep delight 'twould win me,
That with music loud and long,                                                     45

13  *athwart . . . cover:*  Spanning a grove of cedar trees.

I would build that dome in air,
That sunny dome! those caves of ice!
And all who heard should see them there,
And all should cry, Beware! Beware!
His flashing eyes, his floating hair!                                    50
Weave a circle round him thrice,
And close your eyes with holy dread,
For he on honey-dew hath fed,
And drunk the milk of Paradise.

EMILY DICKINSON (1830–1886)

## Much Madness is divinest Sense —                      *ca. 1862*

Much Madness is divinest Sense —
To a discerning Eye —
Much Sense — the starkest Madness —
'Tis the Majority
In this, as All, prevail —
Assent — and you are sane —
Demur — you're straightway dangerous —
And handled with a Chain —

EMILY DICKINSON (1830–1886)

## I know that He exists                                         *ca. 1862*

I know that He exists.
Somewhere — in Silence —
He has hid his rare life
From our gross eyes.

'Tis an instant's play.                                                       5
'Tis a fond Ambush —
Just to make Bliss
Earn her own surprise!

But — should the play
Prove piercing earnest —                                                  10
Should the glee-glaze —
In Death's — stiff — stare —

Would not the fun
Look too expensive!
Would not the jest —                                                           15
Have crawled too far!

## EMILY DICKINSON (1830–1886)

### The Bustle in a House

ca. 1866

The Bustle in a House
The Morning after Death
Is solemnest of industries
Enacted upon Earth —

The Sweeping up the Heart
And putting Love away
We shall not want to use again
Until Eternity.

## JOHN DONNE (1572–1631)

### The Flea

1633

Mark but this flea, and mark in this°
How little that which thou deny'st me is;
It sucked me first, and now sucks thee,
And in this flea our two bloods mingled be;
Thou know'st that this cannot be said                    5
A sin, nor shame, nor loss of maidenhead,
　　Yet this enjoys before it woo,
　　And pampered swells with one blood made of two,
　　And this, alas, is more than we would do.°

Oh stay, three lives in one flea spare,                   10
Where we almost, yea more than, married are.
This flea is you and I, and this
Our marriage bed, and marriage temple is;
Though parents grudge, and you, we're met
And cloistered in these living walls of jet.             15
　　Though use° make you apt to kill me,              *habit*
　　Let not to that, self-murder added be,
　　And sacrilege, three sins in killing three.

Cruel and sudden, hast thou since
Purpled thy nail in blood of innocence?                  20
Wherein could this flea guilty be,
Except in that drop which it sucked from thee?
Yet thou triumph'st, and say'st that thou

___

1 *mark in this:* Take note of the moral lesson in this object.  9 *more than we would*
*do:* That is, if we do not join our blood in conceiving a child.

Find'st not thyself, nor me, the weaker now;
   'Tis true; then learn how false, fears be;        25
   Just so much honor, when thou yield'st to me,
   Will waste, as this flea's death took life from thee.

## RITA DOVE  (B. 1952)

### *Golden Oldie*       *1995*

I made it home early, only to get
stalled in the driveway, swaying
at the wheel like a blind pianist caught in a tune
meant for more than two hands playing.

The words were easy, crooned
by a young girl dying to feel alive, to
     discover
a pain majestic enough
to live by. I turned the air-conditioning off,

Archive Photos/Getty Images.

leaned back to float on a film of sweat,
and listened to her sentiment:
*Baby, where did our love go?*—a lament
I greedily took in

without a clue who my lover
might be, or where to start looking.

## GEORGE ELIOT  (MARY ANN EVANS / 1819–1880)

### *In a London Drawingroom*       *1865*

The sky is cloudy, yellowed by the smoke.
For view there are the houses opposite,
Cutting the sky with one long line of wall
Like solid fog: far as the eye can stretch
Monotony of surface and of form        5
Without a break to hang a guess upon.
No bird can make a shadow as it flies,
For all its shadow, as in ways o'erhung
By thickest canvas, where the golden rays
Are clothed in hemp. No figure lingering      10
Pauses to feed the hunger of the eye
Or rest a little on the lap of life.
All hurry on and look upon the ground
Or glance unmarking at the passersby.

The wheels are hurrying, too, cabs, carriages                          15
All closed, in multiplied identity.
The world seems one huge prison-house and court
Where men are punished at the slightest cost,
With lowest rate of color, warmth, and joy.

# T. S. ELIOT (1888–1965)

## *The Love Song of J. Alfred Prufrock*    *1917*

*S'io credesse che mia risposta fosse*
*A persona che mai tornasse al mondo,*
*Questa fiamma staria senza più scosse.*
*Ma perciocchè giammai di questo fondo*
*Non tornò vivo alcun, s'i'odo il vero,*
*Senza tema d'infamia ti rispondo.°*

    Let us go then, you and I,
When the evening is spread out against the sky

Like a patient etherized upon a table;
Let us go, through certain half-deserted streets,
The muttering retreats                                                5
Of restless nights in one-night cheap hotels
And sawdust restaurants with oyster-shells:
Streets that follow like a tedious argument
Of insidious intent
To lead you to an overwhelming question . . .                        10

Oh, do not ask, "What is it?"
Let us go and make our visit.

In the room the women come and go
Talking of Michelangelo.

    The yellow fog that rubs its back upon the window panes,     15
The yellow smoke that rubs its muzzle on the window panes
Licked its tongue into the corners of the evening,
Lingered upon the pools that stand in drains,

---

Epigraph: *S'io credesse . . . rispondo:* Dante's *Inferno,* 27:58–63. In the Eighth Chasm of the Inferno, Dante and Virgil meet Guido da Montefeltro, one of the False Counselors, who is punished by being enveloped in an eternal flame. When Dante asks Guido to tell his life story, the spirit replies: "If I thought that my answer were to one who might ever return to the world, this flame would shake no more; but since from this depth none ever returned alive, if what I hear is true, I answer you without fear of infamy."

Slipped by the terrace, made a sudden leap,    20
And seeing that it was a soft October night,
Curled once about the house, and fell asleep.

    And indeed there will be time°
For the yellow smoke that slides along the street,
Rubbing its back upon the window panes;    25
There will be time, there will be time
To prepare a face to meet the faces that you meet;
There will be time to murder and create,
And time for all the works and days° of hands
That lift and drop a question on your plate:    30
Time for you and time for me,
And time yet for a hundred indecisions,
And for a hundred visions and revisions,
Before the taking of a toast and tea.

In the room the women come and go    35
Talking of Michelangelo.

    And indeed there will be time
To wonder, "Do I dare?" and, "Do I dare?" —
Time to turn back and descend the stair,
With a bald spot in the middle of my hair —    40
(They will say: "How his hair is growing thin!")
My morning coat, my collar mounting firmly to the chin,
My necktie rich and modest, but asserted by a simple pin —
(They will say: "But how his arms and legs are thin!")
Do I dare    45
Disturb the universe?
In a minute there is time
For decisions and revisions which a minute will reverse.

    For I have known them all already, known them all:
Have known the evenings, mornings, afternoons,    50
I have measured out my life with coffee spoons;
I know the voices dying with a dying fall
Beneath the music from a farther room.
    So how should I presume?

    And I have known the eyes already, known them all —    55
The eyes that fix you in a formulated phrase.
And when I am formulated, sprawling on a pin,
When I am pinned and wriggling on the wall,

---

23 *there will be time:* An allusion to Ecclesiastes 3:1–8: "To everything there is a season, and a time to every purpose under heaven. . . ."

29 *works and days:* Hesiod's eighth-century B.C. poem *Works and Days* gives practical advice on how to conduct one's life in accordance with the seasons.

Then how should I begin
To spit out all the butt-ends of my days and ways?                              60
    And how should I presume?

    And I have known the arms already, known them all —
Arms that are braceleted and white and bare
(But in the lamplight, downed with light brown hair!)
    Is it perfume from a dress                                   65
    That makes me so digress?
Arms that lie along a table, or wrap about a shawl.
    And should I then presume?
    And how should I begin?

    Shall I say, I have gone at dusk through narrow streets,     70
And watched the smoke that rises from the pipes
Of lonely men in shirtsleeves, leaning out of windows? . . .

I should have been a pair of ragged claws
Scuttling across the floors of silent seas.

    And the afternoon, the evening, sleeps so peacefully!         75
Smoothed by long fingers,
Asleep . . . tired . . . or it malingers,
Stretched on the floor, here beside you and me.
Should I, after tea and cakes and ices,
Have the strength to force the moment to its crisis?              80
But though I have wept and fasted, wept and prayed,
Though I have seen my head (grown slightly bald) brought in upon a platter,°
I am no prophet — and here's no great matter;
I have seen the moment of my greatness flicker,
And I have seen the eternal Footman hold my coat, and snicker,   85
    And in short, I was afraid.

    And would it have been worth it, after all,
After the cups, the marmalade, the tea,
Among the porcelain, among some talk of you and me,
Would it have been worth while                                    90
To have bitten off the matter with a smile,
To have squeezed the universe into a ball°
To roll it toward some overwhelming question,
To say: "I am Lazarus,° come from the dead,

---

82 *head . . . upon a platter:* At Salome's request, Herod had John the Baptist decapitated and had the severed head delivered to her on a platter (see Matt. 14:1–12 and Mark 6:17–29).   92 *squeezed the universe into a ball:* See Andrew Marvell's "To His Coy Mistress" (p. 65), lines 41–42: "Let us roll all our strength and all / Our sweetness up into one ball."   94 *Lazarus:* The brother of Mary and Martha who was raised from the dead by Jesus (John 11:1–44). In Luke 16:19–31, a rich man asks that another Lazarus return from the dead to warn the living about their treatment of the poor.

Come back to tell you all, I shall tell you all" —                                           95
If one, settling a pillow by her head,
 Should say: "That is not what I meant at all;
  That is not it, at all."

 And would it have been worth it, after all,
Would it have been worth while,                                                            100
After the sunsets and the dooryards and the sprinkled streets,
After the novels, after the teacups, after the skirts that trail along the floor —
And this, and so much more? —
It is impossible to say just what I mean!
But as if a magic lantern threw the nerves in patterns on a screen:               105
Would it have been worth while
If one, settling a pillow or throwing off a shawl,
And turning toward the window, should say:
 "That is not it at all,
 That is not what I meant, at all."                                                  110

No! I am not Prince Hamlet, nor was meant to be;
Am an attendant lord,° one that will do
To swell a progress,° start a scene or two,                          *state procession*
Advise the prince: withal, an easy tool,
Deferential, glad to be of use,                                                          115
Politic, cautious, and meticulous;
Full of high sentence, but a bit obtuse;
At times, indeed, almost ridiculous —
Almost, at times, the Fool.

I grow old . . . I grow old . . .                                                        120
I shall wear the bottoms of my trousers rolled.
 Shall I part my hair behind? Do I dare to eat a peach?
I shall wear white flannel trousers, and walk upon the beach.
I have heard the mermaids singing, each to each.

I do not think that they will sing to me.                                                125

I have seen them riding seaward on the waves,
Combing the white hair of the waves blown back
When the wind blows the water white and black.

We have lingered in the chambers of the sea
By seagirls wreathed with seaweed red and brown,                                         130
Till human voices wake us, and we drown.

112 *attendant lord:* Like Polonius in Shakespeare's *Hamlet.*

## THOMAS HARDY (1840–1928)

### *Hap*                                                    *1866*

If but some vengeful god would call to me
From up the sky, and laugh: "Thou suffering thing,
Know that thy sorrow is my ecstasy,
That thy love's loss is my hate's profiting!"

Then would I bear it, clench myself, and die,                    5
Steeled by the sense of ire unmerited;
Half-eased in that a Powerfuller than I
Had willed and meted me the tears I shed.

But not so. How arrives it joy lies slain,
And why unblooms the best hope ever sown?                       10
— Crass Casualty obstructs the sun and rain,
And dicing Time for gladness casts a moan. . . .
These purblind Doomsters had as readily strown
Blisses about my pilgrimage as pain.


## FRANCES E. W. HARPER (1825–1911)

### *Learning to Read*                                     *1872*

Very soon the Yankee teachers
    Came down and set up school;
But oh! how the Rebs did hate it, —
    It was agin' their rule

Our masters always tried to hide                                5
    Book learning from our eyes;
Knowledge did'nt agree with slavery —
    'Twould make us all too wise.

But some of us would try to steal
    A little from the book,                                    10
And put the words together,
    And learn by hook or crook.

I remember Uncle Caldwell,
    Who took pot-liquor fat
And greased the pages of his book,                             15
    And hid it in his hat.

And had his master ever seen
    The leaves upon his head,

He'd have thought them greasy papers,
    But nothing to be read.                              20

And there was Mr. Turner's Ben
    Who heard the children spell,
And picked the words right up by heart,
    And learned to read 'em well.

Well the Northern folks kept sending                    25
    The Yankee teachers down
And they stood right up and helped us,
    Though Rebs did sneer and frown,

And, I longed to read my Bible,
    For precious words it said;
But when I begun to learn it,                           30
    Folks just shook their heads,

And said there is no use trying,
    Oh! Chloe, you're too late;
But as I was rising sixty,                              35
    I had no time to wait.

So I got a pair of glasses,
    And straight to work I went,
And never stopped till I could read
    The hymns and Testament.                          40

Then I got a little cabin —
    A place to call my own —
And I felt as independent
    As the queen upon her throne.

# GERARD MANLEY HOPKINS (1844–1889)

## *Pied Beauty*                                        *1877*

Glory be to God for dappled things —
    For skies of couple-color as a brinded cow;
        For rose-moles all in stipple upon trout that swim;
Fresh-firecoal chestnut-falls;° finches' wings;        *fallen chestnut*
    Landscape plotted and pieced — fold, fallow, and plow;    5
        And all trades, their gear and tackle and trim.

All things counter, original, spare, strange;
    Whatever is fickle, freckled (who knows how?)
        With swift, slow; sweet, sour; adazzle, dim;
He fathers-forth whose beauty is past change:          10
    Praise him.

## A. E. HOUSMAN (1859–1936)

### *To an Athlete Dying Young*                                    *1896*

The time you won your town the race
We chaired° you through the marketplace;
Man and boy stood cheering by,
And home we brought you shoulder-high.

Today, the road all runners come,                                    5
Shoulder-high we bring you home,
And set you at your threshold down,
Townsman of a stiller town.

Smart lad, to slip betimes away
From fields where glory does not stay,                               10
And early though the laurel° grows
It withers quicker than the rose.

Eyes the shady night has shut
Cannot see the record cut,
And silence sounds no worse than cheers                             15
After earth has stopped the ears:

Now you will not swell the rout
Of lads that wore their honors out,
Runners whom renown outran
And the name died before the man.                                   20

To set, before its echoes fade,
The fleet foot on the sill of shade,
And hold to the low lintel up
The still-defended challenge-cup.

And round that early-laureled head                                 25
Will flock to gaze the strengthless dead,
And find unwithered on its curls
The garland briefer than a girl's.

2 *chaired*: Carried on the shoulders in triumphal parade.    11 *laurel*: Flowering shrub
traditionally used to fashion wreaths of honor.

## JULIA WARD HOWE (1819–1910)

### *Battle-Hymn of the Republic*                                  *1862*

Mine eyes have seen the glory of the coming of the Lord:
He is trampling out the vintage where the grapes of wrath are stored;
He hath loosed the fateful lightning of his terrible swift sword:
     His truth is marching on.

I have seen Him in the watch-fires of a hundred circling camps;          5
They have builded Him an altar in the evening dews and damps;
I can read His righteous sentence by the dim and flaring lamps.
      His day is marching on.

I have read a fiery gospel, writ in burnished rows of steel:
"As ye deal with my contemners, so with you my grace shall deal;          10
Let the Hero, born of woman, crush the serpent with his heel,
      Since God is marching on."

He has sounded forth the trumpet that shall never call retreat;
He is sifting out the hearts of men before his judgment-seat:
Oh! be swift, my soul, to answer Him! be jubilant, my feet!          15
      Our God is marching on.

In the beauty of the lilies Christ was born across the sea,
With a glory in his bosom that transfigures you and me:
As he died to make men holy, let us die to make men free,
      While God is marching on.          20


## LANGSTON HUGHES  (1902–1967)

### *Harlem*          *1951*

What happens to a dream deferred?

    Does it dry up
    like a raisin in the sun?
    Or fester like a sore —
    And then run?
    Does it stink like rotten meat?          5
    Or crust and sugar over —
    like a syrupy sweet?

    Maybe it just sags
    like a heavy load.          10

    *Or does it explode?*


## GEORGIA DOUGLAS JOHNSON  (1877–1966)

### *Calling Dreams*          *1920*

The right to make my dreams come true,
I ask, nay, I demand of life;
Nor shall fate's deadly contraband
Impede my steps, nor countermand;
Too long my heart against the ground

Has beat the dusty years around;
And now at length I rise! I wake!
And stride into the morning break!


## BEN JONSON (1573–1637)

### *To Celia*                                      *1616*

Drink to me only with thine eyes,
   And I will pledge with mine;
Or leave a kiss but in the cup,
   And I'll not ask for wine.
The thirst that from the soul doth rise                    5
   Doth ask a drink divine;
But might I of Jove's nectar sup,
   I would not change for thine.

I sent thee late a rosy wreath,
   Not so much honoring thee                           10
As giving it a hope that there
   It could not withered be.
But thou thereon didst only breathe,
   And sent'st it back to me;
Since when it grows, and smells, I swear,                  15
   Not of itself but thee.


## JOHN KEATS (1795–1821)

### *To one who has been long in city pent*          *1816*

To one who has been long in city pent,
   'Tis very sweet to look into the fair
   And open face of heaven, — to breathe a prayer
Full in the smile of the blue firmament.
Who is more happy, when, with heart's content,            5
   Fatigued he sinks into some pleasant lair
   Of wavy grass, and reads a debonair
And gentle tale of love and languishment?

Returning home at evening, with an ear
   Catching the notes of Philomel,° — an eye        *A nightingale*   10
Watching the sailing cloudlet's bright career,
   He mourns that day so soon has glided by:
E'en like the passage of an angel's tear
   That falls through the clear ether silently.

JOHN KEATS (1795–1821)

## La Belle Dame sans Merci°                                    *1819*

O what can ail thee, knight-at-arms,
  Alone and palely loitering?
The sedge has withered from the lake,
  And no birds sing.

O what can ail thee, knight-at-arms,       5
  So haggard and so woe-begone?
The squirrel's granary is full,
  And the harvest's done.

I see a lily on thy brow,
  With anguish moist and fever dew,     10
And on thy cheeks a fading rose
  Fast withereth too.

I met a lady in the meads,
  Full beautiful — a faery's child,
Her hair was long, her foot was light,     15
  And her eyes were wild.

I made a garland for her head,
  And bracelets too, and fragrant zone;°    *belt*
She looked at me as she did love,
  And made sweet moan.        20

I set her on my pacing steed,
  And nothing else saw all day long,
For sidelong would she bend, and sing
  A faery's song.

She found me roots of relish sweet,      25
  And honey wild, and manna dew,
And sure in language strange she said,
  "I love thee true."

She took me to her elfin grot,
  And there she wept, and sighed full sore,   30
And there I shut her wild wild eyes
  With kisses four.

And there she lullèd me asleep,
  And there I dreamed — Ah! woe betide!
The latest° dream I ever dreamed     *last* 35
  On the cold hill side.

*La Belle Dame sans Merci:* This title is borrowed from a medieval poem and means "The Beautiful Lady without Mercy."

I saw pale kings and princes too,
    Pale warriors, death-pale were they all;
They cried — "La Belle Dame sans Merci
    Hath thee in thrall!"                    40

I saw their starved lips in the gloam,
    With horrid warning gapèd wide,
And I awoke and found me here,
    On the cold hill's side.

And this is why I sojourn here,               45
    Alone and palely loitering,
Though the sedge has withered from the lake,
    And no birds sing.


## EMMA LAZARUS (1849–1887)

### *The New Colossus*         *1883*

Not like the brazen giant of Greek fame,
With conquering limbs astride from land to land;
Here at our sea-washed, sunset gates shall stand
A mighty woman with a torch, whose flame
Is the imprisoned lightning, and her name        5
Mother of Exiles. From her beacon-hand
Glows world-wide welcome; her mild eyes command
The air-bridged harbor that twin cities frame.
"Keep, ancient lands, your storied pomp!" cries she
With silent lips. "Give me your tired, your poor,      10
Your huddled masses yearning to breathe free,
The wretched refuse of your teeming shore.
Send these, the homeless, tempest-tost to me,
I lift my lamp beside the golden door!"


## AMY LOWELL (1874–1925)

### *A Decade*         *1919*

When you came, you were like red wine and honey,
And the taste of you burnt my mouth with its sweetness.
Now you are like morning bread,
Smooth and pleasant.
I hardly taste you at all for I know your savor;
But I am completely nourished.

## JOHN MILTON (1608–1674)

### *On the Late Massacre in Piedmont°*                          *1655*

Avenge, O Lord, thy slaughtered saints, whose bones
    Lie scattered on the Alpine mountains cold;
    Even them who kept thy truth so pure of old,
When all our fathers worshiped stocks and stones,°
Forget not: in thy book record their groans                         5
    Who were thy sheep, and in their ancient fold
    Slain by the bloody Piedmontese, that rolled
Mother with infant down the rocks.° Their moans
The vales redoubled to the hills, and they
    To heaven. Their martyred blood and ashes sow          10
O'er all the Italian fields, where still doth sway
    The triple Tyrant;° that from these may grow
    A hundredfold, who, having learnt thy way,
Early may fly the Babylonian woe.°

*On the Late Massacre . . . :* Milton's protest against the treatment of the Waldenses, members of a Puritan sect living in the Piedmont region of northwest Italy, was not limited to this sonnet. It is thought that he wrote Oliver Cromwell's appeals to the duke of Savoy and to others to end the persecution.    4 *When . . . stones:* In Milton's Protestant view, English Catholics had worshipped their stone and wooden statues in the twelfth century, when the Waldensian sect was formed.    5–8 *in thy book . . . rocks:* On Easter Day 1655, 1,700 members of the Waldensian sect were massacred in Piedmont by the duke of Savoy's forces.    12 *triple Tyrant:* The Pope, with his three-crowned tiara, has authority on earth and in Heaven and Hell.    14 *Babylonian woe:* The destruction of Babylon, symbol of vice and corruption, at the end of the world (see Rev. 17–18). Protestants interpreted the "Whore of Babylon" as the Roman Catholic Church.

## JOHN MILTON (1608–1674)

### *When I consider how my light is spent*                          *ca. 1655*

When I consider how my light is spent,°
    Ere half my days in this dark world and wide,
    And that one talent° which is death to hide
Lodged with me useless, though my soul more bent

1 *how my light is spent:* Milton had been totally blind since 1651.    3 *that one talent:* Refers to Jesus's parable of the talents (units of money), in which a servant entrusted with a talent buries it rather than invests it and is punished on his master's return (Matt. 25:14–30).

To serve therewith my Maker, and present                        5
  My true account, lest He returning chide;
  "Doth God exact day-labor, light denied?"
I fondly° ask. But Patience, to prevent                    *foolishly*
That murmur, soon replies, "God doth not need
  Either man's work or His own gifts. Who best      10
  Bear His mild yoke, they serve Him best. His state
Is kingly: thousands at His bidding speed,
  And post o'er land and ocean without rest;
  They also serve who only stand and wait."

## CHRISTINA GEORGINA ROSSETTI (1830–1894)

### *Some Ladies Dress in Muslin Full and White*    *ca. 1848*

Some ladies dress in muslin full and
  white,
Some gentlemen in cloth succinct and black;
Some patronise a dog-cart, some a hack,
  Some think a painted clarence only
   right.
  Youth is not always such a pleasing
   sight:
Witness a man with tassels on his back;
Or woman in a great-coat like a sack,
  Towering above her sex with horrid height.
If all the world were water fit to drown,
  There are some whom you would not teach to swim,      10
  Rather enjoying if you saw them sink:
  Certain old ladies dressed in girlish pink,
With roses and geraniums on their gown.
  Go to the basin, poke them o'er the rim —

© Corbis.

## SIEGFRIED SASSOON (1886–1967)

### *"They"*    *1917*

The Bishop tells us: "When the boys come back
They will not be the same; for they'll have fought
In a just cause: they lead the last attack
On Anti-Christ; their comrades' blood has bought

New right to breed an honourable race,                                       5
They have challenged Death and dared him face to face."

"We're none of us the same!" the boys reply.
"For George lost both his legs; and Bill's stone blind;
Poor Jim's shot through the lungs and like to die;
And Bert's gone syphilitic: you'll not find                                  10
A chap who's served that hasn't found *some* change."
And the Bishop said: "The ways of God are strange!"


## WILLIAM SHAKESPEARE (1564–1616)

### *That time of year thou mayst in me behold*                              *1609*

That time of year thou mayst in me behold
When yellow leaves, or none, or few, do hang
Upon those boughs which shake against the cold,
Bare ruined choirs, where late the sweet birds sang.
In me thou see'st the twilight of such day                                   5
As after sunset fadeth in the west;
Which by and by black night doth take away,
Death's second self,° that seals up all in rest.                             *sleep*
In me thou see'st the glowing of such fire,
That on the ashes of his youth doth lie,                                     10
As the deathbed whereon it must expire,
Consumed with that which it was nourished by.
    This thou perceiv'st, which makes thy love more strong,
    To love that well which thou must leave ere long.


## WILLIAM SHAKESPEARE (1564–1616)

### *When, in disgrace with Fortune and men's eyes*                          *1609*

When, in disgrace with Fortune and men's eyes,
I all alone beweep my outcast state,
And trouble deaf heaven with my bootless cries,
And look upon myself and curse my fate,
Wishing me like to one more rich in hope,                                    5
Featured like him, like him with friends possessed,
Desiring this man's art, and that man's scope,
With what I most enjoy contented least,
Yet in these thoughts myself almost despising,
Haply I think on thee, and then my state,                                    10
Like to the lark at break of day arising

From sullen earth, sings hymns at heaven's gate;
   For thy sweet love remembered such wealth brings
   That then I scorn to change my state with kings.

## PERCY BYSSHE SHELLEY (1792–1822)

### *Ozymandias*°                                        *1818*

I met a traveler from an antique land
Who said: Two vast and trunkless legs of stone
Stand in the desert. . . . Near them, on the sand,
Half sunk, a shattered visage lies, whose frown,
And wrinkled lip, and sneer of cold command,                    5
Tell that its sculptor well those passions read
Which yet survive, stamped on these lifeless things,
The hand that mocked them, and the heart that fed:
And on the pedestal these words appear:
"My name is Ozymandias, King of Kings:                          10
Look on my works, ye Mighty, and despair!"
Nothing beside remains. Round the decay
Of that colossal wreck, boundless and bare
The lone and level sands stretch far away.

*Ozymandias:* Greek name for Ramses II, pharaoh of Egypt for sixty-seven years during the thirteenth century B.C. His colossal statue lies prostrate in the sands of Luxor.
Napoleon's soldiers measured it (56 feet long, ear 3$^1/_2$ feet long, weight 1,000 tons). Its
inscription, according to the Greek historian Diodorus Siculus, was "I am Ozymandias,
King of Kings; if anyone wishes to know what I am and where I lie, let him surpass me in
some of my exploits."

## ALFRED, LORD TENNYSON (1809–1892)

### *Ulysses*°                                           *1833*

   It little profits that an idle king,
By this still hearth, among these barren crags,
Matched with an agèd wife,° I mete and dole          *Penelope*
Unequal laws unto a savage race,
That hoard, and sleep, and feed, and know not me.               5
   I cannot rest from travel; I will drink
Life to the lees. All times I have enjoyed
Greatly, have suffered greatly, both with those
That loved me, and alone; on shore, and when

*Ulysses:* Ulysses, the hero of Homer's epic poem the *Odyssey*, is presented by Dante in
*The Inferno*, XXVI, as restless after his return to Ithaca and eager for new adventures.

Through scudding drifts the rainy Hyades°                             10
Vexed the dim sea. I am become a name;
For always roaming with a hungry heart
Much have I seen and known — cities of men
And manners, climates, councils, governments,
Myself not least, but honored of them all —                          15
And drunk delight of battle with my peers,
Far on the ringing plains of windy Troy.
I am a part of all that I have met;
Yet all experience is an arch wherethrough
Gleams that untraveled world, whose margin fades                      20
For ever and for ever when I move.
How dull it is to pause, to make an end,
To rust unburnished, not to shine in use!
As though to breathe were life. Life piled on life
Were all too little, and of one to me                                25
Little remains; but every hour is saved
From that eternal silence, something more,
A bringer of new things; and vile it were
For some three suns to store and hoard myself,
And this gray spirit yearning in desire                              30
To follow knowledge like a sinking star,
Beyond the utmost bound of human thought.

This is my son, mine own Telemachus,
To whom I leave the scepter and the isle —
Well-loved of me, discerning to fulfill                              35
This labor, by slow prudence to make mild
A rugged people, and through soft degrees
Subdue them to the useful and the good.
Most blameless is he, centered in the sphere
Of common duties, decent not to fail                                40
In offices of tenderness, and pay
Meet adoration to my household gods,
When I am gone. He works his work, I mine.

There lies the port; the vessel puffs her sail:
There gloom the dark, broad seas. My mariners,                       45
Souls that have toiled, and wrought, and thought with me —
That ever with a frolic welcome took
The thunder and the sunshine, and opposed
Free hearts, free foreheads — you and I are old;
Old age hath yet his honor and his toil.                             50
Death closes all; but something ere the end,
Some work of noble note, may yet be done,

10 *Hyades:* Five stars in the constellation Taurus, supposed by the ancients to predict
rain when they rose with the sun.

Not unbecoming men that strove with Gods.
The lights begin to twinkle from the rocks;
The long day wanes; the slow moon climbs; the deep       55
Moans round with many voices. Come, my friends.
'Tis not too late to seek a newer world.
Push off, and sitting well in order smite
The sounding furrows; for my purpose holds
To sail beyond the sunset, and the baths       60
Of all the western stars, until I die.
It may be that the gulfs will wash us down;
It may be we shall touch the Happy Isles,°
And see the great Achilles,° whom we knew.
Though much is taken, much abides; and though       65
We are not now that strength which in old days
Moved earth and heaven, that which we are, we are:
One equal temper of heroic hearts,
Made weak by time and fate, but strong in will
To strive, to seek, to find, and not to yield.       70

63 *Happy Isles:* Elysium, the home after death of heroes and others favored by the gods. It was thought by the ancients to lie beyond the sunset in the uncharted Atlantic. 64 *Achilles:* The hero of Homer's *Iliad.*

# WALT WHITMAN (1819–1892)

## *When I Heard the Learn'd Astronomer*       1865

When I heard the learn'd astronomer,
When the proofs, the figures, were ranged in columns before me,
When I was shown the charts and diagrams, to add, divide, and measure them,
When I sitting heard the astronomer where he lectured with much applause
    in the lecture-room,
How soon unaccountable I became tired and sick,
Till rising and gliding out I wandered off by myself,
In the mystical moist night-air, and from time to time,
Looked up in perfect silence at the stars.

# WALT WHITMAN (1819–1892)

## *One's-Self I Sing*       1867

One's-Self I sing, a simple separate person,
Yet utter the word Democratic, the word En-Masse.

Of physiology from top to toe I sing,
Not physiognomy alone nor brain alone is worthy for the Muse, I say the
    Form complete is worthier far,

The Female equally with the Male I sing.

Of Life immense in passion, pulse, and power,
Cheerful, for freest action formed under the laws divine,
The Modern Man I sing.

## WILLIAM WORDSWORTH
(1770–1850)
### *A Slumber Did My Spirit Seal*    *1800*

A slumber did my spirit seal;
  I had no human fears —
She seemed a thing that could not feel
  The touch of earthly years.

No motion has she now, no force;
  She neither hears nor sees;
Rolled round in earth's diurnal course.
  With rocks, and stones, and trees.

Hulton Archive/Getty Images.

## WILLIAM WORDSWORTH   (1770–1850)
### *The Solitary Reaper*°    *1807*

Behold her, single in the field,
Yon solitary Highland lass!
Reaping and singing by herself;
Stop here, or gently pass!
Alone she cuts and binds the grain,                    5
And sings a melancholy strain;
O listen! for the vale profound
Is overflowing with the sound.

No nightingale did ever chaunt
More welcome notes to weary bands                      10
Of travelers in some shady haunt

*The Solitary Reaper:* Dorothy Wordsworth (William's sister) wrote that the poem was suggested by this sentence in Thomas Wilkinson's *Tour of Scotland:* "Passed a female who was reaping alone; she sung in Erse, as she bended over her sickle; the sweetest human voice I ever heard; her strains were tenderly melancholy, and felt delicious, long after they were heard no more."

Among Arabian sands.
A voice so thrilling ne'er was heard
In springtime from the cuckoo-bird,
Breaking the silence of the seas                                          15
Among the farthest Hebrides.

Will no one tell me what she sings? —
Perhaps the plaintive numbers flow
For old, unhappy, far-off things,
And battles long ago.                                                     20
Or is it some more humble lay,
Familiar matter of today?
Some natural sorrow, loss, or pain,
That has been, and may be again?

Whate'er the theme, the maiden sang                                       25
As if her song could have no ending;
I saw her singing at her work,
And o'er the sickle bending —
I listened, motionless and still;
And, as I mounted up the hill,                                            30
The music in my heart I bore
Long after it was heard no more.


# WILLIAM WORDSWORTH  (1770–1850)

## *Mutability*                                                           *1822*

From low to high doth dissolution climb,
And sink from high to low, along a scale
Of awful° notes, whose concord shall not fail;                   ·awe-filled
A musical but melancholy chime,
Which they can hear who meddle not with crime,                            5
Nor avarice, nor over-anxious care.
Truth fails not; but her outward forms that bear
The longest date do melt like frosty rime,
That in the morning whitened hill and plain
And is no more; drop like the tower sublime                              10
Of yesterday, which royally did wear
His crown of weeds, but could not even sustain
Some casual shout that broke the silent air,
Or the unimaginable touch of Time.

# William Butler Yeats

## (1865–1939)

### *Leda and the Swan*°    *1924*

A sudden blow: the great wings beating
    still
Above the staggering girl, her thighs
    caressed
By the dark webs, her nape caught in
    his bill,
He holds her helpless breast upon his
    breast.

How can those terrified vague fingers
    push
The feathered glory from her loosening
    thighs?
And how can body, laid in that white rush,
But feel the strange heart beating where it lies?

A shudder in the loins engenders there
The broken wall, the burning roof and tower       10
And Agamemnon dead.
                   Being so caught up,
So mastered by the brute blood of the air,
Did she put on his knowledge with his power
Before the indifferent beak could let her drop?       15

*Leda and the Swan:* In Greek myth, Zeus in the form of a swan seduced Leda and fathered Helen of Troy (whose abduction started the Trojan War) and Clytemnestra, Agamemnon's wife and murderer. Yeats thought of Zeus's appearance to Leda as a type of annunciation, like the angel appearing to Mary.

# Critical Thinking and Writing about Poetry

# 15

# Critical Strategies
# for Reading

Great literature is simply language
charged with meaning to the
utmost possible degree.
— EZRA POUND

Bettmann/Corbis.

The answers you get from
literature depend upon the
questions you pose.
— MARGARET ATWOOD

© Sophie Bassouls/Sygma/
Corbis.

## CRITICAL THINKING

Maybe this has happened to you: the assignment is to consider a work, let's say Nathaniel Hawthorne's *The Scarlet Letter,* and write an analysis of some aspect of it that interests you, taking into account critical sources that comment on and interpret the work. Having confidently read this frequently assigned novel, you cheerfully begin research in the library but quickly find yourself bewildered by several seemingly unrelated articles. The first traces the thematic significance of images of light and darkness in the novel; the second makes a case for Hester Prynne as a liberated woman; the third argues that Arthur Dimmesdale's guilt is a projection of Hawthorne's own emotions; and the fourth analyzes the introduction, "The Custom House," as an attack on bourgeois values. These disparate treatments may seem random and capricious — a confirmation of your worst suspicions that interpretations of literature are hit-or-miss excursions into areas that you know little about or didn't know even existed. But if you understand that the articles are written from different perspectives — formalist, feminist, psychological, and Marxist — and that the purpose of each is to enhance your understanding of the work by discussing a particular element of it, then you can see that their varying strategies represent potentially interesting ways of opening up the text that might otherwise never have occurred to you. There are many ways to approach a text, and a useful first step is to develop a sense of direction, an understanding of how a perspective — your own or a critic's — shapes a discussion of a text.

This chapter offers an introduction to critical approaches to literature by outlining a variety of strategies for reading poetry, fiction, or drama. The emphasis is, of course, on poetry, and to that end the approaches focus on Robert Frost's "Mending Wall" (p. 260); a rereading of that well-known poem will equip you for the discussions that follow. In addition to the emphasis on this poem to illustrate critical approaches, some fiction and drama examples are also included along the way to demonstrate how these critical approaches can be applied to any genre. These strategies include approaches that have long been practiced by readers who have used, for example, the insights gleaned from biography and history to illuminate literary works as well as more recent approaches, such as those used by feminist, reader-response, and deconstructionist critics. Each of these perspectives is sensitive to image, symbol, tone, irony, and other literary elements that you have been studying, but each also casts those elements in a special light. The formalist approach emphasizes how the elements within a work achieve their effects, whereas biographical and psychological approaches lead outward from the work to consider the author's life and other writings. Even broader approaches, such as historical and sociological perspectives, connect the work to historic, social, and economic forces. Mythological readings represent the broadest approach because they discuss the cultural and universal responses readers have to a work.

Any given strategy raises its own types of questions and issues while seeking particular kinds of evidence to support itself. An awareness of the assumptions and methods that inform an approach can help you understand better the validity and value of a given critic's strategy for making sense of a work. More important, such an understanding can widen and deepen the responses of your own reading.

The critical thinking that goes into understanding a professional critic's approach to a work should not be foreign to you because you have already used essentially the same kind of thinking to understand the work itself. The skills you have developed to produce a literary **analysis** that, for example, describes how a character, symbol, or rhyme scheme supports a theme are also useful for reading literary criticism, because such skills allow you to keep track of how the parts of a critical approach create a particular reading of a literary work. When you analyze a poem, story, or play by closely examining how its various elements relate to the whole, your **interpretation** — your articulation of what the work means to you as supported by an analysis of its elements — necessarily involves choosing what you focus on in the work. The same is true of professional critics.

Critical readings presuppose choices in the kinds of material that are discussed. An analysis of the setting of Robert Frost's "Home Burial" (p. 262) would probably bring into focus the oppressive environment of the couple's domestic life rather than, say, the economic history of New England farming. The economic history of New England farming might be useful to a Marxist critic concerned with how class is revealed in "Home Burial," but for a formalist critic interested in identifying the unifying structures of the poem, such information would be irrelevant.

The following overview is neither exhaustive in the types of critical approaches covered nor complete in its presentation of the complexities inherent in them, but it should help you develop an appreciation of the intriguing possibilities that attend literary interpretation. The emphasis in this chapter is on ways of thinking about literature rather than on daunting lists of terms, names, and movements. Although a working knowledge of critical schools may be valuable and necessary for a fully informed use of a given critical approach, the aim here is more modest and practical. This chapter is no substitute for the shelves of literary criticism that can be found in your library, but it does suggest how readers using different perspectives organize their responses to texts. Moreover, there is no substitute for a careful reading of the text itself.

Successful critical approaches avoid eccentric decodings that reveal so-called hidden meanings; if there is no apparent evidence of a given meaning, this is because it is nonexistent in the text, not because the author has attempted to hide it in some way. For a parody of this sort of critical excess, see "A Parodic Interpretation of 'Stopping by Woods on a Snowy Evening'" (p. 277), in which Herbert R. Coursen Jr. has some fun with a Robert Frost poem and Santa Claus while making a serious point about the dangers of overly ingenious readings. Literary criticism attempts, like any valid hypothesis, to account for phenomena — the text — without distorting or misrepresenting what it describes.

# FORMALIST STRATEGIES

**Formalist critics** focus on the formal elements of a work — its language, structure, and tone. A formalist reads literature as an independent work of art rather than as a reflection of the author's state of mind or as a representation of a moment in history. Historic influences on a work, an author's intentions, or anything else outside the work are generally not treated by formalists (this is particularly true of the most famous modern formalists, known as the **New Critics**, who dominated American criticism from the 1940s through the 1960s). Instead, formalists offer intense examinations of the relationship between form and meaning within a work, emphasizing the subtle complexity of how a work is arranged. This kind of close reading pays special attention to what are often described as *intrinsic* matters in a literary work — diction, irony, paradox, metaphor, and symbol, for instance — as well as larger elements, such as plot, characterization, and narrative technique. Formalists examine how these elements work together to give a coherent shape to a work while contributing to its meaning. The answers to the questions formalists raise about how the shape and effect of a work are related come from the work itself. Other kinds of information that go beyond the text — biography, history, politics, economics, and so on — are typically regarded by formalists as *extrinsic* matters, which are considerably less important than what goes on within the autonomous text.

Poetry especially lends itself to close readings because a poem's relative brevity allows for detailed analyses of nearly all of its words and how they achieve their effects. A formalist reading of Robert Frost's "Mending Wall" leads to an examination of the tensions produced by the poem's diction, repetitions, and images that take us beyond a merely literal reading. The speaker describes how every spring he and his neighbor walk beside the stone wall bordering their respective farms to replace the stones that have fallen during winter. As they repair the wall, the speaker wonders what purpose the wall serves, given that "My apple trees will never get across / And eat the cones under his pines"; his neighbor, however, "only says, 'Good fences make good neighbors.'" The moment described in the poem is characteristic of the rural New England life that constitutes so much of Frost's poetry, but it is also typical of how he uses poetry as a means of "saying one thing in terms of another," as he once put it in an essay titled "Education by Poetry."

Just as the speaker teases his neighbor with the idea that the apple trees won't disturb the pines, so too does Frost tease the reader into looking at what it is "that doesn't love a wall." Frost's use of language in the poem does not simply consist of homespun casual phrases enlisted to characterize rural neighbors. From the opening lines, the "Something . . . that doesn't love a wall" and "That sends the frozen-ground-swell under it" is, on the literal level, a frost heave that causes the stones to tumble from the wall. But after several close readings of the poem, we can see the implicit pun in these lines suggesting that it is *Frost* who objects to the wall, thus aligning the poet's perspective with the speaker's. A careful examination of some of the other formal elements in the poem supports this reading.

In contrast to the imaginative wit of the speaker who raises fundamental questions about the purpose of any wall, the images associated with his neighbor indicate that he is a traditionalist who "will not go behind his father's saying." Moreover, the neighbor moves "like an old-stone savage" in "darkness" that is attributed to his rigid, tradition-bound, walled-in sensibilities rather than to "the shade of trees." Whereas the speaker's wit and intelligence are manifested by his willingness to question the necessity or desirability of "walling in or walling out" anything, his benighted neighbor can only repeat again that "good fences make good neighbors." The stone-heavy darkness of the neighbor's mind is emphasized by the contrasting light wit and agility of the speaker, who speculates: "Before I built a wall I'd ask to know . . . to whom I was like to give offense." The pun on the final word of this line makes a subtle but important connection between giving "offense" and creating "a fence." Frost's careful use of diction, repetition, and images deftly reveals and reinforces thematic significances suggesting that the stone wall serves as a symbol of isolation, confinement, fear, and even savagery. The neighbor's conservative, tradition-bound, mindless support of the wall is a foil to the speaker's — read Frost's — poetic, liberal response, which imagines and encourages the possibilities of greater freedom and brotherhood.

Although this brief discussion of some of the formal elements of Frost's poem does not describe all there is to say about how they produce an effect and create meaning, it does suggest the kinds of questions, issues, and evidence that a formalist strategy might raise in providing a close reading of the text itself. For a sample formalist reading of how a pervasive sense of death is worked into a poem, see "A Reading of Emily Dickinson's 'There's a certain Slant of light' " (p. 363).

# BIOGRAPHICAL STRATEGIES

Knowledge of an author's life can help readers understand his or her work more fully, and such knowledge is the basis of *biographical criticism*. Events in a work might follow actual events in a writer's life just as characters might be based on people known by the author. Ernest Hemingway's "Soldier's Home" is a seven-page short story (frequently anthologized) about the difficulties of a World War I veteran named Krebs returning to his small hometown in Oklahoma, where he cannot adjust to the pious assumptions of his family and neighbors. He refuses to accept their innocent blindness to the horrors he has witnessed during the war. They have no sense of the brutality of modern life; instead they insist he resume his life as if nothing has happened. There is plenty of biographical evidence to indicate that Krebs's unwillingness to lie about his war experiences reflects Hemingway's own responses on his return to Oak Park, Illinois, in 1919. Krebs, like Hemingway, finds he has to leave the sentimentality, repressiveness, and smug complacency that threaten to render his experiences unreal: "[T]he world they were in was not the world he was in."

An awareness of Hemingway's own war experiences and subsequent disillusionment with his hometown can be readily developed through available biographies, letters, and other of his written works. Consider, for example, this passage from *By Force of Will: The Life and Art of Ernest Hemingway,* in which Scott Donaldson describes Hemingway's response to World War I:

> In poems, as in [*A Farewell to Arms*], Hemingway expressed his distaste for the first war. The men who had to fight the war did not die well:
>
> Soldiers pitch and cough and twitch —
>     All the world roars red and black;
> Soldiers smother in a ditch,
>     Choking through the whole attack.

And what did they die for? They were "sucked in" by empty words and phrases—

> King and country,
> Christ Almighty,
> And the rest,
> Patriotism,
> Democracy,
> Honor—

which spelled death. The bitterness of these outbursts derived from the distinction Hemingway drew between the men on the line and those who started the wars that others had to fight.

This kind of information can help deepen our understanding of just how empathetically Krebs is presented in the story. Relevant facts about Hemingway's life will not make "Soldier's Home" a better written story than it is, but such information can make clearer the source of Hemingway's convictions and how his own experiences inform his major concerns as a storyteller.

Some formalist critics—some New Critics, for example—argue that interpretation should be based exclusively on internal evidence rather than on any biographical information outside the work. They argue that it is not possible to determine an author's intention and that the work must stand by itself. Although this is a useful caveat for keeping the work in focus, a reader who finds biography relevant would argue that biography can at the very least serve as a control on interpretation. A reader who, for example, finds Krebs at fault for not subscribing to the values of his hometown would be misreading the story, given both its tone and the biographical information available about the author. Although the narrator never *tells* the reader that Krebs is right or wrong for leaving town, the story's tone sides with his view of things. If, however, someone were to argue otherwise, insisting that the tone is not decisive and that Krebs's position is problematic, a reader familiar with Hemingway's own reactions could refute that argument with a powerful confirmation of Krebs's instincts to withdraw. Hence, many readers find biography useful for interpretation.

However, it is also worth noting that biographical information can complicate a work. For example, readers who interpret "Mending Wall" as a celebration of an iconoclastic sensibility that seeks to break down the psychological barriers and physical walls that separate human beings may be surprised to learn that very few of Frost's other writings support this view. His life was filled with emotional turmoil; he has been described by a number of biographers as egocentric and vindictive rather than as generous and open to others. He once commented that "I always hold that we get forward as much by hating as by loving." Indeed, many facts about Frost's life—as well as many of the speakers in his poems—are typified by depression, alienation, tension, suspicion, jealous competitiveness, and suicidal tendencies. Instead of challenging wall builders, Frost more characteristically built walls of distrust around himself among his family, friends, and colleagues. In this biographical context, it is especially noteworthy that it is the speaker of "Mending Wall" who alone repairs the damage done to the walls by hunters, and it is he who initiates each spring the rebuilding of the wall. However much he may question its value, the speaker does, after all, rebuild the wall between himself and his neighbor. This biographical approach raises provocative questions about the text. Does the poem suggest that boundaries and walls are, in fact, necessary? Are walls a desirable foundation for relationships between people? Although these and other questions raised by a biographical approach cannot be answered here, this kind of biographical perspective certainly adds to the possibilities of interpretation.

Sometimes biographical information does not change our understanding so much as it enriches our appreciation of a work. It matters, for instance, that much of John Milton's poetry, so rich in visual imagery, was written after he became blind; and it is just as significant — to shift to a musical example — that a number of Ludwig van Beethoven's greatest works, including the Ninth Symphony, were composed after he succumbed to total deafness.

# PSYCHOLOGICAL STRATEGIES

Given the enormous influence that Sigmund Freud's psychoanalytic theories had on twentieth-century interpretations of human behavior, it is nearly inevitable that most people have some familiarity with his ideas about dreams, unconscious desires, and sexual repression, as well as his terms for different aspects of the psyche — the id, ego, and superego. Psychological approaches to literature draw on Freud's theories and other psychoanalytic theories to understand more fully the text, the writer, and the reader. **Psychological critics** use such approaches to explore the motivations of characters and the symbolic meanings of events, while biographers speculate about a writer's own motivations — conscious or unconscious — in a literary work. Psychological approaches are also used to describe and analyze the reader's personal responses to a text.

Although it is not feasible to explain psychoanalytic terms and concepts in so brief a space as this, it is possible to suggest the nature of a psychological approach. It is a strategy based heavily on the idea of the existence of a human unconscious — those impulses, desires, and feelings about which a person is unaware but that influence emotions and behavior.

Central to a number of psychoanalytic critical readings is Freud's concept of what he called the **Oedipus complex,** a term derived from Sophocles' tragedy *Oedipus the King.* This complex is predicated on a boy's unconscious rivalry with his father for his mother's love and his desire to eliminate his father in order to take his father's place with his mother. The situation in Frost's "Mending Wall" is not directly related to an Oedipus complex, but the poem has been read as a conflict in which the "father's saying" represents the repressiveness of a patriarchal order that challenges the speaker's individual poetic consciousness. "Mending Wall" has also been read as another kind of struggle with repression. In "Up against the 'Mending Wall': The Psychoanalysis of a Poem by Frost," Edward Jayne offers a detailed reading of the poem as "the overriding struggle to suppress latent homosexual attraction between two men separated by a wall" (*College English* 1973). Jayne reads the poem as the working out of "unconscious homosexual inclinations largely repugnant to Frost and his need to divert and sublimate them." Regardless of whether a reader finds these arguments convincing, it is clear that the poem does have something to do with powerful forms of repression. And what about the reader's response? How might a psychological approach account for different responses from readers who argue that the poem calls for either a world that includes walls or one that dismantles them? One needn't be versed in psychoanalytic terms to entertain this question.

# HISTORICAL STRATEGIES

Historians sometimes use literature as a window onto the past because literature frequently provides the nuances of a historic period that cannot be readily perceived through other sources. The characters in Harriet Beecher Stowe's novel *Uncle Tom's Cabin* (1852) display, for example, a complex set of white attitudes toward blacks in mid-nineteenth-century America that is absent from more traditional historic documents such as census statistics or state laws. Another way of approaching the relationship between literature and history, however, is to use history as a means of understanding a literary work more clearly, as is the case in *historical criticism*. The plot pattern of pursuit, escape, and capture in nineteenth-century slave narratives had a significant influence on Stowe's plotting of action in *Uncle Tom's Cabin*. This relationship demonstrates that the writing contemporary to an author is an important element of the history that helps shape a work. There are many ways to talk about a work's historical and cultural dimensions. Such readings treat a literary text as a document reflecting, producing, or being produced by the social conditions of its time, giving equal focus to the social milieu and the work itself. Four historical strategies that have been especially influential are literary history criticism, Marxist criticism, new historicist criticism, and cultural criticism.

## *Literary History Criticism*

*Literary historians* situate work in the context in which it was written. Hence a literary historian might examine mid-nineteenth-century abolitionist attitudes toward blacks to determine whether Stowe's novel is representative of those views or significantly to the right or left of them. Such a study might even indicate how closely the book reflects racial attitudes of twentieth-century readers. A work of literature may transcend time to the extent that it addresses the concerns of readers over a span of decades or centuries, but it remains for the literary historian a part of the past in which it was composed, a past that can reveal more fully a work's language, ideas, and purposes.

Literary historians move beyond both the facts of an author's personal life and the text itself to the social and intellectual currents in which the author composed the work. They place the work in the context of its time (as do many critical biographers who write "life and times" studies), and sometimes they make connections with other literary works that may have influenced the author. The basic strategy of literary historians is to illuminate the historic background in order to shed light on some aspect of the work itself.

In Hemingway's "Soldier's Home" we learn that Krebs had been at Belleau Wood, Soissons, the Champagne, St. Mihiel, and the Argonne. Although nothing is said of these battles in the story, they were among the most bloody battles of the war; the wholesale butchery and staggering casualties incurred by both sides make credible the way Krebs's unstated but lingering memories have turned him into a psychological prisoner of war. Knowing something about the ferocity of those battles helps us account for Krebs's response in the story. Moreover, we can more fully appreciate Hemingway's refusal to have Krebs lie about the realities of war for the folks back home if we are aware of the numerous poems, stories, and plays published during World War I that presented war as a glorious, manly, transcendent sacrifice for God and country. Juxtaposing those works with "Soldier's Home" brings the differences into sharp focus.

Similarly, a reading of William Blake's poem "London" (p. 92) is less complete if we do not know of the horrific social conditions — the poverty, disease, exploitation, and hypocrisy — that characterized the city Blake laments in the late eighteenth century.

One last example: the potential historical meaning of the wall that is the subject of Frost's "Mending Wall" might be more distinctly seen if it is placed in the context of its publication date, 1914, when the world was on the verge of collapsing into the violent political landscape of World War I. The insistence that "good fences make good neighbors" suggests a grim, ironic tone in the context of European nationalist hostilities that seemed to be moving inexorably toward war. The larger historical context for the poem would have been more apparent to its readers contemporary with World War I, but a historical reconstruction of the horrific tensions produced by shifting national borders and shattered walls during the war can shed some light on the larger issues that may be at stake in the poem. Moreover, an examination of Frost's attitudes toward the war and America's potential involvement in it could help produce a reading of the meaning and value of a world with or without walls.

## Marxist Criticism

Marxist readings developed from the heightened interest in radical reform during the 1930s, when many critics looked to literature as a means of furthering proletarian social and economic goals, based largely on the writings of Karl Marx. **Marxist critics** focus on the ideological content of a work — its explicit and implicit assumptions and values about matters such as culture, race, class, and power. Marxist studies typically aim at not only revealing and clarifying ideological issues but also correcting social injustices. Some Marxist critics have used literature to describe the competing socioeconomic interests that too often advance capitalist money and power rather than socialist morality and justice. They argue that criticism, like literature, is essentially political because it either challenges or supports economic oppression. Even if criticism attempts to ignore class conflicts, it is politicized, according to Marxists, because it supports the status quo.

It is not surprising that Marxist critics pay more attention to the content and themes of literature than to its form. A Marxist critic would more likely be concerned with the exploitive economic forces that cause Willy Loman to feel trapped in Arthur Miller's *Death of a Salesman* than with the playwright's use of nonrealistic dramatic techniques to reveal Loman's inner thoughts. Similarly, a Marxist reading of Frost's "Mending Wall" might draw on the poet's well-known conservative criticisms of President Franklin Delano Roosevelt's New Deal during the 1930s as a means of reading conservative ideology into the poem. Frost's deep suspicions of collective enterprise might suggest to a Marxist that the wall represents the status quo, that is, a capitalist construction that unnaturally divides individuals (in this case, the poem's speaker from his neighbor) and artificially defies nature. Complicit in their own oppression, both farmers, to a lesser and greater degree, accept the idea that "good fences make good neighbors," thereby maintaining and perpetuating an unnatural divisive order that oppresses and is mistakenly perceived as necessary and beneficial. A Marxist reading would see the speaker's and neighbor's conflict as not only an individual issue but also part of a larger class struggle.

## New Historicist Criticism

Since the 1960s, a development in historical approaches to literature known as **new historicism** has emphasized the interaction between the historic context of a work and a modern reader's understanding and interpretation of the work. In contrast to many traditional literary historians, however, new historicists attempt to describe the culture of a period by reading many different kinds of texts that traditional historians might have previously left for sociologists and anthropologists. New historicists attempt to define a period in all of its dimensions, including political, economic, social, and esthetic concerns. For a greater understanding of "Mending Wall," these considerations could be used to explain something about the nature of rural New England life early in the twentieth century. The process of mending the stone wall authentically suggests how this tedious job simultaneously draws the two men together and keeps them apart. Pamphlets and other contemporary writings about farming and maintaining property lines could offer insight into either the necessity or the uselessness of the spring wall-mending rituals.

A new historicist might find useful how advice offered in texts about running a farm reflects or refutes the speaker's or neighbor's competing points of view in the poem.

New historicist criticism acknowledges more fully than traditional historical approaches the competing nature of readings of the past and thereby tends to offer new emphases and perspectives. New historicism reminds us that there is not only one historic context for "Mending Wall." The year before Frost died, he visited Moscow as a cultural ambassador from the United States. During this 1962 visit — only one year after the Soviet Union's construction of the Berlin Wall — he read "Mending Wall" to his Russian audience. Like the speaker in that poem, Frost clearly enjoyed the "mischief" of that moment, and a new historicist would clearly find intriguing the way the poem was both intended and received in so volatile a context. By emphasizing that historical perceptions are governed, at least in part, by our own concerns and preoccupations, new historicists sensitize us to the fact that the history on which we choose to focus is colored by being reconstructed from our own present moment. This reconstructed history affects our reading of texts.

## Cultural Criticism

*Cultural critics,* like new historicists, focus on the historical contexts of a literary work, but they pay particular attention to popular manifestations of social, political, and economic contexts. Popular culture — mass-produced and consumed cultural artifacts, today ranging from advertising to popular fiction to television to rock music — and "high" culture are given equal emphasis. A cultural critic might be interested in looking at how Baz Luhrmann's movie version of *Romeo and Juliet* (1996) was influenced by the fragmentary nature of MTV videos. Adding the "low" art of everyday life to "high" art opens up previously unexpected and unexplored areas of criticism. Cultural critics use widely eclectic strategies drawn from new historicism, psychology, gender studies, and deconstructionism (to name only a handful of approaches) to analyze not only literary texts but also radio talk shows, comic strips, calendar art, commercials, travel guides, and baseball cards. Because all human activity falls within the ken of cultural criticism, nothing is too minor or major, obscure or pervasive, to escape the range of its analytic vision.

Cultural criticism also includes ***postcolonial criticism,*** the study of cultural behavior and expression in relationship to the formerly colonized world. Postcolonial criticism refers to the analysis of literary works by writers from countries and cultures that at one time were controlled by colonizing powers — such as Indian writers during or after British colonial rule. The term also refers to the analysis of literary works written about colonial cultures by writers from the colonizing country. Many of these kinds of analyses point out how writers from colonial powers sometimes misrepresent colonized cultures by reflecting more of their own values: Joseph

Conrad's *Heart of Darkness* (published in 1899) represents African culture differently from the way Chinua Achebe's *Things Fall Apart* (1958) does, for example. Cultural criticism and postcolonial criticism represent a broad range of approaches to examining race, gender, and class in historical contexts in a variety of cultures.

A cultural critic's approach to Frost's "Mending Wall" might emphasize how the poem reflects New England farmers' attitudes toward hunters, or it might examine how popular poems about stone walls contemporary to "Mending Wall" endorse such wall building instead of making problematic the building of walls between neighbors as Frost does. Each of these perspectives can serve to create a wider and more informed understanding of the poem.

# GENDER STRATEGIES

*Gender critics* explore how ideas about men and women — what is masculine and feminine — can be regarded as socially constructed by particular cultures. According to some critics, sex is determined by simple biological and anatomical categories of male or female, and gender is determined by a culture's values. Thus, ideas about gender and what constitutes masculine and feminine behavior are created by cultural institutions and conditioning. A gender critic might, for example, focus on Frost's characterization of the narrator's neighbor as an emotionally frozen son of a father who overshadowed his psychological and social development. The narrator's rigid masculinity would then be seen as a manifestation of socially constructed gender identity in the 1910s. Gender criticism expands categories and definitions of what is masculine or feminine and tends to regard sexuality as more complex than merely masculine or feminine, heterosexual or homosexual. Gender criticism, therefore, has come to include gay and lesbian criticism as well as feminist criticism. Although there are complex and sometimes problematic relationships among these approaches because some critics argue that heterosexuals and homosexuals are profoundly different biologically, gay and lesbian criticism, like feminist criticism, can be usefully regarded as a subset of gender criticism.

## Feminist Criticism

Like Marxist critics, *feminist critics* would also be interested in examining the status quo in "Mending Wall" because they seek to correct or supplement what they regard as a predominantly male-dominated critical perspective with a feminist consciousness. Like other forms of sociological criticism, feminist criticism places literature in a social context, and, like those of Marxist criticism, its analyses often have sociopolitical purposes — purposes that might explain, for example, how images of women in literature reflect the patriarchal social forces that have impeded women's efforts to achieve full equality with men.

Feminists have analyzed literature by both men and women in an effort to understand literary representations of women as well as the writers and cultures that create them. Related to concerns about how gender affects the way men and women write about each other is an interest in whether women use language differently from the way men do. Consequently, feminist critics' approach to literature is characterized by the use of a broad range of disciplines — among them history, sociology, psychology, and linguistics — to provide a perspective sensitive to feminist issues.

A feminist approach to Frost's "Mending Wall" might initially appear to offer few possibilities, given that no women appear in the poem and that no mention or allusion is made about women. And that is precisely the point: the landscape presented in the poem is devoid of women. Traditional gender roles are evident in the poem because it is men, not women, who work outdoors building walls and who discuss the significance of their work. For a feminist critic, the wall might be read as a symbol of patriarchal boundaries that are defined exclusively by men. If the wall can be seen as a manifestation of the status quo built upon the "father's saying[s]," then mending the wall each year and keeping everything essentially the same — with women securely out of the picture — essentially benefits the established patriarchy. The boundaries are reconstructed and rationalized in the absence of any woman's potential efforts to offer an alternative to the boundaries imposed by the men's rebuilding of the wall. Perhaps one way of considering the value of a feminist perspective on this work can be discerned if a reader imagines the speaker or the neighbor as a woman and how that change might extend the parameters of their conversation about the value of the wall.

### Gay and Lesbian Criticism

*Gay and lesbian critics* focus on a variety of issues, including how gays and lesbians are represented in literature, how they read literature, and whether sexuality and gender are culturally constructed or innate. Gay critics have produced new readings and thematic discoveries in writers such as Herman Melville and Henry James, while lesbian critics have done the same with writers such as Emily Dickinson and Sylvia Plath. In "Mending Wall," some readers have found sexual tension between the narrator and his neighbor that is suppressed by both men as they build their wall to fence in forbidden and unbidden desires. Although gay and lesbian readings often raise significant interpretative controversies among critics, they have opened up provocative discussions of seemingly familiar texts.

## MYTHOLOGICAL STRATEGIES

Mythological approaches to literature attempt to identify what in a work creates deep, universal responses in readers. Whereas psychological critics interpret the symbolic meanings of characters and actions in order to understand more fully the unconscious dimensions of an author's mind, a character's motivation, or a reader's response, mythological critics (also frequently referred to as archetypal critics) interpret the hopes, fears, and expectations of entire cultures.

In this context myth is not to be understood simply as referring to stories about imaginary gods who perform astonishing feats in the causes of love, jealousy, or hatred. Nor are myths to be judged as merely erroneous, primitive accounts of how nature runs its course and humanity its affairs. Instead, literary critics use myths as a strategy for understanding how human beings try to account for their lives symbolically. Myths can be a window onto a culture's deepest perceptions about itself because they attempt to explain what otherwise seems unexplainable: a people's origin, purpose, and destiny.

All human beings have a need to make sense of their lives, whether they are concerned about their natural surroundings, the seasons, sexuality, birth, death, or the very meaning of existence. Myths help people organize their experiences; these systems of belief (less formally held than religious or political tenets but no less important) embody a culture's assumptions and values. What is important to the mythological critic is not the validity or truth of those assumptions and values; what matters is that they reveal common human concerns.

It is not surprising that although the details of mythic stories vary enormously, the essential patterns are often similar because these myths attempt to explain universal experiences. There are, for example, numerous myths that redeem humanity from permanent death through a hero's resurrection and rebirth. For Christians the resurrection of Jesus symbolizes the ultimate defeat of death and coincides with the rebirth of nature's fertility in spring. Features of this rebirth parallel the Greek myths of Adonis and Hyacinth, who die but are subsequently transformed into living flowers; there are also similarities that connect these stories to the reincarnation of the Indian Buddha or the rebirth of the Egyptian Osiris. To be sure, important differences exist among these stories, but each reflects a basic human need to limit the power of death and to hope for eternal life.

**Mythological critics** look for underlying, recurrent patterns in literature that reveal universal meanings and basic human experiences for readers regardless of when or where they live. The characters, images, and themes that symbolically embody these meanings and experiences are called **archetypes**. This term designates universal symbols, which evoke deep and perhaps unconscious responses in a reader because archetypes bring with them the heft of our hopes and fears since the beginning of human time. Surely one of the most powerfully compelling archetypes is the death/rebirth theme that relates the human life cycle to the cycle of the seasons. Many others could be cited and would be exhausted only after all human concerns were cataloged, but a few examples can suggest some of the range of plots, images, and characters addressed.

Among the most common literary archetypes are stories of quests, initiations, scapegoats, meditative withdrawals, descents to the underworld, and heavenly ascents. These stories are often filled with archetypal images: bodies of water that may symbolize the unconscious or eternity or baptismal rebirth; rising suns, suggesting reawakening and enlightenment; setting suns, pointing toward death; colors such as green, evocative of growth and fertility, or black, indicating chaos, evil, and death. Along the way are earth mothers, fatal women, wise old men, desert places, and paradisal gardens. No doubt your own reading has introduced you to any number of archetypal plots, images, and characters.

Mythological critics attempt to explain how archetypes are embodied in literary works. Employing various disciplines, these critics articulate the power a literary work has over us. Some critics are deeply grounded in classical literature, whereas others are more conversant with philology, anthropology, psychology, or cultural history. Whatever their emphases, however, mythological critics examine the elements of a work in order to make larger connections that explain the work's lasting appeal.

A mythological reading of Sophocles' *Oedipus the King,* for example, might focus on the relationship between Oedipus's role as a scapegoat and the plague and drought that threaten to destroy Thebes. The city is saved and the fertility of its fields restored only after the corruption is located in Oedipus. His subsequent atonement symbolically provides a kind of rebirth for the city. Thus the plot recapitulates ancient rites in which the well-being of a king was directly linked to the welfare of his people. If a leader were sick or corrupt, he had to be replaced in order to guarantee the health of the community.

A similar pattern can be seen in the rottenness that Shakespeare exposes in Hamlet's Denmark. *Hamlet* reveals an archetypal pattern similar to that of *Oedipus the King:* not until the hero sorts out the corruption in his world and in himself can vitality and health be restored in his world. Hamlet avenges his father's death and becomes a scapegoat in the process. When he fully accepts his responsibility to set things right, he is swept away along with the tide of intrigue and corruption that has polluted life in Denmark. The new order — established by Fortinbras at the play's end — is achieved precisely because Hamlet is willing and finally able to sacrifice himself in a necessary purgation of the diseased state.

These kinds of archetypal patterns exist potentially in any literary period. Frost's "Mending Wall," for example, is set in spring, an evocative season that marks the end of winter and earth's renewal. The action in the poem, however, does not lead to a celebration of new life and human community; instead there is for the poem's speaker and his neighbor an annual ritual to "set the wall between us once again" — a ritual that separates and divides human experience rather than unifying it. We can see that the rebuilding of the wall runs counter to nature itself because the stones are so round that "we have to use a spell to make them balance." The speaker also resists the wall and sets out to subvert it by toying with the idea of challenging his neighbor's assumption that "good fences make good neighbors," a seemingly ancient belief passed down through one "father's saying" to the next. The speaker, however, does not heroically overcome the neighbor's ritual; he merely points out that the wall is not needed where it is. The speaker's acquiescence results in the continuation of a ritual that confirms the old order rather than overthrowing the "old-stone savage," who demands the dark isolation and separateness associated with the "gaps" produced by winter's frost. The neighbor's old order prevails despite nature's and the speaker's protestations. From a mythological critic's perspective, the wall might itself be seen as a "gap," an unnatural disruption of nature and the human community.

# READER-RESPONSE STRATEGIES

Reader-response criticism, as its name implies, focuses on the reader rather than on the work itself. This approach to literature describes what goes on in the reader's mind during the process of reading a text. In a sense, all critical approaches (especially psychological and mythological criticism) concern themselves with a reader's response to literature, but there is a stronger emphasis in reader-response criticism on the reader's active construction of the text. Although many critical theories inform reader-response criticism, all *reader-response critics* aim to describe the reader's experience of a work: in effect, we get a reading of the reader, who comes to the work with certain expectations and assumptions, which are either met or not met. Hence the consciousness of the reader — produced by reading the work — is the subject matter of reader-response critics. Just as writing is a creative act, so is reading, as it also produces a text.

Reader-response critics do not assume that a literary work is a finished product with fixed formal properties, as, for example, formalist critics do. Instead, the literary work is seen as an evolving creation of the reader's as he or she processes characters, plots, images, and other elements while reading. Some reader-response critics argue that this act of creative reading is, to a degree, controlled by the text, but it can produce many interpretations of the same text by different readers. There is no single definitive reading of a work because the crucial assumption is that readers create rather than discover meanings in texts. Readers who have gone back to works they had read earlier in their lives often find that a later reading draws very different responses from them. What earlier seemed unimportant is now crucial; what at first seemed central is now barely worth noting. The reason, put simply, is that two different people have read the same text. Reader-response critics are not after the "correct" reading of the text or what the author presumably intended; instead they are interested in the reader's experience with the text.

These experiences change with readers; although the text remains the same, the readers do not. Social and cultural values influence readings, so that, for example, an avowed Marxist would be likely to come away from Arthur Miller's *Death of a Salesman* with a very different view of American capitalism from that of, say, a successful sales representative, who might attribute Willy Loman's fall more to his character than to the American economic system. Moreover, readers from different time periods respond differently to texts. An Elizabethan — concerned perhaps with the stability of monarchical rule — might respond differently to Hamlet's problems than would a twenty-first-century reader well versed in psychology and concepts of what Freud called the Oedipus complex. This is not to say that anything goes, that Miller's play can be read as an amoral defense of cheating and rapacious business practices or that *Hamlet* is about the dangers of living away from home. The text does, after all, establish some limits that allow us to reject certain readings as erroneous. But reader-response critics do reject formalist approaches that describe a literary work as a self-contained object, the meaning of which can be determined without reference to any extrinsic matters, such as the social and cultural values assumed by either the author or the reader.

Reader-response criticism calls attention to how we read and what influences our readings. It does not attempt to define what a literary work means on the page but rather what it does to an informed reader — a reader who understands the language and conventions used in a given work. Reader-response criticism is not a rationale for mistaken or bizarre readings of works but rather an exploration of the possibilities for a plurality of readings shaped by the readers' experience with the text. This kind of strategy can help us understand how our responses are shaped by both the text and ourselves.

Frost's "Mending Wall" illustrates how reader-response critical strategies read the reader. Among the first readers of the poem in 1914, those who were eager to see the United States enter World War I might have been inclined to see the speaker as an imaginative thinker standing up for freedom rather than antiquated boundaries and sensibilities that don't know what they are "walling in or walling out." But for someone whose son could be sent to the trenches of France to fight the Germans, the phrase "good fences make good neighbors" might sound less like an unthinking tradition and more like solid, prudent common sense. In each instance the reader's circumstances could have an effect on his or her assessment of the value of walls and fences. Certainly the Russians who listened to Frost's reading of "Mending Wall" in 1962, only one year after the construction of the Berlin Wall, had a very different response from the Americans who heard about Frost's reading and who relished the discomfort they thought the reading had caused the Russians.

By imagining different readers, we can imagine a variety of responses to the poem that are influenced by the readers' own impressions, memories, or experiences. Such imagining suggests the ways in which reader-response criticism opens up texts to a number of interpretations. As one final example, consider how readers' responses to "Mending Wall" would be affected if the poem were printed in two different magazines, read in the context of either the *Farmer's Almanac* or the *New Yorker*. What assumptions and beliefs would each magazine's readership be likely to bring to the poem? How do you think the respective experiences and values of each magazine's readers would influence their readings?

## DECONSTRUCTIONIST STRATEGIES

*Deconstructionist critics* insist that literary works do not yield fixed, single meanings. They argue that there can be no absolute knowledge about anything because language can never be limited to what we intend it to mean. Anything we write conveys meanings we did not intend, so the deconstructionist argument goes. Language is not a precise instrument but a power whose meanings are caught in an endless web of possibilities that cannot be untangled. Accordingly, any idea or statement that insists on being understood separately can ultimately be "deconstructed" to reveal its relations and connections to contradictory and opposite meanings.

Unlike other forms of criticism, deconstructionism seeks to destabilize meanings instead of establishing them. In contrast to formalists such as the New Critics, who closely examine a work in order to call attention to how its various components interact to establish a unified whole, deconstructionists try to show how a close examination of a text's language inevitably reveals conflicting, contradictory impulses that "deconstruct" or break down its apparent unity.

Although deconstructionists and New Critics both examine the language of a text closely, deconstructionists focus on the gaps and ambiguities that reveal a text's instability and indeterminacy, whereas New Critics look for patterns that explain how the text's fixed meaning is structured. Deconstructionists painstakingly examine the competing meanings within the text rather than attempt to resolve them into a unified whole.

The questions deconstructionists ask are aimed at discovering and describing how a variety of possible readings are generated by the elements of a text. In contrast to a New Critic's concerns about the ultimate meaning of a work, a deconstructionist's primary interest is in how the use of language — diction, tone, metaphor, symbol, and so on — yields only provisional, not definitive, meanings. Consider, for example, the following excerpt from an American Puritan poet, Anne Bradstreet. The excerpt is from "The Flesh and the Spirit" (1678), which consists of an allegorical debate between two sisters, the body and the soul. During the course of the debate, Flesh, a consummate materialist, insists that Spirit values ideas that do not exist and that her faith in idealism is both unwarranted and insubstantial in the face of the material values that earth has to offer — riches, fame, and physical pleasure. Spirit, however, rejects the materialistic worldly argument that the only ultimate reality is physical reality and pledges her faith in God:

Mine eye doth pierce the heavens and see
What is invisible to thee.
My garments are not silk nor gold,
Nor such like trash which earth doth hold,
But royal robes I shall have on,
More glorious than the glist'ring sun;
My crown not diamonds, pearls, and gold,
But such as angels' heads enfold.
The city where I hope to dwell,
There's none on earth can parallel;
The stately walls both high and strong,
Are made of precious jasper stone;
The gates of pearl, both rich and clear,
And angels are for porters there;
The streets thereof transparent gold,
Such as no eye did e'er behold;
A crystal river there doth run,
Which doth proceed from the Lamb's throne.

A deconstructionist would point out that Spirit's language — her use of material images such as jasper stone, pearl, gold, and crystal — cancels the explicit meaning of the passage by offering a supermaterialistic reward to the spiritually faithful. Her language, in short, deconstructs her intended meaning by using the same images that Flesh would use to describe the rewards of the physical world. A deconstructionist reading, then, reveals the impossibility of talking about the invisible and spiritual worlds without using materialistic (that is, metaphoric) language. Thus Spirit's very language demonstrates a contradiction and conflict in her conviction that the world of here and now must be rejected for the hereafter. Her language deconstructs her meaning.

Deconstructionists look for ways to question and extend the meanings of a text. In Frost's "Mending Wall," for example, the speaker presents himself as being on the side of the imaginative rather than hidebound, rigid responses to life. He seems to value freedom and openness rather than restrictions and narrowly defined limits. Yet his treatment of his Yankee farmer neighbor can be read as condescending and even smug in its superior attitude toward his neighbor's repeating his "father's saying," as if he were "an old-stone savage armed." The condescending attitude hardly suggests a robust sense of community and shared humanity. Moreover, for all the talk about unnecessary conventions and traditions, a deconstructionist would likely be quick to point out that Frost writes the poem in blank verse — unrhymed iambic pentameter — rather than free verse; hence the very regular rhythms of the narrator's speech may be seen to deconstruct its liberationist meaning. As difficult as it is controversial, deconstructionism is not easily summarized or paraphrased.

The preceding summaries of critical approaches are descriptive, not evaluative. Each approach has its advantages and limitations, but those matters are best left to further study. Like literary artists, critics have their personal values, tastes, and styles. The appropriateness of a specific critical approach will depend, at least in part, on the nature of the literary work under discussion as well as on your own sensibilities and experience. However, any approach, if it is to enhance understanding, requires sensitivity, tact, and an awareness of the various literary elements of the text, including, of course, its use of language.

# 16

# Reading and the Writing Process

I can't write five words but that I change seven.

— DOROTHY PARKER

Mary Evans Picture Library / Alamy.

## THE PURPOSE AND VALUE OF WRITING ABOUT LITERATURE

Introductory literature courses typically include three components: reading, discussion, and writing. Students usually find the readings a pleasure, the class discussions a revelation, and the writing assignments — at least initially — a little intimidating. Writing an analysis of the symbolic use of a wall in Robert Frost's "Mending Wall" (p. 260) or in Herman Melville's story "Bartleby, the Scrivener," for example, may seem considerably more daunting than making a case for animal rights or analyzing a campus newspaper editorial that calls for grade reforms. Like Bartleby, you might want to respond with "I would prefer not to." Literary topics are not, however, all that different from the kinds of papers assigned in English composition courses; many of the same skills are required for both. Regardless of the type of paper, you must develop a thesis and support it with evidence in language that is clear and persuasive.

Whether the subject matter is a marketing survey, a political issue, or a literary work, writing is a method of communicating information and perceptions. Writing teaches. But before writing becomes an instrument for informing the reader, it serves as a means of learning for the writer.

An essay is a process of discovery as well as a record of what has been discovered. One of the chief benefits of writing is that we frequently realize what we want to say only after trying out ideas on a page and seeing our thoughts take shape in language.

More specifically, writing about a literary work encourages us to be better readers because it requires a close examination of the elements of a short story, poem, or play. To determine how plot, character, setting, point of view, style, tone, irony, or any number of other literary elements function in a work, we must study them in relation to one another as well as separately. Speed-reading won't do. To read a text accurately and validly — neither ignoring nor distorting significant details — we must return to the work repeatedly to test our responses and interpretations. By paying attention to details and being sensitive to the author's use of language, we develop a clearer understanding of how the work conveys its effects and meanings.

## READING THE WORK CLOSELY

Know the piece of literature you are writing about before you begin your essay. Think about how the work makes you feel and how it is put together. The more familiar you are with how the various elements of the text convey effects and meanings, the more confident you will be explaining whatever perspective on it you ultimately choose. Do not insist that everything make sense on a first reading. Relax and enjoy yourself; you can be attentive and still allow the author's words to work their magic on you. With subsequent readings, however, go more slowly and analytically as you try to establish relations between characters, actions, images, or whatever else seems important. Ask yourself why you respond as you do. Think as you read, and notice how the parts of a work contribute to its overall nature. Whether the work is a short story, poem, or play, you will read relevant portions of it over and over, and you will very likely find more to discuss in each review if the work is rich.

## ANNOTATING THE TEXT AND JOURNAL NOTE TAKING

As you read, get in the habit of annotating your texts. Whether you write marginal notes, highlight, underline, or draw boxes and circles around important words and phrases, you'll eventually develop a system that allows you to retrieve significant ideas and elements from the text. Another way to record your impressions of a work — as with any other experience — is to keep a journal. By writing down your reactions to characters, images, language, actions, and other matters in a reading journal, you can often determine why you like or dislike a work or feel sympathetic or antagonistic to an author or discover paths into a work that might have eluded you if you hadn't preserved your impressions. Your journal notes and annotations may take whatever form you find useful; full sentences and grammatical correctness are not essential (unless they are to be handed in and your instructor requires that), though they might allow you to make better sense of your own reflections days later. The point is simply to put in writing thoughts that you can retrieve when you need them for class discussion or a writing assignment. Consider the following student annotation of the first twenty-four lines of Andrew Marvell's "To His Coy Mistress" and the journal entry that follows it:

## Annotated Text

*If we*
*had*
*time...*

Had we but world enough, and time,
This coyness, lady, were no crime.     *Waste life and you*
We would sit down, and think which way    *steal from yourself.*
To walk, and pass our long love's day.
Thou by the Indian Ganges' side             5
Shouldst rubies find; I by the tide
Of Humber would complain.°    I would     *write love songs*
Love you ten years before the Flood,     *Measurements*
And you should, if you please, refuse    *of time.*
Till the conversion of the Jews.           10
My vegetable love should grow,°
Vaster than empires, and more slow;    *slow, unconscious growth*
An hundred years should go to praise
Thine eyes and on thy forehead gaze,        15
Two hundred to adore each breast,
But thirty thousand to the rest:
An age at least to every part,
And the last age should show your heart.

*Contrast*
*river*
*and*
*desert*
*images.*

For, lady, you deserve this state,          20
Nor would I love at lower rate.
But at my back I always hear      *Lines move faster*
Time's wingèd chariot hurrying near;    *here — tone changes.*
And yonder all before us lie
Deserts of vast eternity.     *This eternity rushes in.*

## Journal Note

    He'd be patient and wait for his "mistress" if they had the time — sing songs, praise her, adore her, etc. But they don't have that much time according to him. He seems to be patient but he actually begins by calling patience — her coyness — a "crime." Looks to me like he's got his mind made up from the beginning of the poem. Where's her response? I'm not sure about him.

This journal note responds to some of the effects noted in the annotations of the poem; it's an excellent beginning for making sense of the speaker's argument in the poem. Taking notes will preserve your initial reactions to the work. Many times first impressions are the best. Your response to a peculiar character, a striking phrase, or a subtle pun might lead to larger perceptions.

You should take detailed notes only after you've read through the work. If you write too many notes during the first reading, you're likely to disrupt your response. Moreover, until you have a sense of the entire work, it will be difficult to determine how connections can be made among its various elements. In addition to recording your first impressions and noting significant passages, images, diction, and so on, you should consult the Questions for Responsive Reading and Writing on page 45. These questions can assist you in getting inside a work as well as organizing your notes.

Inevitably, you will take more notes than you finally use in the paper. Note taking is a form of thinking aloud, but because your ideas are on paper, you don't have to worry about forgetting them. As you develop a better sense of a potential topic, your notes will become more focused and detailed.

## CHOOSING A TOPIC

If your instructor assigns a topic or offers a choice from among an approved list of topics, some of your work is already completed. Instead of being asked to come up with a topic about Emily Dickinson's poems in this anthology, you may be assigned a three-page essay that specifically discusses "Dickinson's Treatment of Grief in 'The Bustle in a House.'" You also have the assurance that a specified topic will be manageable within the suggested number of pages. Unless you ask your instructor for permission to write on a different or related topic, be certain to address yourself to the assignment. An essay that does not discuss grief but instead describes Dickinson's relationship with her father would be missing the point. Notice, too, that there is room even in an assigned topic to develop your own approach. One question that immediately comes to mind is whether grief defeats or helps the speaker in the poem. Assigned topics do not relieve you of thinking about an aspect of a work, but they do focus your thinking.

At some point during the course, you may have to begin an essay from scratch. You might, for example, be asked to write about a poem that somehow impressed you or that seemed particularly well written or filled with insights. Before you start considering a topic, you should have a sense of how long the paper will be because the assigned length can help determine the extent to which you should develop your topic. Ideally, the paper's length should be based on how much space you deem necessary to present your discussion clearly and convincingly, but if you have any doubts and no specific guidelines have been indicated, ask. The question is important; a topic that might be appropriate for a three-page paper could be too narrow for ten pages. Three pages would probably be adequate for a discussion of the speaker's view of death in John Keats's "To Autumn"(p. 98). Conversely, it would be futile to try to summarize Keats's use of sensuality in his poetry in even ten pages; the topic would have to be narrowed to something like "Images of Sensuality in 'La Belle Dame sans Merci.'" Be sure that the topic you choose can be adequately covered in the assigned number of pages.

## DEVELOPING A THESIS

When you are satisfied that you have something interesting to say about a work and that your notes have led you to a focused topic, you can formulate a *thesis*, the central idea of the paper. Whereas the topic indicates what the paper focuses on (the disembodied images in "Prufrock," for example), the thesis explains what you have to say about the topic (the frightening images of eyes, arms, and claws reflect Prufrock's disjointed, fragmentary response to life). The thesis should be a complete sentence (though sometimes it may require more than one sentence) that establishes your topic in clear, unambiguous language. The thesis may be revised as you get further into the topic and discover what you want to say about it, but once the thesis is firmly established, it will serve as a guide for you and your reader because all the information and observations in your essay should be related to the thesis.

One student on an initial reading of Andrew Marvell's "To His Coy Mistress" (p. 65) saw that the male speaker of the poem urges a woman to love now before time runs out for them. This reading gave him the impression that the poem is a simple celebration of the pleasures of the flesh, but on subsequent readings he underlined or noted these images: "Time's wingèd chariot hurrying near"; "Deserts of vast eternity"; "marble vault"; "worms"; "dust"; "ashes"; and these two lines: "The grave's a fine and private place, / But none, I think, do there embrace."

By listing these images associated with time and death, he established an inventory that could be separated from the rest of his notes on point of view, character, sounds, and other subjects. Inventorying notes allows patterns to emerge that you might have only vaguely perceived otherwise. Once these images are grouped, they call attention to something darker and more complex in Marvell's poem than a first impression might suggest.

These images may create a different feeling about the poem, but they still don't explain very much. One simple way to generate a thesis about a literary work is to ask the question "why?" Why do these images appear in the poem? Why does disorder appeal so much to the speaker in Robert Herrick's "Delight in Disorder" (p. 185)? Your responses to these kinds of questions can lead to a thesis.

Writers sometimes use freewriting to help themselves explore possible answers to such questions. It can be an effective way of generating ideas. Freewriting is exactly that: the technique calls for nonstop writing without concern for mechanics or editing of any kind. Freewriting for ten minutes or so on a question will result in fragments and repetitions, but it can also produce some ideas. Here's an example of a student's response to the question about the images in "To His Coy Mistress":

> *He wants her to make love. Love poem. There's little time. Her crime. He exaggerates. Sincere? Sly? What's he want? She says nothing — he says it all. What about deserts, ashes, graves, and worms? Some love poem. Sounds like an old Vincent Price movie. Full of sweetness but death creeps in. Death — hurry hurry! Tear pleasures. What passion! Where's death in this? How can a love poem be so ghoulish? She does nothing. Maybe frightened? Convinced? Why death? Love and death — time — death.*

This freewriting contains several ideas; it begins by alluding to the poem's plot and speaker, but the central idea seems to be death. This emphasis led the student to five potential thesis statements for his essay about the poem:

1. "To His Coy Mistress" is a difficult poem.
2. Death in "To His Coy Mistress."
3. There are many images of death in "To His Coy Mistress."
4. "To His Coy Mistress" celebrates the pleasures of the flesh but it also recognizes the power of death to end that pleasure.
5. On the surface, "To His Coy Mistress" is a celebration of the pleasures of the flesh, but this witty seduction is tempered by a chilling recognition of the reality of death.

The first statement is too vague to be useful. In what sense is the poem difficult? A more precise phrasing, indicating the nature of the difficulty, is needed. The second statement is a topic rather than a thesis. Because it is not a sentence, it does not express a complete idea about how the poem treats death. Although this could be an appropriate title, it is inadequate as a thesis statement. The third statement, like the first one, identifies the topic, but even though it is a sentence, it is not a complete idea that tells us anything significant beyond the fact it states. After these preliminary attempts to develop a thesis, the student remembered his first impression of the poem and incorporated it into his thesis statement. The fourth thesis is a useful approach to the poem because it limits the topic and indicates how it will be treated in the paper: the writer will begin with an initial impression of the poem and then go on to qualify it. However, the fifth thesis is better than the fourth because it indicates a shift in tone produced by the ironic relationship between death and flesh. An effective thesis, like this one, makes a clear statement about a manageable topic and provides a firm sense of direction for the paper.

Most writing assignments in a literature course require you to persuade readers that your thesis is reasonable and supported with evidence. Papers that report information without comment or evaluation are simply summaries. Similarly, a paper that merely pointed out the death images in "To His Coy Mistress" would not contain a thesis, but a paper that attempted to make a case for the death imagery as a grim reminder of how vulnerable flesh is would involve persuasion. In developing a thesis, remember that you are expected not merely to present information but to argue a point.

# ARGUING ABOUT LITERATURE

An argumentative essay is designed to make persuasive your interpretation of a work. Arguing about literature doesn't mean that you're engaged in an angry, antagonistic dispute (though controversial topics do sometimes engender heated debates). Instead, argumentation requires that you present your interpretation of a work (or a portion of it) by supporting your discussion with clearly defined terms, ample evidence, and a detailed analysis of relevant portions of the text.

If you have a choice, it's generally best to write about a topic that you feel strongly about. Even if you don't like snakes, you might find Emily Dickinson's "A Narrow Fellow in the Grass" (p. 2) just the sort of treatment that helps explain why you don't want one. On the other hand, if you're fascinated by snakes the poem may suggest something essential about snakes that you've experienced but have never quite put your finger on. If your essay is to be interesting and convincing, what is important is that it be written from a strong point of view that persuasively argues your evaluation, analysis, and interpretation of a work. It is not enough to say that you like or dislike a work; instead you must give your reader some ideas and evidence that can be accepted or rejected based on the quality of the answers to the questions you raise.

One way to come up with persuasive answers is to generate good questions that will lead you further into the text and to critical issues related to it. The critical strategies for reading summarized in Chapter 15 can be a resource for raising questions that can be shaped into an argument. The following lists of questions for the critical approaches covered in Chapter 15 should be useful for discovering arguments you might make about a poem, short story, or play. The page number that follows each heading refers to the discussion in the anthology for that particular approach.

## Questions for Arguing Critically about Literature

### FORMALIST QUESTIONS (P. 329)

1. How do various elements of the work—plot, character, point of view, setting, tone, diction, images, symbol, and so on—reinforce its meanings?
2. How are the elements related to the whole?
3. What is the work's major organizing principle? How is its structure unified?
4. What issues does the work raise? How does the work's structure resolve those issues?

BIOGRAPHICAL QUESTIONS (P. 331)

1. Are facts about the writer's life relevant to your understanding of the work?

2. Are characters and incidents in the work versions of the writer's own experiences? Are they treated factually or imaginatively?

3. How do you think the writer's values are reflected in the work?

PSYCHOLOGICAL QUESTIONS (P. 333)

1. How does the work reflect the author's personal psychology?

2. What do the characters' or speaker's emotions and behavior reveal about their psychological states? What types of personalities are they?

3. Are psychological matters such as repression, dreams, and desire presented consciously or unconsciously by the author?

HISTORICAL QUESTIONS (P. 334)

1. How does the work reflect the period in which it was written?

2. What literary or historical influences helped shape the work's form and content?

3. How important is the historical context to interpreting the work?

MARXIST QUESTIONS (P. 335)

1. How are class differences presented in the work? Are characters or speakers aware or unaware of the economic and social forces that affect their lives?

2. How do economic conditions determine the characters' or speaker's lives?

3. What ideological values are explicit or implicit?

4. Does the work challenge or affirm the social order it describes?

NEW HISTORICIST QUESTIONS (P. 336)

1. What kinds of documents outside the work seem especially relevant for shedding light on the work?

2. How are social values contemporary to the work reflected or refuted in the work?

3. How does your own historical moment affect your reading of the work and its historical reconstruction?

CULTURAL STUDIES QUESTIONS (P. 337)

1. What does the work reveal about the cultural behavior contemporary to it?

2. How does popular culture contemporary to the work reflect or challenge the values implicit or explicit in the work?

3. What kinds of cultural documents contemporary to the work add to your reading of it?

4. How do your own cultural assumptions affect your reading of the work and the culture contemporary to it?

### GENDER STUDIES QUESTIONS (P. 338)

1. How are the lives of men and women portrayed in the work? Do the men and women in the work accept or reject these roles?

2. Is the work's form and content influenced by the author's gender?

3. What attitudes are explicit or implicit concerning heterosexual or same-sex relationships? Are these relationships sources of conflict? Do they provide resolutions to conflicts?

4. Does the work challenge or affirm traditional ideas about men and women and same-sex relationships?

### MYTHOLOGICAL QUESTIONS (P. 339)

1. How does the work resemble other works in plot, character, setting, or use of symbols?

2. Does the work present archetypes such as quests, initiations, scapegoats, or withdrawals and returns?

3. Does the protagonist undergo any kind of transformation, such as a movement from innocence to experience, that seems archetypal?

4. Do any specific allusions to myths shed light on the text?

### READER-RESPONSE QUESTIONS (P. 342)

1. How do you respond to the work?

2. How do your own experiences and expectations affect your reading and interpretation?

3. What is the work's original or intended audience? To what extent are you similar to or different from that audience?

4. Do you respond in the same way to the work after more than one reading?

### DECONSTRUCTIONIST QUESTIONS (P. 344)

1. How are contradictory and opposing meanings expressed in the work?

2. How does meaning break down or deconstruct itself in the language of the text?

3. Would you say that ultimate definitive meanings are impossible to determine and establish in the text? Why? How does that affect your interpretation?

4. How are implicit ideological values revealed in the work?

(*continued*)

These questions will not apply to all texts, and they are not mutually exclusive. They can be combined to explore a text from several critical perspectives simultaneously. A feminist approach to Anne Bradstreet's "The Author to Her Book" (p. 105) could also use Marxist concerns about class to make observations about the oppression of women's lives in the historical context of the seventeenth century. Your use of these questions should allow you to discover significant issues from which you can develop an argumentative essay that is organized around clearly defined terms, relevant evidence, and a persuasive analysis.

## ORGANIZING A PAPER

After you have chosen a manageable topic and developed a thesis — a central idea about it — you can begin to organize your paper. Your thesis, even if it is still somewhat tentative, should help you decide what information will need to be included and provide you with a sense of direction.

Consider again the sample thesis in the section on developing a thesis:

> On the surface, "To His Coy Mistress" is a celebration of the pleasures of the flesh, but this witty seduction is tempered by a chilling recognition of the reality of death.

This thesis indicates that the paper can be divided into two parts: the pleasures of the flesh and the reality of death. It also indicates an order: because the central point is to show that the poem is more than a simple celebration, the pleasures of the flesh should be discussed first so that another, more complex reading of the poem can follow. If the paper began with the reality of death, its point would be anticlimactic.

Having established such a broad and informal outline, you can draw on your underlinings, margin notations, and notecards for the subheadings and evidence required to explain the major sections of your paper. This next level of detail might look like the following:

1. Pleasures of the flesh
    Part of the traditional tone of love poetry
2. Recognition of death
    Ironic treatment of love
        Diction
        Images
        Figures of speech
        Symbols
        Tone

This list was initially a jumble of terms, but the student arranged the items so that each of the two major sections leads to a discussion of tone. (The student also found it necessary to drop some biographical information from his notes because it was irrelevant to the thesis.) The list indicates that the first part of the paper will establish the traditional tone of love poetry that celebrates the pleasures of the flesh, while the second part will present a more detailed discussion about the ironic recognition of death. The emphasis is on the latter because that is the point to be argued in the paper. Hence the thesis has helped organize the parts of the paper, establish an order, and indicate the paper's proper proportions.

The next step is to fill in the subheadings with information from your notes. Many experienced writers find that making lists of information to be included under each subheading is an efficient way to develop paragraphs. For a longer paper (perhaps a research paper), you should be able to develop a paragraph or more on each subheading. On the other hand, a shorter paper may require that you combine several subheadings in a paragraph. You may also discover that while an informal list is adequate for a brief paper, a ten-page assignment could require a more detailed outline. Use the method that is most productive for you. Whatever the length of the essay, your presentation must be in a coherent and logical order that allows your reader to follow the argument and evaluate the evidence. The quality of your reading can be demonstrated only by the quality of your writing.

## WRITING A DRAFT

Be flexible. Your outline should smoothly conduct you from one point to the next, but do not permit it to railroad you. If a relevant and important idea occurs to you now, work it into the draft. By using the first draft as a means of thinking about what you want to say, you will very likely discover more than your notes originally suggested. Plenty of good writers don't use outlines at all but discover ordering principles as they write. Do not attempt to compose a perfectly correct draft the first time around. Grammar, punctuation, and spelling can wait until you revise. Concentrate on what you are saying. Good writing most often occurs when you are in hot pursuit of an idea rather than in a nervous search for errors.

Once you have a first draft on paper, you can delete material that is unrelated to your thesis and add material necessary to illustrate your points and make your paper convincing. The student who wrote "Disembodied Images in T. S. Eliot's 'The Love Song of J. Alfred Prufrock'" (p. 367) wisely dropped a paragraph that questioned whether Prufrock displays chauvinistic attitudes toward women. Although this could be an interesting issue, it has nothing to do with the thesis, which explains how the images reflect Prufrock's inability to make a meaningful connection to his world.

Remember that your initial draft is only that. You should go through the paper many times — and then again — working to substantiate and clarify your ideas. You may even end up with several entire versions of the paper. Rewrite. The sentences within each paragraph should be related to a single topic. Transitions should connect one paragraph to the next so that there are no abrupt or confusing shifts. Awkward or wordy phrasing or unclear sentences and paragraphs should be mercilessly poked and prodded into shape.

## Writing the Introduction and Conclusion

After you have clearly and adequately developed the body of your paper, pay particular attention to the introductory and concluding paragraphs. It's probably best to write the introduction — at least the final version of it — last, after you know precisely what you are introducing. Because this paragraph is crucial for generating interest in the topic, it should engage the reader and provide a sense of what the paper is about. There is no formula for writing effective introductory paragraphs because each writing situation is different — depending on the audience, topic, and approach — but if you pay attention to the introductions of the essays you read, you will notice a variety of possibilities. The introductory paragraph to the Prufrock paper, for example, is a straightforward explanation of why the disembodied images are important for understanding Prufrock's character. The rest of the paper then offers evidence to support this point.

Concluding paragraphs demand equal attention because they leave the reader with a final impression. The conclusion should provide a sense of closure instead of starting a new topic or ending abruptly. In the final paragraph about the disembodied images in "Prufrock," the student explains their significance in characterizing Prufrock's inability to think of himself or others as complete and whole human beings. We now see that the images of eyes, arms, and claws are reflections of the fragmentary nature of Prufrock and his world. Of course, the body of your paper is the most important part of your presentation, but do remember that first and last impressions have a powerful impact on readers.

## Using Quotations

Quotations can be a valuable means of marshaling evidence to illustrate and support your ideas. A judicious use of quoted material will make your points clearer and more convincing. Here are some guidelines that should help you use quotations effectively.

1. Brief quotations (four lines or fewer of prose or three lines or fewer of poetry) should be carefully introduced and integrated into the text of your paper with quotation marks around them.

> According to the narrator, Bertha "had a reputation for strictness." He tells us that she always "wore dark clothes, dressed her hair simply, and expected contrition and obedience from her pupils" (quoted in Jackson).

For brief poetry quotations, use a slash to indicate a division between lines.

> The concluding lines of Blake's "The Tyger" pose a disturbing question: "What immortal hand or eye / Dare frame thy fearful symmetry?" (Meyer 187).

Lengthy quotations should be separated from the text of your paper. More than three lines of poetry should be double-spaced and centered on the page. More than four lines of prose should be double-spaced and indented ten spaces from the left margin, with the right margin the same as for the text. Do *not* use quotation marks for the passage; the indentation indicates that the passage is a quotation. Lengthy quotations should not be used in place of your own writing. Use them only if they are absolutely necessary.

2. If any words are added to a quotation, use brackets to distinguish your addition from the original source.

> "He [Young Goodman Brown] is portrayed as self-righteous and disillusioned."

Any words inside quotation marks and not in brackets must be precisely those of the author. Brackets can also be used to change the grammatical structure of a quotation so that it fits into your sentence.

> Smith argues that Chekhov "present[s] the narrator in an ambivalent light."

If you drop any words from the source, use an ellipsis (three spaced periods) to indicate that the omission is yours.

> "Early to bed . . . makes a man healthy, wealthy, and wise."

Use a period followed by an ellipsis to indicate an omission at the end of a sentence.

> Franklin wrote: "Early to bed and early to rise makes a man healthy. . . ."

Use a single line of spaced periods to indicate the omission of a line or more of poetry or more than one paragraph of prose.

> Nothing would sleep in that cellar, dank as a ditch,
> Bulbs broke out of boxes hunting for chinks in the dark,
>
> . . . . . . . . . . . . . . . . . .
>
> Nothing would give up life:
> Even the dirt kept breathing a small breath.

3. You will be able to punctuate quoted material accurately and confidently if you observe these conventions.

Place commas and periods inside quotation marks.

> "Even the dirt," Roethke insists, "kept breathing a small breath."

Even though a comma does not appear after "dirt" in the original quotation, it is placed inside the quotation mark. The exception to this rule occurs when a parenthetical reference to a source follows the quotation.

> "Even the dirt," Roethke insists, "kept breathing a small breath" (11).

Punctuation marks other than commas or periods go outside the quotation marks unless they are part of the material quoted.

What does Roethke mean when he writes that "the dirt kept breathing a small breath"?

Yeats asked, "How can we know the dancer from the dance?"

# REVISING AND EDITING

Put some distance — a day or so if you can — between yourself and each draft of your paper. The phrase that seemed just right on Wednesday may be revealed as all wrong on Friday. You'll have a better chance of detecting lumbering sentences and thin paragraphs if you plan ahead and give yourself the time to read your paper from a fresh perspective. Through the process of revision, you can transform a competent paper into an excellent one.

Begin by asking yourself if your approach to the topic requires any rethinking. Is the argument carefully thought out and logically presented? Are there any gaps in the presentation? How well is the paper organized? Do the paragraphs lead into one another? Does the body of the paper deliver what the thesis promises? Is the interpretation sound? Are any relevant and important elements of the work ignored or distorted to advance the thesis? Are the points supported with evidence? These large questions should be addressed before you focus on more detailed matters. If you uncover serious problems as a result of considering these questions, you'll probably have quite a lot of rewriting to do, but at least you will have the opportunity to correct the problems — even if doing so takes several drafts.

The following checklist offers questions to ask about your paper as you revise and edit it. Most of these questions will be familiar to you; however, if you need help with any of them, ask your instructor or review the appropriate section in a composition handbook.

---

### Questions for Revising and Editing

1. Is the topic manageable? Is it too narrow or too broad?

2. Is the thesis clear? Is it based on a careful reading of the work?

3. Is the paper logically organized? Does it have a firm sense of direction?

4. Is your argument persuasive? Do you use evidence from the text to support your main points?

5. Should any material be deleted? Do any important points require further illustration or evidence?

6. Does the opening paragraph introduce the topic in an interesting manner?

7. Are the paragraphs developed, unified, and coherent? Are any too short or long?

8. Are there transitions linking the paragraphs?

9. Does the concluding paragraph provide a sense of closure?

10. Is the tone appropriate? Is it unduly flippant or pretentious?

11. Is the title engaging and suggestive?

12. Are the sentences clear, concise, and complete?

13. Are simple, complex, and compound sentences used for variety?

14. Have technical terms been used correctly? Are you certain of the meanings of all of the words in the paper? Are they spelled correctly?

15. Have you documented any information borrowed from books, articles, or other sources? Have you quoted too much instead of summarizing or paraphrasing secondary material?

16. Have you used a standard format for citing sources (see p. 383)?

17. Have you followed your instructor's guidelines for the manuscript format of the final draft?

18. Have you carefully proofread the final draft?

When you proofread your final draft, you may find a few typographical errors that must be corrected but do not warrant printing an entire page again. Provided there are not more than a handful of such errors throughout the paper, they can be corrected as shown in the following passage. This example condenses a short paper's worth of errors; no single passage should be this shabby in your essay.

To add a letter or word, use a caret on the line where the addition is needed. To delete a word draw a single line through ~~through~~ it. Run-on words are separated by a vertical line, and inadvertent spaces are closed like this. Transposed letters are indicated this way. New paragraphs are noted with the sign ¶ in front of where the next paragraph is to begin. ¶ Unless you . . .

These sorts of errors can be minimized by proofreading on the screen and simply entering corrections as you go along.

## MANUSCRIPT FORM

The novelist and poet Peter De Vries once observed in his characteristically humorous way that he very much enjoyed writing but that he couldn't bear the "paper work." Behind this playful pun is a half-serious impatience with the mechanics of it all. You may feel some of that too, but this is not the time to allow a thoughtful, carefully revised paper to trip over minor details that can be easily accommodated. The final draft you hand in to your instructor should not only read well but also look neat. If your instructor does not provide specific instructions concerning the paper's format, follow these guidelines.

1. Papers (particularly long ones) should be typed, double-spaced, on 8½ × 11–inch paper. Be certain that the printout is legible. If your instructor accepts handwritten papers, write legibly in ink on only one side of a wide-lined page.

2. Use a one-inch margin at the top, bottom, and sides of each page. Unless you are instructed to include a separate title page, type your name, instructor's name, course number and section, and date on separate lines one inch below the upper-left corner of the first page. Double-space between these lines and then center the title below the date. Do not italicize or put quotation marks around your paper's title, but do use quotation marks around the titles of poems, short stories, or other brief works, and italicize the titles of books and plays (a sample paper title: "Mending Wall" and Other Boundaries in Frost's *North of Boston*). Begin the text of your paper two spaces below the title. If you have used secondary sources, center the heading "Notes" or "Works Cited" one inch from the top of a separate page and then double-space between it and the entries.

3. Number each page consecutively, beginning with page 1, a half inch from the top of the page in the upper-right corner.

4. Gather the pages with a paper clip rather than staples, folders, or some other device. That will make it easier for your instructor to handle the paper.

## TYPES OF WRITING ASSIGNMENTS

The types of papers most frequently assigned in literature classes are explication, analysis, and comparison and contrast. Most writing about literature involves some combination of these skills. This section includes a sample explication, an analysis, and a comparison-and-contrast paper. For a sample research paper that demonstrates a variety of strategies for documenting outside sources, see page 392. For other examples of student papers, see pages 364, 368, and 374.

### *Explication*

The purpose of this approach to a literary work is to make the implicit explicit. **Explication** is a detailed explanation of a passage of poetry or prose. Because explication is an intensive examination of a text line by line, it is mostly used to interpret a short poem in its entirety or a brief passage from a long poem, short story, or play. Explication can be used in any kind of paper when you want to be specific about how a writer achieves a certain effect. An explication pays careful attention to language: the connotations of words, allusions, figurative language, irony, symbol, rhythm, sound, and so on. These elements are examined in relation to one another and to the work's overall effect and meaning.

The simplest way to organize an explication is to move through the passage line by line, explaining whatever seems significant. It is wise to avoid, however, an assembly-line approach that begins each sentence with "In line. . . ." Instead, organize your paper in whatever way best serves your thesis. You might find that the right place to start is with the final lines, working your way back to the beginning of the poem or passage. The following sample explication on Emily Dickinson's "There's a certain Slant of light" does just that. The student's opening paragraph refers to the final line of the poem in order to present her thesis. She explains that though the poem begins with an image of light, it is not a bright or cheery poem but one concerned with "the look of Death." Because the last line prompted her thesis, that is where she begins the explication.

You might also find it useful to structure a paper by discussing various elements of literature so that you have a paragraph on connotative words followed by one on figurative language and so on. However your paper is organized, keep in mind that the aim of an explication is not simply to summarize the passage but to comment on the effects and meanings produced by the author's use of language in it. An effective explication (the Latin word *explicare* means "to unfold") displays a text to reveal how it works and what it signifies. Although writing an explication requires some patience and sensitivity, it is an excellent method for coming to understand and appreciate the elements and qualities that constitute literary art.

# A SAMPLE EXPLICATION

## *A Reading of Emily Dickinson's*
## *"There's a certain Slant of light"*

The sample paper by Bonnie Katz is the result of an assignment calling for an explication of about 750 words on any poem by Emily Dickinson. Katz selected "There's a certain Slant of light."

## EMILY DICKINSON (1830–1886)

### *There's a certain Slant of light*                    *ca. 1861*

There's a certain Slant of light,
Winter Afternoons —
That oppresses, like the Heft
Of Cathedral Tunes —

Heavenly Hurt, it gives us —                              5
We can find no scar,
But internal difference,
Where the Meanings, are —

None may teach it — Any —
'Tis the Seal Despair —                                    10
An imperial affliction
Sent us of the Air —

When it comes, the Landscape listens —
Shadows — hold their breath —
When it goes, 'tis like the Distance                       15
On the look of Death —

This essay comments on every line of the poem and provides a coherent reading that relates each line to the speaker's intense awareness of death. Although the essay discusses each stanza in the order that it appears, the introductory paragraph provides a brief overview explaining how the poem's images contribute to its total meaning. In addition, the student does not hesitate to discuss a line out of sequence when it can be usefully connected to another phrase. This is especially apparent in the third paragraph, in her discussion of stanzas 2 and 3. The final paragraph describes some of the poem's formal elements. It might be argued that this discussion could have been integrated into the previous paragraphs rather than placed at the end, but the student does make a connection in her concluding sentence between the pattern of language and its meaning.

Several other matters are worth noticing. The student works quotations into her own sentences to support her points. She quotes exactly as the words appear in the poem, even Dickinson's irregular use of capital letters. When something is added to a quotation to clarify it, it is enclosed in brackets so that the essayist's words will not be mistaken for the poet's: "Seal [of] Despair." A slash is used to separate line divisions as in "imperial affliction / Sent us of the Air."

Bonnie Katz

Professor Quiello

English 109–2

26 October 2015

A Reading of Emily Dickinson's

"There's a certain Slant of light"

Because Emily Dickinson did not provide titles for her poetry, editors follow

the customary practice of using the first line of a poem as its title. However, a

more appropriate title for "There's a certain Slant of light," one that suggests what the speaker in the poem is most concerned about, can be drawn from the poem's last line, which ends with "the look of Death." Although the first line begins with an image of light, nothing bright, carefree, or cheerful appears in the poem. Instead, the predominant mood and images are darkened by a sense of despair resulting from the speaker's awareness of death.

> *Thesis providing overview of explication.*

In the first stanza, the "certain Slant of light" is associated with "Winter Afternoons" (lines 1-2), a phrase that connotes the end of a day, a season, and even life itself. Such light is hardly warm or comforting. Not a ray or beam, this slanting light suggests something unusual or distorted and creates in the speaker a certain slant on life that is consistent with the cold, dark mood that winter afternoons can produce. Like the speaker, most of us have seen and felt this sort of light: it "oppresses" (3) and pervades our sense of things when we encounter it. Dickinson uses the senses of hearing and touch as well as sight to describe the overwhelming oppressiveness that the speaker experiences. The light is transformed into sound by a simile that tells us it is "like the Heft / Of Cathedral Tunes" (3-4). Moreover, the "Heft" of that sound—the slow, solemn measures of tolling church bells and organ music—weighs heavily on our spirits. Through the use of shifting imagery, Dickinson evokes a kind of spiritual numbness that we keenly feel and perceive through our senses.

> *Line-by-line explication of first stanza, focusing on connotations of words and imagery, in relation to mood and meaning of poem as a whole; supported with references to the text.*

By associating the winter light with "Cathedral Tunes," Dickinson lets us know that the speaker is concerned about more than the weather. Whatever it is that "oppresses" is related by connotation to faith, mortality, and God. The second and third stanzas offer several suggestions about this connection. The pain caused by the light is a "Heavenly Hurt" (5). This "imperial affliction / Sent us of the Air—" (11-12) apparently comes from God above, yet it seems to be part of the very nature of life. The oppressiveness we feel is in the air, and it can neither be specifically identified at this point in the poem  nor be eliminated, for "None may teach it—Any" (9). All we know is that existence itself seems depressing under the weight of this "Seal [of] Despair" (10). The impression left by this "Seal" is stamped within the mind or soul rather than externally. "We can find no scar" (6), but once experienced this oppressiveness challenges our faith in life and its "Meanings" (8).

> *Explication of second, third, and fourth stanzas, focusing on connotations of words and imagery in relation to mood and meaning of poem as a whole; supported with references to the text.*

The final stanza does not explain what those "Meanings" are, but it does make clear that the speaker is acutely aware of death. As the winter daylight fades, Dickinson projects the speaker's anxiety onto the surrounding landscape and shadows, which will soon be engulfed by the darkness that follows this light: "the Landscape listens— / Shadows—hold their breath" (13-14). This image firmly aligns the winter light in the first stanza with darkness. Paradoxically, the light in this poem illuminates the nature of darkness. Tension is released when the light is completely gone, but what remains is the despair that the "imperial affliction" has imprinted on the speaker's sensibilities, for it is "like the Distance / On the look of Death" (15-16). There can be no relief from what that "certain Slant of light" has revealed because what has been experienced is permanent—like the fixed stare in the eyes of someone who is dead.

> **Explication of the elements of rhythm and sound throughout poem.**

The speaker's awareness of death is conveyed in a thoughtful, hushed tone. The lines are filled with fluid *l* and *s* sounds that are appropriate for the quiet, meditative voice in the poem. The voice sounds tentative and uncertain— perhaps a little frightened. This seems to be reflected in the slightly irregular meter of the lines. The stanzas are trochaic with the second and fourth lines of each stanza having five syllables, but no stanza is identical because each works a slight variation on the first stanza's seven syllables in the first and third lines. The rhymes also combine exact patterns with variations. The first and third lines of each stanza are not exact rhymes, but the second and fourth lines are exact so that the paired words are more closely related: *Afternoons, Tunes; scar, are; Despair, Air;* and *breath, Death*. There is a pattern to the poem, but it is unobtrusively woven into the speaker's voice in much the same way that "the look of Death" is subtly present in the images and language of the poem.

> **Conclusion tying explication of rhythm and sound with explication of words and imagery in previous paragraphs.**

## Work Cited

Dickinson, Emily. "There's a certain Slant of light." *Thinking and Writing about Poetry.* Ed. Michael Meyer. Boston: Bedford/St. Martin's, 2016. 363. Print.

## Analysis

The preceding sample essay shows how an explication examines in detail the important elements in a work and relates them to the whole. An *analysis*, however, usually examines only a single element — such as diction, character, point of view, symbol, tone, or irony — and relates it to the entire work. An analytic topic separates the work into parts and focuses on a specific one; you might consider "Point of View in 'The Love Song of J. Alfred Prufrock,'" "Patterns of Rhythm in Robert Browning's 'My Last Duchess,'" or "Irony in 'The Road Not Taken.'" The specific element must be related to the work as a whole or it will appear irrelevant. It is not enough to point out that there are many death images in Andrew Marvell's "To His Coy Mistress"; the images must somehow be connected to the poem's overall effect.

Whether an analytic paper is just a few pages or many, it cannot attempt to discuss everything about the work it is considering. Only those elements that are relevant to the topic can be treated. This kind of focusing makes the topic manageable; this is why most papers that you write will probably be some form of analysis. Explications are useful for a short passage, but a line-by-line commentary on a story, play, or long poem simply isn't practical. Because analysis allows you to consider the central effect or meaning of an entire work by studying a single important element, it is a useful and common approach to longer works.

# A SAMPLE ANALYSIS

## Disembodied Images in T. S. Eliot's "The Love Song of J. Alfred Prufrock"

Beth Hart's paper analyzes some of the images in T. S. Eliot's "The Love Song of J. Alfred Prufrock" (the poem appears on p. 304). The assignment simply called for an essay of approximately 750 words on a poem written in the twentieth century. The approach was left to the student.

The idea for this essay began with Hart asking herself why there are so many fragmentary, disjointed images in the poem. The initial answer to this question was that "the disjointed images are important for understanding Prufrock's character." This answer was the rough beginning of a tentative thesis. What still had to be explained, though, was how the images are important. To determine the significance of the disjointed images, Hart jotted down some notes based on her underlinings and marginal notations.

| Prufrock | Images |
|---|---|
| odd name — nervous, timid? | fog |
| "indecisions," "revisions" | lost, wandering |
| confessional tone, self- | watching eyes |
| conscious | ladies' arms |

| | |
|---|---|
| "bald spot" | polite talk, meaningless talk |
| "afraid" | "ragged claws" that scuttle |
| questioning, tentative | oppressive |
| "I am not Prince Hamlet" | distorted |
| "I grow old" | weary longing |
| wake — to drown | entrapped — staircase |

From these notes Hart saw that the images — mostly fragmented and disjointed — suggested something about Prufrock's way of describing himself and his world. This insight led eventually to the final version of her thesis statement: "Eliot's use of frightening disembodied images such as eyes, arms, and claws reflects Prufrock's terror at having to face a world to which he feels no meaningful connection." Her introductory paragraph concludes with this sentence so that her reader can fully comprehend why she then discusses the images of eyes, arms, and claws that follow.

The remaining paragraphs present details that explain the significance of the images of eyes in the second paragraph, the arms in the third, the claws in the fourth, and in the final paragraph all three images are the basis for concluding that Prufrock's vision of the world is disconnected and disjointed.

Hart's notes certainly do not constitute a formal outline, but they were useful to her in establishing a thesis and recognizing what elements of the poem she needed to cover in her discussion. Her essay is sharply focused, well organized, and generally well written (though some readers might wish for a more engaging introductory paragraph that captures a glint of Prufrock's "bald spot" or some other small detail in order to generate some immediate interest in his character).

Hart 1

Beth Hart
Professor Lucas
English 110–3
30 March 2015

Disembodied Images in T. S. Eliot's
"The Love Song of J. Alfred Prufrock"

T. S. Eliot's poem "The Love Song of J. Alfred Prufrock" addresses the dilemma of a man who finds himself trapped on the margins of the social world, unable to make any meaningful interpersonal contact because of his deep-seated fear of rejection and misunderstanding. Prufrock feels acutely disconnected from society, which makes him so self-conscious that he is frightened into a state of social paralysis. His overwhelming self-consciousness, disillusionment with social circles, and lack of connection with those around him are revealed through Eliot's use of fragmented imagery. Many of the predominant images are disembodied pieces of a whole, revealing that Prufrock sees the world not as fully whole or complete, but as disjointed, fragmented parts of the whole. Eliot's use of frightening disembodied images such as eyes, arms, and claws reflects Prufrock's terror at having to face a world to which he feels no meaningful connection.

    Eliot suggests Prufrock's acute self-consciousness through the fragmentary image of eyes. Literally, these eyes merely represent the people who surround Prufrock, but this disembodied image reveals his obsessive fear of being watched and judged by others. His confession that "I have known the eyes already, known them all— / The eyes that fix you in a formulated phrase" (lines 55-56) suggests how deeply he resists being watched, and how uncomfortable he is with himself, both externally—referring in part to his sensitivity to the "bald spot in the middle of my hair" (40)—and internally—his relentless self-questioning "'Do I dare?' and, 'Do I dare?'" (38). The disembodied eyes force the reader to recognize the oppression of being closely watched, and so to share in Prufrock's painful self-awareness. Prufrock's belief that the eyes have the terrifying and violent power to trap him like a specimen insect "pinned and wriggling on the wall" (58), to be scrutinized in its agony, further reveals the terror of the floating, accusatory image of the eyes.

    The disembodied image of arms also reflects Prufrock's distorted vision of both himself and others around him. His acknowledgment that he has "known the arms already, known them all— / Arms that are braceleted and white and bare" (62-63) relates to the image of the eyes, yet focuses on a very different aspect of the people surrounding Prufrock. Clearly, the braceleted arms belong to women, and that these arms are attached to a perfumed dress (65) suggests that these arms belong to upper-class, privileged women. This is partially what makes the disembodied image of the arms so frightening for Prufrock: He is incapable of connecting with a woman the way he, as a man, is expected to. The image of the arms, close enough to Prufrock to reveal their down of "light brown hair" (64), suggests the potential for reaching out and possibly touching Prufrock. The

*Thesis providing overview of writer's analysis.*

*Analysis of the meaning of fragmented imagery in the poem.*

*Close analysis of "eyes" supported with references to the text.*

*Close analysis of "arms" supported with references to the text.*

terrified self-consciousness that the image elicits in him leads Prufrock to wish that he could leave his own body and take on the characteristics of yet another disembodied image.

Close analysis of "claws" supported with references to the text.

Prufrock's despairing declaration, "I should have been a pair of ragged claws / Scuttling across the floors of silent seas" (73-74), offers yet another example of his vision of the world as fragmented and incomplete. The "pair of claws" that he longs to be not only connotes a complete separation from the earthly life that he finds so threatening, so painful, and so meaningless, but also suggests an isolation from others that would allow Prufrock some freedom and relief from social pressures. However, this image of the claws as a form of salvation for Prufrock in fact offers little suggestion of actual progress from his present circumstances; crabs can only "scuttle" from side to side and are incapable of moving directly forward or backward. Similarly, Prufrock is trapped in a situation in which he feels incapable of moving either up or down the staircase (39). Thus, this disembodied image of the claws serves to remind the reader that Prufrock is genuinely trapped in a life that offers him virtually no hope of real connection or wholeness.

Conclusion of analysis echoes the thesis and draws in points made in previous paragraphs.

The fragmented imagery that pervades "The Love Song of J. Alfred Prufrock" emphasizes and clarifies Prufrock's vision of the world as disconnected and disjointed. The fact that Prufrock thinks of people in terms of their individual component parts (specifically, eyes and arms) suggests his lack of understanding of people as whole and complete beings. This reflects his vision of himself as a fragmentary self, culminating in his wish to be not a whole crab, but merely a pair of disembodied claws. By use of these troubling images, Eliot infuses the poem with the pain of Prufrock's self-awareness and his confusion at the lack of wholeness he feels in his world.

## Work Cited

Eliot, T. S. "The Love Song of J. Alfred Prufrock." *Thinking and Writing about Poetry.* Ed. Michael Meyer. Boston: Bedford/St. Martin's, 2016. 304–07. Print.

Hart's essay suggests a number of useful guidelines for analytic papers:

1. Only those points related to the thesis are included. In another type of paper the significance of Eliot's epigraph from Dante, for example, might have been more important than the imagery.
2. The analysis keeps the images in focus while at the same time indicating how they are significant in revealing Prufrock's character.
3. The title is a useful lead into the paper; it provides a sense of what the topic is.
4. The introductory paragraph is direct and clearly indicates that the paper will argue that the images serve to reveal Prufrock's character.
5. Brief quotations are deftly incorporated into the text of the paper to illustrate points. We are told what we need to know about the poem as evidence is provided to support ideas. There is no unnecessary summary.
6. The paragraphs are well developed, unified, and coherent. They flow naturally from one to another. Notice, for example, the smooth transition worked into the final sentence of the third paragraph and the first sentence of the fourth paragraph.
7. Hart makes excellent use of her careful reading and notes by finding revealing connections among the details she has observed.
8. As events in the poem are described, the present tense is used. This avoids awkward tense shifts and lends an immediacy to the discussion.
9. The concluding paragraph establishes the significance of why the images should be seen as a reflection of Prufrock's character and provides a sense of closure by relating the images of Prufrock's disjointed world with the images of his fragmentary self.
10. In short, Hart has demonstrated that she has read the work closely, has understood the function of the images in the revelation of Prufrock's sensibilities, and has argued her thesis convincingly by using evidence from the poem.

## Comparison and Contrast

Another essay assignment in literature courses often combined with analytic topics is the type that requires you to write about similarities and differences between or within works. You might be asked to discuss "How Sounds Express Meanings in May Swenson's 'A Nosty Fright' and Lewis Carroll's 'Jabberwocky'" or "Love and Hate in Robert Frost's 'Fire and Ice.'" A *comparison* of either topic would emphasize their similarities, while a *contrast* would stress their differences. It is possible, of course, to include both perspectives in a paper if you find significant likenesses and differences. A comparison of Andrew Marvell's "To His Coy Mistress" (p. 65) and Ann Lauinger's "Marvell Noir" (p. 67) would, for example, yield similarities because each poem describes a man urging his lover to make the most of their precious time together; however, important differences also exist in the tone and theme of each poem that would constitute a contrast. (You should, incidentally, be aware that the term *comparison* is sometimes used inclusively to refer to both similarities and differences as it is in the discussion and writing suggestions in this book. If you are assigned a comparison of two works, be sure that you understand what your instructor's expectations are; you may be required to include both approaches in the essay.)

When you choose your own topic, the paper will be more successful — more manageable — if you write on works that can be meaningfully related to each other. Although Robert Herrick's "To the Virgins, to Make Much of Time" (p. 63) and T. S. Eliot's "The Love Song of J. Alfred Prufrock" (p. 304) both have something to do with hesitation, the likelihood of anyone making a connection between the two that reveals something interesting and important is remote — though perhaps not impossible if the topic were conceived imaginatively and tactfully. Choose a topic that encourages you to ask significant questions about each work; the purpose of a comparison or contrast is to understand the works more clearly for having examined them together.

Choose works to compare or contrast that intersect with each other in some significant way. They may, for example, be written by the same author or about the same subject. Perhaps you can compare their use of some technique, such as irony or point of view. Regardless of the specific topic, be sure to have a thesis that allows you to organize your paper around a central idea that argues a point about the two works. If you merely draw up a list of similarities or differences without a thesis in mind, your paper will be little more than a series of observations with no apparent purpose. Keep in the foreground of your thinking what the comparison or contrast reveals about the works.

There is no single way to organize comparative papers as each topic is likely to have its own particular issues to resolve, but it is useful to be aware of two basic patterns that can be helpful with a comparison, a contrast, or a combination of both. One method that can be effective for relatively short papers consists of dividing the paper in half, first discussing one work and then the other. Here, for example, is a partial informal outline for a discussion of Tony Hoagland's "America" (p. 291) and Tato Laviera's "AmeRícan" (p. 232); the topic is a comparison and contrast:

"Two Views of America by Hoagland and Laviera"

1.  "America"
    a. Diction
    b. Images
    c. Allusions
    d. Themes
2.  "AmeRícan"
    a. Diction
    b. Images
    c. Allusions
    d. Themes

This organizational strategy can be effective provided that the second part of the paper combines the discussion of "AmeRícan" with references to "America" so that the thesis is made clear and the paper is unified without being repetitive. If the two poems were treated entirely separately, then the discussion would be merely parallel rather than integrated. In a lengthy paper, this organization probably would not work well because a reader would have difficulty remembering the points made in the first half as he or she reads on.

Thus for a longer paper it is usually better to create a more integrated structure that discusses both works as you take up each item in your outline. Shown here in partial outline is the second basic pattern using the elements just cited.

1. Diction
   a. "America"
   b. "AmeRícan"
2. Images
   a. "America"
   b. "AmeRícan"
3. Allusions
   a. "America"
   b. "AmeRícan"
4. Themes
   a. "America"
   b. "AmeRícan"

This pattern allows you to discuss any number of topics without requiring that your reader recall what you first said about the diction of "America" before you discuss the diction of "AmeRícan" many pages later. However you structure your comparison or contrast paper, make certain that a reader can follow its elements and keep track of its thesis.

## A SAMPLE COMPARISON

### Andrew Marvell and Sharon Olds Seize the Day

The following paper responds to an assignment that required a comparison and contrast — about 1,000 words — of two assigned poems. The student chose to write an analysis of two very different *carpe diem* poems.

In the following comparison essay, Christina Smith focuses on the male and female *carpe diem* voices of Andrew Marvell's "To His Coy Mistress" (p. 65) and Sharon Olds's "Last Night" (p. 69). After introducing the topic in the first paragraph, she takes up the two poems in a pattern similar to the first outline suggested for "Two Views of America by Hoagland and Laviera." Notice how Smith works in subsequent references to Marvell's poem as she discusses Olds's so that her treatment is integrated and we are reminded why she is comparing the two works. Her final paragraph sums up her points without being repetitive and reiterates the thesis with which she began.

Christina Smith

English 109-10

Professor Monroe

2 April 2015

Andrew Marvell and Sharon Olds Seize the Day

In her 1996 poem "Last Night," Sharon Olds never mentions Andrew
Marvell's 1681 poem "To His Coy Mistress." Through a contemporary lens,
however, she firmly qualifies Marvell's seventeenth-century masculine
perspective. Marvell's speaker attempts to woo a young woman and convince her
to have sexual relations with him. His seize-the-day rhetoric argues that "his
mistress" should let down her conventional purity and enjoy the moment, his
logic being that we are grave bound anyway, so why not? Although his poetic
pleading is effective, both stylistically and argumentatively, Marvell's speaker
obviously assumes that the coy mistress will succumb to his grasps at her
sexuality. Further, and most important, the speaker takes for granted that the
female must be persuaded to love. His smooth talk leaves no room for a feminine
perspective, be it a slap in the face or a sharing of his *carpe diem* attitudes. Olds
accommodates Marvell's masculine speaker but also deftly takes poetic license in
the cause of female freedom and sensuously lays out her own scenario. Through
describing a personal sexual encounter both erotically and with jarring rawness,
Olds's female speaker demonstrates that women have just as many lustful urges
as the men who would seduce them; she presents sex as neither solely a male
quest nor a female sacrifice. "Last Night" takes a female perspective on sex and
fully explores it at its most raw and basic level.

"To His Coy Mistress" is in a regular rhyme scheme, as each line rhymes
with the next—almost like a compilation of couplets. And this, accompanied
by traditional iambic pentameter, lays the foundation for a forcefully flowing
speech, a command for the couple to just do it. By the end of the poem the
speaker seems to expect his mistress to capitulate. Marvell's speaker declares at
the start that if eternity were upon them, he would not mind putting sex aside
and paying her unending homage:

> Had we but world enough, and time,
>
> This coyness, lady, were no crime.
>
> We would sit down, and think which way
>
> To walk, and pass our long love's day. (lines 1-4)

He proclaims that he would love her "ten years before the Flood" (8) and concedes that she "should, if you please, refuse / Till the conversion of the Jews" (9-10). This eternal love-land expands as Marvell asserts that his "vegetable love should grow / Vaster than empires, and more slow" (11-12). Every part of her body would be admired for an entire "age" (17) because "lady, you deserve this state, / Nor would I love at lower rate" (19-20). He would willingly wait but, alas, circumstances won't let him. She'll have to settle for the here and now, and he must show her that life is not an eternity but rather an alarm clock.

The speaker laments that "at my back I always hear / Time's wingèd chariot hurrying near" (21-22). He then cleverly draws a picture of what exactly eternity does have in store for them, namely barren "Deserts" where her "beauty shall no more be found" (24, 25) while "worms shall try / That long preserved virginity" (27-28) and her "quaint honor turn to dust" (29). This death imagery is meant to frighten her for not having lived enough. He astutely concedes that "The grave's a fine and private place, / But none, I think, do there embrace" (31-32), thereby making even more vivid the nightmare he has just laid before her. Although he must make his grim argument, he does not want to dampen the mood, so he quickly returns to her fair features.

"Now," the speaker proclaims,

> while the youthful hue
> Sits on thy skin like morning dew,
> And while thy willing soul transpires
> At every pore with instant fires,
> Now let us sport us while we may. (33-37)

The speaker has already made the decision for her. Through sex, their energies will become one—they will "roll" their "strength" and "sweetness up into one ball" (41-42) as they "tear [their] pleasures with rough strife" (43). If the two of them cannot have eternity and make the "sun / Stand still" (45-46), then they will seize the day, combine and celebrate their humanity, and "make [the sun] run" (46). The speaker makes a vivid case in favor of living for the moment. His elaborate images of the devotion his mistress deserves, the inevitability of death, and the vivaciousness of human life are compelling. Three hundred years later, however, Sharon Olds demonstrates that women no longer need—or may never have needed— this lesson because they share the same desires.

Olds's poem may be read as a contemporary response, though likely unintentional, to "To His Coy Mistress." This poet's "fine and private place" is not the grave, as it was in Marvell's poetic persuasion (31), but rather her own sexual encounter. The hard language of the poem, describing this act of sex as a "death-grip / holding to life" (Olds 13-14), suggests a familiarity with Marvell's own implications of death. More importantly, her speaker needs no rationale to live fully; she just does. She has sex on her own, willingly, knowingly, and thoroughly.

Unlike "To His Coy Mistress," "Last Night" has no rhyme scheme and has little meter or conventional form. The free verse tells the sexual story in an unconfined, open way. The poem flows together with urgent, sexual images drawn from a place in which nothing exists but biological instinct. It is organic at its most raw, basic level. The speaker and her lover unite "like dragonflies / in the sun, 100 degrees at noon, / the ends of their abdomens stuck together" (Olds 2-4). Whereas Marvell's lovers race against time, Olds's seem unaware of it altogether. The only sense of time in the poem is in reference to the morning after sex; the act itself is suspended in an unmeasured space in the speaker's memory. Any descriptive details are reserved for the encounter itself, and the setting is undefined. So it is the language of biology—

> something twisting and
> twisting out of a chrysalis,
> enormous, without language, all
> head, all shut eyes (6-9)

—that evokes erotic images. There is no foreplay, "No kiss, / no tenderness" (12-13), but the poem does not hint at a power struggle either. The speaker suggests mutuality, describing the lovers as "like violent hands clasped tight" (15). The two are "barely moving" (16), and when they "[start] / to die" (18-19), they do so together.

Afterward, they return to themselves, away from the sensual, all-consuming world in which they reveled. However, the speaker has not literally or figuratively exhausted the natural world yet. She describes their hairlines as "wet as the arc of a gateway after / a cloudburst" (25-26). The cloudburst is itself a sudden, almost violent phenomenon, not unlike this sexual moment, and though she emerges from the encounter, it stays with her as a vivid memory.

Revisiting memories of the experience the next day allows the speaker to examine the moment, and she reflects in line 26 that it ended in peaceful sleep. The last lines stand in contrast to those of Marvell's speaker, whose desperate, pleading tone is filled with tension rather than the relief of consummation. As Olds's poem draws to a close (26-29), we see that this sexual encounter is an experience that, however raw, is rooted in tenderness. The erotic language of biology is in her own voice as she describes the two waking in the morning "clasped, fragrant, buoyant" (28). Olds's subject does not have to be persuaded by an excited man to be a sexual being; her sexuality seeps into her normal life, she wakes the next morning "almost afraid" (1) of it, and we marvel at its depth. Unlike Marvell's speaker, who remains eternally poised to "tear our pleasures" (43), Olds's speaker is steeped in those pleasures.

## Works Cited

Marvell, Andrew. "To His Coy Mistress." Meyer. 65–66.

Meyer, Michael, ed. *Thinking and Writing about Poetry*. Boston: Bedford/St. Martin's, 2016. Print.

Olds, Sharon. "Last Night." Meyer. 69.

# 17

# The Literary Research Paper

© Nancy Crampton.

Does anyone know a good poet who's a vegetarian?

—DONALD HALL

## WRITING A LITERARY RESEARCH PAPER

A close reading of a primary source such as a short story, poem, or play can give insights into a work's themes and effects, but sometimes you will want to know more. A published commentary by a critic who knows the work well and is familiar with the author's life and times can provide insights that otherwise may not be available. Such comments and interpretations — known as *secondary sources* — are, of course, not a substitute for the work itself, but they often can take you into a work further than if you made the journey by yourself.

After imagination, good sense, and energy, perhaps the next most important quality for writing a research paper is the ability to organize material. A research paper on a literary topic requires a writer to take account of quite a lot at once: the text, ideas, sources, and documentation techniques all make demands on one's efforts to present a topic clearly and convincingly.

The following list should give you a sense of what goes into creating a research paper. Although some steps on the list can be folded into one another, they offer an overview of the work that will involve you.

1. Choosing a topic
2. Finding sources

3. Evaluating sources
4. Taking notes
5. Developing a thesis
6. Organizing an outline
7. Writing drafts
8. Revising
9. Documenting sources
10. Preparing the final draft and proofreading

Even if you have never written a research paper, you most likely have already had experience choosing a topic, developing a thesis, organizing an outline, and writing a draft that you then revised, proofread, and handed in. Those skills represent six of the ten items on the list. This chapter briefly reviews some of these steps and focuses on the remaining tasks, unique to research paper assignments.

## CHOOSING A TOPIC

Chapter 16 discusses the importance of reading a work closely and taking careful notes as a means of generating topics for writing about literature. If you know a work well and record your understanding of it in notes, you'll have impressions and ideas to choose from for potential topics. You may find it useful to review the information on pages 348–50 before reading the advice in this chapter about putting together a research paper.

The student author of the sample research paper "Individuality and Community in Frost's 'Mowing' and 'Mending Wall'" (p. 393) was asked to write a five-page paper that demonstrated some familiarity with published critical perspectives on two Robert Frost poems of her choice. Before looking into critical discussions of the poems, she read them several times, taking notes and making comments in the margin of her textbook on each reading.

What prompted her choice of "Mending Wall," for example, was a class discussion that focused on the poem's speaker's questioning the value and necessity of the wall in contrast to his neighbor's insistence on it. At one point, however, the boundaries of the discussion opened up to the possibility that the wall is important to both characters in the poem rather than only the neighbor. It is, after all, the speaker, not the neighbor, who repairs the damage to the wall caused by hunters and who initiates the rebuilding of the wall. Why would he do that if he wanted the wall down? Only after having thoroughly examined the poem did the student go to the library to see what professional critics had to say about this question.

## FINDING SOURCES

Whether your college library is large or small, its reference librarians can usually help you locate secondary sources about a particular work or author. Unless you choose a very recently published poem, play, or essay about which little or nothing has been written, you should be able to find out more about a literary work efficiently and quickly. Even if a work has been published recently, you can probably find relevant information on the Internet.

## *Electronic Sources*

Researchers can locate materials in a variety of sources, including card catalogs, specialized encyclopedias, bibliographies, and indexes to periodicals. Library Web sites also provide online databases that you can access from home. This can be an efficient way to establish a bibliography on a specific topic. Consult a reference librarian about how to use your library's online resources to determine how they will help you research your topic.

In addition to the many electronic databases ranging from your library's computerized holdings to the many major sources for articles and books on literary topics, such as *MLA International Bibliography*, the Internet also connects millions of sites with primary sources (the full texts of stories, poems, plays, and essays) and secondary sources (biography or criticism). If you have not had practice with research on the Web, it is a good idea to get guidance from your instructor or a librarian and to use your library's home page as a starting point. Browsing on the Internet can be absorbing as well as informative, but unless you have plenty of time to spare, don't wait until the last minute to locate your electronic sources. You might find yourself trying to find reliable, professional sources among thousands of sites if you enter an unqualified entry such as "Robert Frost."

Here are several especially useful electronic databases that will provide you with bibliographic information in literature studies. Your school's English Department home page may offer online support as well.

*Internet Public Library Online Criticism.* <http://ipl.org/div/litcrit/>. Maintained by the University of Michigan, this site provides links to literary criticism by author, work, country, or period.

*JSTOR.* An index as well as abstracts of journal articles on language and literature.

*Literary Resources.* <http://people.virginia.edu/~jbh/literaryresources .html>. An extensive list of Internet literary resources for students and scholars.

*MLA International Bibliography.* This standard resource on literary subjects allows topical and keyword searches.

*Voice of the Shuttle.* <http://vos.ucsb.edu>. Maintained by the University of California, this site is a wide-ranging resource for British and American literature studies.

Do remember that your own college library offers a broad range of electronic sources. If you're feeling uncertain, intimidated, and profoundly unplugged, your reference librarians are there to help you get started.

# EVALUATING SOURCES AND TAKING NOTES

Evaluate your sources for their reliability and the quality of their evidence. Check to see if an article or a book has been superseded by later studies; try to use up-to-date sources. A popular magazine article will probably not be as authoritative as an article in a scholarly journal. Sources that are well documented with primary and secondary materials usually indicate that the author has done his or her homework. Books printed by university presses and established trade presses are preferable to books privately printed. But there are always exceptions. If you are uncertain about how to assess a book, try to find out something about the author. Are there any other books listed in the catalog that indicate the author's expertise? What do book reviews say about the work? Three valuable indexes to book reviews of literary studies are *Book Review Digest, Book Review Index,* and *Index to Book Reviews in the Humanities.* Your reference librarian can show you how to use these important tools for evaluating books. Reviews can be a quick means to get a broad perspective on writers and their works because reviewers often survey previous approaches to the topic under discussion.

A cautionary note: assessing online sources can be more problematic than evaluating print sources because anyone with a computer and online access can publish on the Internet. Be sure to determine the nature of your sources and their authority. Is the site the work of a professional or an amateur? Is the information likely to be reliable? Is it biased? Is it documented? Before placing your trust in an Internet source, make sure that it warrants your confidence.

As you prepare a list of reliable sources relevant to your topic, record the necessary bibliographic information so that it will be available when you make up the list of works cited for your paper. For a book include the author, complete title, place of publication, publisher, and date. For an article include author, complete title, name of periodical, volume number, date of issue, and page numbers. For an Internet source include the author, complete title, database title, periodical or site name, date of posting of the site (or last update), name of institution or organization, date when you accessed the source, and the network address (URL).

Once you have assembled a tentative bibliography, you will need to take notes on your readings. Be sure to keep track of where the information comes from by recording the author's name and page number. If you use more than one work by the same author, include a brief title as well as the author's name.

# DEVELOPING A THESIS AND ORGANIZING THE PAPER

As the notes on "Mowing" and "Mending Wall" accumulated, the student sorted them into topics including

1. Publication history of the poems
2. Frost's experiences as a farmer
3. Critics' readings of the poems
4. The speaker's attitude toward the wall
5. The neighbor's attitude toward the wall
6. Mythic elements in the poems
7. Does the wall have any positive value?
8. How do the speaker and neighbor characterize themselves?
9. Humor and tone in the poems
10. Frost as a regional poet

The student quickly saw that items 1, 2, 6, and 10 were not directly related to her topic concerning why the speaker initiates the rebuilding of the wall. The remaining numbers (3–5, 7–9) are the topics taken up in the paper. The student had begun her reading of secondary sources with a tentative thesis that stemmed from her question about why the poem's speaker helps his neighbor rebuild the wall. That "why" shaped itself into the expectation that she would have a thesis something like this: "The speaker helps rebuild the wall because . . ."

She assumed she would find information that indicated some specific reason. But the more she read, the more she discovered that there was no single explanation provided by the poem or by critics' readings of the poem. Instead, through the insights provided by her sources, she began to see that the wall had several important functions in the poem. The perspective she developed into her thesis — that the wall "provided a foundation upon which the men build a personal sense of identity" — allowed her to incorporate a number of the critics' insights into her paper in order to shed light on why the speaker helps rebuild the wall.

Because the assignment was relatively brief, the student did not write up a formal outline but instead organized her stacks of usable notecards and proceeded to write the first draft from them.

## REVISING

After writing your first draft, you should review the advice and the Questions for Revising and Editing on pages 360–61 so that you can read your paper with an objective eye. Two days after writing her next-to-last draft, the writer of "Individuality and Community in Frost's 'Mowing' and 'Mending Wall'" realized that she had allotted too much space for critical discussions of the humor in the poem that were not directly related to her approach. She realized that it was not essential to point out and discuss the puns in the poem; hence she corrected this by simply deleting most references to the poem's humor. The point is that she saw this herself after she took some time to approach the paper from a fresh perspective.

# DOCUMENTING SOURCES AND AVOIDING PLAGIARISM

You must acknowledge the use of a source when you (1) quote someone's exact words, (2) summarize or borrow someone's opinions or ideas, or (3) use information and facts that are not considered to be common knowledge. The purpose of this documentation is to acknowledge your sources, to demonstrate that you are familiar with what others have thought about the topic, and to provide your reader access to the same sources. If your paper is not adequately documented, it will be vulnerable to a charge of *plagiarism* — the presentation of someone else's work as your own. Conscious plagiarism is easy to avoid; honesty takes care of that for most people. However, there is a more problematic form of plagiarism that is often inadvertent. Whether inadequate documentation is conscious or not, plagiarism is a serious matter and must be avoided. Papers can be evaluated only by what is on the page, not by their writers' intentions.

Let's look more closely at what constitutes plagiarism. Consider the following passage quoted from A. R. Coulthard, "Frost's 'Mending Wall,'" *Explicator* 45 (Winter 1987): 40:

> "Mending Wall" has many of the features of an "easy" poem aimed at high-minded readers. Its central symbol is the accessible stone wall to represent separation, and it appears to oppose isolating barriers and favor love and trust, the stuff of Golden Treasury of Inspirational Verse.

Now read this plagiarized version:

> "Mending Wall" is an easy poem that appeals to high-minded readers who take inspiration from its symbolism of the stone wall, which seems to oppose isolating barriers and support trusting love.

Though the writer has shortened the passage and made some changes in the wording, this paragraph is basically the same as Coulthard's. Indeed, several of his phrases are lifted almost intact. (Notice, however, that the plagiarized version seems to have missed Coulthard's irony and, therefore, misinterpreted and misrepresented the passage.) Even if a parenthetical reference had been included at the end of the passage and the source included in "Works Cited," the language of this passage would still be plagiarism because it is presented as the writer's own. Both language and ideas must be acknowledged.

Here is an adequately documented version of the passage:

> A. R. Coulthard points out that "high-minded readers" mistakenly assume that "Mending Wall" is a simple inspirational poem that uses the symbolic wall to reject isolationism and to support, instead, a sense of human community (40).

This passage makes absolutely clear that the observation is Coulthard's, and it is written in the student's own language with the exception of one quoted phrase. Had Coulthard not been named in the passage, the parenthetical reference would have included his name: (Coulthard 40).

Some mention should be made of the notion of common knowledge before we turn to the standard format for documenting sources. Observations and facts that are widely known and routinely included in many of your sources do not require documentation. It is not necessary to cite a source for the fact that Alfred, Lord Tennyson, was born in 1809 or that Frost writes about New England. Sometimes it will be difficult for you to determine what common knowledge is for a topic that you know little about. If you are in doubt, the best strategy is to supply a reference.

There are two basic ways to document sources. Traditionally, sources have been cited in footnotes at the bottom of each page or in endnotes grouped together at the end of the paper. Here is how a portion of the sample paper on "Mending Wall" would look if footnotes were used instead of parenthetical documentation:

> It remains one of Frost's more popular poems, and, as Douglas Wilson notes, "one of the most famous in all of American poetry."[1]

> [1]Douglas L. Wilson, "The Other Side of the Wall," *Iowa Review* 10 (Winter 1979): 65. Print.

Unlike endnotes, which are double-spaced throughout and grouped under the title "Notes" at the end of the paper, footnotes appear four spaces below the text. They are single-spaced, with an extra space between notes.

No doubt you will have encountered these documentation methods in your reading. A different style is recommended, however, in the Modern Language Association's *MLA Handbook for Writers of Research Papers,* 7th ed. (2009). The MLA style uses parenthetical references within the text of the paper; these are keyed to an alphabetical list of works cited at the end of the paper. This method is designed to be less distracting for the reader. Unless you are instructed to follow the footnote or endnote style for documentation, use the parenthetical method explained in the next section.

## The List of Works Cited

Items in the list of works cited are arranged alphabetically according to the author's last name and indented five spaces after the first line. This allows the reader to locate quickly the complete bibliographic information for the author's name cited within the parenthetical reference in the text. The following are common entries for literature papers and should be used as models. If some of your sources are of a different nature, consult the *MLA Handbook for Writers of Research Papers,* 7th ed. (New York: MLA, 2009); or, for the latest updates, check MLA's Web site at mlahandbook.org.

The following entries include examples to follow when citing electronic sources. For electronic sources, include as many of the following elements as apply and as are available:

- Author's name
- Title of work (if it's a book, italicize; if it's a short work, such as an article or a poem, use quotation marks)
- Title of the site (or of the publication, if you're citing an online periodical, for example), italicized
- Sponsor or publisher of the site (if not named as the author)
- Date of publication or last update
- Medium of publication
- Date you accessed the source

### A book by one author

Hendrickson, Robert. *The Literary Life and Other Curiosities*. New York: Viking, 1981.
    Print.

### An online book

Frost, Robert. *A Boy's Will*. New York: Holt, 1915. *Bartleby.com: Great Books Online*. Bartleby
    .com, 1999. Web. 4 Feb. 2015.

### Part of an online book

Frost, Robert. "Into My Own." *A Boy's Will*. New York: Holt, 1915. *Bartleby.com: Great Books
    Online*. Bartleby.com, 1999. Web. 19 Sept. 2015.

Notice that the author's name is in reverse order. This information, along with the full title, place of publication, publisher, and date, should be taken from the title and copyright pages of the book. The title is italicized and is also followed by a period. If the city of publication is well known, it is unnecessary to include the state. Use the publication date on the title page; if none appears there, use the copyright date (after ©) on the back of the title page. Include the medium of publication.

### A book by two authors

Horton, Rod W., and Herbert W. Edwards. *Backgrounds of American Literary Thought*.
    3rd ed. Englewood Cliffs: Prentice, 1974. Print.

Only the first author's name is given in reverse order. The edition number appears after the title.

### A book with more than three authors

Gates, Henry Louis, Jr., et al., eds. *The Norton Anthology of African American Literature*.
    New York: Norton, 1997. Print.

(Note: The abbreviation *et al.* means "and others.")

### A work in a collection by the same author

O'Connor, Flannery. "Greenleaf." *The Complete Stories*. By O'Connor. New York: Farrar, 1971.
    311-34. Print.

Page numbers are given because the reference is to only a single story in the collection.

### A work in a collection by a different writer

Frost, Robert. "Design." *Thinking and Writing about Poetry*. Ed. Michael Meyer. Boston:
    Bedford/St. Martin's, 2016. 271. Print.

### Cross-reference to a collection

Frost, Robert. "Design." Meyer. 891.

Meyer, Michael, ed. *The Compact Bedford Introduction to Literature*. 10th ed. Boston:
    Bedford/St. Martin's, 2014. Print.

O'Connor, Flannery. "Revelation." Meyer. 381-95.

Sun, Nilaja. *No Child*. . . . Meyer. 1363-1381.

When citing more than one work from the same collection, use a cross-reference to avoid repeating the same bibliographic information that appears in the main entry for the collection.

### A translated book

Grass, Günter. *The Tin Drum*. Trans. Ralph Manheim. New York: Vintage-Random, 1962. Print.

### An introduction, preface, foreword, or afterword

Johnson, Thomas H. Introduction. *Final Harvest: Emily Dickinson's Poems*. By Emily
    Dickinson. Boston: Little, 1961. vii-xiv. Print.

This cites the introduction by Johnson. Notice that a colon is used between the book's main title and subtitle. To cite a poem in this book, use this method:

Dickinson, Emily. "A Tooth upon Our Peace." *Final Harvest: Emily Dickinson's Poems*. Ed.
    Thomas H. Johnson. Boston: Little, 1961. 110. Print.

### An entry in an encyclopedia

"Wordsworth, William." *The New Encyclopedia Britannica*. 1984 ed. Print.

Because this encyclopedia is organized alphabetically, no page number or other information is given, only the edition number (if available) and date.

**An article in a magazine**

Morrow, Lance. "Scribble, Scribble, Eh, Mr. Toad." *Time* 24 Feb. 1986: 84. Print.

**An article from an online magazine**

Wasserman, Elizabeth. "The Byron Complex." *Atlantic Online*. Atlantic Monthly Group,
22 Sept. 2002. Web. 4 Feb. 2015.

The citation for an unsigned article would begin with the title and be alpha-
betized by the first word of the title other than "a," "an," or "the."

**An article in a scholarly journal with continuous pagination
beyond a single issue**

Mahar, William J. "Black English in Early Blackface Minstrelsy: A New Interpretation of the
Sources of Minstrel Show Dialect." *American Quarterly* 37.2 (1985): 260-85. Print.

Because this journal uses continuous pagination instead of separate pagination for each issue, it is not necessary to include the month, season, or number of the issue. Only one of the quarterly issues will have pages numbered
260–85. If you are not certain whether a journal's pages are numbered con-
tinuously throughout a volume, supply the month, season, or issue number,
as in the next entry.

**An article in a scholarly journal with separate pagination
for each issue**

Updike, John. "The Cultural Situation of the American Writer." *American Studies
International* 15 (Spring 1977): 19-28. Print.

By noting the spring issue, the entry saves a reader from looking through
each issue of the 1977 volume for the correct article on pages 19 to 28.

**An article from an online scholarly journal**

Mamet, David. "Secret Names." *Threepenny Review* 96 (Winter 2004): n. pag. Web. 8 Apr. 2015.

The following citation indicates that the article appears on page 1 of
section 7 and continues onto another page.

**An article in a newspaper**

Ziegler, Philip. "The Lure of Gossip, the Rules of History." *New York Times* 23 Feb. 1986: sec.
7: 1+. Print.

**An article from an online newspaper**

Brantley, Ben. "Souls Lost and Doomed Enliven London Stages." *New York Times*. New York
Times, 4 Feb. 2004. Web. 6 Mar. 2015.

## A lecture

Tilton, Robert. "The Beginnings of American Studies." English 270 class lecture. University
    of Connecticut, Storrs. 12 Mar. 2010. Lecture.

## Letter, e-mail, or interview

Vellenga, Carolyn. Letter to the author. 9 Oct. 2015.

Harter, Stephen P. E-mail to the author. 28 Dec. 2013.

McConagha, Bill. Personal interview. 6 Mar. 2014.

Following are additional examples for citing electronic sources.

## Work from a subscription service

Libraries pay for access to databases such as *Lexis-Nexis, ProQuest Direct,*
and *Expanded Academic ASAP.* When you retrieve an article or other work
from a subscription database, cite your source based on this model:

Vendler, Helen Hennessey. "The Passion of Emily Dickinson." *New Republic* 3 Aug. 1992:
    34-38. *Expanded Academic ASAP.* Web. 17 Apr. 2015.

## A document from a Web site

When citing sources from the Internet, include as much publication information as possible (see guidelines on pp. 384–85). In some cases, as in the
following example, a date of publication for the document "Dickens in
America" is not available. The entry provides the author, title of document,
title of site, sponsor of the site, the date of publication or "n.d." if there is
none, the medium, and access date:

Perdue, David. "Dickens in America." *David Perdue's Charles Dickens Page.* David A.
    Perdue, n.d. Web. 13 Feb. 2015.

## An entire Web site

Perdue, David. *David Perdue's Charles Dickens Page.* David A. Perdue, 1 Apr. 2009. Web.
    13 Feb. 2015.

Treat a CD-ROM as you would any other source, but name the medium
before the publication information.

## A work from a CD-ROM

Aaron, Belèn V. "The Death of Theory." *Scholarly Book Reviews* 4.3 (1997): 146-47.
    CD-ROM. *ERIC.* SilverPlatter. Dec. 1997.

## An online posting

Shuck, John. "Hamlet." PBS Discussions. PBS, 16 May 2005. Web. 13 Oct. 2015.

## *Parenthetical References*

A list of works cited is not an adequate indication of how you have used sources in your paper. You must also provide the precise location of quotations and other information by using parenthetical references within the text of the paper. You do this by citing the author's name (or the source's title if the work is anonymous) and the page number.

> Collins points out that "Nabokov was misunderstood by early reviewers of his work" (28).

or

> Nabokov's first critics misinterpreted his stories (Collins 28).

Either way a reader will find the complete bibliographic entry in the list of works cited under Collins's name and know that the information cited in the paper appears on page 28. Notice that the end punctuation comes after the parentheses.

If you have listed more than one work by the same author, you would add a brief title to the parenthetical reference to distinguish between them. You could also include the full title in your text.

> Nabokov's first critics misinterpreted his stories (Collins, "Early Reviews" 28).

or

> Collins points out in "Early Reviews of Nabokov's Fiction" that Nabokov's early work was misinterpreted by reviewers (28).

There can be many variations on what is included in a parenthetical reference, depending on the nature of the entry in the list of works cited. But the general principle is simple enough: provide enough parenthetical information for a reader to find the work in "Works Cited." Examine the sample research paper for more examples of works cited and strategies for including parenthetical references. If you are puzzled by a given situation, ask your reference librarian to show you the *MLA Handbook*.

## *Incorporating Secondary Sources*

The questions on page 390 can help you incorporate materials from critical or biographical essays into your own writing about a literary work. You may initially feel intimidated by the prospect of responding to the arguments of professional writers in your own paper. However, the process will not defeat you if you have clearly formulated your own response to the literary work and are able to distinguish it from the critics' perspectives. Reading what other people have said about a work can help you develop your own ideas — perhaps, to cite just two examples, by using their ideas as supporting evidence or by arguing with them in order to clarify or qualify their points about the literary work. As you write and discover how to advance your thesis, you'll find yourself participating in a dialogue with the critics. This sort of conversation will help you to improve your thinking and hone your argument.

Keep in mind that the work of professional critics is a means of enriching your understanding of a literary work rather than a substitution for your own analysis and interpretation of that work. Quoting, paraphrasing, or summarizing someone else's perspective does not relieve you of the obligation of choosing a topic, organizing information, developing a thesis, and arguing your point of view by citing sufficient evidence from the text you are examining. These matters are discussed in further detail in Chapter 16. You should also be familiar with the methods for documenting sources that are explained in this chapter, and keep in mind how important it is to avoid plagiarism.

No doubt you won't find everything you read about a work equally useful: some critics' arguments won't address your own areas of concern; some will be too difficult for you to get a handle on; and some will seem wrongheaded. However, much of the criticism you read will serve to make a literary work more accessible and interesting to you, and disagreeing with others' arguments will often help you develop your own ideas about a work. When you use the work of critics in your own writing, you should consider the following questions. Responding to these questions will help you develop a clear understanding of what a critic is arguing about a work, decide to what extent you agree with that argument, and plan how to incorporate and respond to the critic's reading in your own paper. The more questions you can ask yourself in response to this list or as a result of your own reading, the more you'll be able to think critically about how you are approaching both the critics and the literary work under consideration.

## Questions for Incorporating Secondary Sources

1. Have you read the poem carefully and taken notes of your own impressions before reading any critical perspectives so that your initial insights are not lost to the arguments made by the critics? Have you articulated your own responses to the work in a journal entry prior to reading the critics?

2. Are you sufficiently familiar with the poem that you can determine the accuracy, fairness, and thoroughness of the critic's use of evidence from the work?

3. Have you read the critic's piece carefully? Try summarizing the critic's argument in a brief paragraph. Do you understand the nature and purpose of the critic's argument? Which passages are especially helpful to you? Which seem unclear? Why?

4. Is the critic's reading of the poem similar to or different from your own reading? Why do you agree or disagree? What generational, historical, cultural, or biographical considerations might help to account for any differences between the critic's responses and your own?

5. How has your reading of the critic influenced your understanding of the poem? Do issues that previously seemed unimportant now seem significant? What are these issues, and how does a consideration of them affect your reading of the work?

6. Are you too quickly revising or even discarding your own reading because the critic's perspective seems so polished and persuasive? Are you making use of your reading notes and the responses in your journal entries?

7. How would you classify the critic's approach? Through what kind of lens does the critic view the poem? Is the critical approach formalist, biographical, psychological, historical, mythological, reader-response, deconstructionist, or some combination of these or possibly other strategies? (For a discussion of these approaches, see Chapter 15.)

8. What biases, if any, can you detect in the critic's approach? How might, for example, a southern critic's reading of "Mending Wall" differ from a northern critic's?

9. Can you determine how other critics have responded to the critic's work? Is the critic's work cited and taken seriously in other critics' books and articles? Is the work dated by having been superseded by subsequent studies?

10. Are any passages or topics that you deem important left out by the critic? Do these omissions qualify or refute the critic's argument?

11. What judgments does the critic seem to make about the work? Is the work regarded, for example, as significant, unified, representative, trivial, inept, or irresponsible? Do you agree with these judgments? If not, can you develop and support a thesis about your difference of opinion?

12. What important disagreements do critics reveal in their approaches to the work? Do you find one perspective more convincing than another? Why? Is there a way of resolving their conflicting views that could serve as a thesis for your paper?

13. Can you extend or qualify the critic's argument to matters in the literary text that are not covered by the critic's perspective? Will this allow you to develop your own topic while acknowledging the critic's useful insights?

14. Have you quoted, paraphrased, or summarized the critic accurately and fairly? Have you avoided misrepresenting the critic's arguments in any way?

15. Are the critic's words, ideas, opinions, and insights adequately acknowledged and documented in the correct format? Do you understand the difference between common knowledge and plagiarism? Have you avoided quoting excessively? Are the quotations smoothly integrated into your own text?

16. Are you certain that your incorporation of the critic's work is for the purpose of developing your paper's thesis rather than for name-dropping or padding your paper? How can you explain to yourself why the critic's work is useful for your argument?

# A SAMPLE RESEARCH PAPER

## Individuality and Community in Robert Frost's "Mowing" and "Mending Wall"

As you read the paper by Stephanie Tobin on Robert Frost's "Mowing" (p. 259) and "Mending Wall" (p. 260), pay special attention to how she documents outside sources and incorporates other people's ideas into her own argument. How strong do you think her final thesis is? Is it effectively supported by the sources? Has she integrated the sources fully into the paper? How does the paper enhance your understanding of the two poems?

Stephanie's paper follows the format described in the *MLA Handbook for Writers of Research Papers*, 7th ed. This format is discussed in the preceding section on documentation in this chapter (p. 383) and in Chapter 16 in the section on manuscript form (p. 361). Though the sample paper is short, it illustrates many of the techniques and strategies useful for writing an essay that includes secondary sources — including online databases, a Web site, books, and journals.

Stephanie Tobin

Professor Bass

Poetry 100

17 November 2015

Individuality and Community in

Frost's "Mowing" and "Mending Wall"

We think of Robert Frost as a poet of New England who provides portraits of the rural landscape and communities. But it was not until Frost's second book, *North of Boston* (1914), that he truly gave voice to a community—in dramatic monologues, dialogues, and narrative poems. The poems in his first book, *A Boy's Will* (1913), are mainly personal lyrics in which the poet encounters the world and defines it for himself through the writing of poetry, establishing both an individual perspective and an aesthetic. A poem from the first book, "Mowing," illustrates the theme of individualism, against which a poem from the second book, "Mending Wall," can be seen as a widening of the thematic lens to include other perspectives.

In *A Boy's Will*, Frost explores the idea of man as a solitary creature, alone, at work in the natural world. Poems such as "Mowing" capture the essence of this perspective in the very first lines: "There was never a sound beside the wood but one, / And that was my long scythe whispering to the ground" (lines 1-2). Jay Parini describes "Mowing" as a poem in which the "poet cultivates a private motion" (121)—the motions both of farmwork, done to support oneself, and the motion of the individual mind expressed in the poem as it moves down the page. The sense of privacy and of an individually defined world captured in "Mowing" is central to the book itself.

The dramatic change in perspective evident in *North of Boston* illustrates Frost's development as a writer. Although the second collection was published just one year later, Frost expresses a different perception and understanding of human nature in *North of Boston*. W. S. Braithwaite wrote in 1915, in a review of the two books, that *A Boy's Will* and *North of Boston* "represent a divergent period of development. The earlier book expresses an individuality, the later interprets a community" (2). The focus on community is best demonstrated by the poem "Mending Wall," which presents the reader with an image of two men, separated literally and metaphorically by a wall, yet joined by their dedication to the task they must undertake and the basic human need for boundaries that compels them. The speaker in "Mending Wall" does not forfeit his own individuality but rather comes to understand it more fully in the context of the society in which he lives, with its traditions and requirements, some of which he tries to see as a game: "Oh, just another kind of outdoor game, / One on a side" (21-22), while still allowing for deeper implications.

Individuality can be defined by one's differences from others, as well as by the creative work of defining, and self-defining, done in poetry. Frost's own experience of life in New England helped shape the perspectives of both individualism and community exemplified in his first two books. When Frost wrote "Mowing," his perspective on life in New England leaned more toward isolation than community. The first few years of farm life were arduous and lonely, and the stark environment provided an atmosphere far more suitable for self-realization than socialization. Prior to the publication of *A Boy's Will*, Frost had spent "five years of self-enforced solitude" (Meyers 99). "Mowing," which Frost considered to be the best poem in the collection, exemplifies this feeling of isolation and the need for self-exploration. While the poem is, in the literal sense, about the act of cutting grass in order to make hay, it is metaphorically rooted in the idea that man finds meaning and beauty in the world alone. Parini suggests that the idea that "a man's complete meaning is derived alone, at work . . . is a consistent theme in Frost and one that could be explored at length in all his work" (14).

"Mowing" begins with the speaker's observation of the silence that surrounds him as he works. The only sound is the hushed whisper of his scythe as he mows. He writes, "What was it it whispered? I knew not well myself" (3). The possibility that its meaning could be found in some fanciful imagination of the task is dismissed: "It was no dream of the gift of idle hours, / Or easy gold at the hand of fay or elf" (Frost, "Mowing" 7-8). For Frost, an exaggeration of the action would imply that meaning cannot be found in objective reality, an idea continually argued by his poems.

Instead, this poem asserts a faith in nature as it is, and in the labor necessary to support and define oneself—labor in the natural world, and in the making of poems. This idea is brought forth in the next lines: "Anything more than the truth would have seemed too weak / To the earnest love that laid the swale in rows" (9-10). Whether the "fact" that is "the sweetest dream that labour knows" (13) is the actual act of cutting the grass or the verse that is inspired by the simple action, it is something that must be achieved in solitude.

This faith in the work of the individual demonstrated in *A Boy's Will* is not lost in *North of Boston* but is redefined. Meyers writes that *North of Boston* "signaled Frost's change of emphasis from solitary to social beings" (112). In Frost's dedication to his wife, he called *North of Boston* "This Book of People." The poems in this collection demonstrate an understanding of the individual as well as the community in which he lives. This shift seems a natural development after a book in which Frost so carefully established his sense of self and his particular poetic vision and aims.

"Mending Wall," a poem in *North of Boston*, illustrates Frost's shift in focus from the solitary individual to the interacting society. In the poem, the speaker and his neighbor set out to perform the annual task of mending a wall that divides their properties. From the very beginning, the speaker's tone—at once humorous and serious—indicates that the real subject of the poem is not the mending of the wall, which he describes almost lightheartedly, but the "mending" of the subtle boundaries between the speaker and his neighbor. The poem begins, "Something there is that doesn't love a wall, / That sends the frozen-ground-swell under it" (Frost, "Mending" 1-2), yet this "something," mentioned twice in the poem, refers to more than the seasonal frost that "spills the upper boulders in the sun" (3). Peter Stanlis writes in a commentary on "Mending Wall" that "the central theme falls within the philosophical polarities of the speaker and his neighbor" (1). The man's statement that "good fences make good neighbors" (Frost, "Mending" 27) implies his belief that boundaries between people will maintain the peace between them, but the speaker questions this need for boundaries: "Before I built a wall I'd ask to know / What I was walling in or walling out" (32-33). With this he brings the wall into the figurative realm to decipher its meaning.

His neighbor feels no need for such analysis. But while articulating a figurative barrier of noncommunication and different values between the men, the poem is as much about community as individuality; the wall is what connects as well as separates them. Marie Borroff argues that "the story told in the poem is not about a one-man rebellion against wall mending but about an attempt to communicate" (66). However individuated the men may perceive themselves to be, the common task they must undertake and the ethos it represents join them in a particular social community, the assumptions of which Frost articulates in this poem by both participating in and questioning them.

For the speaker, the task of mending the wall provides an opportunity for thought and questioning rather than serving a utilitarian purpose. While the tradition unites the men "by marking their claims to private property through mutual respect," it is still a barrier (Stanlis 3). Both joined and separated by the fence, the two neighbors walk together and alone, isolated by the physical boundary but connected by their maintenance of the relationship and tradition that created it. As James R. Dawes points out, these "men can only interact when reassured by the constructed alienation of the wall" (300). They keep the wall in place, and thereby keep in place their separate senses of self.

While the speaker is explicitly and lightheartedly critical of the ritual, it is he who "insists on the yearly ritual, as if civilization depends upon the collective activity of making barriers. . . . One senses a profound commitment to the act of creating community in the speaker" (Parini 139). Unwilling to placate his neighbor by performing the task in silence, the speaker makes a playful attempt at communication. Explaining that "My apple trees will never get across / And eat the cones under his pines" (Frost, "Mending" 25-26), he asks why the wall is necessary. But rather than contemplate the logic behind the boundary, the neighbor rejects the invitation to communicate: "He only says, 'Good fences make good neighbors'" (27). By refusing to think about the speaker's question, and choosing to hide behind his own father's words, he closes any possible window of communication between them (Monteiro 127), not crossing the barrier of the wall literally or psychologically. And even while the speaker jokes about the wall's uselessness, he keeps his deeper questions to himself. Rather than threaten the agreed-upon terms of community, he is complicit in keeping them there in actuality, only privately articulating and upending them, in poetry.

Mark Van Doren wrote in 1951 that Robert Frost's poems "are the work of a man who has never stopped exploring himself" (2); he never stopped exploring the psychology of others, either. "Mowing," which illustrates his initial focus on individualism, was only a starting point in Frost's understanding of his place in the world as a poet. The change of perspective evident in "Mending Wall" demonstrates his enriched idea of man as an individual within a community. Having established a singular voice and his own moral aesthetic—"The fact is the sweetest dream that labour knows" ("Mowing" 13)—Frost has the confidence to incorporate different voices into his poems and to allow his "facts" and values to encounter those of others, as the two men in "Mending Wall" do across the wall, each maintaining his own and the other's sense of personal identity.

## Works Cited

Borroff, Marie. "Robert Frost's New Testament: The Uses of Simplicity." *Modern Critical Views: Robert Frost*. Ed. Harold Bloom. New York: Chelsea House, 1986. 63-83. Print.

Braithwaite, W. S. "A Poet of New England." *Boston Evening Transcript* 28 Apr. 1915. *Robert Frost: Poems, Life, Legacy*. New York: Holt, 1997. CD-ROM.

Dawes, James R. "Masculinity and Transgression in Robert Frost." *American Literature* 65 (June 1993): 297-312. Print.

Frost, Robert. "Mending Wall." *Thinking and Writing about Poetry*. Ed. Michael Meyer. Boston: Bedford/St. Martin's, 2016. 260-61. Print.

---. "Mowing." Meyer. 259-60.

Meyers, Jeffrey. *Robert Frost: A Biography*. New York: Houghton, 1996. Print.

Monteiro, George. *Robert Frost and the New England Renaissance*. Lexington: UP of Kentucky, 1988. Print.

Parini, Jay. *Robert Frost: A Life*. New York: Holt, 1999. Print.

Stanlis, Peter J. "Commentary: 'Mending Wall.'" *Robert Frost: Poems, Life, Legacy*. New York: Holt, 1997. CD-ROM.

Van Doren, Mark. "Robert Frost's America." *Atlantic Monthly*. Atlantic Unbound, June 1951. Web. 26 Oct. 2015.

# 18

# Taking Essay Examinations

You must write. It's not enough to start by thinking. You become a writer by writing.

—R. K. NARAYAN

© Dinodia Photos/Alamy.

## PREPARING FOR AN ESSAY EXAM

### *Keep Up with the Reading*

The best way to prepare for an examination is to keep up with the reading. If you begin the course with a commitment to completing the reading assignments on time, you will not have to read in a frenzy and cram just days before the test. The readings will be a pleasure, not a frantic ordeal. Moreover, you will find that your instructor's comments and class discussion will make more sense to you and that you'll be able to participate in class discussion. As you prepare for the exam, you should be rereading texts rather than reading for the first time. It may not be possible to reread everything, but you'll at least be able to scan a familiar text and reread passages that are particularly important.

## Take Notes and Annotate the Text

Don't rely exclusively on your memory. The typical literature class includes a hefty amount of reading, so unless you take notes, annotate the text with your own comments, and underline important passages, you're likely to forget material that could be useful for responding to an examination question (see pp. 348–50 for a discussion of these matters). The more you can retrieve from your reading, the more prepared you'll be for reviewing significant material for the exam. Your notes can be used to illustrate points that were made in class. By briefly quoting an important phrase or line from the text, you can provide supporting evidence that will make your argument convincing. Consider, for example, the difference between writing that "Marvell's speaker in 'To His Coy Mistress' says that they won't be able to love after they die" and writing that "the speaker intones that 'The grave's a fine and private place, / But none, I think, do there embrace.'" No one expects you to memorize the entire poem, but recalling a few lines here and there can transform a sleepy generality into an illustrative, persuasive argument.

## Anticipate Questions

As you review the readings, keep in mind the class discussions and the focus provided by your instructor. Very often class discussions and the instructor's emphasis become the basis for essay questions. You may not see the exact same topics on the exam, but you might find that the matters you've discussed in class will serve as a means of responding to an essay question. If, for example, class discussion of Robert Frost's "Mending Wall" (see p. 260) centered on the poem's rural New England setting, you could use that conservative, traditional setting to answer a question such as "Discuss how the conflicts between the speaker and his neighbor are related to the poem's theme." A discussion of the neighbor's rigidity and his firmly entrenched conservative New England attitudes could be connected to his impulse to rebuild the wall between himself and the poem's speaker. The point is that you'll be well prepared for an essay exam when you can shape the material you've studied so that it is responsive to whatever kinds of reasonable questions you encounter on the exam. Reasonable questions? Yes, your instructor is more likely to offer you an opportunity to demonstrate your familiarity with and understanding of the text than to set a trap that, for instance, demands that you discuss how Frost's work experience as an adolescent informs the poem when no mention was ever made of that in class or in your reading.

You can also anticipate questions by considering the Questions for Responsive Reading and Writing about poetry (p. 45) and the Questions for Arguing Critically about Literature (p. 353), along with the Questions for Writing about an Author in Depth (p. 250). Not all of these questions will necessarily be relevant to every work that you read, but they cover a wide range of concerns that should allow you to organize your reading, note taking, and reviewing so that you're not taken by surprise during the exam.

Studying with a classmate or a small group from class can be a stimulating and fruitful means of discovering and organizing the course's major topics and themes. This method of brainstorming can be useful not only for studying for exams but also through the semester as a way to understand and review course readings. And, finally, you needn't be shy about asking your instructor what types of questions might appear on the exam and how best to study for them. You may not get a very specific reply, but almost any information is more useful than none.

## TYPES OF EXAMS

### *Closed-Book versus Open-Book Exams*

Closed-book exams require more memorization and recall than open-book exams, which permit you to use your text and perhaps even your notes to answer questions. Obviously, dates, names, definitions, and other details play less of a role in an open-book exam. An open-book exam requires no less preparation, however, because you'll need to be intimately familiar with the texts and the major ideas, themes, and issues that you've studied in order to quickly and efficiently support your points with relevant, specific evidence. Because every student has the same advantage of having access to the text, preparation remains the key to answering the questions. Some students find open-book exams more difficult than closed-book tests because they risk spending too much time reading, scanning, and searching for material and not enough time writing a response that draws on the knowledge and understanding that their reading and studying have provided them. It's best to limit the time you allow yourself to review the text or notes so that you devote an adequate amount of time to getting your ideas down on paper.

### *Essay Questions*

Essay questions generally fall within one of the following categories. If you can recognize quickly what is being asked of you, you will be able to respond to the question more efficiently.

   **1. Explication.**  Explication calls for a line-by-line explanation of a passage of poetry or prose that considers, for example, diction, figures of speech, symbolism, sound, form, and theme in an effort to describe how language creates meaning. (For a more detailed discussion of explication, see p. 362.)

   **2. Definition.**  Defining a term and then applying it to a writer or work is a frequent exam exercise. Consider: "Define *Romanticism*. To what extent can Keats's 'Ode on a Grecian Urn' (p. 75) be regarded as a Romantic poem?" This sort of question requires that you first describe what constitutes a

Romantic literary work and then explain how "Ode on a Grecian Urn" does (or doesn't) fit the bill.

**3. Analysis.** An analytical question focuses on a particular part of a literary work. You might be asked, for example, to analyze the significance of images in Sharon Olds's poem "Last Night" (p. 69). This sort of question requires you not only to discuss a specific element of the poem but also to explain how that element contributes to the poem's overall effect. (For a more detailed discussion of analysis, see p. 367.)

**4. Comparison and Contrast.** Comparison and contrast calls for a discussion of the similarities or differences between writers, works, or elements of works. For example: "Compare and contrast the tone of the *carpe diem* arguments made by the speaker in Ann Lauinger's 'Marvell Noir' and in Andrew Marvell's 'To His Coy Mistress.'" Despite the nearly three hundred years that separate these two poems in setting and circumstances, a discussion of the tone of the speakers' arguments reveals some intriguing similarities and differences. (For a more detailed discussion of comparison and contrast, see p. 371.)

**5. Discussion of a Critical Perspective.** A brief quotation by a critic about a work is usually designed to stimulate a response that requires you to agree with, disagree with, or qualify a critic's perspective. Usually it is not so important whether you agree or disagree with the critic; what matters is the quality of your argument. Think about how you might wrestle with this assessment of Robert Frost written by Lionel Trilling: "The manifest America of Mr. Frost's poems may be pastoral; the actual America is tragic." With some qualifications (surely not all of Frost's poems are "tragic"), this could provide a useful way of talking about a poem such as "Mending Wall" (p. 260).

**6. Imaginative Questions.** To a degree, every question requires imagination regardless of whether it's being asked or answered. However, some questions require more imaginative leaps to arrive at the center of an issue than others do. Consider, for example, the intellectual agility needed to respond to this question: "Discuss the speakers' attitudes toward the power of imagination in Emily Dickinson's 'To make a prairie it takes a clover and one bee,' Robert Frost's 'Mending Wall,' and Philip Larkin's 'A Study of Reading Habits.'" As tricky as this thematic triangulation may seem, there is plenty to say about the speakers' varied, complicated, and contradictory attitudes toward the power of an individual's imagination. Or try a simpler but no less interesting version: "How do you think Frost would review Marvell's 'To His Coy Mistress' and Olds's 'Last Night'?" Such questions certainly require detailed, reasoned responses, but they also leave room for creativity and even wit.

# STRATEGIES FOR WRITING ESSAY EXAMS

Your hands may be sweaty and your heart pounding as you begin the exam, but as long as you're prepared and you keep in mind some basic strategies for writing essay exams, you should be able to respond to questions with confidence and a genuine sense of accomplishment.

1. Before you begin writing, read through the entire exam. If there are choices to be made, make certain you know how many questions must be answered (for instance, only one out of four, not two). Note how many points each question is worth; spend more time on the two worth forty points each and perhaps leave the twenty-point question for last.

2. Budget your time. If there are short-answer questions, do not allow them to absorb you so that you cannot do justice to the longer essay questions. Follow the suggested time limits for each question; if none is offered, then create your own schedule in proportion to the points allotted for each question.

3. Depending on your own sensibilities, you may want to begin with the easiest or hardest questions. It doesn't really matter which you begin with as long as you pace yourself to avoid running out of time.

4. Be sure that you understand the question. Does it ask you to compare or contrast, define, analyze, explicate, or use some other approach? Determine how many elements there are to the question so that you don't inadvertently miss part of the question. Do not spend time copying the question.

5. Make some brief notes about how you plan to answer the question; even a simple list of what you'll need to cover can serve as a useful outline.

6. Address the question; avoid unnecessary summaries or irrelevant asides. Focus on the particular elements enumerated or implied by the question.

7. After beginning the essay, write a clear thesis that describes the major topics you will discuss: for example, "Mending Wall" is typical of Frost's concerns as a writer owing to its treatment of setting, tone, and theme.

8. Support and illustrate your answer with specific, relevant references to the text. The more specificity — the more you demonstrate a familiarity with the text (rather than simply providing a summary) — the better the answer.

9. Don't overlap and repeat responses to questions; your instructor will recognize such padding. If two different questions are about the same work or writer, demonstrate the breadth and depth of your knowledge of the subject.

10. Allow time to proofread and to qualify and to add more supporting material if necessary. At this final stage, too, it's worth remembering that Mark Twain liked to remind his readers that the difference between the right word and the almost right word is the difference between lightning and a lightning bug.

# Glossary of Literary Terms

**Accent** The emphasis, or STRESS, given a syllable in pronunciation. We say "*syl*lable" not "syl*lable*," "*em*phasis" not "em*pha*sis." Accents can also be used to emphasize a particular word in a sentence: *Is* she con*tent* with the *con*tents of the *yel*low *pack*age? See also METER.

**Allegory** A narration or description usually restricted to a single meaning because its events, actions, characters, settings, and objects represent specific abstractions or ideas. Although the elements in an allegory may be interesting in themselves, the emphasis tends to be on what they ultimately mean. Characters may be given names such as Hope, Pride, Youth, and Charity; they have few if any personal qualities beyond their abstract meanings. These personifications are not symbols because, for instance, the meaning of a character named Charity is precisely that virtue. See also SYMBOL.

**Alliteration** The repetition of the same consonant sounds in a sequence of words, usually at the beginning of a word or stressed syllable: "*d*escending *d*ew *d*rops"; "*l*uscious *l*emons." Alliteration is based on the sounds of letters, rather than the spelling of words; for example, "*k*een" and "*c*ar" alliterate, but "*c*ar" and "*c*ite" do not. Used sparingly, alliteration can intensify ideas by emphasizing key words, but when used too self-consciously, it can be distracting, even ridiculous, rather than effective. See also ASSONANCE, CONSONANCE.

**Allusion** A brief reference to a person, a place, a thing, an event, or an idea in history or literature. Allusions conjure up biblical authority, scenes from Shakespeare's plays, historic figures, wars, great love stories, and anything else that might enrich an author's work. Allusions imply reading and cultural experiences shared by the writer and reader, functioning as a kind of shorthand whereby the recalling of something outside the work supplies an emotional or intellectual context, such as a poem about current racial struggles calling up the memory of Abraham Lincoln.

**Ambiguity** Allows for two or more simultaneous interpretations of a word, phrase, action, or situation, all of which can be supported by the context of a work. Deliberate ambiguity can contribute to the effectiveness and richness of a work. However, unintentional ambiguity obscures meaning and can confuse readers.

**Anagram** A word or phrase made from the letters of another word or phrase, as *heart* is an anagram of *earth*. Anagrams have often been considered merely an exercise of one's ingenuity, but sometimes writers use anagrams to conceal proper names or veiled messages or to suggest important connections between words, as in *hated* and *death*.

**Analysis**  Usually examines only a single element of a work such as diction, character, point of view, symbol, tone, or irony and relates it to the entire work.

**Anapestic meter**  See FOOT.

**Apostrophe**  An address, either to someone who is absent and therefore cannot hear the speaker or to something nonhuman that cannot comprehend. Apostrophe often provides a SPEAKER the opportunity to think aloud.

**Approximate rhyme**  See RHYME.

**Archetype**  A term used to describe universal symbols that evoke deep and sometimes unconscious responses in a reader. In literature, characters, images, and themes that symbolically embody universal meanings and the basic experiences of humans, regardless of when or where they live, are considered archetypes. Common literary archetypes include stories of quests, initiations, scapegoats, descents to the underworld, and ascents to heaven. See also MYTHOLOGICAL CRITICISM.

**Assonance**  The repetition of internal vowel sounds in nearby words that do not end the same, for example, "asl*ee*p under a tr*ee*," or "*ea*ch *e*vening." Similar endings result in rhyme, as in "asl*ee*p in the d*ee*p." Assonance is a strong means of emphasizing important words in a line. See also ALLITERATION, CONSONANCE.

**Ballad**  Traditionally, a ballad is a song, transmitted orally from generation to generation, that tells a story and that eventually is written down. As such, ballads usually cannot be traced to a particular author or group of authors. Typically, ballads are dramatic, condensed, and impersonal narratives, such as "Bonny Barbara Allan." A **literary ballad** is a narrative poem written in deliberate imitation of the language, form, and spirit of the traditional ballad, such as John Keats's "La Belle Dame sans Merci." See also BALLAD STANZA, QUATRAIN.

**Ballad stanza**  A four-line stanza, known as a QUATRAIN, consisting of alternating eight- and six-syllable lines. Usually only the second and fourth lines rhyme (an *abcb* pattern). Coleridge adopted the ballad stanza in "The Rime of the Ancient Mariner":

All in a hot and copper sky
The bloody Sun, at noon,
Right up above the mast did stand,
No bigger than the Moon.

See also BALLAD, QUATRAIN.

**Biographical criticism**  An approach to literature that suggests that knowledge of the author's life experiences can aid in the understanding of his or her work. While biographical information can sometimes complicate one's interpretation of a work, and some formalist critics (such as the New Critics) disparage the use of the author's biography as a tool for textual interpretation, learning about the life of the author can often enrich a reader's appreciation for that author's work. See also FORMALIST CRITICISM, NEW CRITICISM.

**Blank verse**   Unrhymed iambic pentameter. Blank verse is the English verse form closest to the natural rhythms of English speech and therefore is the most common pattern found in traditional English narrative and dramatic poetry from Shakespeare to the early twentieth century. Shakespeare's plays use blank verse extensively. See also IAMBIC PENTAMETER.

**Cacophony**   Language that is discordant and difficult to pronounce, such as this line from John Updike's "Player Piano": "never my numb plunker fumbles." Cacophony ("bad sound") may be unintentional in the writer's sense of music, or it may be used consciously for deliberate dramatic effect. See also EUPHONY.

**Caesura**   A pause within a line of poetry that contributes to the rhythm of the line. A caesura can occur anywhere within a line and need not be indicated by punctuation. In scanning a line, we indicate caesuras by a double vertical line (||). See also METER, RHYTHM, SCANSION.

**Canon**   Those works generally considered by scholars, critics, and teachers to be the most important to read and study, which collectively constitute the "masterpieces" of literature. Since the 1960s, the traditional English and American literary canon, consisting mostly of works by white male writers, has been rapidly expanding to include many female writers and writers of varying ethnic backgrounds.

**Carpe diem**   The Latin phrase meaning "seize the day." This is a very common literary theme, especially in lyric poetry, which emphasizes that life is short, time is fleeting, and one should make the most of present pleasures. Robert Herrick's poem "To the Virgins, to Make Much of Time" uses the *carpe diem* theme.

**Cliché**   An idea or expression that has become tired and trite from overuse, its freshness and clarity having worn off. Clichés often anesthetize readers and are usually a sign of weak writing. See also SENTIMENTALITY, STOCK RESPONSES.

**Colloquial**   Refers to a type of informal diction that reflects casual, conversational language and often includes slang expressions. See also DICTION.

**Comparison and contrast**   A discussion or an essay about similarities and differences between or within works. The term *comparison* is sometimes used to refer to both similarities and differences, so it is important to be aware of the expectations embedded in the assignment.

**Connotation**   Associations and implications that go beyond a word's literal meaning and deriving from how the word has been commonly used and the associations people make with it. For example, the word *eagle* connotes ideas of liberty and freedom that have little to do with the word's literal meaning. See also DENOTATION.

**Consonance** A common type of near rhyme that consists of identical consonant sounds preceded by different vowel sounds: *home, same; worth, breath.* See also RHYME.

**Contextual symbol** See SYMBOL.

**Controlling metaphor** See METAPHOR.

**Convention** A characteristic of a literary genre (often unrealistic) that is understood and accepted by readers because it has come, through usage and time, to be recognized as a familiar technique. For example, the use of METER and RHYME are poetic conventions.

**Conventional symbol** See SYMBOL.

**Cosmic irony** See IRONY.

**Couplet** Two consecutive lines of poetry that usually rhyme and have the same meter. A **heroic couplet** is a couplet written in rhymed IAMBIC PENTAMETER.

**Cultural criticism** An approach to literature that focuses on the historical as well as social, political, and economic contexts of a work. Popular culture—mass-produced and -consumed cultural artifacts ranging from advertising and popular fiction to television to rock music—is given the same emphasis as "high culture." Cultural critics use widely eclectic strategies such as new historicism, psychology, gender studies, and deconstructionism to analyze not only literary texts but also everything from radio talk shows, comic strips, calendar art, commercials, to travel guides and baseball cards. See also HISTORICAL CRITICISM, MARXIST CRITICISM, POSTCOLONIAL CRITICISM.

**Dactylic meter** See FOOT.

**Deconstructionism** An approach to literature that suggests that literary works do not yield fixed, single meanings because language can never say exactly what we intend it to mean. Deconstructionism seeks to destabilize meaning by examining the gaps and ambiguities of a text's language. Deconstructionists pay close attention to language in order to discover and describe how a variety of possible readings are generated by the elements of a text. See also NEW CRITICISM.

**Denotation** The dictionary meaning of a word. See also CONNOTATION.

**Dialect** A type of informal diction. Dialects are spoken by definable groups of people from a particular geographic region, economic group, or social class. Writers use dialect to contrast and express differences in their characters' educational, class, social, and regional backgrounds. See also DICTION.

**Diction** A writer's choice of words, phrases, sentence structures, and figurative language, which combine to help create meaning. **Formal diction**

consists of a dignified, impersonal, and elevated use of language; it follows the rules of syntax exactly and is often characterized by complex words and lofty tone. **Middle diction** maintains correct language usage but is less elevated than formal diction; it reflects the way most educated people speak. **Informal diction** represents the plain language of everyday use and often includes idiomatic expressions, slang, contractions, and many simple, common words. **Poetic diction** refers to the way poets sometimes use an elevated diction that deviates significantly from the common speech and writing of their time, choosing words for their supposedly inherent poetic qualities. Since the eighteenth century, however, poets have been incorporating all kinds of diction in their work, and so there is no longer an automatic distinction between the language of a poet and the language of everyday speech. See also DIALECT.

**Didactic poetry**  Poetry designed to teach an ethical, moral, or religious lesson. Michael Wigglesworth's Puritan poem *Day of Doom* is an example of didactic poetry.

**Doggerel**  A derogatory term used to describe poetry whose subject is trite and whose rhythm and sounds are monotonously heavy-handed.

**Dramatic irony**  See IRONY.

**Dramatic monologue**  A type of lyric poem in which a character (the SPEAKER) addresses a distinct but silent audience imagined to be present in the poem in such a way as to reveal a dramatic situation and, often unintentionally, some aspect of his or her temperament or personality. See also LYRIC.

**Elegy**  A mournful, contemplative lyric poem written to commemorate someone who is dead, often ending in a consolation. Tennyson's *In Memoriam,* written on the death of Arthur Hallam, is an elegy. *Elegy* may also refer to a serious meditative poem produced to express the SPEAKER's melancholy thoughts. See also LYRIC.

**End rhyme**  See RHYME.

**End-stopped line**  A poetic line that has a pause at the end. End-stopped lines reflect normal speech patterns and are often marked by punctuation. The first line of John Keats's "Endymion" is an example of an end-stopped line; the natural pause coincides with the end of the line and is marked by a period:

A thing of beauty is a joy forever.

**English sonnet**  See SONNET.

**Enjambment**  In poetry, when one line ends without a pause and continues into the next line for its meaning. This is also called a **run-on line**. The transition between the first two lines of William Wordsworth's "My Heart Leaps Up" demonstrates enjambment:

My heart leaps up when I behold
  A rainbow in the sky:

**Envoy**  See SESTINA.

**Epic**  A long narrative poem, told in a formal, elevated style, that focuses on a serious subject and chronicles heroic deeds and events important to a culture or nation. John Milton's *Paradise Lost,* which attempts to "justify the ways of God to man," is an epic. See also NARRATIVE POEM.

**Epigram**  A brief, pointed, and witty poem that usually makes a satiric or humorous point. Epigrams are most often written in couplets but take no prescribed form.

**Euphony**  *Euphony* ("good sound") refers to language that is smooth and musically pleasant to the ear. See also CACOPHONY.

**Exact rhyme**  See RHYME.

**Explication**  A detailed explanation and line-by-line interpretation of a poem or brief passage of prose that carefully considers its use of literary elements such as connotation, allusion, symbol, tone, and sound.

**Extended metaphor**  See METAPHOR.

**Eye rhyme**  See RHYME.

**Falling meter**  See METER.

**Feminine rhyme**  See RHYME.

**Feminist criticism**  An approach to literature that seeks to correct or supplement what may be regarded as a predominantly male-dominated critical perspective with a feminist consciousness. Feminist criticism places literature in a social context and uses a broad range of disciplines, including history, sociology, psychology, and linguistics, to provide a perspective sensitive to feminist issues. Feminist theories also attempt to understand representation from a woman's point of view and to explain women's writing strategies as specific to their social conditions. See also GENDER CRITICISM.

**Figures of speech**  Ways of using language that deviate from the literal, denotative meanings of words in order to suggest additional meanings or effects. Figures of speech say one thing in terms of something else, such as when an eager funeral director is described as a vulture. See also METAPHOR, SIMILE.

**Fixed form**  A poem that may be categorized by the pattern of its lines, meter, rhythm, or stanzas. A SONNET is a fixed form of poetry because by definition it must have fourteen lines. Other fixed forms include LIMERICK, SESTINA, and VILLANELLE. However, poems written in a fixed form may not always fit into categories precisely because writers sometimes vary traditional forms to create innovative effects. See also OPEN FORM.

**Foot**  The metrical unit by which a line of poetry is measured. A foot usually consists of one stressed and one or two unstressed syllables. An **iambic**

foot, which consists of one unstressed syllable followed by one stressed syllable (ăwáy), is the most common metrical foot in English poetry. A **trochaic** foot consists of one stressed syllable followed by an unstressed syllable (lóvelў). An **anapestic** foot is two unstressed syllables followed by one stressed syllable (ŭnděrstánd). A **dactylic** foot is one stressed syllable followed by two unstressed syllables (déspěrăte). A **spondee** is a foot consisting of two stressed syllables (dèad sèt) but is not a sustained metrical foot and is used mainly for variety or emphasis. See also IAMBIC PENTAMETER, LINE, METER. A **pyrrhic** foot consists of two unstressed symbols, as in Shakespeare's "A horse! A horse! My kingdŏm fŏr a horse!" Pyrrhic feet are typically variants for iambic verse rather than predominant patterns in lines.

**Form**  The overall structure or shape of a work, which frequently follows an established design. Forms may refer to a literary type (narrative form, lyric form) or to patterns of meter, lines, and rhymes (stanza form, verse form). See also FIXED FORM, OPEN FORM.

**Formal diction**  See DICTION.

**Formalist criticism**  An approach to literature that focuses on the formal elements of a work, such as its language, structure, and TONE. Formalist critics offer intense examinations of the relationship between FORM and meaning in a work, emphasizing the subtle complexity in how a work is arranged. Formalists pay special attention to DICTION, IRONY, METAPHOR, PARADOX, and SYMBOL, as well as larger elements such as plot, characterization, and narrative technique. Formalist critics read literature as an independent work of art rather than as a reflection of the author's state of mind or as a representation of a moment in history. Therefore anything outside of the work, including historical influences and authorial intent, is generally not examined by formalist critics. See also NEW CRITICISM.

**Found poem**  An unintentional poem discovered in a nonpoetic context, such as a conversation, news story, or advertisement. Found poems serve as reminders that everyday language often contains what can be considered poetry or that poetry is definable as any text read as a poem.

**Free verse**  Also called *open form poetry,* free verse refers to poems characterized by their nonconformity to established patterns of meter, rhyme, and stanza. Free verse uses elements such as speech patterns, grammar, emphasis, and breath pauses to determine line breaks and usually does not rhyme. See OPEN FORM.

**Gay and lesbian criticism**  An approach to literature that focuses on how gays and lesbians are represented in literature, how they read literature, and whether sexuality, as well as gender, is culturally constructed or innate. See also FEMINIST CRITICISM, GENDER CRITICISM.

**Gender criticism**  An approach to literature that explores how ideas about men and women — what is masculine and feminine — can be regarded as socially constructed by particular cultures. Gender criticism expands categories and definitions of what is masculine or feminine and tends to regard sexuality as more complex than merely masculine or feminine, heterosexual or homosexual. See also FEMINIST CRITICISM, GAY AND LESBIAN CRITICISM.

**Genre**   A French word meaning "kind" or "type." The major genres in literature are poetry, fiction, drama, and essays. *Genre* can also refer to more specific types of literature such as comedy, tragedy, epic poetry, or science fiction.

**Haiku**   A style of lyric poetry borrowed from the Japanese that typically presents an intense emotion or vivid image of nature, which, traditionally, is designed to lead to a spiritual insight. Haiku is a fixed poetic form, consisting of seventeen syllables organized into three unrhymed lines of five, seven, and five syllables. Today, however, many poets vary the syllabic count in their haiku. See also FIXED FORM.

**Heroic couplet**   See COUPLET.

**Historical criticism**   An approach to literature that uses history as a means of understanding a literary work more clearly. Such criticism moves beyond both the facts of an author's personal life and the text itself in order to examine the social and intellectual currents in which the author composed the work. See also CULTURAL CRITICISM, MARXIST CRITICISM, NEW HISTORICISM, POSTCOLONIAL CRITICISM.

**Hyperbole**   A boldly exaggerated statement that adds emphasis without intending to be literally true, as in the statement "He ate everything in the house." Hyperbole (also called *overstatement*) may be used for serious, comic, or ironic effect. See also FIGURES OF SPEECH.

**Iambic meter**   See FOOT.

**Iambic pentameter**   A metrical pattern in poetry that consists of five iambic feet per line. (An iamb, or iambic foot, consists of one unstressed syllable followed by a stressed syllable.) See also FOOT, METER.

**Image**   A word, phrase, or figure of speech (especially a SIMILE or a METAPHOR) that addresses the senses, suggesting mental pictures of sights, sounds, smells, tastes, feelings, or actions. Images offer sensory impressions to the reader and also convey emotions and moods through their verbal pictures. See also FIGURES OF SPEECH.

**Implied metaphor**   See METAPHOR.

**Informal diction**   See DICTION.

**Internal rhyme**   See RHYME.

**Interpretation**   An explanation of what a literary work means that is supported by an analysis of its elements.

**Irony**  A literary device that uses contradictory statements or situations to reveal a reality different from what appears to be true. It is ironic for a firehouse to burn down or for a police station to be burglarized. **Verbal irony** is a figure of speech that occurs when a person says one thing but means the opposite. **Sarcasm** is a strong form of verbal irony that is calculated to hurt someone through, for example, false praise. **Dramatic irony** creates a discrepancy between what a character believes or says and what the reader or audience member knows to be true. **Situational irony** exists when there is an incongruity between what is expected to happen and what actually happens owing to forces beyond human comprehension or control. The suicide of the seemingly successful main character in Edwin Arlington Robinson's poem "Richard Cory" is an example of situational irony. **Cosmic irony** occurs when a writer uses God, destiny, or fate to dash the hopes and expectations of a character or of humankind in general. In cosmic irony, a discrepancy exists between what a character aspires to and what universal forces provide. Stephen Crane's poem "A Man Said to the Universe" is a good example of cosmic irony because the universe acknowledges no obligation to the man's assertion of his own existence.

**Italian sonnet**  See SONNET.

**Jargon**  The use of words or phrases by particular groups such as professions or trades. Lawyers, doctors, the military, and educators serve as examples of groups that use language specific to their fields. Brainstorming with your peers in the learning center will yield more examples.

**Limerick**  A light, humorous style of fixed form poetry. Its usual form consists of five lines with the rhyme scheme *aabba;* lines 1, 2, and 5 contain three feet, while lines 3 and 4 usually contain two feet. Limericks range in subject matter from the silly to the obscene, and since Edward Lear popularized them in the nineteenth century, children and adults have enjoyed these comic poems. See also FIXED FORM.

**Line**  A sequence of words printed as a separate entity on the page. In poetry, lines are usually measured by the number of feet they contain. The names for various line lengths are as follows:

| | |
|---|---|
| monometer: one foot | pentameter: five feet |
| dimeter: two feet | hexameter: six feet |
| trimeter: three feet | heptameter: seven feet |
| tetrameter: four feet | octameter: eight feet |

The number of feet in a line, coupled with the name of the foot, describes the metrical qualities of that line. See also END-STOPPED LINE, ENJAMBMENT, FOOT, METER.

**Literary ballad**  See BALLAD.

**Literary historians**  See HISTORICAL CRITICISM.

**Literary symbol**  See SYMBOL.

**Litotes**  See UNDERSTATEMENT.

**Lyric**  A type of brief poem that expresses the personal emotions and thoughts of a single speaker. It is important to realize, however, that although the lyric is uttered in the first person, the SPEAKER is not necessarily the poet. There are many varieties of lyric poetry, including the DRAMATIC MONOLOGUE, ELEGY, HAIKU, ODE, and SONNET forms.

**Marxist criticism**  An approach to literature that focuses on a work's ideological content — its explicit and implicit assumptions and values about matters such as culture, race, class, and power. Marxist criticism, based largely on the writings of Karl Marx, typically aims at not only revealing and clarifying ideological issues but also correcting social injustices. Some Marxist critics use literature to describe the competing socioeconomic interests that too often advance capitalist interests such as money and power rather than socialist interests such as morality and justice. They argue that literature and literary criticism are essentially political because they either challenge or support economic oppression. Because of this strong emphasis on the political aspects of texts, Marxist criticism focuses more on the content and themes of literature than on its form. See also CULTURAL CRITICISM, HISTORICAL CRITICISM, SOCIOLOGICAL CRITICISM.

**Masculine rhyme**  See RHYME.

**Metaphor**  A metaphor is a FIGURE OF SPEECH that makes a comparison between two unlike things without using the words *like* or *as*. Metaphors assert the identity of dissimilar things, as when Macbeth asserts that life *is* a "brief candle." Metaphors can be subtle and powerful and can transform people, places, objects, and ideas into whatever the writer imagines them to be. An **implied metaphor** is a more subtle comparison; the terms being compared are not so specifically explained. For example, to describe a stubborn man unwilling to leave, one could say that he was "a mule standing his ground." This is a fairly explicit metaphor; the man is being compared to a mule. But to say that the man "brayed his refusal to leave" is to create an implied metaphor, because the subject (the man) is never overtly identified as a mule. Braying is associated with the mule, a notoriously stubborn creature, and so the comparison between the stubborn man and the mule is sustained. Implied metaphors can slip by inattentive readers who are not sensitive to such carefully chosen, highly concentrated language. An **extended metaphor** is a sustained comparison in which part or all of a poem consists of a series of related metaphors. Robert Francis's poem "Catch" relies on an extended metaphor that compares poetry to playing catch. A **controlling metaphor** runs through an entire work and determines its form or nature. The controlling metaphor in Anne Bradstreet's poem "The Author to Her Book" likens her book to a child. **Synecdoche**

is a kind of metaphor in which a part of something is used to signify the whole, as when a gossip is called a "wagging tongue" or when ten ships are called "ten sails." Sometimes, synecdoche refers to the whole being used to signify the part, as in the phrase "Boston won the baseball game." Clearly, the entire city of Boston did not participate in the game; the whole of Boston is being used to signify the individuals who played and won the game. **Metonymy** is a type of metaphor in which something closely associated with a subject is substituted for it. In this way, we speak of the "silver screen" to mean motion pictures, "the crown" to stand for the king, "the White House" to stand for the activities of the president. See also FIGURES OF SPEECH, PERSONIFICATION, SIMILE.

**Meter**   When a rhythmic pattern of stresses recurs in a poem, it is called *meter*. Metrical patterns are determined by the type and number of feet in a line of verse; combining the name of a line length with the name of a foot concisely describes the meter of the line. **Rising meter** refers to metrical feet that move from unstressed to stressed sounds, such as the iambic foot and the anapestic foot. **Falling meter** refers to metrical feet that move from stressed to unstressed sounds, such as the trochaic foot and the dactylic foot. See also ACCENT, FOOT, IAMBIC PENTAMETER, LINE.

**Metonymy**   See METAPHOR.

**Middle diction**   See DICTION.

**Mythological criticism**   An approach to literature that seeks to identify what in a work creates deep, universal responses in readers, by paying close attention to the hopes, fears, and expectations of entire cultures. Mythological critics (sometimes called *archetypal critics*) analyze literature for underlying, recurrent patterns that reveal universal meanings and basic human experiences for readers regardless of when and where they live. These critics attempt to explain how archetypes (the characters, images, and themes that symbolically embody universal meanings and experiences) are embodied in literary works in order to make larger connections that explain a particular work's lasting appeal. Mythological critics may specialize in areas such as classical literature, philology, anthropology, psychology, and cultural history, but they all emphasize the assumptions and values of various cultures. See also ARCHETYPE.

**Narrative poem**   A poem that tells a story. A narrative poem may be short or long, and the story it relates may be simple or complex. See also BALLAD, EPIC.

**Near rhyme**   See RHYME.

**New Criticism**   An approach to literature made popular between the 1940s and the 1960s that evolved out of formalist criticism. New Critics suggest that detailed analysis of the language of a literary text can uncover important layers of meaning in that work. New Criticism consciously downplays the historical influences, authorial intentions, and social contexts that surround texts in order to focus on explication — extremely close textual analysis. See also FORMALIST CRITICISM.

**New historicism**  An approach to literature that emphasizes the interaction between a work's historical context and a modern reader's understanding and interpretation of the work. New historicists attempt to describe the culture of a period by reading many different kinds of texts and paying close attention to many different dimensions of a culture, including political, economic, social, and esthetic concerns. They regard texts not simply as a reflection of the culture that produced them but also as producing that culture by playing an active role in the social and political conflicts of an age. New historicism acknowledges and then explores various versions of "history," sensitizing us to the fact that the history on which we choose to focus has been reconstructed from our present circumstances. See also HISTORICAL CRITICISM.

**Octave**  A poetic stanza of eight lines, usually forming one part of a sonnet. See also SONNET, STANZA.

**Ode**  A relatively lengthy lyric poem that often expresses lofty emotions in a dignified style. Odes are characterized by a serious topic, such as truth, art, freedom, justice, or the meaning of life; their tone tends to be formal. There is no prescribed pattern that defines an ode; some odes repeat the same pattern in each stanza, while others introduce a new pattern in each stanza. See also LYRIC.

**Oedipus complex**  A Freudian term derived from Sophocles' tragedy *Oedipus the King*. It describes a psychological complex that is predicated on a boy's unconscious rivalry with his father for his mother's love and his desire to eliminate his father in order to take his father's place with his mother.

**Off rhyme**  See RHYME.

**Onomatopoeia**  A term referring to the use of a word that resembles the sound it denotes. *Buzz, rattle, bang,* and *sizzle* all reflect onomatopoeia. Onomatopoeia can also consist of more than one word; writers sometimes create lines or whole passages in which the sound of the words helps convey their meanings.

**Open form**  Sometimes called *free verse*, open form poetry does not conform to established patterns of METER, RHYME, and STANZA. Such poetry derives its rhythmic qualities from the repetition of words, phrases, or grammatical structures; from the arrangement of words on the printed page; or by some other means. The poet E. E. Cummings wrote open form poetry; his poems do not have measurable meters, but they do have RHYTHM. See also FIXED FORM.

**Overstatement**  See HYPERBOLE.

**Oxymoron** A condensed form of paradox in which two contradictory words are used together, as in "sweet sorrow" or "jumbo shrimp." See also PARADOX.

**Paradox** A statement that initially appears to be contradictory but then, on closer inspection, turns out to make sense. For example, John Donne ends his sonnet "Death, Be Not Proud" with the paradoxical statement "Death, thou shalt die." To solve the paradox, it is necessary to discover the sense that underlies the statement. Paradox is useful in poetry because it arrests a reader's attention by its seemingly stubborn refusal to make sense.

**Paraphrase** A prose restatement of the central ideas of a work, in your own language.

**Parody** A humorous imitation of another, usually serious, work. It can take any fixed or open form, because parodists imitate the tone, language, and shape of the original in order to deflate the subject matter, making the original work seem absurd. Anthony Hecht's poem "Dover Bitch" is a famous parody of Matthew Arnold's well-known "Dover Beach." Parody may also be used as a form of literary criticism to expose the defects in a work. But sometimes parody becomes an affectionate acknowledgment that a well-known work has become both institutionalized in our culture and fair game for some fun. For example, Ann Lauinger's "Marvell Noir" gently mocks Andrew Marvell's "To His Coy Mistress."

**Persona** Literally, a *persona* is a mask. In literature a *persona* is a speaker created by a writer to tell a story or to speak in a poem. A persona is not a character in a story or narrative nor does a persona necessarily directly reflect the author's personal voice. A persona is a separate self, created by and distinct from the author, through which he or she speaks.

**Personification** A form of metaphor in which human characteristics are attributed to nonhuman things. Personification offers the writer a way to give the world life and motion by assigning familiar human behaviors and emotions to animals, inanimate objects, and abstract ideas. For example, in John Keats's "Ode on a Grecian Urn," the speaker refers to the urn as an "unravished bride of quietness." See also METAPHOR.

**Petrarchan sonnet** See SONNET.

**Picture poem** A type of open form poetry in which the poet arranges the lines of the poem so as to create a particular shape on the page. The shape of the poem embodies its subject; the poem becomes a picture of what the poem is describing. Michael McFee's "In Medias Res" is an example of a picture poem. See also OPEN FORM.

**Poetic diction** See DICTION.

**Postcolonial criticism** An approach to literature that focuses on the study of cultural behavior and expression in relationship to the colonized world.

Postcolonial criticism refers to the analysis of literary works by writers from countries and cultures that at one time have been controlled by colonizing powers — such as Indian writers during or after British colonial rule. Post-colonial criticism also refers to the analysis of literary works written about colonial cultures by writers from the colonizing country. Many of these kinds of analyses point out how writers from colonial powers sometimes misrepresent colonized cultures by reflecting their own values. See also CULTURAL CRITICISM, HISTORICAL CRITICISM, MARXIST CRITICISM.

**Prose poem**  A kind of open form poetry that is printed as prose and represents the most clear opposite of fixed form poetry. Prose poems are densely compact and often make use of striking imagery and figures of speech. See also FIXED FORM, OPEN FORM.

**Prosody**  The overall metrical structure of a poem. See also METER.

**Psychological criticism**  An approach to literature that draws on psychoanalytic theories, especially those of Sigmund Freud or Jacques Lacan, to understand more fully the text, the writer, and the reader. The basis of this approach is the idea of the existence of a human unconscious — those impulses, desires, and feelings about which a person is unaware but which influence emotions and behavior. Critics use psychological approaches to explore the motivations of characters and the symbolic meanings of events, while biographers speculate about a writer's own motivations — conscious or unconscious — in a literary work. Psychological approaches are also used to describe and analyze the reader's personal responses to a text.

**Pun**  A play on words that relies on a word's having more than one meaning or sounding like another word. Shakespeare and other writers use puns extensively for serious and comic purposes; in *Romeo and Juliet* (3.2.101) the dying Mercutio puns, "Ask for me tomorrow and you shall find me a grave man." Puns have serious literary uses, but since the eighteenth century they have been used almost purely for humorous effect.

**Pyrrhic**  See FOOT.

**Quatrain**  A four-line stanza. Quatrains are the most common stanzaic form in the English language; they can have various meters and rhyme schemes. See also METER, RHYME, STANZA.

**Reader-response criticism**  An approach to literature that focuses on the reader rather than the work itself, by attempting to describe what goes on in the reader's mind during the reading of a text. Hence the consciousness of the reader — produced by reading the work — is the actual subject of reader-response criticism. These critics are not after a "correct" reading of the text or what the author presumably intended; instead, they are interested in the reader's individual experience with the text. Thus there is no single definitive reading of a work because readers create rather than discover absolute meanings in texts. However, this approach is not a rationale for mistaken or bizarre readings but rather an exploration of the possibilities for a plurality of readings. This kind of strategy calls attention to how we read, what influences our readings, and what that reveals about us.

**Rhyme** The repetition of identical or similar concluding syllables in different words, most often at the ends of lines. Rhyme is predominantly a function of sound rather than spelling; thus words that end with the same vowel sounds rhyme (for instance, *day, prey, bouquet, weigh*), and words with the same consonant ending rhyme (for instance *vain, feign, rein, lane*). Words do not have to be spelled the same way or look alike to rhyme. In fact, words may look alike but not rhyme at all. This is called **eye rhyme**, as with *bough* and *cough*, or *brow* and *blow*. **End rhyme** is the most common form of rhyme in poetry; the rhyme comes at the end of the lines:

It runs through the reeds
  And away it proceeds,
Through meadow and glade,
  In sun and in shade.

The **rhyme scheme** of a poem describes the pattern of end rhymes. Rhyme schemes are mapped out by noting patterns of rhyme with small letters: the first rhyme sound is designated *a*, the second becomes *b*, the third *c*, and so on. Thus the rhyme scheme of the preceding stanza is *aabb*. **Internal rhyme** places at least one of the rhymed words within the line, as in "Dividing and gliding and sliding" or "In mist or cloud, on mast or shroud." **Masculine rhyme** describes the rhyming of single-syllable words, such as *grade* or *shade*. Masculine rhyme also occurs in rhyming words of more than one syllable when the same sound occurs in a final stressed syllable, as in *defend* and *contend, betray* and *away*. **Feminine rhyme** consists of a rhymed stressed syllable followed by one or more identical unstressed syllables, as in *butter, clutter; gratitude, attitude; quivering, shivering*. All of the examples so far have illustrated **exact rhymes**, because they share the same stressed vowel sounds as well as sharing sounds that follow the vowel. In **near rhyme** (also called **off rhyme**, **slant rhyme**, and **approximate rhyme**) the sounds are almost but not exactly alike. A common form of near rhyme is CONSONANCE, which consists of identical consonant sounds preceded by different vowel sounds: *home, same; worth, breath*.

**Rhyme scheme** See RHYME.

**Rhythm** A term used to refer to the recurrence of stressed and unstressed sounds in poetry. Depending on how sounds are arranged, the rhythm of a poem may be fast or slow, choppy or smooth. Poets use rhythm to create pleasurable sound patterns and to reinforce meanings. Rhythm in prose arises from pattern repetitions of sounds and pauses that create looser rhythmic effects. See also METER.

**Rising meter**  See METER.

**Run-on line**  See ENJAMBMENT.

**Sarcasm**  See IRONY.

**Satire**  The literary art of ridiculing a folly or vice in order to expose or correct it. The object of satire is usually some human frailty; people, institutions, ideas, and things are all fair game for satirists. Satire evokes attitudes of amusement, contempt, scorn, or indignation toward its faulty subject in the hope of somehow improving it. See also IRONY, PARODY.

**Scansion**  The process of measuring the stresses in a line of verse to determine the metrical pattern of the line. See also LINE, METER.

**Sentimentality**  A pejorative term used to describe the effort by an author to induce emotional responses in the reader that exceed what the situation warrants. Sentimentality especially pertains to such emotions as pathos and sympathy; it cons readers into falling for the mass murderer who is devoted to stray cats, and it requires that readers do not examine such illogical responses. CLICHÉS and STOCK RESPONSES are the key ingredients of sentimentality in literature.

**Sestet**  A STANZA consisting of exactly six lines.

**Sestina**  A type of FIXED FORM poetry consisting of thirty-six lines of any length divided into six sestets and a three-line concluding stanza called an **envoy.** The six words at the end of the first sestet's lines must also appear at the ends of the other five sestets, in varying order. These six words must also appear in the envoy, where they often resonate important themes. An example of this highly demanding form of poetry is Algernon Charles Swinburne's "Sestina." See also SESTET.

**Setting**  The physical and social context in which the action of a poem occurs. The major elements of setting are the time, the place, and the social environment that frame the poem. Setting can be used to evoke a mood or atmosphere that will prepare the reader for what is to come, as in Robert Frost's "Home Burial."

**Shakespearean sonnet**  See SONNET.

**Simile**  A common figure of speech that makes an explicit comparison between two things by using words such as *like, as, than, appears,* and *seems:* "A sip of Mrs. Cook's coffee is like a punch in the stomach." The effectiveness of this simile is created by the differences between the two things compared. There would be no simile if the comparison were stated this way: "Mrs. Cook's coffee is as strong as the cafeteria's coffee." This is a literal translation because Mrs. Cook's coffee is compared with something like it — another kind of coffee. See also FIGURES OF SPEECH, METAPHOR.

**Situational irony**  See IRONY.

**Slant rhyme**  See RHYME.

**Sonnet**  A fixed form of lyric poetry that consists of fourteen lines, usually written in iambic pentameter. There are two basic types of sonnets, the Italian and the English. The **Italian sonnet**, also known as the **Petrarchan sonnet**, is divided into an octave, which typically rhymes *abbaabba,* and a sestet, which may have varying rhyme schemes. Common rhyme patterns in the sestet are *cdecde, cdcdcd,* and *cdccdc.* Very often the octave presents a situation, attitude, or problem that the sestet comments on or resolves, as in John Keats's "On First Looking into Chapman's Homer." The **English sonnet**, also known as the **Shakespearean sonnet**, is organized into three quatrains and a couplet, which typically rhyme *abab cdcd efef gg.* This rhyme scheme is more suited to English poetry because English has fewer rhyming words than Italian. English sonnets, because of their four-part organization, also have more flexibility with respect to where thematic breaks can occur. Frequently, however, the most pronounced break or turn comes with the concluding couplet, as in Shakespeare's "Shall I compare thee to a summer's day?" See also COUPLET, IAMBIC PENTAMETER, LINE, OCTAVE, QUATRAIN, SESTET.

**Speaker**  The voice used by an author to tell a story or speak a poem. The speaker is often a created identity and should not automatically be equated with the author's self. See also PERSONA.

**Spondee**  See FOOT.

**Stanza**  In poetry, *stanza* refers to a grouping of lines, set off by a space, that usually has a set pattern of meter and rhyme. See also LINE, METER, RHYME.

**Stock responses**  Predictable, conventional reactions to language, characters, symbols, or situations. The flag, motherhood, puppies, God, and peace are common objects used to elicit stock responses from unsophisticated audiences. See also CLICHÉ, SENTIMENTALITY.

**Stress**  The emphasis, or ACCENT, given a syllable in pronunciation.

**Style**  The distinctive and unique manner in which a writer arranges words to achieve particular effects. Style essentially combines the idea to be expressed with the author's individuality. These arrangements include individual word choices as well as matters such as the length of sentences, their structure, tone, and use of irony. See also DICTION, IRONY, TONE.

**Symbol**  A person, an object, an image, a word, or an event that evokes a range of additional meaning beyond and usually more abstract than its literal significance. Symbols are educational devices for evoking complex ideas without having to resort to painstaking explanations that would make a story more like an essay than an experience. **Conventional symbols** have meanings that are widely recognized by a society or culture.

Some conventional symbols are the Christian cross, the Star of David, a skull and crossbones, or a nation's flag. Writers use conventional symbols to reinforce meanings. For example, a spring setting might suggest a renewed sense of life. A **literary** or **contextual symbol** can be a setting, a character, an action, an object, a name, or anything else in a work that maintains its literal significance while suggesting other meanings. Such symbols go beyond conventional symbols; they gain their symbolic meaning within the context of a specific story. For example, the urn in John Keats's "Ode on a Grecian Urn" takes on multiple symbolic meanings in the work, but these meanings do not automatically carry over into other poems about urns. The meanings suggested by Keats's urn are specific to that text; therefore it becomes a contextual symbol. See also ALLEGORY.

**Synecdoche** See METAPHOR.

**Syntax** The ordering of words into meaningful verbal patterns such as phrases, clauses, and sentences. Poets often manipulate syntax, changing conventional word order, to place certain emphasis on particular words. Emily Dickinson, for instance, writes about being surprised by a snake in her poem "A narrow Fellow in the Grass" and includes this line: "His notice sudden is." In addition to the alliterative hissing *s*-sounds here, Dickinson also effectively manipulates the line's syntax so that the verb *is* appears unexpectedly at the end, making the snake's hissing presence all the more "sudden."

**Tercet** A three-line stanza. See also STANZA, TRIPLET.

**Terza rima** An interlocking three-line rhyme scheme: *aba, bcb, cdc, ded*, and so on. Dante's *Divine Comedy* and Robert Frost's "Acquainted with the Night" are written in terza rima. See also RHYME, TERCET.

**Theme** The central meaning or dominant idea in a literary work. A theme provides a unifying point around which the plot, characters, setting, point of view, symbols, and other elements of a work are organized. It is important not to mistake the theme for the work's actual subject; the theme refers to the abstract concept that is made concrete through the images, characterization, and action of the text. In nonfiction, however, the theme generally refers to the main topic of the discourse.

**Thesis** The central idea of an essay. The thesis is a complete sentence (although sometimes it may require more than one sentence) that establishes the topic of the essay in clear, unambiguous language.

**Tone** The author's implicit attitude toward the reader or the people, places, and events in a work as revealed by the elements of the author's style. Tone may be characterized as serious or ironic, sad or happy, private or public, angry or affectionate, bitter or nostalgic, or any other attitudes and feelings that human beings experience. See also STYLE.

**Triplet**  A TERCET in which all three lines rhyme.

**Trochaic meter**  See FOOT.

**Understatement**  The opposite of hyperbole, *understatement* (or litotes) refers to a figure of speech that says less than is intended. Understatement usually has an ironic effect, and it sometimes may be used for comic purposes, as in Mark Twain's statement, "The reports of my death are greatly exaggerated." See also HYPERBOLE, IRONY.

**Verbal irony**  See IRONY.

**Verse**  A generic term used to describe poetic lines composed in a measured, rhythmical pattern that are often, but not necessarily, rhymed. See also LINE, METER, RHYME, RHYTHM.

**Villanelle**  A type of fixed form poetry consisting of nineteen lines of any length divided into six stanzas: five tercets and a concluding quatrain. The first and third lines of the initial tercet rhyme; these rhymes are repeated in each subsequent tercet (*aba*) and in the final two lines of the quatrain (*abaa*). Line 1 appears in its entirety as lines 6, 12, and 18, while line 3 reappears as lines 9, 15, and 19. Dylan Thomas's "Do not go gentle into that good night" is a villanelle. See also FIXED FORM, QUATRAIN, RHYME, TERCET.

## Acknowledgments (continued from p. iv)

Sherman Alexie. "The Facebook Sonnet." Copyright © 2011 by Sherman Alexie. Originally appeared in the May 16, 2011, issue of the *New Yorker*. Used by permission of Nancy Stauffer Associates.

A. R. Ammons. "Coward" from *Diversifications* by A. R. Ammons. Copyright © 1975 by A. R. Ammons. Used by permission of W. W. Norton & Company, Inc.

Richard Armour. "Going to Extremes" from *Light Armour* by Richard Armour. Permission to reprint this material is given courtesy of the family of Richard Armour.

Margaret Atwood. "you fit into me" from *Power Politics* by Margaret Atwood. Copyright © 1971, 1996 by Margaret Atwood. Reprinted by permission of House of Anansi Press, Toronto.

W. H. Auden. "The Unknown Citizen" from *W. H. Auden: Collected Poems* by W. H. Auden. Copyright © 1940 and renewed 1968 by W. H. Auden. Used by permission of Random House, an imprint and division of Penguin Random House LLC. All rights reserved. Any third party use of this material, outside of this publication, is prohibited. Interested parties must apply directly to Penguin Random House LLC for permission.

William Baer. "Letter of Resignation" from *"Bocage" and Other Sonnets* by William Baer. Texas Review Press, 2008. Copyright © 2008 by William Baer. Reprinted by permission.

Regina Barreca. "Nighttime Fires" from *The Minnesota Review* (Fall 1986). Reprinted by permission of the author.

Matsuo Bashō. "Under cherry trees," trans. by Peter Beilenson, published in *Japanese Haiku*. Copyright © 1955–1956 by Peter Pauper Press. Used by permission of Peter Pauper Press, www.peterpauper.com.

Ellen Bass. "Gate C22" from *The Human Line*. Copyright © 2007 by Ellen Bass. Reprinted with the permission of The Permissions Company, Inc., on behalf of Copper Canyon Press, www.coppercanyonpress.org.

Elizabeth Bishop. "Manners" from *Complete Poems 1927–1979* by Elizabeth Bishop. Copyright © 1979, 1983 by Alice Helen Methfessel. Reprinted by permission of Farrar, Straus and Giroux, LLC.

Billie Bolton. "Memorandum." Copyright © 2006 by Billie Bolton. Reprinted by permission of the author.

Allen Braden. "The Hemlock Tree" from *A Wreath of Down and Drops of Blood* by Allen Braden. University of Georgia Press, 2010. Copyright © 2010. Reprinted by permission of the University of Georgia Press.

Gwendolyn Brooks. "We Real Cool" from *Blacks* by Gwendolyn Brooks. Copyright © 1991 by Gwendolyn Brooks. Reprinted by consent of Brooks Permissions.

Helen Chasin. "The Word *Plum*" from *Coming Close and Other Poems* by Helen Chasin. Copyright © 1968 by Yale University Press. Reprinted by permission of Yale University Press.

Michael Chitwood. "Men Throwing Bricks" from *From Whence* by Michael Chitwood. Copyright © 2007 by Michael Chitwood. Reprinted by permission of the author and Louisiana State University Press.

John Ciardi. "Suburban" from *For Instance* by John Ciardi. Copyright © 1979 by John Ciardi. Used by permission of W. W. Norton & Company, Inc.

Billy Collins. "Introduction to Poetry" from *The Apple That Astonished Paris*. Copyright © 1988, 1996 by Billy Collins. Reprinted with the permission of The Permissions Company, Inc., on behalf of the University of Arkansas Press, www.uapress.com.

Edmund Conti. "Pragmatist" from *Light Year '86*. Reprinted by permission of the author.

Sally Croft. "Home-Baked Bread" from *Light Year '86*. Reprinted by permission of Bruce Croft.

E. E. Cummings. "l(a" from *Complete Poems: 1904–1962* by E. E. Cummings, edited by George J. Firmage. Copyright © 1958, 1986, 1991 by the Trustees for the E. E. Cummings Trust. "may I feel said he" from *Complete Poems: 1904–1962* by E. E. Cummings, edited by George J. Firmage. Copyright © 1935, 1963, 1991 by the Trustees for the E. E. Cummings Trust. Copyright © 1978 by George James Firmage. "next to of course god america i" from *Complete Poems: 1904–1962* by E. E. Cummings, edited by George J. Firmage. Copyright © 1926, 1954, © 1991 by the Trustees for the E. E. Cummings Trust. Copyright © 1985 by George James Firmage. Used by permission of Liveright Publishing Corporation.

Joanne Diaz. "On My Father's Loss of Hearing," *The Southern Review* 42, no. 3 (Summer 2006). Copyright © 2006 by Joanne Diaz. Reprinted by permission of the author.

Emily Dickinson. "A Bird came down the Walk —," "Much Madness is divinest Sense —," "A narrow Fellow in the Grass," and "There's a certain Slant of light." Reprinted by permission of the publishers and the Trustees of Amherst College from *The Poems of Emily Dickinson*, Thomas H. Johnson, ed., Cambridge, Mass.: The Belknap Press of Harvard University Press. Copyright © 1951, 1955, 1979, 1983 by the President and Fellows of Harvard College.

Rita Dove. "Golden Oldie" from *Mother Love* by Rita Dove. Copyright © 1995 by Rita Dove. Used by permission of W. W. Norton & Company, Inc.

Denise Duhamel. "How It Will End" from *Blowout* by Denise Duhamel. Copyright © 2013. "The Language Police" from *Ka-Ching!* by Denise Duhamel. First published in *Sentence: A Journal of Prose Poetics* No. 4 (2006). Copyright © 2009. Reprinted by permission of the University of Pittsburgh Press.

Cornelius Eady. "The Supremes" from *The Gathering of My Name*. Copyright © 1991 by Cornelius Eady. Reprinted with the permission of The Permissions Company, Inc., on behalf of Carnegie Mellon University Press.

Martín Espada. "The Community College Revises Its Curriculum in Response to Changing Demographics" from *A Mayan Astronomer in Hell's Kitchen* by Martín Espada. Copyright © 2000 by Martín Espada. Used by permission of the author and W. W. Norton & Company, Inc. "Latin Night at the Pawn Shop" from *Rebellion Is the Circle of a Lover's Hands / Rebelión es el giro de manos del amante* by Martín Espada. Copyright © 1990 by Martín Espada. Translation copyright © by Camilo Pérez-Bustillo and Martín Espada. First printed in 1990 by Curbstone Press. Reprinted with the permission of Northwestern University Press.

Ruth Fainlight. "Crocuses" from *New & Collected Poems* by Ruth Fainlight (Bloodaxe Books, 2011). Copyright © 2011 by Ruth Fainlight. Reprinted by permission of Bloodaxe Books Ltd.

Blanche Farley. "The Lover Not Taken" from *Light Year '86*. Reprinted by permission of the author.

Kenneth Fearing. "AD" from *Kenneth Fearing Complete Poems,* ed. by Robert Ryely (Orono, ME: National Poetry Foundation, 1997). Copyright © 1938 by Kenneth Fearing, renewed in 1966 by the Estate of Kenneth Fearing. Reprinted by the permission of Russell & Volkening as agents for the author.

Ruth Forman. "Poetry Should Ride the Bus." From *We Are the Young Magicians* (Boston: Beacon Press, 1993). Copyright © 1993 by Ruth Forman. Reprinted with the permission of the author.

Robert Francis. "Catch" from *The Orb Weaver*. Copyright © 1960 by Robert Francis. Published by Wesleyan University Press and used by permission. "On 'Hard' Poetry." Reprinted from *The Satirical Rogue on Poetry* by Robert Francis. Copyright © 1968 by Robert Francis and published by the University of Massachusetts Press. Used by permission.

Robert Frost. "Acquainted with the Night" from *The Poetry of Robert Frost,* edited by Edward Connery Lathem. Copyright © 1923, 1928, 1969 by Henry Holt and Company, copyright © 1936, 1951, 1956 by Robert Frost, copyright © 1964 by Lesley Frost Ballantine. "Design" from *The Poetry of Robert Frost,* edited by Edward Connery Lathem. Copyright © 1923, 1928, 1969 by Henry Holt and Company, copyright © 1936, 1951, 1956 by Robert Frost, copyright © 1964 by Lesley Frost Ballantine. "Dust of Snow" from *The Poetry of Robert Frost,* edited by Edward Connery Lathem. Copyright © 1923, 1928, 1969 by Henry Holt and Company, copyright © 1936, 1951, 1956 by Robert Frost, copyright © 1964 by Lesley Frost Ballantine. "Fire and Ice" from *The Poetry of Robert Frost,* edited by Edward Connery Lathem. Copyright © 1923, 1928, 1969 by Henry Holt and Company, copyright © 1936, 1951, 1956 by Robert Frost, copyright © 1964 by Lesley Frost Ballantine. "Stopping by Woods on a Snowy Evening" from *The Poetry of Robert Frost,* edited by Edward Connery Lathem. Copyright © 1923, 1928, 1969 by Henry Holt and Company, copyright © 1936, 1951, 1956 by Robert Frost, copyright © 1964 by Lesley Frost Ballantine. Reprinted by permission of Henry Holt and Company, LLC. "The Figure a Poem Makes" from *The Selected Prose of Robert Frost,* edited by Hyde Cox and Edward Connery Lathem, copyright 1939, 1967 by Henry Holt and Company. Reprinted by permission of Henry Holt and Company, LLC. "On the Way to Read a Poem" from "Poetry and School" by Robert Frost in *The Atlantic Monthly,* June 1951. Reprinted by permission of the Estate of Robert Lee Frost.

Brendan Galvin. "An Evel Knievel Elegy" from *Shenandoah* 58.2 (2008), p. 6. Copyright © 2008. Reprinted by permission of the author.

Gary Gildner. "First Practice" from *Blue Like the Heavens: New and Selected Poems* by Gary Gildner. Copyright © 1984. Reprinted by permission of the University of Pittsburgh Press.

R. S. Gwynn. "Shakespearean Sonnet." Originally appeared in *Formalist* 12.2 (2001). Copyright © 2001 by R. S. Gwynn. Reprinted by permission of the author.

H.D. [Hilda Doolittle]. "Heat" from *Collected Poems, 1912–1944.* Copyright 1982 by The Estate of Hilda Doolittle. Reprinted by permission of New Directions Publishing Corp.

Richard Hague. "Directions for Resisting the SAT" from *Ohio Teachers Write* (Ohio Council of Teachers of English, 1996). Copyright © 1996 by Richard Hague. Reprinted by permission of the author.

Mark Halliday. "Graded Paper," *Michigan Quarterly Review.* Reprinted by permission of the author.

William Hathaway. "Oh, Oh" from *Light Year '86.* This poem was originally published in the *Cincinnati Poetry Review.* Reprinted by permission of the author.

Robert Hayden. "Those Winter Sundays," copyright © 1966 by Robert Hayden, from *Collected Poems of Robert Hayden* by Robert Hayden, edited by Frederick Glaysher. Used by permission of Liveright Publishing Corporation.

Judy Page Heitzman. "The Schoolroom on the Second Floor of the Knitting Mill." Copyright © 1991 by Judy Page Heitzman. Originally appeared in the *New Yorker,* December 2, 1992, p. 102. Reprinted by permission of the author.

William Heyen. "The Trains" from *The Host: Selected Poems 1965–1990* by William Heyen. Copyright © 1994 by Time Being Press. Reprinted by permission of the author.

Bob Hicok. "Making it in poetry," copyright © 2004 by Bob Hicok. "Making it in poetry" first appeared in the *Georgia Review* 58.2 (Summer 2004), and is reprinted here with the acknowledgment of the editors and the permission of the author.

Tony Hoagland. "America," from *What Narcissism Means to Me.* Copyright © 2003 by Tony Hoagland. Reprinted with the permission of The Permissions Company, Inc., on behalf of Graywolf Press, Minneapolis, Minnesota, www.graywolfpress.org.

Langston Hughes. "Harlem" [2] from *The Collected Poems of Langston Hughes* by Langston Hughes, edited by Arnold Rampersad with David Roessel, Associate Editor. Copyright © 1994 by the Estate of Langston

Edna St. Vincent Millay. "I will put Chaos into fourteen lines" from *Collected Poems*. Copyright 1954 and renewed © 1982 by Norma Millay Ellis. Reprinted with the permission of The Permissions Company, Inc., on behalf of Holly Peppe, Literary Executor, The Millay Society, www.millay.org.

Janice Townley Moore. "To a Wasp" first appeared in *Light Year*, Bits Press. Reprinted by permission of the author.

Thomas R. Moore. "At the Berkeley Free Speech Café" from *The Bolt-Cutters* by Thomas R. Moore. Copyright © 2010. Reprinted by permission of Fort Hemlock Press and Thomas R. Moore.

Robert Morgan. "Mountain Graveyard" and "Overalls" from *Sigodlin*. Copyright © 1990 by Robert Morgan. Reprinted by permission of the author.

Harryette Mullen. "Blah-Blah" and "Dim Lady" from *Sleeping with the Dictionary* by Harryette Mullen. Copyright © 2002 by Harryette Mullen. Reprinted by permission of the Regents of the University of California and the publisher, the University of California Press.

Joan Murray. "We Old Dudes," copyright © 2006 by Joan Murray. First appeared in the July/August 2006 issue of *Poetry* magazine. Reprinted by permission of the author.

Marilyn Nelson. "How I Discovered Poetry" from *The Fields of Praise: New and Selected Poems* by Marilyn Nelson. Copyright © 1997 by Marilyn Nelson. Reprinted by permission of the author and Louisiana State University Press.

John Frederick Nims. "Love Poem" from *Selected Poems*. Copyright © 1982 by the University of Chicago. Reprinted by permission of the University of Chicago Press.

Sharon Olds. "Last Night" from *Wellspring: Poems* by Sharon Olds. Copyright © 1996 by Sharon Olds. Used by permission of Alfred A. Knopf, an imprint of the Knopf Doubleday Publishing Group, a division of Penguin Random House LLC. All rights reserved. Any third party use of this material, outside of this publication, is prohibited. Interested parties must apply directly to Penguin Random House LLC for permission.

Mary Oliver. "The Poet with His Face in His Hands" from *New and Selected Poems, Vol. 2* by Mary Oliver. Copyright © 2005 by Mary Oliver. Published by Beacon Press, Boston. Reprinted by permission of the Charlotte Sheedy Literary Agency, Inc.

Lisa Parker. "Snapping Beans," from the collection *This Gone Place* by Lisa Parker. Originally appeared in *Parnassus* 23, no. 2 (1998). Reprinted by permission of the author.

Laurence Perrine. "The limerick's never averse." Copyright © Laurence Perrine. Reprinted by permission of Douglas Perrine.

Kevin Pierce. "Proof of Origin" from *Light 50* (Autumn 2005). Copyright © 2005 by Kevin Pierce. Reprinted with the permission of the author.

Henry Reed. "Naming of Parts" from *Henry Reed: Collected Poems,* ed. Jon Stallworthy. Copyright © 1946, 1947, 1970, 1991, 2007 by the Executor of Henry Reed's Estate. Reprinted by permission of Carcanet Press Ltd.

Alberto Ríos. "Seniors" from *Five Indiscretions*. Copyright © 1985 by Alberto Ríos. Reprinted by permission of the author.

Theodore Roethke. "My Papa's Waltz," copyright 1942 by Hearst Magazines, Inc., from *Collected Poems* by Theodore Roethke. Used by permission of Doubleday, an imprint of the Knopf Doubleday Publishing Group, a division of Penguin Random House LLC. All rights reserved. Any third party use of this material, outside of this publication, is prohibited. Interested parties must apply directly to Penguin Random House LLC for permission.

Kay Ryan. "Turtle" from *Flamingo Watching* by Kay Ryan. Copyright © 1994 by Kay Ryan. Used by permission of Copper Beech Press.

Sonia Sanchez. "c'mon man hold me" from *Like the Singing Coming Off the Drums: Love Poems* by Sonia Sanchez. Copyright © 1998 by Sonia Sanchez. Reprinted by permission of Beacon Press, Boston.

Peter Schmitt. "Friends with Numbers" from *Hazard Duty*. Copyright © 1995 by Peter Schmitt. Used by permission of Copper Beech Press.

Karl Shapiro. "Lower the Standard" from *Collected Poems, 1940–1978* by Karl Shapiro. Copyright © 1978 by Karl Shapiro. Reprinted by permission of Harold Ober Associates Incorporated.

David Shumate. "Shooting the Horse" from *High Water Mark: Prose Poems* by David Shumate. Copyright © 2004. Reprinted by permission of the University of Pittsburgh Press.

Anya Krugovoy Silver. "French Toast" from *The Ninety-Third Name of God* by Anya Krugovoy Silver. Copyright © 2010 by Anya Krugovoy Silver. Reprinted by permission of Louisiana State University Press.

Charles Simic. "The Storm" from *The Virginia Quarterly Review* vol. 84, no. 2 (Spring 2008), p. 92. Copyright © 2008 by Charles Simic. Reprinted by permission of the author.

David R. Slavitt. "Titanic" from *Change of Address: Poems New and Selected* by David R. Slavitt. Copyright © 2005 by David R. Slavitt. Reprinted by permission of Louisiana State University Press.

Ernest Slyman. "Lightning Bugs" from *Sometime the Cow Kick Your Head, Light Year '88/'89*. Reprinted by permission of the author.

Patricia Smith. "What It's Like to Be a Black Girl (For Those of You Who Aren't)" from *Life According to Motown* by Patricia Smith. Copyright © 1991 by Patricia Smith. Reprinted by permission of the author.

Gary Snyder. "How Poetry Comes to Me" from *No Nature* by Gary Snyder. Copyright © 1992 by Gary Snyder. Used by permission of Pantheon Books, an imprint of the Knopf Doubleday Publishing Group, a

# Index of First Lines

# Index of Authors and Titles

# Index of Terms